VIOLENT CRIME

CLINICAL AND SOCIAL IMPLICATIONS

CHRISTOPHER J.
FERGUSON
Texas A&M International University
EDITOR

 **SAGE**

Los Angeles • London • New Delhi • Singapore • Washington DC

For information:

SAGE Publications, Inc.
2455 Teller Road
Thousand Oaks, California 91320
E-mail: order@sagepub.com

SAGE Publications, India Pvt. Ltd.
B 1/I 1 Mohan Cooperative
  Industrial Area
Mathura Road, New Delhi 110 044
India

SAGE Publications, Ltd.
1 Oliver's Yard
55 City Road
London EC1Y 1SP
United Kingdom

SAGE Publications, Asia-Pacific Pte. Ltd.
33 Pekin Street #02-01
Far East Square
Singapore 048763

Printed in the United States of America

Library of Congress Cataloging-in-Publication Data

Violent crime : clinical and social implications / editor, Christopher J. Ferguson.
    p. cm.
Includes bibliographical references and index.
ISBN 978-1-4129-5992-6 (cloth)
ISBN 978-1-4129-5993-3 (pbk.)
    1. Violent crimes—Sociological aspects. 2. Violent crimes—Research.
3. Violent crimes—Psychological aspects. I. Ferguson, Christopher J.

HV6493.V57 2009
364.2—dc22   2008031844

This book is printed on acid-free paper.

12   13   10   9   8   7   6   5   4   3

Acquisitions Editor:	Jerry Westby
Associate Editor:	Deya Saoud
Editorial Assistant:	Eve Oettinger
Production Editor:	Catherine M. Chilton
Copy Editor:	Diana Breti
Typesetter:	C&M Digitals (P) Ltd.
Proofreader:	William H. Stoddard
Indexer:	Hyde Park Publishing Services LLC
Cover Designer:	Candice Harman
Marketing Manager:	Christy Guilbault

Brief Contents

Contents

Preface

Violent criminal behavior, despite being on a precipitous decline in the United States, Canada, the UK, and most other Western countries for a decade and a half, remains a cultural and academic area of fascination. In the media, crime shows such as *CSI: Crime Scene Investigation* and *Law and Order* remain among the top-rated shows, giving birth to a dizzying array of spinoffs and copycats. At universities, courses and majors in criminology, criminal justice, and forensic psychology are among the most popular. Indeed, if every student in these majors obtained a job in the field, there arguably would be more criminologists than criminals. Many students come to my office and inquire about careers in law enforcement, predictably voicing an interest in criminal profiling or "CSI" jobs. Clearly, there is much desire for information on violent crime. Yet, in a field that is arguably rampant with politics and ideology, there is a risk that the information widely available may be what is expedient or, indeed, politically correct rather than empirically supported. That was the genesis for this book: I envisioned it as a book that would break through the old tropes, adages, and false paths of society's understanding of violent crime and return the discussion to the science of violence and the current direction of research.

Science is inherently self-correcting. However, sometimes it takes its time to do so. I think that societal understanding, and even academic understanding, of violent criminal behavior may linger in the past at times. I submit that social science still labors, despite the "nature/nurture compromise," under decades of behavioral and social learning dogma. This is not to say that these paradigms don't enjoy some window on the "truth" of human behavior, but at least some proponents of this view have set up unnecessary roadblocks to our understanding of the biological and genetic roots of violent behavior. Similarly, old theories that should have been laid to rest may continue to exert considerable influence, despite the limits of their empirical support. First, I set out to develop this book to be a core, introductory text on the current science of violent crime. Second, I view this text as a catalyst for discussion of what we think we know, how we study violence, and where the research may take us in the future. This book is not wedded to a single theoretical viewpoint or even an overarching paradigm, such as social constructionist or biological essentialist perspectives. Theory is important, and the major views are presented in the first part of this book, yet the single most important question in the development of this book was "What does the research say?"

This text may differ in some notable ways from other texts in this area. First, I have observed that most texts and theorists focus on sociological or social constructionist perspectives of violent crime. Although these approaches are important to examine, the comparative lack of coverage of biological and genetic influences is a major oversight. Thus, this text includes a more thorough examination of biological theories of aggression than is common in most similar works. Second, violent criminals are not treated as a homogenous group. Specific chapters are dedicated to major categories of criminals, from sex offenders to domestic violence perpetrators to serial murderers. Attention is focused on similarities and differences between male and female perpetrators, particularly in areas related to domestic violence and homicide. Third, the text examines the clinical implications of violent crime with respect to treatment of offenders and the experience of victims.

This book is designed to be an introductory text to the research on violent crime. This makes this text suitable for academic classes on criminal violence, criminal justice, forensic psychology, criminal offending and profiling, violence and victimology, and sociology and social work classes focused on violence. Broader classes on criminology or criminological theory may also benefit from this book, perhaps as a secondary text. This book has several features that I believe distinguish it:

- *An interdisciplinary focus:* Chapter authors consider multiple theoretical frameworks, and they are experts in criminal justice, criminology, sociology, psychology, psychiatry, and medicine.
- *An international focus:* Chapter authors are from the United States, Canada, England, Greece, and Spain, providing a wider perspective on criminal violence.
- *Discussion of biological theories:* One of my concerns in writing this book is that biological theories of violence continue to be given short shrift in the criminological literature. To my reading, this is unfortunate, given that current data to support biological causes of violence are strong. The inclusion of this data, at least as a springboard for discussion, is essential for any complete understanding of criminal violence.
- *Relevant case studies:* Empirical and theoretical data in each chapter are highlighted by relevant case studies from the historical record or the authors' case files. It is my opinion that the inclusion of these case

studies enhances the reader's experience, both by giving real-world examples of the material discussed in the chapters and by appealing to the reader's fascination with criminal violence. In other words, these case studies help draw readers in so they become interested in reading the empirical material.

- *Internet resources:* Each chapter includes a list of Internet resources that readers may use to learn more about the topics. They include links to law enforcement agencies, advocacy groups, and even some of the original empirical papers that are freely available on the Internet.

Not surprisingly, there are a number of people whom I would like to acknowledge for their contributions to this book. First, the chapter authors who have contributed their knowledge and expertise, not to mention their time and effort, to this project. Without them, this book simply could not have been possible. This book also benefited from several stages of reviews that provided excellent suggestions and feedback. I would like to thank the reviewers for their thoughtful comments and for their time and hard work: Chris Anderson, Concorde College; Geri Brandt, Maryville University; Sara Broaders, Northwestern University; Delores Craig-Moreland, Wichita State University; Stan Crowder, Kennesaw State University; Mitch Eisen, California State University, Los Angeles; Kelly Goodness, University of Texas at Dallas; Christopher Hale, Southern Connecticut State University; Chandrika Kelso, National University; Kay King, Johnson County Community College; Travis Langley, Henderson State University; Hua-Lun Huang, University of Louisiana, Lafayette; David Myers, Indiana University of Pennsylvania; Douglas Peters, University of North Dakota; Allan Roscoe, University of Massachusetts, Lowell; Ira Sommers, California State University, Los Angeles; Amy Thistlethwaite, Northern Kentucky University; Louis Schlesinger, John Jay College of Criminal Justice; Stephen Schnebly, Arizona State University; Mike Stevenson, University of Toledo; Lori Van Wallendael, University of North Carolina at Charlotte; Mark Winton, University of Central Florida at Daytona Beach.

My university has been very supportive of this effort. In particular, Roberto Heredia, John Kilburn, and Dean Champion have all given me time and advice on the book editing process. So, too, has my colleague and former mentor, Charles Negy. Jerry Westby and Deya Saoud at Sage deserve a thank you for their patience and for guiding me through this process. Last, and certainly not least, I want to acknowledge my family: my wife Diana; my son, Roman; and my parents, Stuart and Denise. Their support has been immeasurable in importance. After thinking about violence all day at work, it's nice to come home to a warm and supportive family. Their positive influence is what keeps me grounded.

Supporting researchers for more than 40 years

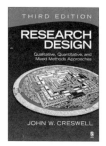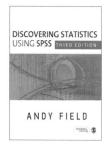

PART I

Causes of Crime

CHAPTER 1

Violent Crime Research

An Introduction

Christopher J. Ferguson

On August 1, 1966, Charles Whitman stabbed to death his wife and mother, then climbed the University of Texas at Austin clock tower, where he perpetrated one of the most famous mass murders in American history. He first clubbed to death a university receptionist; then he fired on a group of tourists who were climbing up the tower after him, killing two. Over the next several hours, Whitman, an ex-marine and student at the university, fired a high-powered rifle down on the campus below. Ultimately, 16 people died, including one of the officers who responded to the scene and the unborn child of a wounded female victim. Thirty-one people were wounded, several of whom experienced lifelong disabilities as a consequence of their injuries. Whitman was successful in keeping a police airplane at bay using his rifle, and he hid behind the tower ramparts to avoid returned fire from police officers and armed civilians below. Finally, two police officers emerged on the observation deck of the clock tower and shot Whitman point blank, killing him.

The tale of Charles Whitman, in and of itself, is an interesting, if tragic story about a school shooting from 40 years ago. However, Whitman's story ends with an important twist. Upon autopsy, it was found that Charles Whitman had a tumor in the hypothalamus region of his brain. Could this tumor have contributed to Whitman's mental state, leading him to become more aggressive and irrational than he otherwise would have been, or is the presence of this tumor simply a coincidence? Most violent criminals don't have brain tumors, after all.

Questions about the causes of violence have been with us for centuries. Many famous cases offer tantalizing clues to the origins of violent crime, but are these clues reliable or merely false paths? Consider the following cases:

- Before being executed in Florida, Ted Bundy, who had raped and murdered approximately 30 young women in the United States, claimed that exposure to pornography had helped mold him into a serial killer.
- In 2001, Andrea Yates drowned her five children in Texas. Although initially convicted of murder, Yates was found not guilty by reason of insanity in a second trial, due to a documented history of psychotic illness.
- In 2004, 14-year-old Cody Posey shot to death his father and step-mother. Posey had allegedly experienced years of physical and sexual abuse, yet he also was a player of the violent video game *Grand Theft Auto*. The makers of *Grand Theft Auto* were sued for "wrongful death" for allegedly contributing to Posey's development as a murderer, but the suit was ultimately dismissed.
- In June, 2007, professional wrestler Chris Benoit strangled to death his wife and son, then hanged himself. Allegations that Benoit had used illegal steroids surfaced, leading to speculation that "'roid rage" may have been responsible for the homicides, although these speculations were not confirmed. During subsequent examination, it was alleged by neurosurgeons at West Virginia University that Benoit's brain was severely damaged, possibly from multiple concussive injuries sustained as a wrestler.

These cases and many famous cases like them appear to offer hints at the origins of violence, whether brain injuries, tumors, family violence exposure, or exposure to the media. However, for each case in which one potential cause appears relevant, another case appears to disconfirm that case. For instance, Aileen Wuornos, a female serial killer who shot men, had a long history of exposure to violence and abuse prior to committing her crimes. By contrast, Karla Homolka, who along with her husband raped and murdered four young girls including her own sister, appeared to come from a privileged background. The purpose of this book is to examine the phenomenon of violent crime in order to separate the "wheat from the chaff." In other words, what does the evidence *really* say about the origins of violent crime?

CASE STUDY: TED BUNDY

Handsome, charming, and intelligent, Ted Bundy (birth name: Theodore Robert Cowell) garnered notoriety in the United States as one of the most vicious serial murderers of the late 20th century. The reason for Bundy's string of vicious rapes and murders, during which he killed 30 or more young women, remains a constant source of speculation.

Bundy's upbringing is most notable for the circumstances of his parentage. His mother was young and unmarried when she gave birth in 1946. In order to avoid the stigma of having an unwed mother, Bundy was raised by his maternal grandparents as if he were their own son, and his biological mother pretended to be his sister. Bundy did not find out about this state of affairs until his late teens. Although no evidence of abuse in the family is reported, Bundy later claimed that his grandfather was bullying and could fly into violent rages. Bundy appears to have been shy and introverted as a teen, got in minor trouble with the law (the records were expunged), and later reported being fascinated with sex and death even during his teenage years.

Bundy was initially something of an underachiever during his early college years. This was noticed by his girlfriend Stephanie Brooks (a pseudonym used to protect her real identity), who broke off their relationship due to his lack of drive and ambition. After the loss of this relationship, he turned things around, becoming socially and politically active and gaining admittance to law school. He began dating Brooks again and proposed to her late in 1973. After she accepted his proposal, he dumped her without explanation. Soon after, his killing spree began.

Beginning in Washington State, Bundy began attacking young women, often bludgeoning or strangling them to death, engaging in rape or necrophilia, and dumping their bodies in the woods. Many victims showed signs of brutal beatings to the head. Most of the women who went missing were young, slender, and attractive. Reportedly, Bundy used clever tactics to gain the sympathy of some of his victims, such as appearing to struggle with heavy books or a broken-down car while wearing a cast on one arm (a tactic borrowed by the film *Silence of the Lambs*). He then moved on to kill in Utah and Colorado.

The police investigating the string of murders got their first break in Utah, where Bundy attempted to kidnap Carol DaRonch. Masquerading as a security guard, he informed DaRonch that her car had been broken into and asked her to accompany him to inspect her car and fill out a report. He showed her a badge and offered to drive her to police headquarters. DaRonch became fearful once the man drove her away from police headquarters and stopped the car. Although he pulled a gun on her, DaRonch managed to escape and flag down a passing motorist, while still wearing handcuffs that he had forced on her. Although Bundy escaped and continued killing women, DaRonch became an important witness later.

In 1975, Bundy was pulled over for a traffic violation. Inspecting his car, police found that the passenger seat was missing and in the car were a crowbar, handcuffs, a ski mask, and other suspicious paraphernalia. He was quickly arrested and identified by DaRonch as the man who had briefly kidnapped her. Police were able to find other evidence linking him to many of the murders and disappearances. Hairs matching several victims were found in his VW Bug. Impressions in the skull of one victim matched the crowbar found in his car.

In 1976, Bundy was put on trial for kidnapping DaRonch and convicted. Facing a murder trial, Bundy decided to represent himself and was granted unsupervised time at a courthouse library to plan his own defense. On one such outing, he jumped out of a library window and escaped but was soon apprehended. Seven months later he escaped again, crawling up

(Continued)

(Continued)

through the ceiling of the jail and leaving through a janitor's apartment. This escape was more successful than the first.

On the run, Bundy managed to make his way down to Tallahassee, Florida. In January of 1978, he entered the Chi Omega sorority house on Florida State University campus. Most of the women were out for the night, although a few were home. Bundy killed two, Lisa Levy and Margaret Bowman, while they slept, beating them over the head with a log and strangling them. Levy was also raped and bitten so badly that one nipple was nearly severed from her breast. A third woman was injured but survived, and a fourth saw Bundy as he left the house, a ski mask covering his face.

Bundy's last victim was 13-year-old Kimberly Leach, who was much younger than most of his victims. Her decomposed body was found eight weeks after she went missing. Bundy was arrested soon after, driving a stolen VW Bug. Leach's blood was found in a van Bundy had previously used, and Bundy's biological material was found in her underwear. A shoe print matching Bundy was also found near the body's dump site. Bite marks on Lisa Levy's body were found to match Bundy's teeth. He was put on trial for murder, convicted, and sentenced to death in Florida. During the sentencing phase of the Kimberly Leach trial, Bundy married a female admirer.

Bundy attempted to appeal his convictions but was unsuccessful. He later admitted to the killings and stated that, in fact, there were more dead women that had yet to be identified. He offered to help authorities find the bodies in exchange for avoiding the death penalty. The authorities were not interested.

Just prior to his execution, Bundy gave an interview that received considerable attention. Bundy claimed that exposure to pornography (he claimed that his grandfather kept a considerable collection of pornography), particularly violent pornography, had helped mold his personality. Naturally, these claims were highlighted by antipornography activists. Particularly in the 1980s, there were many concerns that consumption of pornography might be associated with sex crimes or other violence toward women. Ultimately, however, research evidence failed to find any relationship between pornography and sex crimes (Diamond & Uchiyama, 1999). Bundy was executed January 24, 1989.

Where Is the Research on Violent Crime Going?

At the turn of the 20th century, the predominating classical school of criminology (which posits that criminal actions are freely chosen) was challenged by Cesare Lombroso, who argued that it was biology and evolution that determined criminal behavior. Lombroso argued that criminals were regressed evolutionary throwbacks to less-civilized hominid ancestors. Such throwbacks could potentially be identified by their primitive ape-like features. Lombroso's work came to be involved with the pseudoscientific enterprise of *forensic craniometry* (predicting criminality based on the shape and size of the skull) and eugenics and was subsequently discredited. Yet, was Lombroso's basic belief that evolution plays a role in violent behavior wrong? If not, and if violence is caused by forces beyond an individual's control, what does this mean for the classical assumption of free will, upon which most Western criminal justice systems are based? Should all violent criminals be considered diseased in some way and thus not held responsible for their actions?

In the biological sciences, evolutionary theory has enjoyed a relatively unbroken dominance in thought, beginning in the 19th century with Charles Darwin. However, in the social sciences, this was not the case. By the mid-20th century, the focus in the social sciences had shifted away from biological and evolutionary theories of human behavior, including violent behavior, to socialization and learning explanations of behavior. For instance, the American Psychological Association's (APA) pamphlet on youth violence states, "There is no gene for violence. Violence is a learned behavior" (APA, 1996). During the mid-20th century, some important risk factors for violence were identified, including poverty, family violence, and community cohesion. During much of the later half of the 20th century, theories suggesting that biology or evolution may contribute to violent crime remained controversial and were actively resisted (Wasserman & Wachbroit, 2001).

By the beginning of the 21st century, increased awareness of powerful genetic, biological, and evolutionary factors influencing violent crime came to light. As can be seen in Table 1.1, the single most powerful predictor of violent and antisocial behavior is genetics. There are other factors, both social and biological, that are also important to consider, but none can singularly account for as much variance as genetics can. Also, several genes have been specifically linked to violent behavior (see Chapters 4 and 5). Thus, we can say that claims such as those made by the APA (1996) are simply out of date. The complex interactions between genetic and nongenetic factors remain a subject of intense study, and future research is likely to focus on complex interactions between multiple causal factors including genetics, family environment, poverty and unemployment, and policing strategies and neighborhoods. More and more, researchers understand that violence is complex, multifaceted, and best understood from a multivariate perspective.

Where does all this leave the classical theory, with its emphasis on free will? Not surprisingly, as both biological and social factors that influence violent behavior have come to light, perpetrators have argued that they are not guilty by reason of mental defect due to biological or social influences outside their control. The case of Dan White presents one infamous example. White assassinated the mayor of San Francisco and the city supervisor in November, 1978. During his trial, his defense team argued that White's consumption of Twinkies and Coca-Cola and generally poor diet made his existing mood swings more difficult to control. Believing

Table 1.1 Effect Sizes in Medical and Criminal Justice Research

Relationship	Effect Size (r)
Smoking on Lung Cancer	.90
Genetic Influences on Antisocial Behavior	.75
Salk Vaccine on Polio Prevention	.74
Self-Control and Perceptions of Criminal Opportunity on Crime	.58
Protective Effect of Community Institutions on Neighborhood Crime	.39
Violent Video Game Playing on Visuospatial Cognitive Ability	.36
Firearms Ownership on Crime	.35
Incarceration Use as a Deterrent on Crime	.33
Aggressive Personality and Violent Crime	.25
Poverty on Crime	.25
Childhood Physical Abuse and Adult Violent Crime	.22
Child Witnessing Domestic Violence on Future Aggression	.18
Television Violence on Violent Crime	.10
Violent Video Game Playing on Aggressive Behavior	.04
Parental Spanking on Child Aggression	.03

SOURCE: Data are from Baumrind, Larzelere, and Cowan (2002); Block and Crain (2007); Ferguson (2007); Ferguson (in press); Ferguson, Rueda, Cruz, Ferguson, Fritz, and Smith (2008); Francis et al. (1955); Kizman, Gaylord, Holt, and Kenny (2003); Paik and Comstock (1994); Pratt and Cullen (2000, 2005); Rhee and Waldman (2002); Wynder and Graham (1950).

he was thus incapable of premeditating the violent crime, the jury found White guilty of manslaughter rather than murder. White served five years in prison for the two homicides and ultimately committed suicide at home in 1985.

In the case of serious mental illness such as schizophrenia, of course arguments regarding diminished capacity or mental defect are worth considering. But in most other cases, in the absence of a well-documented mental illness, these arguments have generally not convinced juries. Historically, science has not been friendly to the notion of free will. It's not hard to see why; science seeks to define clear cause-and-effect relationships in which individuals have no choice. Yet, slowly, researchers are beginning to see that the issue of free will is not black or white. Many social scientists now argue that biology, evolution, and the social environment all do exert some causal effects on our behavior, but we also retain some degree of free will; this perspective is sometimes called "soft determinism." For instance, as a chocolate lover, my love for sweets likely has genetic and evolutionary origins. Thus, my drive for naughty food is biological in nature. Yet, when I see a doughnut, I still retain the ability to resist my desires. In the end, I am still responsible for my decision should I decide to "give in" to my biologically derived craving. Thus, I would argue that the classical theory is not incompatible with scientific theories such as evolutionary theory or social modeling.

Studying Violence

In the biblical book of Genesis, Cain, the first son of Adam and Eve, kills his brother Abel during a fit of jealousy, suggesting that violent crimes have been with humanity since the beginning of our history. Naturally, academic researchers turn to science in an attempt to understand violent behavior, and there is debate regarding the point in our evolutionary history when intraspecies violence (violent acts by humans against other humans) became commonplace. However, it is probably safe to say that violence is nothing new to humanity and certainly has been part of human existence throughout recorded history. Since humans began scientifically studying human behavior, violence has been a topic of keen interest. What are the origins of human violence? How can we predict who is likely to become violent, and how might we prevent violent behavior? How can the law enforcement, corrections, and social science communities best intervene in violent crimes to prevent future crimes and to protect the public?

Generally, I suspect that people would prefer rather easy answers along the lines of "Violent crime is caused by X and Y and all that we have to do to prevent violence is Z." Unfortunately, there are no simple answers in regard to any facet of violent criminal behavior. Indeed, one of the ideas that I hope readers will take away from this book is that there are many predictors and potential causes of violent crime, and the etiological (or causal) path that leads one individual to commit violent crimes may be very different from the etiological path followed by another individual. It is the goal of this book to introduce research on violent crime from multiple disciplines and from varying perspectives to present, in effect, a "state of the research" on violent crime, its causes, and preventive efforts.

At the outset, before discussions of the theories of violent crime, types of violent criminals, and preventive and intervention efforts, I would like to mention a few things that I believe are important for readers to consider as they digest this material. First, I believe it is important to remember that violent crime is, in many ways, both an emotional and highly politicized issue. It is probably not terribly surprising for me to suggest that discussions of violent crime by politicians or advocacy groups often attempt to communicate a particular "message" and convince the public of a particular moral or legal stance. It is perhaps more controversial for me to suggest that scientists, while attempting to be more objective than politicians or advocates of one cause or another, ultimately are as human as anyone else.

Although it may be that, discipline wide, opinions will converge and self-correct into "consensus," others have pointed out that discipline-wide biases may exist in science. For example, some authors have argued that disciplines such as psychology demonstrate a "liberal" political and social bias and may systematically interpret information in accordance with this bias (Redding, 2001). Outside the purely political realm, others (Kuhn, 1970) have observed that science itself may latch onto certain ideas and defend them "dogmatically" despite evidence against those ideas. In other words, I believe it is important for readers always to consider the perspective that a particular author takes on a topic and what "message" he or she is trying to convey. This doesn't mean that science is valueless—quite the contrary—however, science is a human endeavor and, as with any human endeavor, rendered imperfect by natural human foibles.

Not surprising, the result is numerous debates within the scientific community about the nature of violent crime, many of which will be covered in this book. For instance, does genetics contribute to violent crime, or is violence entirely a learned behavior? Have certain behaviors, such as assault or even rape, evolved through natural selection in (hopefully) a minority of the members of our species? Does media violence or spanking children contribute to violent crime? Do interventions for violent criminals really work, or is incarceration the only solution? Probably even before you read this book you will have many opinions on these topics. The information provided in this book may give you fuel for further thought to challenge or confirm your opinions. The authors included in this book have presented thoughtful discussions on the "state of the research" in each of their disciplines. Yet I hope you will digest this material beyond simply memorizing it (or indeed becoming indoctrinated by it!), and, instead, you will analyze it critically. Indeed, should you reject some (or all!) of the conclusions made throughout this book, but do so based on an informed view and critical thinking (as opposed to, say, an emotional response), I will consider this book to have met its primary objective.

With that in mind, there are three main questions that I think would be valuable for readers to consider as they read through the chapters. The following is by no means a conclusive list, but I think it will help set the tone for critical thinking.

How Are Aggression and Violence Defined and Measured?

First, let me note that the terms *aggression, violence,* and *violent crime* are related, but they are not exactly the same. *Aggressive behavior* has been defined as behavior intended to cause harm or humiliation to another person who is not a consenting participant (Baron & Richardson, 1994). *Violent behavior* has been defined as physical force used against oneself or another resulting in injury, death, or other significant harm (World Health Organization, 2007). Thus, while all violent behavior is aggressive, many aggressive behaviors, such as calling rude names, withdrawing affection, using sarcasm, or sabotaging, are not violent. Violent behaviors that specifically violate a relevant legal code are considered violent crimes, although not all violent behaviors are violent crimes; for instance, the actions of police officers or soldiers or people defending themselves from harm are not violent crimes.

Indeed, in one sense we all know what violence is, yet defining it satisfactorily may be difficult. Attempting to measure violent and aggressive behaviors can be even more complex. For instance, most of us would likely agree that hitting another person is "aggression," but what about two children who are playing "cops and robbers" using toy guns? Are they behaving aggressively? Alternatively, if two adults consent to play a reaction time game in which they can "punish" each other for losing by using non-painful bursts of white noise (like an untuned radio), would you consider them to be engaging in aggressive behavior? If you hear of a study that suggests, for example, "Eating plantains leads to aggression," the first thing you should ask is "How did the scientists measure aggression?"

Aggression and violence can both be difficult to measure. There are certain ethical constraints that are probably rather obvious. It's simply not ethical in experimental settings to provoke people into engaging in behaviors that would be violently criminal. In experimental settings, the solution has been to employ proxy or ad hoc measures of aggression, which can vary widely from experiment to experiment (the white noise machine described above is one of them). When considering an individual experimental study, it's always worth knowing what kind of measure of aggression was used, particularly because many have been criticized for having low validity (Tedeschi & Quigley, 1996). In other words, does the measure of aggression reasonably look anything like aggressive behavior?

In nonexperimental (or correlational) research, a number of different outcomes may be employed: arrest records, victim reports, self-reports of perpetration, or psychological measures of antisocial tendencies or externalizing behaviors. Arguably, all of these forms of data have weaknesses. For instance, arrest data is largely contingent (with the obvious exception of homicides) on people reporting their victimization to the police. It is widely understood that for many violent crimes, such as rape, only a fraction of victims report being victimized to police (Tjaden & Thoennes, 2006). As such, arrest records may tend to underestimate overall perpetration of crimes. So, for example, if you were to hear that "only 10% of offenders who receive treatment X engage in further crimes within five years" and that information is based on arrest records, it would be reasonable to wonder whether the outcome data may be underestimating further crimes (recidivism).

Self-report measures of perpetration, victimization, and psychological problems may not underestimate the number of crimes in the same way that arrest records do; however, they are weakened by people's natural tendency to lie. Naturally, many of the surveys relevant to criminal justice research ask about sensitive or embarrassing topics such as illegal activities, violent behaviors, sexual behaviors, and antisocial attitudes. For instance, if I were to ask a group of children or adults the question, "True or false: I have stolen something within the past year," many, and perhaps most, would prefer to answer "false." However, I suspect that most individuals, if answering honestly, would have to report "true" to that question because most individuals have taken office supplies, illegally downloaded a song, or failed to report all income on tax day. Some groups of individuals, such as criminal offenders, may have ulterior motives for answering questions in a certain way. For example, if you were to hear that 42% of pedophiles reported being sexually abused themselves as children (Greenberg, Bradford, & Curry, 1993), you may wonder whether a sample of pedophiles is being honest in reporting past abuse or whether they might lie about past abuse in order to make themselves appear less culpable. Asking questions about the definition and measurement of constructs related to violent behavior may help you put the results into perspective.

What Is the Effect Size of the Research?

Most people who read newspapers or other articles on science have at least passing familiarity with the term *statistical significance.* This term gives the impression that in science, things either are important or they are not. Unfortunately, although statistical significance is, indeed, an "up or down" vote (a study's result either is or is not statistically significant), this is not really a good reflection of reality. Indeed, some researchers have been pointing out for years that statistical significance is an inadequate way of testing hypotheses (Cohen, 1994; Loftus, 1996). Part of the problem is the issue of sample size: With small samples, important effects may be missed because they don't reach statistical significance, and with very large samples, almost any relationship, no matter how trivial or unimportant, may appear statistically significant.

A better way of understanding the relative importance of a research finding is through another reported statistic: effect size. The *effect size* of a research finding can be thought of as the size of the impact of one variable on another. For example, I may look at the effects of eating fresh blueberries on mood. With a large sample, I may find a statistically significant relationship (although my example here is hypothetical) but find that the effect size is actually very tiny, nearly zero, perhaps. In other words, statistical significance does not always translate into practical significance. Reporting effect sizes is one way to understand the practical impact of a research finding.

There are many ways to report effect size, but I'll mention one important way very briefly. The Pearson r should be familiar to anyone who has taken a statistics course and remembers correlation coefficients. Even experimental research can be translated to an effect size r (which ranges from 0 to 1.00, usually with two decimal points reported), making r an easily understood measure of effect size. The r statistic can also be squared and multiplied by 100 ($r^2 \times 100$) to give an indication of shared variance. So, if you discover that the relationship between variable X and variable Y is $r = .20$, then you know that their shared variance overlaps by 4%, which is not very much. In other words, although X and Y do predict each other a little, it's not a strong predictive relationship. In the social sciences, values of r from .1 to .3 are considered to be small, values from .3 to .5 are considered to be moderate, and above .5 are considered to be large (Rosnow & Rosenthal, 2003). In Table 1.1, I have produced a list of common effect sizes seen in criminal justice research, as well as several effect sizes calculated from medical epidemiological research, which serve as a contrast. The smoking/lung cancer research sets the "gold standard" for effect size, with other effects ranging from large to nearly zero. As can be seen from Table 1.1, some research that gets a lot of public attention, such as the effects of media violence or spanking by parents, appears to have very little actual impact on violent crime. It should be noted that calculating effect size r from medical epidemiological research can be tricky due to differing methods used in social science and medical research, and some scholars have been concerned that efforts to convert medical effect sizes to r may have resulted in underestimates in the past (Block & Crain, 2007).

Public Perceptions of Violent Crime

The scientific community does not live in a vacuum, cut off from the rest of society. Scientists are exposed to the same communitywide beliefs, biases, and messages as everyone else. Indeed, the scientific endeavor itself is highly influenced by political forces, which may fund certain scientific projects and not others and may be highly active in setting scientific agendas. Also, as Kuhn (1970) noted, scientists may be influenced by the dictates and dogmas of their own scientific communities. It is worth understanding the effects of community on the scientific endeavor and how this may change the kinds of questions that scientists may ask as well as how they interpret their results (Shapin, 1995).

What can we say, then, about the way in which Western cultures, and particular the United States, perceive violent crime? Let's consider first the issue of how much crime there is in the United States. In Gallup opinion polls, the majority of respondents continue to express the belief that crime is worsening in the United States (Gallup, 2004). How violent is the United States in reality? The truth is that violent crime has been decreasing significantly in the United States since the early 1990s (Federal Bureau of Investigation, 1951–2004). Although rates for individual years tend to fluctuate up and down, and one can expect the raw rates of violent crimes to increase gradually as the population increases, these data demonstrate a remarkable decline in violent crimes. The data is consistent for adults and juveniles (Federal Interagency Forum on Child and Family Statistics, 2007). Nonetheless, I would argue that many politicians, advocacy groups, and individuals speak about violent crime as if rates have been continuing to rise dramatically rather than decline significantly. Some authors (e.g., Surette, 2006) have argued that this may be due, in part, to the way in which crime is presented in the media. For instance, news media tend to report images of violent crimes, as opposed to reporting positive news stories. As a result, people may be given the impression that violent crimes are more common than they actually are because such crimes are always being reported in the news.

Another concern about the way in which crime is understood in the culture, or perhaps presented in the media, is the degree to which stereotypes of violent crime are endorsed. For example, some scholars note that certain ethnic groups, such as Hispanics/Latinos, tend to be more often portrayed as perpetrators of crime in the media (Rivadeneyra, 2006). Others have noted essentially the opposite effect; many crime shows, particularly those focused on murders, portray perpetrators who are very distinct from actual crime perpetrators (Surette, 2006). For instance, if you watch a show such as *CSI: Miami*, you may be led to suspect that most perpetrators of violent crimes are young, wealthy, motivated by greed or sex, and, additionally, are more physically attractive than the average person. Similarly, murder shows such as *Murder She Wrote* would lead one to suspect that middle-aged wealthy Caucasians were particularly prone to committing homicides. In many shows, males and females appear equally likely to commit homicides, when in fact about 85% of violent crimes are committed by males, usually against other males. More often than not, violent crimes in real life are motivated by trivial matters, not complicated plots; occur among lower-SES individuals; and are moderated by alcohol or drug use (Holmes & Holmes, 2001).

These overarching cultural views about crime, particularly related to the actual prevalence of crime, can have an impact on the scientific community, as well. This is particularly true when scientists, like other groups, must convince others that their area of research is "important." It thus may be beneficial for scientists to portray violent crime as an increasing social problem because this approach is more likely to secure funding and attention than is pointing out that violent crimes are on the decline. This need not imply unethical behavior on the part of scientists; rather, my argument is that this is simply human nature and is encouraged by the cultural context in which science is practiced.

It is also important to point out that certain ideas, both within the scientific community and within the general culture, become "popular" and difficult to undo even in the presence of contradictory data. When these beliefs permeate (or originate in) the scientific community, they can result in *dogma,* which is entrenched scientific belief that resists contradictory evidence. In some cases, dogma may serve to protect the scientific endeavor from "crackpot" ideas, but in other cases, it may make the process of accommodating new data difficult (Kuhn, 1970). For example, much of social science in the latter 20th century became focused on a model of behavior that, generally speaking, focused on human behavior as a product of the environment (e.g., Skinner, 1987). Arguably, this view permeated many avenues of social science, from child development to feminist theory to criminal justice research. Put generally, in relation to violent crime, such theories would imply that criminals learned to become criminals, quite possibly as a consequence of exposure to negative environments or abuse as children (e.g., Straus & Yodanis, 1996). Arguably, one side effect of this focus, whether intentional or unintentional, has been a disinclination for researchers to focus on biological, and particularly genetic and evolutionary, explanations of violent and aggressive behavior (Pinker, 2002).

As a result, discussions of violence that focus on evolutionary explanations are often met with a much greater emotional reaction than are those that focus on environmental explanations. For example, Thornhill and Palmer (2000) published a book that argued that the common belief that "rape is not about sex" is wrong and that some males may have developed rape behavior essentially through evolutionary processes (perhaps as a byproduct, rather than a true adaptation). Whatever one's particular thoughts are about this thesis, the book contained enough supportive data that it arguably was as worthy of consideration and debate as any other text on the matter. Nonetheless, it is argued here that the reaction from some scholars to this text was much more emotional than is seen in typical scientific discourse (e.g., Travis, 2003). This affair was, itself, much milder than the collision of science and culture that occurred over a particularly controversial article (Rind, Tromovitch, & Bauserman, 1998). The article examined studies of child sexual abuse and argued that most victims of child sexual abuse don't suffer negative long-term consequences. Naturally, this argument went over like a lead balloon, with vocal complaints from many members of the scientific community and even Congress. Although the APA published the study, they later repudiated it when it became politically expedient to do so (see Dallam, 2001 for a full timeline of the controversy surrounding this article). Although it is certainly worthy to examine the methodology used in such a study, many of the criticisms came from groups who appeared to have not even read the original report and thus responded from emotional opposition rather than scientific opposition.

With these cautionary notes in mind, I hope that you will find this book to be informative and interesting. The chapters are organized in three main Parts. Part I focuses on potential causes of violent crime. Chapters range from potential sociological and environmental causes of crime to biological and evolutionary causes of crime. Part II of the book focuses on specific types of violent crimes, from youth violence to domestic violence to serial murder. Finally, issues related to victimology, prevention, and treatment of violent crime are considered in Part III. In general, the hope for this book is that it will present a "state of the research" on violent crime, including what is known and directions for future research. Like any single piece of information, this book can ultimately provide only one perspective on violent crime, and, as such, the reader is encouraged to seek out other perspectives and information. With this in mind, each chapter provides Internet Resources for further information and reading. I hope that by the end of this book you emerge feeling as if you are better acquainted with the research, theories, and debates on violent crime and perhaps will take an active role, as a researcher, student, or simply a concerned citizen, in deciding future directions for violent crime research.

References

American Psychological Association. (1996). *An APA brochure on youth violence.* Retrieved February 7, 2007, from http://www.apa.org/ppo/issues/pbviolence.html.

Baron, R., & Richardson, D. (1994). *Human aggression.* New York: Plenum Press.

Baumrind, D., Larzelere, R., & Cowan, P. (2002). Ordinary physical punishment: Is it harmful? Comment on Gershoff, 2002. *Psychological Bulletin, 128*(4), 580–589.

Block, J., & Crain, B. (2007). Omissions and errors in "Media violence and the American public." *American Psychologist, 62*, 252–253.

Cohen, J. (1994). The earth is round ($p < .05$). *American Psychologist, 49*, 997–1003.

Dallam, S. (2001). Science or propaganda: An examination of Rind, Tromovitch & Bauserman (1998). *Journal of Child Sexual Abuse, 9*, 109–134.

Diamond, M., & Uchiyama, A. (1999). Pornography, rape and sex crimes in Japan. *International Journal of Law and Psychiatry, 22*, 1–22.

Federal Bureau of Investigation. (1951–2004). *Uniform crime reports.* Washington, DC: Government Printing Office.

Federal Interagency Forum on Child and Family Statistics. (2007). *America's children: Key national indicators of well-being, 2007.* Retrieved July 28, 2007, from http://childstats.gov/americaschildren/index.asp.

Ferguson, C. J. (in press). Genetic contributions to antisocial personality and behavior (APB): A meta-analytic review (1996–2006) from an evolutionary perspective. *Journal of Social Psychology.*

Ferguson, C. J. (2007). The good, the bad and the ugly: A meta-analytic review of positive and negative effects of violent video games. *Psychiatric Quarterly, 78,* 309–316.

Ferguson, C. J., Rueda. S., Cruz, A., Ferguson, D., Fritz, S., & Smith, S. (2008). Violent video games and aggression: Causal relationship or byproduct of family violence and intrinsic violence motivation? *Criminal Justice and Behavior, 35,* 311–332.

Francis, T., Korns, R., Voight, R., Boisen, M., Hemphill, F., Napier, J., et al. (1955). An evaluation of the 1954 poliomyelitis vaccine trials: Summary report. *American Journal of Public Health, 45,* 1–63.

Gallup, G., Jr. (Ed). (2004). *The Gallup Poll: Public opinion 2003.* Lanham, MD: Rowman & Littlefield.

Greenberg, D., Bradford, J., & Curry, S. (1993). A comparison of sexual victimization in the childhoods of pedophiles and hebephiles. *Journal of Forensic Sciences, 2,* 432–436.

Holmes, R., & Holmes, S. (2001). *Murder in America.* Thousand Oaks, CA: Sage.

Kizman, K., Gaylord, N., Holt, A., & Kenny, E. (2003). Child witnesses to domestic violence: A meta-analytic review. *Journal of Consulting and Clinical Psychology, 71,* 339–353.

Kuhn, T. (1970). *The structure of scientific revolutions.* Chicago: Chicago University Press.

Loftus, G. (1996). Psychology will be a much better science when we change the way we analyze data. *Current Directions in Psychological Science, 5,* 161–171.

Paik, H., & Comstock, G. (1994). The effects of television violence on antisocial behavior: A meta-analysis. *Communication Research, 21,* 516–539.

Pinker, S. (2002). *The blank slate: The modern denial of human nature.* New York: Penguin.

Pratt, T., & Cullen, C. (2000). The empirical status of Gottfredson and Hirschi's general theory of crime: A meta-analysis. *Criminology, 38,* 931–964.

Pratt, T., & Cullen, C. (2005). Assessing macro-level predictors and theories of crime: A meta-analysis. In M. Tomry (Ed.), *Crime and justice: A review of research* (Vol. 32, pp. 373–450). Chicago: University of Chicago Press.

Redding, R. (2001). Sociopolitical diversity in psychology: The case for pluralism. *American Psychologist, 56,* 205–215.

Rhee, S., & Waldman, I. (2002). Genetic and environmental influences on antisocial behavior: A meta-analysis of twin and adoption studies. *Psychological Bulletin, 128,* 490–529.

Rind, B., Tromovitch, P., & Bauserman, R. (1998). A meta-analytic examination of assumed properties of child sexual abuse using college samples. *Psychological Bulletin, 124,* 22–53.

Rivadeneyra, R. (2006). Do you see what I see? Latino Americans' perceptions of the images on television. *Journal of Adolescent Research, 21,* 393–414.

Rosnow, R., & Rosenthal, R. (2003). Effect sizes for experimenting psychologists. *Canadian Journal of Experimental Psychology, 57,* 221–237.

Shapin, S. (1995). Here and everywhere: Sociology of scientific knowledge. *Annual Review of Sociology, 21,* 289–231.

Skinner, B. (1987). Whatever happened to psychology as the science of behavior. *American Psychologist, 42,* 780–786.

Straus, M., & Yodanis, C. (1996). Corporal punishment in adolescence and physical assaults on spouses in later life: What accounts for the link? *Journal of Marriage and the Family, 58,* 825–841.

Surette, R. (2006). *Media, crime, and criminal justice: Images, realities and policies.* Florence, KY: Wadsworth.

Tedeschi, J., & Quigley, B. (1996). Limitations of laboratory paradigms for studying aggression. *Aggression & Violent Behavior, 2,* 163–177.

Thornhill, R., & Palmer, C. (2000). *A natural history of rape.* Cambridge: MIT Press.

Tjaden, P., & Thoennes, N. (2006). *Extent, nature and consequences of rape victimization: Findings from the National Violence Against Women Survey.* Washington, DC: National Institute of Justice.

Travis, C. (2003). *Evolution, gender and rape.* Cambridge: MIT Press.

Wasserman, D., & Wachbroit, R. (2001). *Genetics and criminal behavior.* New York: Cambridge University Press.

World Health Organization. (2007). *Definition and typology of violence.* Retrieved September 28, 2007, from http://www.who.int/violenceprevention/approach/definition/en/index.html.

Wynder, F., & Graham, E. (1950). Tobacco smoking as a possible etiological factor in brochiogenic carcinoma. *Journal of the American Medical Association, 143,* 329–336.

CHAPTER 2

Family and Social Influences on Violent Crime

John C. Kilburn, Jr., and Jenifer Lee

The issue of violent crime remains a pressing facet of American society that affects a number of aspects of our lives. Various researchers (DuBow, McCabe, & Kaplan, 1979; Kilburn & Shrum, 1998; Lavrakas, 1981) have discussed numerous ways that people alter their lives in hope of providing security or protection against criminal victimization. Many individuals take precautions such as avoiding going out at night, staying away from certain "high-risk" places, using home security measures, and carrying guns for protection. In addition, some neighborhoods combine resources to provide protection for their members, such as neighborhood watches. Municipal governments also provide protection in the form of policing, and the federal government provides national defense and homeland security. However, truly protecting ourselves from violent crime cannot occur without an adequate understanding of the social forces that place certain individuals and neighborhoods at risk for increased violence.

In an effort to understand and examine the social causes of violence, the American Sociological Association (ASA) formed a study group in the 1990s. Among the conclusions drawn were that "violence is a social behavior that reflects long- and short-term socialization effects, occurs in the context of at least two people, and it is more probable under certain social situations and conditions than others" (Levine & Rosich, 1996, p. 3). Another finding of the ASA study group involved how individuals define and perceive violence. The

ASA found that "individual and group perceptions of violence and its seriousness are mediated by social change and by cultural and social norms about what constitutes acceptable and unacceptable behavior" (p. 3). Put more simply, different individuals and cultures define violence differently.

Varying definitions of violence can influence issues ranging from estimating the prevalence of violence, justification for funding specific research studies, designing violence prevention programs, funding battered women's shelters, setting school discipline policies, to setting sentencing guidelines for violent offenders. As such, what constitutes violence may differ depending on the motives of the individual offering the definition. Activist groups, for instance, may define violence quite broadly, attempting to draw attention to a "crisis."

CASE STUDY: TIMOTHY MCVEIGH AND THE BOMBING OF THE MURRAH FEDERAL BUILDING

On April 19, 1995, approximately 9 a.m., a 20-foot-long yellow Ryder Rental truck was parked just outside of the Alfred P. Murrah Federal Building. The driver got out of the truck and walked away. Minutes later a massive explosion came from the truck, destroying a large portion of the building. One hundred and sixty-eight people, including nineteen children, were killed. More than 500 others were injured as a large portion of the building collapsed. Twenty-seven-year-old Timothy James McVeigh got in his 1977 yellow Mercury Grand Marquis and drove north on I-35. McVeigh had earlier removed the license plate from the vehicle in order to reduce identifying information, but the lack of a license plate was noticed by an Oklahoma Patrol Officer, Charlie Hanger. McVeigh was pulled over and had no vehicle registration or proof of insurance. When McVeigh produced his driver's license, the officer noticed that McVeigh had a 9 mm Glock, an ammunition clip, and a knife on his body. McVeigh was arrested, though there was very little indication at the time that he was responsible for the horrendous act that had taken place just 90 minutes before. Preliminary checks showed that McVeigh had no criminal record, and a search of his vehicle yielded nothing suspicious.

Due to a substantial court backlog, McVeigh was held for his suspicious weapons and vehicle offense. At the time, investigative teams were working feverishly, attempting to discover clues related to the bombing. Some suspected foreign terrorists, while others saw significance in the date, April 19, which was the second anniversary of the government raid on the Branch Davidian compound in Waco, Texas. Although the explosion was massive, the truck's license plate and identifying information from the truck's rear axle provided evidence that the truck was rented by Robert Kling, an alias used by McVeigh when he reserved the vehicle at Elliott's Body Shop in Junction City, Kansas. The truck was picked up on April 17 and fitted with over two tons of an ammonium nitrate and fuel explosive.

Sketch artists were able to create two drawings of the two men who picked up the truck, and the manager of the nearby Dreamland Motel was able to link one of the sketches to a man who registered under the name Timothy McVeigh. McVeigh had parked both a Ryder truck and a yellow Grand Marquis in the parking lot.

McVeigh's Motivation

There is nothing in McVeigh's early life history that indicates that he would eventually commit such a horrendous act. He was born on April 23, 1968 and raised in the small town of Pendleton, New York. His father was a blue-collar laborer. Like many other young boys in the United States, he enjoyed hunting and the outdoors and developed an interest in guns. His childhood was described as happy; he worked at Burger King during high school and he graduated from high school with honors (Serrano, 1998). McVeigh did face some degree of family discord, as his parents divorced in 1986.

With time, McVeigh's interest in guns began to grow. He spent more time learning about issues related to the Second Amendment to the Constitution. He took a job as an armed security guard for an armored truck service. He was considered a good employee, and no suspicious incidents occurred during his service on the job. It was at this time that McVeigh is believed to have read *The Turner Diaries*, a book in which the main character truck-bombs the Washington FBI headquarters to protest the imposition of gun-control laws. He was also enamored with *Red Dawn*, a movie about a young makeshift militia that defends the nation from communist troops invading the United States.

Shortly after his 20th birthday, McVeigh enlisted in the Army. His service was distinguished and his tour of duty during the 1991 Gulf War earned him numerous decorations, including the Bronze Star. McVeigh attempted to join the Special Forces shortly after returning from Iraq, but he failed to make the cut. He left the Army shortly afterward. However, in basic training McVeigh met two men who would change his life tremendously: Terry Nichols and Michael Fortier. McVeigh was disillusioned with many aspects of the American government. He had read numerous accounts of the government attempting to limit the rights of gun owners. McVeigh earned part of his income by charging a fee to purchase guns for people who did not want their names listed on the gun purchase forms. Guns were a key part of his life. McVeigh vowed revenge for the government raid on the Branch Davidians. Enlisting the assistance of his Army buddies, Nichols and Fortier, McVeigh designed a plot to attack the Murrah building and kill federal law enforcement agents.

Throughout his arrest and trail, McVeigh showed no remorse. He frequently mentioned that he considered his actions patriotic (Michel & Herbeck, 2001). Even with his opportunity to make a final statement, McVeigh offered no apology for his actions.

How Could This Have Been Prevented?

Some people could argue that because of his significant record of accomplishment and lack of criminal record, McVeigh's actions were unpredictable. He was a good student, and he had respectable employment and military service records. While being the child of divorced parents and not making the cut for the U.S. Army Special Forces may be considered setbacks, numerous people experience these hardships without turning to crime or terrorism. The only clues were those related to suspicious activities that may have taken place shortly before the bombing. The significant purchase of materials that were used for the bomb may have been suspected and possibly he may have displayed some erratic behaviors. However, neither large purchases of fertilizer nor erratic behavior can serve as justification for preventive detention. At best, crime prevention can monitor actions of groups and individuals who speak in subversive and terroristic terms.

To address violent crime, do we focus our energies on treating or pun-ishing the offender, supporting the victim, or changing society? Of course, all aspects of the problem should be addressed, and in an ideal world with infinite resources to address every significant variable related to violence, we may be able to drastically reduce the problem of violence in society. However, the stark reality is that resources, time, and energy to focus on the problem are finite.

In an effort to determine what course(s) of action should or need to be taken, the causes of violence must be investigated. Many different disciplines have devoted significant time and resources to understanding the phenomenon of violence. Sociologists, criminologists, and psychologists are just a few of the groups attempting to understand various aspects of violence. In this chapter, we examine violent crime from a social perspective. We begin first by examining several leading social theories of violence. Second, we examine trends in violent crime in the United States and discuss how violent crime is measured. Finally, we discuss important family, school, and neighborhood influences on violent crime.

Theories of Violence

Considerable scientific and policy resources have been directed at the problem of violence in an attempt to isolate its "true cause." Gradually, most scientists have come to understand that there is simply no one cause that leads to violence and that different individuals may become violent for different reasons. However, we do have some theoretical frameworks that offer some explanations of violent behavior. These theories focus on neighborhoods, family environments, and social environments in addition to other sociological, criminological, and psychological influences.

Strain Theory

Strain Theory was largely advanced by the work of Robert Merton (1938). Merton's theory focuses on societal goals (culturally defined goals) and the socially approved methods of attaining those goals. For example, society may dictate that individuals should seek financial resources through socially sanctioned work. As human beings, we all have some self-interest and goals that have developed from this self-interest. Societies then establish culturally approved procedures for attaining those goals. Merton developed roles or modes of adaptation to society based upon how an individual rejects or accepts the goals and methods of achieving those goals. Those who accepted and followed the standard goals of society and went about achieving those goals through generally acceptable means were considered *conformists*. Conformists, according to Merton, generally avoided crime. According to Merton's adaptations, the groups most likely to be involved in crime were those he labeled as *innovators*. This group accepted the goals of society yet rejected the socially approved means to attain them. Such an individual may still seek financial resources but does so through burglary or theft rather than through work.

One disadvantage of this particular approach to or explanation of crimes of violence is that it focuses on the actions of the poor and disadvantaged. As such, it does not explain phenomena such as white-collar crime or other crimes by well-to-do individuals. Also, this theory may not provide a comprehensive explanation for violence because violence may not always be motivated by culturally defined goals (e.g., economic success). A serial murderer who is motivated by sexual pleasure derived from torturing victims is an example of an offender who does not fit well within strain theory.

Social Learning Theory

Social Learning Theory is based on the idea that we learn from the interactions we have with others and model the behaviors or attitudes of others viewed during that interaction. These behaviors and attitudes come from interactions with family, friends, coworkers, and others, and each of these may support or oppose criminal behavior. The greater frequency with which a particular behavior is viewed, particularly when viewed during interactions with close associates, the more likely the behavior is to be modeled.

Rational Choice Theory

Rational Choice Theory is among the least complicated explanations for any action and involves a simple cost-benefit analysis. A violent individual gains some benefit from either threatening violence or acting out violently. If he or she does not receive, or fear receiving, some significant punishment, then he or she is more likely to act on his or her drive to act out in a violent manner (Cornish & Clarke, 1986).

Subculture of Violence

The notion of a subculture of violence, such as among Southern men or smaller communities within a city, has been investigated and explored through the use of crime mapping. Crime mapping offers the opportunity to study the nature of crime in terms of geographic clusters of offenses as well as the location of the offenders. While modern Geographic Information Systems may be used to study trends, this process of investigating the connection between crime and location dates back many years to the simple placement of pins on a map to represent significant events. This particular approach to understanding violence and crime has found that certain crimes are more likely to occur in certain regions or areas of a community.

For example, in their analysis of residences of juvenile offenders in Chicago, Shaw and McKay (1969) noted that residences of juvenile offenders were concentrated in the industrial areas of the city just outside the central business district. Wolfgang and Ferracuti (1982) drew on their observations of homicide patterns in Philadelphia to note that residents of some areas saw violence as more acceptable than did others.

Symbolic Interactionism

While many theories of violence focus on the internal motivation of offenders, there are situational aspects to violence that explain why some individuals act out violently. Research is clear that some individuals are more prone to violence than others. However, how can we understand when an individual with a history of violence does or does not act out violently? While the previously mentioned theories examine the patterns of violence and the rates of violent acts through quantitative (or statistical) analysis of crime data, other scholars argue that understanding the situation and the meaning of the act is essential to explaining why violent acts occur (Athens, 1997; Sommers & Baskin, 1993).

Lonnie Athens (1997) approaches the study of violent acts from a symbolic interactionist perspective. According to this perspective, each actor involved in a potential confrontation interprets the meaning of the situation, makes a judgment, and then takes action. Athens argues that this methodology does not look for the cause of the violent actions or characteristics of the specific violent offender. Instead, his research methodology offers the opportunity to understand the situation and interactive elements of what was going on at the time the act took place. For example, what was the offender thinking when he or she participated in the violent act?

There are certain advantages to this methodology. Aggregate studies (i.e., those based on group differences) examine characteristics of the offender. While there are numerous characteristics of offenders that may lead us to some interesting conclusions, knowledge of these characteristics rarely are sufficient in themselves to understand the immediate cause of a violent act. For example, in looking at correlates of violent behavior, it is recognized that young adult males are more likely to act violently than are older males. However, the simple relationship of age and violent behavior offers little explanation of why a particular violent act may have occurred.

According to symbolic interactionism, violence is a product of the offender's interpretation of the situation. Athens (1997, p. 34) shares an account of victim-precipitated violence. For example, one offender describes the circumstances leading to his violent actions:

I was sitting at a bar drinking beer when this guy sitting next to me went to play the pinball machine. When he came back to the bar, he said, "You've been drinking my beer. I had a full can of beer when I went over to that pinball machine." I said, "I ain't drank none of your beer." He said, "You better buy me another can of beer." I said, "Shit no, I ain't." At first I didn't know whether he really thought I had drank some of his beer or was trying to bluff me into buying him a can, but when he later said, "You're gonna buy me another fucking can of beer," I knew then he was handing me that to start some crap, so I knew for sure that I wasn't gonna buy him any beer. He told me again to buy him a beer. I said, "Hell no." I figured if I showed him that I wasn't gonna buy him a beer, he wouldn't push it, but then he said, "You better go on and buy me another fucking beer." All I said was, "I don't want any trouble; I'm just out of the pen, so go on and leave me alone, 'cause I ain't about to buy you any beer." He just kept looking. Then I started thinking he was out to do something to me. He pulled out a knife and made for me, and I shot him once in the arm. He kept on coming, so I had to finish him off. He was out to kill me.

Other circumstances that Athens (1997) writes about include individuals who act violently out of frustration or interpret events through a lens of hatred. He noted that some violent offenders view themselves as gaining status by being violent. Individuals may also gain power in their personal, romantic, or intimate relationships by harming their partners. In sum, motivations for violent actions may be dependent on the situation and the interpretation of events by the individual offender.

Crime Statistics

Violent crime trends in the United States follow an interesting path. Since the government started keeping records in the 1930s, we have seen a pattern of rising and declining murder rates, though there is no definitive agreement on

Table 2.1   Changes in Crime Rates in the United States From 1995 to 2005

Year	VC Rate	Murder and Manslaughter	Assault	Rape
1995	758.2	9.8	433.4	42.3
2005	469.2	5.6	291.1	31.7

NOTE: VC Rate = violent crime rate per 100,000

the causes of this variation. In recent years, most violent crime rates have dropped substantially (see Table 2.1).

One of the most commonly used sets of national crime statistics is the Federal Bureau of Investigation's Uniform Crime Reports (UCR). The UCR is a record of crimes reported to and recorded by the various policing agencies across the United States. While the UCR is frequently used to compare crime statistics among cities, one major criticism is that those reports only capture crimes that are reported to the police. Much of the information provided in and by the UCR is used to investigate and understand offending behavior or crimes that have been committed. Though the UCR is the official crime statistics of the United States, there are significant issues and shortcomings with using this information to gain knowledge of the nature and extent of crime victimization. For instance, many crimes, such as rape or domestic violence, may not be reported to the police. Even simple thefts may not be reported often, due to the expectation that police will have little interest in minor crimes. There are several possible reasons that an individual may fail to report or be reluctant to report being a crime victim to the police. These can include fear of reprisals, embarrassment, involvement in the criminal act, and distrust of law enforcement officials. In order to address the shortfalls of the UCR, national victimization surveys have been developed. National victimization surveys are a relatively new phenomenon that provides additional information about crime and victimization in the United States.

Victimization surveys focus specifically on criminal victimization that takes place in the United States. The 1975 and 1985 National Family Violence Surveys, in addition to the National Crime Victimization Survey (NCVS), provided a great deal of the initial information on criminal victimization in the United States. Since the development of the NCVS in the early 1970s, it has become a primary source of information on crime victims. The NCVS provides information on the victims of crime and also provides information on the offense, the victim-offender relationship, and any injury suffered by the victim.

While victimization surveys are likely to gather information on many violent actions that are never reported to the police, these studies are still criticized for failing to provide a complete picture of criminal victimization. One of the major difficulties with gaining information about victimization is obtaining this information from victims. Many victims are reluctant to discuss their victimization, even in anonymous surveys. Also, because households are studied and victims of violence are likely to be more transient than those not victimized, there is a potential undercount of victims of violent crime who do not reside in households (Gottfredson & Hindelang, 1981).

As with all surveys, self-report surveys such as the NCVS have shortcomings, such as the reasons listed above for people's reluctance to report being the victim of a crime. While there are some advantages to using self-report surveys (e.g., they may capture many incidents that were not reported to the police), the shortcomings do need to be addressed.

Self-report surveys of victimization (such as the NCVS) are subject to some degree of inaccuracy due to a number of factors including the victim's memory, potential relationship between the victim and offender (e.g., a battered wife is unlikely to discuss being attacked by her husband with a stranger on the phone, particularly if her husband is standing nearby), fear, and embarrassment. Researchers have noted that human memories are far from perfect (Loftus, 1996; Loftus & Palmer, 1974), and this fact may negatively impact the ability of victims to provide researchers with accurate information. If the victim has some type of relationship with the offender (e.g., acquaintance, coworker, classmate, spouse, relative), this may lead to a greater likelihood that the victimization will go unreported than if the victim and offender were strangers (Hindelang, 1976).

Family-Related Potential Causes of Crime

Poverty and the Breakdown of the Family

Geographical analyses have routinely identified substantially higher crime rates in certain sections of urban areas, which apparently shows that some areas are very dangerous while other areas are safe. Blau and Blau (1982) argue that the frustration over income inequality leads to tensions that create conditions for violence. LaFree (1999), who studied trends of violence over the long term, notes that circumstances influencing crime rates seem to change over time. His explanation suggests that if we want to simplify the argument that economic conditions create circumstances that lead to higher rates of violent crime, we must then carefully define the economic variables that influence violent behavior. One measure, referred to as an *absolute measure* of economic well-being, relates to how well individuals or groups fare in terms of measures like income and unemployment.

Another measure LaFree (1999) uses to explain the economic impact on crime is *relative measure*, which focuses on how well a person is doing compared to other groups. LaFree argues that absolute measures seemed to influence crime rates in the years immediately following World War II. However, as the United States entered the second half of the 20th century and the debates on inequality in America came to the forefront, relative measures were more effective at explaining longitudinal crime rates in the postwar United States. This may mean that the frustrations felt are not due to being an individual lacking economic well-being but, instead, are due to having less than others. In other words, it may not be low-income status, per se, that predisposes one to crime, but rather coming from a low-income background and feeling resentment when viewing others from a high-income background.

Most urban regions in the United States have faced a loss of inner-city jobs with the process of deindustrialization and jobs moving abroad. This process led to significant urban family disruption and an increase in the concentration of urban single-parent households (Wilson, 1987). Many of these areas with a large percentage of single-parent households face conditions for family disruption and disorder in neighborhoods (Sampson, 1987; Shihadeh & Ousey, 1996; Shihadeh & Steffensmeir, 1994). This loss of jobs translates to social disorder and disorganization. Numerous researchers link the concentration of single-parent mothers with high crime due to the economic hardship that low-income areas face (Bennett & Fraser, 2000; Sampson & Laub, 1994; Shihadeh & Steffensmeir, 1994).

Government resources should see family support programs as assisting in the war on crime. Interventions along these lines call for the revitalization of urban environments. By providing well-paying jobs for workers in the region, we are creating more equality and contributing to the resources that build families, home ownership, and stable communities.

In sociology, we often state that the family is the primary unit of socialization. We spend a significant amount of our time with our families during our early developmental stages. We develop our identities through the family's social status and our neighborhood of residence. Children who are well-integrated and accepting of conventional rules are less likely to act in a delinquent manner (Braithwaite, 1989). But while families are sometimes considered safe, protective environments, there is sometimes a dark side of violence in various dating and family relationships.

Witnessing Violence

The issue of the impact of witnessing violence on a child's behavior is one that has a long history of interest and research. Witnessing abuse or violence cannot be considered a sole cause of a person's violent behavior. However, even one-year-old infants reflect much of the distress related to conflict when they are exposed to angry verbal disagreements (De Jonghe, Bogat, Levendosky, Von Eye, & Davidson, 2005). Also, exposure to verbal or physical conflicts may hinder children's development and verbal abilities (Feerick & Haugaard, 1999). These and other long-term effects may be only some of the consequences for children who witness violence and abuse. Long-term effects are difficult to study because other life experiences take place over time that may attenuate or enhance the effects of what an individual experienced in early childhood. In other words, because violent behavior is likely caused by multiple factors, it is difficult to separate early childhood influences from later influences, or family influences (such as witnessing family violence) from other social factors (such as a dysfunctional peer group).

One question is whether domestic violence perpetrators are created by witnessing acts of domestic violence between their parents (or stepparents) during their childhood. Some research has found that men exposed to parental violence are substantially more likely to be violent toward their spouse than are men not exposed to parental violence (Barnett, Miller-Perrin, & Perrin, 1997). Additionally, research has found that females exposed to parental violence could be slightly more likely to be victims of partnership violence (Barnett et al., 1997). This is a complex question because exposure to violence does not take place in a vacuum. Those who see physical violence also may be exposed to other disadvantages such as varying degrees of trauma, psychological maltreatment, physical abuse, and neglect. Bevan and Higgins (2002) found that witnessing violence, in and of itself, is not significantly related to acting out violently.

Corporal Punishment

One hotly debated issue is that of parents spanking their children. An October, 2002 ABC News Poll showed that 65% of Americans approve of spanking children; however, only 27% thought that spanking should be permitted in school (Crandall, 2002). Of those who were parents with minor children residing in their home, 50% admitted to spanking their children while 45% claimed they did not. However, in terms of region of the country, 62% of Southerners reported spanking their children as compared to 41% of those residing in other regions. This seems to fit with other research that demonstrates that Southerners in general have a wider acceptance of various types of violent actions (Ellison, 1991).

Several generations of schoolchildren (up to the 1960s) were subjected to some form of corporal punishment in the schools. While there are various statutes governing what schools may or may not do to discipline children, this issue continues to be debated by various school boards, advocacy groups, and parents. Popular arguments supporting corporal punishment frequently develop along the lines that discipline is lost in the modern school, and corporal punishment, along with parents' support of the use of corporal punishment, may be effective in creating a more disciplined environment in the schools. However, 28 states currently ban corporal punishment in the schools (Hague, 2006). Opponents of corporal punishment in the schools frequently evoke parental responsibility for discipline and question the effectiveness of such disciplinary actions in controlling the behavior of school-aged children in the school environment.

Straus (2001) considers one of the root causes of violence in America to be the wide practice of corporal punishment. People are introduced to violence at an early age, and they grow up attempting to solve conflicts through violence. The extension of this idea is that those individuals who were spanked as children learned that there are certain circumstances in which violence is acceptable. This may lead to many offenders feeling justified in their violent behavior, given that they have been taught that violence is an acceptable way of asserting authority. Current research on spanking effects has been mixed, and it has proven difficult to separate spanking from more serious forms of physical abuse (Baumrind, Larzelere, & Cowan, 2002). One parent may follow very clear spanking guidelines while another parent may get out of control and cause physical or emotional damage to a child. Parents causing serious harm may very well think that their actions were performed with the best of intentions in controlling the children's behavior. Again, the perspective of the one inflicting the harm may differ from the perspective of the one experiencing the harm/violence.

School-Related Potential Causes of Crime

Bullying

While defining bullying is difficult, most definitions include a wide range of verbal and physical offending behaviors, such as those described by Olweus (2003):

> A person who intentionally inflicts, or attempts to inflict, injury or discomfort on someone else is engaging in negative actions, a term similar to the definition of aggressive behavior in the social sciences. People carry out negative actions through physical contact, with words, or in more indirect ways, such as making mean faces or gestures, spreading rumors, or intentionally excluding someone from the group. (p. 12)

Based on this definition of the problem, the Olweus Bullying Prevention Program was developed to reduce aggressive behaviors and develop prosocial skills. This program focuses on creating a nurturing school environment with clear rules and feedback from positive role models.

Several of the programs that attempt to develop prosocial skills are not clearly dealing with the significant causes of bullying behavior. This may be due, in part, to our general lack of understanding regarding what truly causes violence in adults and adolescents. Also, another area of concern is the general issue of defining violence and, in this case, bullying.

Teaching Anti-Bullying in Schools

There are various governmental responses to bullying in schools. While this issue has been documented for many years (Shulman, 1930; Thrasher, 1933), the 1994 renaming of the Drug-Free Schools and Community Act (DFSCA) as the Safe and Drug-Free Schools Act (SDFSCA) was a significant landmark event, in that this program provided federal funds to states offering treatment and intervention programs. While many people support the idea of nonviolence programs, criticisms regarding the effectiveness of these programs have led to a reduction in funds for these programs (Sherman, 2000).

While these programs are politically popular due to the general public's demand for somebody to do something about this violence, the effectiveness of these programs continues to be subject to debate. Some argue that these programs have been successful (Farrell, Meyer, Sullivan, & Kung, 2003; Olweus, 1993) while others argue that these programs have a minimal effect on reducing violent behavior (Ferguson, San Miguel, Kilburn, & Sanchez, 2007).

Neighborhood-Related Causes of Crime

Subculture of Violence

Residents in a specific geographic location develop their own norms and definitions about appropriate actions. Wolfgang and Ferracuti (1982) claim that some portions of the population of a region develop values that are more tolerant of violent acts.

From this work, Anderson (1999) describes an action referred to as the "Code of the Street."

> The street culture has evolved a "code of the street," which amounts to a set of informal rules governing interpersonal public behavior, particularly violence. The rules prescribe both proper comportment and the proper way to respond if challenged. They regulate the use of violence and so supply a rationale allowing those who are inclined to aggression to precipitate violent encounters in an approved way. The rules have been established and are enforced mainly by the street-oriented; but on the streets the distinction between street and decent is often irrelevant. Everybody knows that if the rules are violated, there are penalties. Knowledge of the code is thus largely defensive, and it is literally necessary for operating in public. Therefore, though families with a decency orientation are usually opposed to the values of the code, they often reluctantly encourage their children's familiarity with it in order to enable them to negotiate the inner-city environment. (p. 33)

Once again, while the aggregations of quantitative data may show that a larger percentage of residents in one community may be more likely to act in a violent manner than those residing in another community, how do we explain violent actions that occur in relatively "safe" communities?

While violence may be common in society, most violent people do not act violently on a daily basis, nor do they harm everyone they come into contact with. Even the most violent offenders may, at times, express caring and nurturing for others. For example, L.A. gangster Sanyika Shakur, a.k.a. Monster, of the Eight-Trey Crips gang, showed genuine compassion for his mother and his brother at the same time he was participating in the most violent acts on the street. There were circumstances that encouraged his violent behavior. Most violent acts are directed at particular individuals, at a specific time and place.

Sanyika Shakur (1993) recounts how he earned his gang nickname, "Monster."

> In the neighborhood, respect was forthcoming. In 1977, when I was thirteen, while robbing a man I turned my head and was hit in the face. The man tried to run, but was tripped by Tray Ball, who then held him for me. I stomped him for twenty minutes before leaving him unconscious in the alley. Later that night, I learned that the man had lapsed into a coma and was disfigured from my stomping. The police told bystanders that the person responsible for this was a "monster." The name stuck, and I took that as a moniker over my birth name. As Monster, however, I had to consistently be more vicious and live up to my name. (p. 13)

Other offenders claim they were generally frustrated when they struck out to do their crime. While this approach to understanding violent behavior may yield detailed information about specific incidents of violence, designing appropriate methods for prevention of violent actions and intervention continues to challenge scholars.

Several specific types of violence have emerged and garnered the attention of the general public, policymakers, researchers, and the criminal justice system. While these forms of violence have existed for years, it has only been recently that these particular types of violence have gained widespread recognition. One example of this is hate crimes.

Hate Crimes

Hate crimes are defined by the Federal Bureau of Investigation as "criminal offenses that are motivated, in whole or in part, by the offender's bias against a race, religion, sexual orientation, ethnicity/national origin, or disability and are committed against persons, property, or society" (U.S. Department of Justice, 2006). The FBI has been charged with collecting and disseminating information on hate crimes since the passage of the Hate

Crime Statistics Act of 1990. According to the FBI's UCR Hate Crime Statistics, there were 6 hate crime murder or nonnegligent manslaughter victims in 2005. There were 5 murder/nonnegligent manslaughter victims in 2004; 14 in 2003; and 11 in 2002. There were a total of 7,163 hate crime incidents reported by 2,073 law enforcement agencies in 2005. Of those, 4,208 were crimes against persons (almost 60% of all hate crimes). In light of the 1,390,695 violent crimes recorded by the UCR, these numbers do not seem to be highly significant. However, the sentiment related to these crimes clearly contributes to the sense of intimidation among various groups in the United States, and the data suggest that there are numerous social inequalities, vulnerabilities, and a sense of subordination in society (Grattet & Jenness, 2001).

There are some critics of hate crime legislation who argue that these laws selectively favor some groups over others; therefore, these crimes do not warrant an entire new set of laws and legislation ("Troopers won't back," 2001). However, proponents of the legislation argue that crimes taking place because of an individual's membership in a particular group are particularly harmful because they violate the societal values of inclusion and diversity (Lee, 2006).

As with most crimes, hate crimes suffer from underreporting. Reasons for underreporting these offenses likely mirror reasons for underreporting other types of crimes. Hate crime victims may fail to report because of embarrassment, fear of retaliation, or the real/perceived lack of interest on the part of law enforcement officials (Lee, 2006). As noted earlier, only 2,073 out of 12,417 participating agencies submitted a report of a hate crime incident in their jurisdiction. This means just under 17% of all participating law enforcement agencies in the United States recorded and reported a hate crime. While it is possible this is an accurate reflection of the frequency of hate crimes, it is likely that police are actually underreporting hate crime incidents in their jurisdictions. Agencies could underreport because of lack of clarity on the definition of a hate crime, confusion over how to identify a hate crime, lack of victim cooperation, or personal/agency bias against members of groups likely to be targeted.

Conclusion

If the problem of violence were easy to understand or solve, violent crime would have been largely eradicated already. However, violence has been a continuous social problem throughout history. Attempts to explain all aspects of violence, ranging from genetic predisposition, social encounters, violence in relationships, variable crime rates in neighborhoods, to differences between regions of the country, are essential to understanding the phenomenon of violent behavior.

Attempts to scientifically study the problem of violent crime may have led to the development of policies that have contributed to the reduction of overall rates of violence in the United States over the past 30 years. Though the impact of most social policies and programs are truly difficult to measure, it is essential to understand the facts regarding the impact of a policy without getting bogged down in personal opinions and politics (Rossi & Freeman, 1993). Building policy from a solid grounding in social facts may lead to a reduction in violent behavior. We cannot simplify our understanding of violence by offering simple political solutions and focusing on only one aspect of the problem without continued dialogue about the various potential causes of violence.

Discussion Questions

1. How should violence be defined? Should it depend on who is defining it (e.g., victims, advocates, researchers, CJS officials) and why they are seeking to do so (e.g., support services, acquisition of knowledge about the issue, creation of laws)?

2. How do you think the definition of crime by a victim, a researcher, and a criminal justice official would differ? What would each definition include and how would they differ?

3. Would you consider violence at a sporting event a criminal offense? Think about the high-profile fight during an NBA game between the Pacers and Pistons in 2004 and the sideline-clearing fight that took place during a college football game between two Florida teams. Also, consider fights that take place during hockey games or bench-clearing brawls during major league baseball games. Are these not criminal acts? Do we excuse them because of the context in which they take place? Should we?

4. Using examples of violent acts included in this chapter, choose two sociological, criminological, and/or psychological theories to explain violence. Why would you select these particular theories?

Internet Resources

American Society of Criminology: http://www.asc41.com/

American Sociological Association: http://www.asanet.org/

Bullying UK: http://www.bullying.co.uk/

Federal Bureau of Investigations Page on Hate Crimes: http://www.fbi .gov/hq/cid/civilrights/hate.htm

Stop Family Violence: http://www.stopfamilyviolence.org/

References

Anderson, E. (1999). *Code of the street.* New York: Norton.

Athens, L. (1997). *Violent criminal acts and actors revisited.* Urbana: University of Illinois Press.

Barnett, O. W., Miller-Perrin, C. L., & Perrin, R. D. (1997). *Family violence across the lifespan: An introduction.* Thousand Oaks, CA: Sage.

Baumrind, D., Larzelere, R. E., & Cowan, P. E. (2002). Ordinary physical punishment. Is it harmful? Comment on Gershoff. *Psychological Bulletin, 128*(4), 580–589.

Bennett, M. D., & Fraser, M. W. (2000). Urban violence among African American males: Integrating family, neighborhood, and peer perspectives. *Journal of Sociology and Social Welfare, 27*(3), 93–117.

Bevan, E., & Higgins, D. J. (2002). Is domestic violence learned? The contribution of five forms of child maltreatment to men's violence and adjustment. *Journal of Family Violence, 17,* 223–245.

Blau, J. R., & Blau, P. M. (1982). The cost of inequality: Metropolitan structure and violent crime. *American Sociological Review, 47,* 114–129.

Braithwaite, J. (1989). *Crime, shame, and reintegration.* Melbourne: Cambridge University Press.

Cornish, D., & Clarke, R. V. (1986). Introduction. In D. Cornish & R. V. Clarke (Eds.), *The reasoning criminal* (pp. 1–16). New York: Springer-Verlag.

Crandall, J. (2002, October 29). Most say spankings OK by parents but not by grade-school teachers. abcnews.com. Retrieved October 30, 2007, from http://www.icrsurvey.com/ Studyaspx?f=ABC_Spanking_1102.html.

DeJonghe, E. S., Bogat, A., Levendosky, A. A., Von Eye, A., & Davidson, W. S., II. (2005). Infant exposure to domestic violence predicts heightened sensitivity to adult verbal conflict. *Infant Mental Health Journal, 26,* 268–281.

DuBow, F., McCabe, E., & Kaplan, G. (1979). *Reactions to crime: A critical review of the literature.* Washington, DC: U.S. Department of Justice.

Ellison, C. G. (1991). An eye for an eye? A note on the southern subculture of violence thesis. *Social Forces, 69,* 1223–1239.

Farrell, A., Meyer, A., Sullivan, T., & Kung, E. (2003). Evaluation of the responding in peaceful and positive ways (RIPP) seventh-grade violence prevention curriculum. *Journal of Child and Family Studies, 12*(1), 101–120.

Feerick, M. M., & Haugaard, J. J. (1999). Long-term effects of witnessing marital violence for women: The contribution of childhood physical and sexual abuse. *Journal of Family Violence, 14,* 377–398.

Ferguson, C. J., San Miguel, C., Kilburn, J., & Sanchez, P. (2007). The effectiveness of school-based anti-bullying programs: A meta-analytic review. *Criminal Justice Review, 32*(4), 401–414.

Gottfredson, M., & Hindelang, M. J. (1981). Sociological aspects of criminal victimization. *Annual Review of Sociology, 7,* 107–128.

Grattet, R., & Jenness, V. (2001). Examining the boundaries of hate crime law: Disabilities and the dilemma of difference. *The Journal of Criminal Law and Criminology, 91,* 653–698.

Hague, D. R. (2006). The Ninth Amendment: A constitutional challenge to corporal punishment in public schools. *Kansas Law Review, 55,* 429–461.

Hindelang, M. (1976). *Criminal victimization in eight American cities: A descriptive analysis of common theft and assault.* Cambridge, MA: Ballinger.

Kilburn, J., & Shrum, W. (1998). Private and collective protection in urban areas. *Urban Affairs Review, 33,* 790–812.

LaFree, G. (1999). Declining violent crime rates in the 1990s: Predicting crime booms and busts. *Annual Review of Sociology, 25,* 145–168.

Lavrakas, P. J. (1981). Impact of crime on households. In D. A. Lewis (Ed.), *Reactions to crime* (pp. 67–85). Beverly Hills, CA: Sage.

Lee, J. (2006). Judging the hate crime victim: Law school student perceptions and the effects of individual and law school factors. *Dissertation Abstracts International, 67*(1). (UMI No. 3205809)

Levine, F. J., & Rosich, K. J. (1996). *Social causes of violence: Crafting a science agenda.* Washington, DC: American Sociological Association.

Loftus, E. F. (1996). *Eyewitness testimony.* Cambridge, MA: Harvard University Press.

Loftus, E. F., & Palmer, J. C. (1974). Reconstruction of automobile destruction: An example of the interaction between language and memory. *Journal of Verbal Learning and Verbal Behavior, 13,* 585–589.

Merton, R. K. (1938). Social structure and anomie. *American Sociological Review, 3,* 672–682.

Michel, L., & Herbeck, D. (2001). *American terrorist.* New York: HarperCollins.

Olweus, D. (1993). *Bullying at school: What we know and what we can do.* Oxford, UK: Blackwell.

Olweus, D. (2003, March). A profile of bullying at school. *Educational Leadership,* 12–17.

Rossi, P. H., & Freeman, H. E. (1993). *Evaluation: A systematic approach.* Newbury Park, CA: Sage.

Sampson, R. J. (1987). Urban black violence: The effect of male joblessness and family disruption. *American Journal of Sociology, 93,* 348–382.

Sampson, R. J., & Laub, J. H. (1994). Urban poverty and the family context of delinquency: A new look at the structure and process in a classic study. *Child Development, 65,* 523–540.

Serrano, R. A. (1998). *One of ours: Timothy McVeigh and the Oklahoma City bombing.* New York: W.W. Norton.

Shakur, S. (1993). *Monster: The autobiography of an L.A. gang member.* New York: Penguin.

Shaw, C., & McKay, H. (1969). *Juvenile delinquency in urban areas.* Chicago: University of Chicago Press.

Sherman, L. W. (2000). The safe and drug-free schools program. *Brookings Papers on Education Policy,* 125–156.

Shihadeh, E. S., & Ousey, G. (1996). Industrial restructuring and violence: The link between entry-level jobs, economic deprivation, and black and white homicide. *Social Forces, 77,* 185–206.

Shihadeh, E. S., & Steffensmeir, D. (1994). Economic inequality, family disruption, and the urban black violence: Cities as units of stratification and social control. *Social Forces, 73*(2), 729–751.

Shulman, H. (1930). Crime prevention and the public schools. *Journal of Educational Sociology, 4*(2), 69–81.

Sommers, I., & Baskin, D. R. (1993). The situational context of violent female offending. *Journal of Research in Crime and Delinquency, 30*(2), 136–162.

Straus, M. A. (2001). *Beating the devil out of them: Corporal punishment in American families and its effects on children.* New Brunswick, NJ: Transaction.

Thrasher, F. (1933). Juvenile delinquency and crime prevention. *Journal of Educational Sociology, 6*(8), 500–509.

Troopers won't back hate-crime statute. (2001, March 23). *Organized Crime Digest,* p. 6.

U.S. Department of Justice. (2006). *Hate crime statistics.* Retrieved July 28, 2008, from http://www.fbi.gov/ucr/hc2006/methodology.html

Wilson, W. J. (1987). *The truly disadvantaged.* Chicago: University of Chicago Press.

Wolfgang, M., & Ferracuti, F. (1982). *The subculture of violence.* Thousand Oaks, CA: Sage.

CHAPTER 3

Media Violence Effects and Violent Crime

Good Science or Moral Panic?

Christopher J. Ferguson

Whether exposure of children or adults to violent media is a cause of aggression and violent behavior has been one of the most intensely debated issues in criminal justice and the broader populace. Debates about the effects of media ranging from books to video games have a long history (Trend, 2007). Even religious writings such as the Bible have been the target of criticism, from early Christian writings in the Roman Empire to "native" language translations of the Bible in the late medieval period. In fact, the Bible recently came back in the spotlight with a study suggesting that reading passages from the Bible with violent content provokes aggression in the same manner as violent video games or television allegedly do (Bushman, Ridge, Das, Key & Busath, 2007). The 20th century has seen many other examples, from Harry Potter teaching witchcraft, to the concern (largely evaporated) that playing Dungeons and Dragons would lead to Satanism or mental illness, to the Hays Code "taming" of Betty Boop (which, by forcing her to put on more clothes, doomed the comic strip). Concerns have come and gone that media such as comic books, jazz, rock, rap, role-playing games, and books, as well as television and movies, would lead to waves of rebelliousness, violence, and moral degradation. New media such as video games and the Internet inevitably stoke the flames of fear with waves of advocates and politicians expressing concern over the fate of supposedly vulnerable children and teens.

Opinions on the matter of media violence effects are wide ranging. Some scholars (Anderson et al., 2003) claim that media violence effects have been conclusively demonstrated, so much so that the certainly equals that of smoking and lung cancer (Bushman & Anderson, 2001). By contrast, other scholars have claimed that the entire media violence research field has been mismanaged, with weak, inconsistent results; poor measures of aggression; a mismatch between the theories and actual crime data; and failure to consider alternative causes of aggression such as personality, evolution, or family violence (e.g., Freedman, 2002; Olson, 2004; Savage, 2004). Several medical doctors have recently questioned the data behind the supposed similarities between media violence research and research on smoking and lung cancer (Block & Crain, 2007), and indeed, as demonstrated in Chapter 1, the effect sizes for smoking and for media violence are nearly on opposite sides of the spectrum. Wherein lies the truth? I suspect that, as happens all too often in the social sciences, "truth" is subjective. With that in mind, it is the goal of this chapter to discuss, bluntly and directly, the research on media violence. I will discuss not only what study authors say they found but how they measured constructs such as aggression, and I will examine their results in greater detail than has been customary in most reviews. The goal is to give the reader an "insider" view of media violence research, from a media violence researcher, so that readers can construct their own informed opinion.

CASE STUDY: VIRGINIA TECH

On the morning of April 16, 2007, the Virginia Tech campus in Blacksburg, VA became the site of the worst school shooting in American history. The attacks began at approximately 7:15 a.m., when two students, Emily Hilscher and Ryan Clark, were shot and killed in a dorm building. At the time of this writing there is no evidence that the shooter, Seung-Hui Cho, had a prior relationship with either of these individuals or any other of his victims. These shootings, like the rest, appear to have been fairly random.

Cho then mailed a "manifesto" to NBC, including videotapes he had taken of himself ranting and posing with weapons. The final massacre in Norris Hall occurred two hours after the initial shootings. The Virginia Tech campus has subsequently been criticized for communication failures in failing to adequately warn students about the initial shootings. Warning students that a shooting had occurred or canceling classes might have prevented or reduced the number of subsequent deaths. However, in all fairness, it is likely that many similar institutions would have stumbled under similar shocking and unforeseen circumstances. Most of us are just not prepared, outfitted, or equipped to deal with events as rare as this one.

Cho then entered Norris hall wielding two handguns and chained shut the main exit doors. Cho went to the second floor of the building and began the second, much more deadly portion of his massacre, shooting faculty and students in their classrooms. Nine minutes later, 30 people were dead (32 dead total) and 17 had been wounded. There were individual stories of bravery during the shooting, such as Professor Liviu Librescu, who barricaded a classroom door with his own body while most of his students were able to escape through a window. Librescu was killed after being shot through the door. Police responded to the scene swiftly but initially had difficulty entering the building due to the chained doors. As police entered the building, Cho killed himself with a gunshot to the head.

Within hours of the massacre, before the name of the perpetrator had even been released, several pundits had begun suggesting that violent video games were behind the massacre. Jack Thompson, a Florida lawyer and anti-video game activist, blamed video games for teaching children to kill. Dr. Phil McGraw (Dr. Phil) appeared on *Larry King Live* to assert that violent video games and other violent media are turning children into mass murderers. The *Washington Post* included a paragraph suggesting that Cho might have been an avid player of the violent game "Counter-Strike," and then quickly removed that paragraph from an online article without explanation.

None of these assertions proved true, however. In fact, in the final report by the Virginia state review panel commissioned by the Governor, Tim Kaine, video games were entirely and specifically exonerated. Cho, it turned out, was not a gamer. In fact, unusual for a young male, there was little evidence to suggest that he played video games at all, aside perhaps from the nonviolent game "Sonic the Hedgehog" (Virginia Tech Review Panel, 2007). The review panel stated that "He was enrolled in a Tae Kwon Do program for awhile, watched TV, and played video games like Sonic the Hedgehog. None of the video games were war games or had violent themes. He liked basketball and had a collection of figurines and remote controlled cars" and "Cho's roommate never saw him play video games." There were other indications that all was not well with Cho: a long history of mental health problems and stalking behavior toward two female students. Yet, if Cho was odd in any respect in his video game playing habits, it's because he played them rarely and violent games not at all.

Research Methods in Media Violence

If you are curious whether media violence contributes to violent crime, the simple answer to that is we really don't know. In defense of media violence researchers, there are some very good reasons for this. Foremost among them is that studying violent crime experimentally—that is to say, attempting to manipulate some research participants into committing violent crimes—is clearly unethical. That leaves us with correlational research only (e.g., self-reported violent acts or arrest records). Media violence researchers have responded to this experimental problem by instead studying aggression; because not all aggressive acts are illegal or particularly damaging to others, they can ethically be studied experimentally. If studies can experimentally demonstrate a causal effect of media violence on aggression in the laboratory and media violence is correlated with violent crime in the real world, then an argument can be made that the two phenomena are similar enough to warrant concern.

If we can't ethically examine violent behaviors, how can we measure aggression in the laboratory? One common method for measuring aggression in the laboratory (I've used it myself) is the modified Taylor Competitive Reaction Time Test (TCRTT; Anderson & Dill, 2000; Ferguson, Rueda, Cruz, Ferguson, Fritz, & Smith, 2008). After being exposed to some form of media (e.g., either a violent or nonviolent television program or video game), research participants are told that they will play a reaction time game against a human opponent. In this game, participants are instructed to press the mouse button as quickly as they can whenever a central square on their screen turns red. They are told that their opponent is also trying to press his mouse button quickly (two computers are supposedly linked up through Ethernet or similar connection and are playing against each other). Before each trial, the human participant is told that he or she can set a noise blast punishment for his or her opponent should the opponent lose. This noise blast can be set (from 0 to 10) in terms of both intensity (loudness) and duration. Even the loudest settings are not painful to the human ear; rather, they are more irritating, like the white noise of a television set. Naturally, the opponent is also supposedly setting punishments that the research participant will receive should he or she lose the match. The punishments can be reset after each match, and there are approximately 25 matches in total.

In reality, of course, there is no human opponent, and the participant is just playing against the computer. In theory, people who set louder and longer noise blasts for their supposed opponent are behaving aggressively. This isn't really a measure of violence because the noise blasts obviously aren't damaging, but how does it function as a measure of aggression? It seems intuitive, but despite years of use, the measure has never been shown to be predictive of real-world aggression, let alone violent crime.

One problem with the TCRTT is that, in the past, it has not been used in a standardized way. There are actually many ways to measure aggression with this test: You could measure the number of punishments that are above a certain arbitrary level (say 8 out of 10), or you could take the mean of all 25 matches, or you could just use the mean after win trials or the mean after lose trials. With a little creativity, you could likely think of dozens of ways to use the test to measure aggression, and this is not a good thing. This means that the test lacks standardization. Without a standardized test, researchers can measure aggression however they want and, indeed, can pick the outcomes that best support their hypotheses and ignore outcomes that don't support their hypotheses.

These kinds of problems with laboratory measures are not unique to the TCRTT, and some scholars have questioned the validity of all laboratory measures of aggression (Tedeschi & Quigley, 1996). Aside from instruments such as the TCRTT, other laboratory measures of aggression have included asking children whether they wanted to pop a balloon (Mussen & Rutherford, 1961), asking college students whether they would like to have a graduate student confederate (who had just insulted them) as an instructor in a course (Berkowitz, 1965), asking subjects to interpret the actions of a character in a story (Bushman & Anderson, 2002), and asking subjects to sentence criminals in an analog (i.e., made up) scenario (Deselms & Altman, 2003). To study aggression in children, researchers can observe children at play, although it has proven difficult to distinguish between aggressive play (e.g., playing cowboys and Indians) and true aggression (e.g., pushing a child down to steal lunch money).

Both correlation and experimental designs can make use of surveys. Surveys may include self-reported violent criminal activity, self-reported aggression, or symptoms of a psychiatric disorder related to crime, such as antisocial personality disorder. To study young children, parent report measures can be used. Child peer ratings of aggression have also been attempted, but it is not entirely clear whether children have enough insight to actually rate each others' aggressive behaviors rather than turn any negative-sounding set of questions into a popularity contest. Many surveys, such as the Buss Aggression Questionnaire (Buss & Warren, 2000; a measure of aggressive personality traits), are standardized and reliable and have demonstrated validity. One obvious problem with survey measures is that people can easily lie on them. Also, it is not enough to merely label a set of questions "aggression"; they must be tested for validity. For example, Table 3.1

Table 3.1   Items From the Lefkowitz, Eron, Walder, and Huesmann Measure of Aggression

---

 1. Who does not obey the teacher?
 2. Who often says, "Give me that"?
 3. Who gives dirty looks or sticks out their tongue at other children?
 4. Who makes up stories and lies to get other children into trouble?
 5. Who does things that bother others?
 6. Who starts a fight over nothing?
 7. Who pushes or shoves other children?
 8. Who is always getting into trouble?
 9. Who says mean things?
10. Who takes other children's things without asking?

---

presents a list of peer-rating questions used in some television studies of aggression (Lefkowitz, Eron, Walder, & Huesmann, 1977). Many of the items appear related to naughtiness, but only a few involve actual violent behaviors.

Aside from the validity of aggression measures, one other issue that bears mentioning is the absence on most aggression measures of a clinical cut-off. A *clinical cut-off score* is a score above which a person likely has a particular disorder. For instance, the Minnesota Multiphasic Personality Inventory (a common test for mental illnesses) uses clinical cut-off *t*-scores of 65 (a *t*-score mean is 50, with standard deviation of 10) to indicate the likely presence of mental health problems. A person who scores under 65 is within the "normal" range; above 65 a person is at increasing risk for a mental disorder. Thus, if you were to take a sample of individuals and expose them to some phenomenon (say, media violence) and their scores went from a normal average of 50 past the clinical cut-off to a mean of 70, it would be reasonable to suggest that exposure to this phenomenon put them at significant risk for a mental health problem. Most aggression measures, even well-researched ones, don't have a clinical cut-off, however. Thus, even if one group scores higher on a measure than another group, does that mean that the first group is at risk of becoming aggressive? This is particularly important because effect sizes in media violence research tend to be very small (with *r* values typically ranging from 0 to .2). If Group A is exposed to media violence and their mean aggression scores are found to be a *t*-score of 52, whereas Group B is not exposed to media violence and maintains the typical mean *t*-score of 50 (and these differences in score are about typical for media violence research), can we really say that media violence has "caused aggression" if none of the participants is pushed over any clinical cut-off?

Theories of Media Violence

Historically, there have been two main approaches to understanding potential media violence effects: the social learning approaches and the catharsis model. In recent years, most researchers have preferred to work from the social learning model. Briefly, this model suggests that individuals are likely to imitate what they see. For instance, a child learning to tie her shoes is likely to first watch an adult do it and then attempt to model the viewed behavior. Social learning models of aggression, such as the General Aggression Model (Bushman & Anderson, 2002), suggest that watching violent media leads to the development of violent *scripts*. People who watch more violent media develop more and stronger violent scripts than those who do not consume violent media. In real life, when presented with hostile or even ambiguous circumstances, people with more violent scripts are more likely to respond violently. Although such models may allow for individual differences due to biology or personality, biology and personality are seldom discussed much in these models, so they are, by and large, tabula rasa models (meaning they consider everyone to be about equal or "blank slates" prior to environmental learning).

By contrast, catharsis models suggest that aggression is primarily a biological drive that requires expression (Lorenz, 1963). According to the catharsis model, media violence may provide an outlet or release for aggressive drives. As such, people who consume violent media would be expected to become less aggressive. Many media violence researchers today take a dim view of the catharsis hypothesis (Bushman, 2002).

To date, which of these models does the research seem to support? In short, neither. Social learning models of aggression, given their popularity in recent decades, have been subjected to frequent (although perhaps not rigorous) testing. Results have been weak, inconsistent, and compromised by poor research methods (Freedman, 2002; Savage, 2004). Meta-analytic studies of media violence effects have consistently demonstrated that links between media violence exposure and increased aggression are close to zero. In the most famous (probably because it is most positive) of these meta-analyses, the effect size for media violence and violent criminal behavior is $r = .1$ (Paik & Comstock, 1994). Results for nonviolent measures of aggression, such as the TCRTT, were slightly higher, with $r = .2$. Most other meta-analyses suggest that even Paik and Comstock's data may be too high. For instance, Hogben (1998) finds $r = .11$ for the relationship between television viewing and general aggression measures. Bushman and Anderson (2001) find results ranging from $r = .14$ to $r = .2$. Note that these effects are for general measures of aggression, not violent crime, which tends to get even weaker effects. Results for video games have been weaker still (e.g., Sherry, 2001; Ferguson, 2007). Ferguson (2007) found that publication bias (the tendency for scientific journals to publish articles that support a particular hypothesis and not publish those that do not) was a significant problem for video game articles (no similar analysis has been conducted for television) and that unstandardized, poorly constructed measures of aggression tended to produce higher effects than better measures of aggression (perhaps because they allow researchers to pick the results that best support their hypotheses). No support was found for the link between video game playing and higher aggression.

Results have not been kind to the catharsis model either. Although a few early studies initially provided weak support for the catharsis model (e.g., Feshbach, 1961), more recent researchers haven't given much credence to these early studies. Indeed, in the last few decades, although evidence to support the social learning theories of media violence has been very weak, evidence supporting the catharsis hypothesis has been virtually absent. Arguably, this may be due to the fact that few researchers actually test the catharsis hypothesis. To do so, a researcher would have to begin by irritating participants, make them angry, and then see whether violent or nonviolent media calm them down. Very few media studies do this. Virtually all media violence studies take the opposite tack; they begin with a (presumably) nonirritated individual and expose him or her to violent or nonviolent media to see whether his or her aggression increases. Thus, arguably, the present body of literature provides little evidence for or against the catharsis model. A few authors have begun to suggest that the catharsis hypothesis should be investigated with more care. For instance, Sherry (2007) has noted that individuals exposed to longer periods of play with violent video games have less aggression than those exposed to shorter periods of play with violent video games. In other words, the longer you play violent video games, the less aggressive you become. While this certainly calls the social learning theories into question, it doesn't truly support the catharsis hypothesis. It is just as likely (more likely, I'd argue) that some people who participate in video game studies are unfamiliar with the games they are randomized to play. This unfamiliarity fosters frustration that diminishes over time once the player becomes accustomed to the game. Studies that include only a short exposure may see increased aggression, but this is due to game familiarity issues rather than violent content (violent video games do tend to be more complex to play than nonviolent games). Similarly, the drop in aggression scores over time is not due to catharsis but rather increasing familiarity. Nonetheless, Sherry (2007) recommends more diligent study of catharsis.

Two recent studies with video games have added a bit of credence to the catharsis model, although not yet enough to engender widespread confidence in it. Unsworth, Devilly, and Ward (2007) found that effects of violent video game play varied from player to player, with some players showing cathartic effects after playing violent games. Most players showed no effect, and a small group also became more aggressive. Thus, it may be hard to make conclusive statements regarding whether violent media exerts a cathartic or noncathartic effect, as there is much variation between individuals. In another recent study, Olson, Kutner, and Warner (2008) reported that adolescent boys commonly reported feeling calmer and less angry subsequent to violent video game play and used violent video games to reduce aggression. The authors suggest that the catharsis model should be better examined in future research.

Both the social learning theory and the catharsis model continue to have advocates, although thus far, research evidence for either is weak. Ferguson

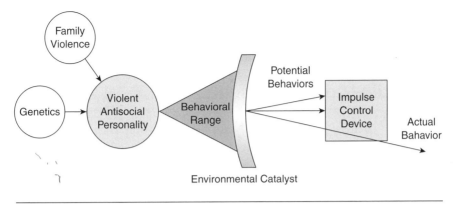

Figure 3.1   A Catalyst Model for Violent Antisocial Behavior

et al. (2008) have proposed an alternative model (the Catalyst Model) of aggression (Figure 3.1) that attempts to explain the interaction between biological and external forces on aggression. At least half of the variance in violent and antisocial behavior can be explained by genetics (Ferguson, in press; Rhee & Waldman, 2002); thus, this Catalyst Model is an evolutionary model. Antisocial personalities develop through the interaction between genetics and physical abuse early in life, an observation consistent with research data (e.g., Caspi et al., 2002). Aggression is a normal response to hostile provocation. Restraining aggression is also adaptive because aggression can carry risks of injury or ostracism from the community; consequently, humans have also evolved an *impulse control device*, which restrains aggressive (and other) impulses. This impulse control device appears to be located in the frontal lobes of the brain; damage to these areas increases aggression (see Chapter 6). Either an aggressive personality or damage to the impulse control devices can result in increased aggressive responses, particularly under periods of increased environmental stress (e.g., loss of job, divorce). These environmental stressors are *catalysts* for violence; they don't *cause* violence, but they may stimulate specific violent acts in a particular individual who is already prone to violent behavior. According to this model, media violence neither is a cause of violent crime nor stimulates it, but may act as a *stylistic catalyst*. This means that individuals who decide to act aggressively may sometimes do so in a way similar to what they have seen in the media (e.g., someone who watches *CSI: Crime Scene Investigation* may decide to use bleach to remove blood evidence from a weapon when she wouldn't have thought of that on her own). Were the media influence removed, the person would still act violently, albeit in a slightly different way (i.e., not using the bleach). Initial testing of the Catharsis Model (Ferguson et al., 2008) demonstrated favorable results in comparison to the social learning model on a dataset involving violent criminal activity, although further testing of this model will be required.

Examples of Media Violence Research

Reviews of media violence research are fairly plentiful and take different tacks. Anderson et al. (2003) presents the research as essentially flawless, while other reviewers (Freedman, 1984, 2002; Olson, 2004; Savage, 2004) have pointed out systematic problems with media violence research as it exists today. Thus, the quality of the research seems to be something of a matter of perspective. Below I've included a detailed description of three influential and often-cited studies of television and video game effects. These studies are fairly representative of the existing research on media violence effects and are representative of systemic strengths and weaknesses in the field. Understanding these studies should be helpful in understanding media violence data.

One common point raised by critics of media violence research is that other countries with media as violent as (or even more violent than) in the United States have not seen violent crime waves like those that occurred in the United States in the 1970s through the early 1990s. If the introduction of violent television set off massive crime waves in the U.S., why not also in the countries of Europe or Asia where media violence is also commonplace? Huesmann and Eron (1986) examined the effects of media violence on children in multiple countries, including boys and girls in the United States, Australia, Finland, Israel (both a city sample and a kibbutz sample), and Poland. A Dutch group dropped out of the study and published their results separately (Wiegman & Kuttschreuter, 1992), apparently out of concern regarding methodological and interpretive differences. The intent of this study was to examine whether television viewing habits would predict aggressive behaviors in children at a later age (3 years later) while controlling for *trait aggression* (aggressive personality). Out of all six countries (including the Netherlands), significant results based on the original model were found only for American girls. In no other case were significant results reported for television violence exposure and later aggression. Given that the authors did not control error due to multiple comparisons (using something called a Bonferroni correction), it's possible even this one finding could be due to "error." The authors then develop an additional measure in which they compile television viewing habits with a personality measure ("identification with aggressive characters"). This latter personality characteristic is highly correlated with aggressive personality and, as a result, aggressive personality can no longer be teased out from television viewing habits in this study (Savage, 2004). In other words, it isn't very surprising to find that aggressive individuals behave aggressively. Ultimately, results from differing countries use differing measures of television exposure, many of which include this personality variable. Even with this personality measure combined with television viewing substituting for television viewing habits alone (which was the actual study hypothesis), the end results were mixed, with some groups showing weak effects and others (such as the Dutch and Australians, children on the Israeli kibbutz, and girls in Poland or Finland) still showing no effects. Although Huesmann and Eron (1986) nonetheless interpret the results as supportive of the link between television violence and aggression cross-nationally, the Dutch authors came to the opposite conclusion (Wiegman & Kuttschreuter, 1992). However, if we return to the question of whether viewing television violence was associated with aggressive behavior, the study found evidence for this only in American girls and possibly Israeli city children, not in American boys or in children from Poland, Australia, the Netherlands, or the Israeli kibbutz. One other concern with this study is that it does not attempt to control for the potential effects of exposure to family violence. It is quite possible, given the weak effects found for even the few significant results, that no effects would have been found had family violence been adequately controlled.

One often-cited study is by Friedrich and Stein (1973); it implies that children who watch violent programs (such as *Batman* or *Superman*) are more interpersonally aggressive. The authors included five measures of aggression (including one composite of two of the basic aggression measures) and provide a number of analyses to attempt to support this view. Generally, the results did not support the hypothesis that exposure to violent programs increased any form of aggression, including hitting other children, verbal aggression, or fantasy aggression. The only significant finding was an interaction between initial aggressiveness and violent programs. However, had a Bonferroni correction for multiple analyses been appropriately applied (it was not), this finding would not have been significant. Furthermore, once gender was added to this analysis, this interaction was no longer significant. Thus, once gender is properly controlled, there were no significant findings to suggest that exposure to violent programs resulted in more violent behavior.

Within the realm of video games, one of the most often-cited studies is Anderson and Dill (2000), who used the TCRTT. In their laboratory study of violent video game effects, the authors computed four methods of measuring aggression using the TCRTT (noise intensity and duration after both win and loss trials), without applying the appropriate Bonferroni correction to their analyses. Only one of the four measures of aggression (noise duration after loss trials) was reported as significant, although had a Bonferroni correction been appropriately applied, this index also would have been nonsignificant. Remember also that the noise duration indices appear not to work (Ferguson, Smith, Miller-Stratton, Fritz, & Heinrich, in press) as a valid measure of aggression. Nonetheless, this study is often cited as one of the leading studies indicating a link between video game violence exposure and aggressive behavior in the lab. Examined closely, however, it appears to indicate quite the opposite. The authors include a correlational analyses as well, and though they find a relationship between violent video game play and violent acts, they did not control for family violence exposure. In at least one study, controlling for family violence exposure has been found to eliminate all predictive value of violent game exposure (Ferguson et al., 2008). Thus, it would appear to be that family violence exposure predicts violent behaviors, not exposure to violent video games.

The above studies present a fairly representative mix of the kind of studies conducted in the media violence realms. Strengths and weaknesses are fairly systematic across most media violence studies and are, perhaps, part of the reason some scholars question the utility of such studies in attempting to examine the media violence hypothesis (i.e., Freedman, 2002; Savage, 2004).

Violent Crime Data

In the end, perhaps the ultimate question we should be asking is whether media violence research can explain real-world phenomena. Does violent media availability and exposure in a culture relate to levels of violence in that culture? If so, then removing or restricting violent media would appear to be an easy way to reduce societal violence. Disappointingly, the answer is clearly "no." In the 1970s through the 1990s, a surge in violent crime in the United States led some researchers to conclude that the introduction of television may have been at least partially responsible (Bushman & Anderson, 2001), but this now appears not to have been the case. First, comparing the 1980s to the 1950s (a period of remarkably low crime in the United States) was probably too limited in scope. In fact, violent crime waves in the 1930s and late 1800s and early 1900s were worse than those of the peak years of the 1980s, despite the relative absence of violent mass media (Bureau of Justice Statistics, 1988; National Commission on the Causes and Prevention of Violence, 1969). As such, the surge in violent crimes in the latter half of the 20th century, although unfortunate, was not terribly remarkable in the landscape of American crime trends.

More remarkably, as noted in Chapter 1 (and throughout this book), the United States experienced a dramatic plummet in violent crime rates beginning in the early 1990s, to the point that current rates are about the same as in the late 1960s and early 1970s (Federal Bureau of Investigation, 1951–2004). In other words, despite television, movies, and even music becoming more graphically violent and despite the introduction of violent video games, actual violent crime rates have experienced a massive decline, and the United States is the safest it has been in 40 years. Figure 3.2 presents trends in the overall violent crime rate across time, whereas Figure 3.3 presents trends in the per capita rate of murders and nonnegligent homicides (Bureau of Justice Statistics, 2007). As mentioned earlier, the introduction of television and video games in other countries (particularly in Europe and Asia) was never associated with any wave of violent crimes. From this, we can say that violent media is not precipitating an epidemic of violent crime (or youth violence, as violent crime data is similar for youth and adults) because there is no epidemic of violent crime. It is only a short further step to conclude that, despite the reasonableness of concern regarding media violence and violent crime, media violence is not related to violent crime; the data simply conflict (Olson, 2004).

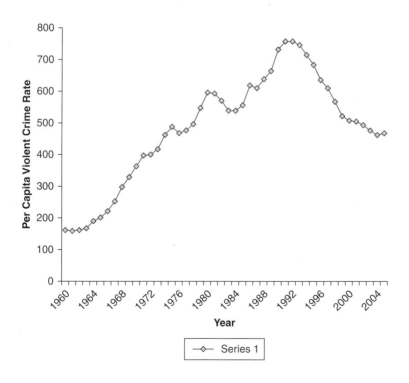

Figure 3.2   Per Capita Violent Crime Rates in the United States by Year

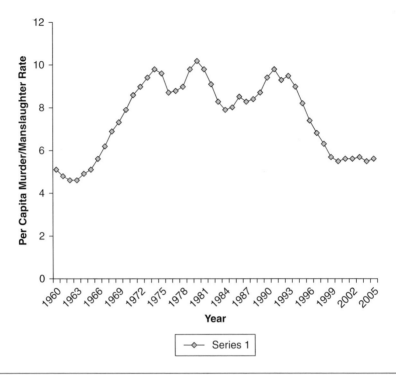

Figure 3.3 Per Capita Murder/Nonnegligent Manslaughter Rates in the United States by Year

If research on media violence is generally flawed with weak results, and violent crime data don't support the conclusion that media violence is an important contributor to violent behavior, you may wonder why media violence is so hotly debated in the United States. Trend (2007) refers to a "media hysteria cycle," of which scientists are a part. Basically, this is how it happens: A rare but well-covered (in terms of the news) violent event occurs. Because the event seems so unexplainable, experts are asked for their opinions. In truth, of course, experts have a great deal of difficulty predicting and explaining serious violent acts, but media violence sounds reasonable and suffices to make the unexplainable seem explainable in the short term. Trend also notes that blaming "media" for all manner of societal vices is nothing new and has probably been practiced through history, often as a means of rationalizing government control over expression. Scientists are not immune from this phenomenon and may stimulate it. There may be some unique cultural and political factors at play in the United States in particular. Media violence is one issue that appeals to many individuals on both the extreme left and right of the political spectrum. Thus, politicians can use "protecting the children" to appeal to voters from both sides of the spectrum, while simultaneously implying that their opponents are not concerned with child welfare. Despite this "hysteria," Kutner, Olson, Warner, and Hertzog (2008) found that most parents are not terribly concerned that violent media such as video games will lead to aggression in their own children. Thus the hysteria may be relegated more to special interest groups than the general population. My own impression (admittedly subjective) is that this hysteria is rather uniquely American and that Europeans and other people (including non-American scientists) consider the matter much less dire.

Response of the Criminal Justice System

The media violence hypothesis has received its greatest support from professional organizations such as the American Psychological Association and the American Academy of Pediatrics. Perhaps the most striking is the American Academy of Pediatrics (AAP) testimony before Congress:

> Since the 1950s more than 3500 research studies in the United States and around the world using many investigative methods have examined whether there is an association between exposure to media violence and subsequent violence behavior. All but 18 have shown a positive correlation between media exposure and violent behavior. (Cook, 2000)

This statement is a blatant misrepresentation of the facts. Similar statements from the American Psychiatric Association and American Psychological Association provide scientists and laypersons alike, who are not familiar with the literature, with the impression that thousands of conclusive studies exist. Although no reviews conducted by researchers familiar with the field make such claims (e.g., Paik & Comstock, 1994 included about 200 studies in their meta-analysis), neither are they vocal in challenging this misconception.

Freedman's (2002) review of the literature noted that there are actually approximately 200 empirical studies of media violence effects. This is still an impressive number, although nowhere near the figure cited by the AAP. Of greater concern, however, is that of the studies available that conducted empirical research regarding a link (correlational or causal) between media violence and actual violent behavior, more than half of them failed to support this link. From this analysis it appears that, far from being "unequivocal," the research is highly inconsistent.

The standpoint of the criminal justice system has been far more critical. For instance, a recent Secret Service study of school shooting cases found that, despite all the attention paid to video games and other media following these events, violent media consumption was not a useful predictor (United States Secret Service & United States Department of Education, 2002). More interesting, perhaps, has been the response of the judicial system to legislation and criminal tort cases involving media violence. In tort cases, video games, television shows, or musical acts such as Ozzy Osbourne have been accused of causing specific violent acts (such as a youth's suicide, in the case of Ozzy Osbourne). Legislative bodies at the state and federal level have also moved to censor media with violent content. At the time of this writing, the Federal government is considering options to regulate violent content on television, and there have been at least 10 state legislative efforts to regulate the sale of violent video games. In each case, these efforts (tort cases and censorship) have failed, both on First Amendment grounds and on the weaknesses of the scientific evidence. In many of these rulings, the judges have been critical of the media violence literature and specifically note that the scientific literature does not meet the courts' standards for conclusive evidence (e.g., Entertainment Software Association, Video Software Dealers Association, and Illinois Retail Merchants Association v. Blagojevich, Madigan, and Devine, 2005). Thus, the case for media violence effects has not passed the inspection of judges, who are perhaps the most neutral observers we could hope to find on this debate.

Conclusion

Much debate remains regarding the impact of media violence on aggressive and violent behavior. At present, the evidence for short-term increases in minor aggression remains inconclusive and a subject of continued debate. However, at present, the weight of evidence does not support a link between media violence and acts of serious aggression or violent crime. Persistent focus on this debate may potentially risk loss of attention to more pressing social causes of crime including poverty, family violence, social inequality, and the drug trade.

Discussion Questions

1. What motivated people to blame video games so quickly following the Virginia Tech Massacre? What does this say about our culture or society?

2. The belief in media violence effects has persisted among many members of the scientific community despite consistently weak evidence of effects. What does this say about the standards of scientific evidence that we use in the social sciences? How might these standards of evidence be improved?

3. One issue that has not been examined yet in media violence research is whether specific groups of individuals or adults may be at risk for aggression in response to media violence. Is it possible that such groups of individuals exist, and what characteristics would they likely have?

4. What factors in our culture contribute to higher violent crime levels compared to other Western cultures? Why have violent crime rates in the United States been declining dramatically over the past 15 years?

5. Does the catharsis hypothesis have any merit? How would you design a study to test the catharsis hypothesis?

Internet Resources

Bureau of Justice Statistics crime data: http://www.ojp.usdoj.gov/bjs/cvict_c.htm

Entertainment Software Association data on video games and gaming: http://www.theesa.com/facts/index.asp

Secret Service report on school shootings: http://www.secretservice.gov/ntac/ssi_final_report.pdf

Video Games: The Latest Scapegoat for Violence, by Christopher J. Ferguson (*Chronicle of Higher Education* essay): http://members.aol.com/dukearagon/VideoGames.html

Virginia Tech Review Panel Final Report: http://www.governor.virginia.gov/TempContent/techPanelReport.cfm

References

Anderson, C., Berkowitz, L., Donnerstein, E., Heusmann, L. R., Johnson, J., Linz, D., et al. (2003). The influence of media violence on youth. *Psychological Science in the Public Interest, 4*, 81–110.

Anderson, C., & Dill, K. (2000). Video games and aggressive thoughts, feelings and behavior in the laboratory and in life. *Journal of Personality and Social Psychology, 78*, 772–790.

Berkowitz, L. (1965). Some aspects of observed aggression. *Journal of Personality and Social Psychology, 2*, 359–369.

Block, J., & Crain, B. (2007). Omissions and errors in "Media violence and the American public." *American Psychologist, 62*, 252–253.

Bureau of Justice Statistics. (1988). *Report to the nation on crime and justice.* Washington, DC: Government Printing Office.

Bureau of Justice Statistics. (2007). *Reported crimes in the United States—Total.* Retrieved November 12, 2007, from http://bjsdata.ojp.usdoj.gov/dataonline/Search/Crime/State/StatebyState.cfm.

Bushman, B. (2002). Does venting anger feed or extinguish the flame? Catharsis, rumination, distraction, anger and aggressive responding. *Personality and Social Psychology Bulletin, 6*, 724–731.

Bushman, B., & Anderson, C. (2001). Media violence and the American public. *American Psychologist, 56*, 477–489.

Bushman, B., & Anderson, C. (2002). Violent video games and hostile expectations: A test of the General Aggression Model. *Personality and Social Psychology Bulletin, 28*, 1679–1686.

Bushman, B., Ridge, R., Das, E., Key, C., & Busath, G. (2007). When God sanctions killing: Effect of scriptural violence on aggression. *Psychological Science, 18*, 204–207.

Buss, A. H., & Warren, W. L. (2000). *Aggression questionnaire manual.* Los Angeles: Western Psychological Services.

Caspi, A., McClay, J., Moffitt, T., Mill, J., Martin, J., Craig, I., et al. (2002). Role of genotype in the cycle of violence in maltreated children. *Science, 297*, 851–854.

Cook, D. (2000). *Testimony of the American Academy of Pediatrics on media violence before the U.S. Senate Commerce Committee.* Elk Grove Village, IL: American Academy of Pediatrics. Retrieved November 12, 2007, from http://www.aap.org/advocacy/releases/mediaviolencetestimony.pdf.

Deselms, J., & Altman, J. (2003). Immediate and prolonged effects of videogame violence. *Journal of Applied Social Psychology, 33*, 1553–1563.

Entertainment Software Association, Video Software Dealers Association, and Illinois Retail Merchants Association v. Blagojevich, Madigan, and Devine, No. 05 C 4265 (N.D. Ill. 2005).

Federal Bureau of Investigation. (1951–2004). *Uniform crime reports.* Washington, DC: Government Printing Office.

Ferguson, C. J. (2007). Evidence for publication bias in video game violence effects literature: A meta-analytic review. *Aggression and Violent Behavior, 12*, 470–482.

Ferguson, C. J. (in press). Genetic contributions to antisocial personality and behavior (APB): A meta-analytic review (1996–2006) from an evolutionary perspective. *Journal of Social Psychology.*

Ferguson, C. J., Rueda. S., Cruz, A., Ferguson, D., Fritz, S., & Smith, S. (2008). Violent video games and aggression: Causal relationship or byproduct of family violence and intrinsic violence motivation? *Criminal Justice and Behavior, 35*, 311–332.

Ferguson, C. J., Smith, S., Miller-Stratton, S., Fritz, S., & Heinrich, E. (in press). Aggression in the laboratory: Problems with the validity of the modified Taylor Competitive Reaction Time Test as a measure of aggression in media violence studies. *Journal of Aggression, Maltreatment, and Trauma*.

Feshbach, S. (1961). The stimulating versus cathartic effect of vicarious aggressive activity. *Journal of Abnormal and Social Psychology, 63*, 381–385.

Freedman, J. (1984). Effect of television violence on aggressiveness. *Psychological Bulletin, 96*, 227–245.

Freedman, J. (2002). *Media violence and its effect on aggression: Assessing the scientific evidence*. Toronto: University of Toronto Press.

Friedrich, L., & Stein, A. (1973). Aggressive and prosocial television programs and the natural behavior of preschool children. *Monographs of the Society for Research in Child Development, 38*, 63.

Heusmann, L., & Eron, L. (1986). *Television and the aggressive child: A cross-national comparison*. Hillsdale, NJ: Erlbaum.

Hogben, M. (1998). Factors moderating the effect of television aggression on viewer behavior. *Communication Research, 25*, 220–247.

Kutner, L., Olson, C., Warner, D., & Hertzog, S. (2008). Parents' and sons' perspectives on video game play: A qualitative study. *Journal of Adolescent Research, 23*, 76–96.

Lefkowitz, M. M., Eron, L. D., Walder, L. O., & Huesmann, L. R. (1977). *Growing up to be violent: A longitudinal study of the development of aggression*. New York: Pergamon.

Lorenz, K. (1963). *On aggression*. New York: Harcourt, Brace and World.

Mussen, P., & Rutherford, E. (1961). Effects of aggressive cartoons on children's aggressive play. *Journal of Abnormal and Social Psychology, 62*, 461–464.

National Commission on the Causes and Prevention of Violence. (1969). *To establish justice, to insure domestic tranquility*. New York: Award Books.

Olson, C. (2004). Media violence research and youth violence data: Why do they conflict? *Academic Psychiatry, 28*, 144–150.

Olson, C., Kutner, L., & Warner, D. (2008). The role of violent video game play in adolescent development: Boys' perspectives. *Journal of Adolescence Research, 23*, 55–75.

Paik, H., & Comstock, G. (1994). The effects of television violence on anti-social behavior: A meta-analysis. *Communication Research, 21*, 516–546.

Rhee, S., & Waldman, I. (2002). Genetic and environmental influences on antisocial behavior: A meta-analysis of twin and adoption studies. *Psychological Bulletin, 128*, 490–529.

Savage, J. (2004.) Does viewing violent media really cause criminal violence? A methodological review. *Aggression and Violent Behavior, 10*, 99–128.

Sherry, J. (2001). The effects of violent video games on aggression: A meta-analysis. *Human Communication Research, 27*, 409–431.

Sherry, J. (2007). Violent video games and aggression: Why can't we find links? In R. Preiss, B. Gayle, N. Burrell, M. Allen, & J. Bryant (Eds.), *Mass media effects research: Advances through meta-analysis* (pp. 231–248). Mahwah, NJ: Lawrence Erlbaum.

Tedeschi, J., & Quigley, B. (1996). Limitations of laboratory paradigms for studying aggression. *Aggression & Violent Behavior, 2*, 163–177.

Trend, D. (2007). *The myth of media violence*. Malden, MA: Blackwell.

United States Secret Service & United States Department of Education. (2002). *The *final report and findings of the Safe School Initiative: Implications for the prevention of school attacks in the United States.* Retrieved November 12, 2007, from http://www.secretservice.gov/ntac/ssi_final_report.pdf.

Unsworth, G., Devilly, G., & Ward, T. (2007). The effect of playing violent videogames on adolescents: Should parents be quaking in their boots? *Psychology, Crime and Law, 13,* 383–394.

Virginia Tech Review Panel. (2007). *Report of the Virginia Tech Review Panel.* Retrieved November 11, 2007, from http://www.governor.virginia.gov/TempContent/techPanelReport.cfm.

Wiegman, O., & Kuttschreuter, M. (1992). A longitudinal study of the effects of television viewing on aggressive and prosocial behaviors. *British Journal of Social Psychology, 31,* 147–164.

CHAPTER 4

Evolutionary and Genetic Explanations of Violent Crime

Martin Gottschalk

Lee Ellis

Nothing in biology makes sense except in the light of evolution.

—Theodosius Dobzhansky (1997)

Most people can recall images of violence and aggression between wild animals. You may have seen nature programs on TV in which a leopard hunts an impala. Using stealth to get close to its prey, the leopard springs with deadly force and suffocates the impala with a sustained bite to the throat. Another form of violence you may have seen involves male bighorn sheep slamming their heads together in contests over potential mates, their massive curled horns absorbing several thousand pounds of force with each blow. Closer to home, you may have poked a stick in an anthill and watched as an army of ants attacked the invading object in defense of their home.

Aggression in the animal kingdom helps animals to obtain food, compete for access to a mate, and protect territory. These forms of aggressive behavior have been favored by a process called *natural selection* because they facilitate the reproduction of genes in the aggressive animals, either directly, as in the case of the bighorn sheep competing for a mate, or more indirectly, by aiding survival so that an animal or its close kin can reproduce later, as in the cases of the hunting leopard and the territory-defending ants.

CASE STUDY: MURDER AMONG CHIMPS

Since 1975, primatologist Frans de Waal has been studying the social organization of a colony of chimpanzees at the Arnhem Zoo in the Netherlands (de Waal, 1998). The shifting alliances and coalitions among the chimpanzees, and the complex behavioral mechanisms that regulated these relationships, were a revelation to de Waal. While physical conflicts, including slaps, thrown objects, and bites, did occur, the intricate and nuanced nature of the colony's social life is what really stands out when one reads *Chimpanzee Politics,* de Waal's account of his time at Arnhem. The Arnhem chimpanzees appeared to be much more sophisticated than the popular image of the playful and "silly" chimp. They also shattered their peaceful reputation because in 1980, "during the night of 12–13 September, the males' nightcages turned red with blood" (de Waal, 1986, p. 243). When attendants inspected, they found that the dominant male, Luit,

showed numerous deep gashes on [his] head, flanks, back, around the anus, and in the scrotum. His feet, in particular, were badly injured (from one foot one toe was missing, from the other foot, several toes). He also had sustained bites in this hands (several nails were missing). The most gruesome discovery was that he had lost both testicles. All missing body parts were later found on the cage floor (de Waal, 1986, p. 243).

Luit died later that day.

Over the course of several years, the three most prominent males—Yoroen, Luit, and Nikkie—had been jockeying for the alpha, or most dominant, position within the Arnhem colony. With this position came not only a considerable degree of deferential behavior from the other chimpanzees in the group, but, most important, the largest number of matings. Yoroen, the oldest, had once been the alpha male in the group before he was unseated by Luit with the help of Nikkie. Yoroen subsequently began courting Nikkie, ultimately allowing Nikkie to ascend to the top spot in the colony. Ten weeks prior to the attack, however, Yoroen had withdrawn his support for Nikkie, allowing Luit to once again gain alpha status, until the fatal night described above. Since neither Nikkie nor Yoroen had any major injuries, it appears that Yoroen had once again switched sides and joined Nikkie in the lethal attack on Luit.

Yoroen had skillfully played Luit and Nikkie against each other. As the kingmaker and "favorite" to whichever alpha he was supporting at the time, Yoroen was able to acquire a large number of matings within the colony. However, while much attention has been paid to the males in the group, de Waal makes clear that the females also played an essential role in regulating the status hierarchy of the males. The males regularly courted the support of the females with embraces, grooming behavior, and kisses. Threatening gestures and physical conflicts for "betrayals" also regulated relationships within the colony. For example, Puist—a female who was particularly close to Luit—attacked Nikkie and chased him up a tree the day that Luit died and kept him there for 10 minutes with threatening, violent behavior.

Modern sexual selection theory suggests that in some social species, like chimpanzees and humans, because of differential parental investment (i.e., females invest more) as well as the great variability of fecundity among males (i.e., some males have lots of children and other males have none), competition for social status and, thus, mating opportunities might be quite intense, and consequently more violence might occur. This is why we observe much more violence among men in all human societies as well as among the chimpanzees in the Arnhem colony.

It is easy to see a parallel between the killing of Luit and the assassination of a Mafia boss or a gang leader by ambitious and ruthless underlings striving for power. However, status competition appears to play a large role in more commonplace acts of violence among men. As Daly and Wilson (1988) have argued, "a large proportion of the homicides in America . . . have to be understood as the rare, fatal consequences of a ubiquitous competitive struggle among men for status and respect" (p. 146). Moreover, the type of moralistic, retributive aggression that Puist demonstrated in her attack on Nikkie can sometimes be entangled in human status competitions. It is difficult to ignore the fact that the perpetrators of school shootings, such as those at Columbine and Virginia Tech, seem so often to be motivated by a desire for revenge or retaliation against those who they feel have "degraded" or diminished their status.

Of course, humans are different from chimpanzees. We gain some insight into the general patterns of human behavior by observing our closest cousins, the chimpanzees. However, humans also employ mechanisms other than those used by chimpanzees to regulate status and power competitions—the law, for example. Because we use the law to regulate our competitions, we see a greater use of violence in those areas of our society where the law does not reach, such as gangs and the Mafia.

Here are three more acts of aggression that will strike a familiar chord if you've watched the news. First, consider a young man attacking another young man on the street, beating him unconscious and then robbing him of his wallet. Second, imagine two men in a bar arguing over the affections of a women. This type of event is common enough that it should not be too hard to picture. During this dispute, one of the men pulls out a gun and shoots the other man dead. Third, members of a street gang notice that members of a rival gang are hanging out on a street corner in a neighborhood where they "don't belong." To make clear that these rivals are trespassing, the gang members open fire on them.

Like the first set of examples, these acts of human aggression also may exist because of the reproductive consequences that aggressive behavior had for our ancestors. In fact, it is conceivable that acts of human aggression have served reproductive functions that are not too dissimilar from those in the animal examples. For example, the mugging that was just described secured money that may be used to purchase, among other things, food, clothing, or housing. The barroom shooting occurred over the affections of a potential "mate." Finally, our hypothetical gang warfare involved, at least implicitly, the defense of territory.

These human acts of aggression are certainly more complicated than our animal examples, given the very subtle and sophisticated nature of human social life. Nonetheless, these human acts of aggression may have been naturally selected to a similar degree as aggression in animals. If so, many acts of human aggression and violence exist because of the role they have played in passing genes on to future generations. At least under some circumstances, aggressive individuals may have passed their genes on at higher rates than relatively passive individuals. These possibilities will be the focus of this chapter.

This chapter will acquaint you with an amazing possibility: The tendencies humans have toward violence, including that which is considered criminal, have evolutionary and genetic roots. In the first section, this chapter will describe the process of natural selection in order to show how this evolutionary force may have impinged upon tendencies toward aggression. Next, we will explain how a special type of natural selective model, known as sexual selection, may have also played a role in making males more violent than females, especially during their most active reproductive years. Following that, we will discuss efforts to isolate genetic influences on violent behavior and will briefly describe several genes that have been identified in relation to violence. Before we continue, however, a couple of introductory remarks are in order.

First, it is important to remember that simply because humans may have a naturally evolved capacity for violence and aggression does not mean that violence is a good thing, nor does it mean that society cannot and should not try to control such behavior. Humans also have a naturally evolved susceptibility to tooth decay and bacterial infections, but these conditions can and should be controlled for our well-being. Likewise, humans do not simply have violent tendencies; we can also cooperate, empathize, negotiate, and live in harmony. In fact, we have used our evolved intellect to construct a network of legal and administrative procedures—the criminal justice system—to reduce violence and maintain social order (Ellis, 1990).

It is the large number and sophistication of our evolved capacities—what evolutionists refer to as *adaptations*—that make human behavior, criminal or otherwise, so difficult to understand. As an example of the large number of evolved capacities that can be brought to bear in a criminal enterprise, consider the infamous serial killer Ted Bundy, who lured some of his female victims by faking an injury and then asking for their assistance in order to get them into a vulnerable position. His violent tendencies, combined with human capacities for language use, deception, and cunning, resulted in a horrific series of rapes and murders. To understand these capabilities, which exist in nearly all of us to some degree, a theoretical framework is needed. Increasingly, criminologists are turning to biology for guidance.

Darwin's theory of evolution is a valuable tool for understanding the physical appearance of animals as well as their behavior, including violent behavior. This is the point that the great geneticist Theodosius Dobzhansky makes in the epigraph at the beginning of this chapter. The theory of evolution by natural selection has become the central organizing principle for understanding why living things are the way they are and why they do what they do.

While the concept of natural selection is rather simple, it can be dauntingly subtle and far reaching in its applications. Let us briefly examine the concept and how it helps us to understand the evolution of life.

Evolution by Natural Selection

Biologically speaking, *evolution* just means change within lineages of organisms over the course of successive generations. The so-called "fossil record" provides irrefutable evidence that life forms have radically changed over the passage of eons.

While there has undoubtedly been evolutionary change in the forms of life over geologic time, the process that really does the "designing" was a major biological mystery. In the mid-19th century, Charles Darwin (1859) proposed a theory in which the driving force behind the evolution of species was identified as *natural selection*. It is a concept that can be explained in a variety of ways, but it basically means differential survival and reproduction of organisms depending upon the influence of their genes.

Natural selection can be thought of in terms of two interlocking steps. The first step is the production and existence of genetic variation in a population of organisms. The second step is the differential survival and reproduction of these genetically variable organisms. In order to more clearly understand this process, let us consider the hypothetical leopards discussed earlier.

A population of leopards, like all populations, will exhibit variation in traits and abilities, some of which is attributable to genetic factors. When we talk about genetics or genes, we are referring to organic molecules that are inherited by offspring from their parents and that constitute the recipe for constructing the proteins out of which living things are made—most of your dry weight is protein. All of the leopards will differ from each other in terms of things like lung capacity, muscle mass, volume and connectivity of nervous system fibers, and so on, all of which are influenced by the slightly different genes possessed by the leopards in this population. This is the first step from above—genetic variation in the population.

The genetic variation ultimately comes from *mutations,* which are simply slight errors that occur in the copying of the genetic material that is passed from parents to offspring. For example, you, like all humans, possess roughly 100 to 200 unique genetic mutations (Nachman, 2004); that is, there are roughly 100 to 200 points along the 23 chromosomes that you inherited from each of your parents at which you are uniquely different from either your mother or father. While 100 to 200 mutations might seem like a lot, it is useful to remember that you have approximately 3 billion nucleotide base pairs in the DNA you received from your parents (3 billion points at which your DNA can differ from either of your parents), so 100 to 200 mutations is a small fraction of your total DNA. The vast majority of these mutations have no effect whatsoever. In fact, much of your DNA does not seem to do much of anything, and many of these mutations occur in this noncoding DNA (it is sections of this noncoding DNA that are used for DNA fingerprinting). However, many genetic mutations might be harmful to the organisms possessing them, while other mutations may be beneficial to the organisms bearing them.

Genetic variation in a population is also created by sexual reproduction— or recombination—which ensures an almost limitless supply of genetic variation for natural selection to work upon. In fact, sexual reproduction itself may have been an adaptation to deal with the harmful accumulation of deleterious mutations in the genetic makeup of organisms (Kondrashov, 1982). At any rate, when it comes to genetic variation in a population, because of sexual recombination, an offspring will often mix the genetic mutations of its mother and father. So each member of our hypothetical population of leopards is slightly different from every other member genetically, and these genetic differences influence things like muscle mass, visual acuity, lung capacity, and so on. Now for the second step in the process: differential survival and reproduction.

This second step is natural selection itself. Because of the slight differences in our population of leopards in terms of things like muscle mass, lung capacity, and nervous system function, some leopards will be better than others at hunting and feeding, and some of these differences will be due to genetic differences. These differences in genetic endowment will not be concentrated in a single individual. Different leopards will have different strengths and weaknesses that aid them in hunting. However, those leopards that hunt and feed better, for whatever reason, will tend to live longer and reproduce more, thus passing on more copies of the genes that gave them their muscle mass, stamina, and vision. Notice that it is *reproduction* that really matters here— reproduction, not survival, is the gold standard of natural selection.

In the course of evolution, whatever genetic variation that exists in a population is run through a natural sieve. Environmental selection forces, such as the speed of impalas and the distance at which a leopard can identify an impala as a possible dinner source, are "selecting" which leopards will feed, survive, and, ultimately, reproduce, thus passing on their genes for greater speed, better vision, stamina, and all the other functional characteristics that leopards possess. Over many generations, this process will produce a population of leopards that are, on average, faster, have better sight, and so on.

As we discuss evolutionary explanations of violence, it is necessary to bear in mind that we are always talking about selection *in the past* for characteristics that humans display *today*. Selection has sculpted behavioral characteristics by "choosing" the genes that underlie a given behavior. But, genes do not code for behavior directly; instead, they code for the construction of all the different types of proteins of which an organism is composed. The mind-boggling complexity of an organism like yourself with your many interacting parts—your skin and heart and liver and brain—is made possible because your genes are making the different proteins that compose the cells of your skin, liver, heart, and brain that, in turn, compose you.

Of special importance to behavior is the fact that your brain, which controls your behavior, is constructed the way that it is because of genes. This genetic influence continues throughout your life. In fact, as you read this chapter, a cascade of neurological changes is taking place in you, among them the turning on of genes that help strengthen the connections between neurons that create new images and memories (Kandel, 2006). In a sense, you are constantly being rewired, all of which is made possible by your genes.

But, what about violence? What about a case like that of Joel Zellmer, who was arrested in 2007 for drowning his stepdaughter, Ashley McLellan, in his pool? According to court documents, Zellmer had a history of violence against the children of unwed mothers whom he had dated or been engaged to, including two previous nonbiological children who nearly drowned while with him and a third who suffered broken bones while under his care (Hagey, 2007; Johnson, 2007). However, none of his biological children were ever harmed (Johnson, 2007). The question for researchers working within the evolutionary tradition is this: Has our evolutionary history selected genetic variants that underlie this behavior? The challenge, in short, is to discover whether or not, and to what extent, violent behavior is under genetic influence. There are two broad research traditions evolutionary theorists engage in that attempt to address this issue.

Population Genetics and Violent Crime

Ever since the gene-based theory of evolution by natural selection was ushered in with what is called the *modern synthesis,* population genetics has been central to evolutionary biology. When evolutionary theorists observe some phenomenon among a natural population, like the elevated levels of violence among human males compared to females, they begin to ask whether or not this phenomenon might be an adaptation produced by natural selection. Population genetics is a mathematical tool that is used to see whether or not it is theoretically possible for hypothesized genes underlying a phenomenon (such as violence) to have spread in the population over multiple generations, under the influence of natural selection. In other words, the type of question that population geneticists are concerned with is this: If a particular genetic variant—called an *allele*—appears in a population, and if it has certain types of hypothetical effects, will it become more common in the population over time because of its selective advantage? The theorizing of criminologists who have been inspired by evolutionary theory has been greatly influenced by population genetics thinking.

If you think back to the examples at the beginning of this chapter, you will notice that all of the crimes depicted involved male offenders. This is neither unintentional nor unrealistic. Crimes of violence are overwhelmingly committed by men. Here are some relevant statistics to consider. In the United States in 2002, there were 9,015 men arrested for murder and nonnegligent manslaughter compared to 1,092 women; 19,884 men were arrested for forcible rape while only 278 women were; 69,369 men were arrested for robbery and women accounted for a mere 7,973 arrests; and, finally, 270,905 men were arrested for aggravated assault compared to 68,532 women (Pastore & Maguire, 2005). In sum, for violent crimes in the U.S. in 2002, men were nearly five times as likely to be arrested as women. This same general pattern is consistent across time and across societies.

The question is why would males dominate in the commission of nearly all types of offenses, not just in the United States but throughout the world? Using a population genetic style of reasoning, we can ask, Are there any reasons to believe that any genes in the population that increase male aggressiveness would become more common in males over time? When it comes to understanding the heightened levels of violence among males, population genetics thinking, as well as a specialized version of natural selection that Darwin (1859, 1871) referred to as *sexual selection*, have been particularly important.

Sexual selection theory says that just as the speed of impalas, for example, led to selection for characteristics that increased the speed of leopards, males and females in a population can select for characteristics of the other sex. So, for example, as females choose which males to mate with, they are choosing the genetically influenced characteristics of those males; those characteristics thus become more common in the population. These mating decisions can be thought of as cost/benefit choices, although the choices are largely unconscious. Particularly important to the unconscious calculation of mate choice is the amount of parental investment (time, effort, and resources) that each sex must make in order to produce offspring who will mature and go on to reproduce successfully themselves.

Robert Trivers (1972), who created the concept of parental investment, noted that "in the vast majority of species, the male's only contribution to the survival of his offspring is his sex cells. In these species, female contribution clearly exceeds male and by a large ratio" (p. 141). Human males, generally speaking, make a considerable investment in their offspring, but it is women, not men, who carry the developing offspring for nine months until birth. Trivers, like Bateman (1948) before him, realized that the sex that invests the most in offspring (usually females) will be more discriminating when it comes to mating. The sex that invests the least (usually males) will tend to favor quantity over quality of mates and will compete more intensely; that is, males will compete with other males to be chosen. Often accompanying this male-male competition will be intense aggression and risk taking.

Theorizing About Violent Crime

A number of criminologists operating in the evolutionary tradition have used the above lines of reasoning to produce theories of criminal behavior, with a special emphasis on violent offenses. They include David Rowe (1990, 1996), Linda Mealey (1995), and Lee Ellis (2003, 2004, 2005). Below is a basic sketch of arguments they have made in common:

People, especially males, vary in their tendencies to invest time and energy in caring for offspring, and this variation is partly the result of genetic factors. In other words, some males appear to be biologically less inclined to devote time and energy to ensuring the welfare and happiness of their children.

Males who want to invest heavily in parenthood are the sort of men most women would like to have father their children, so these men are called *dads*. The men who are not inclined to make this investment beyond the donation of sperm are referred to as *cads*.

If evolutionary theory is correct, both types of males need to have offspring if their genes are to be represented in subsequent generations. This means that both dads and cads must find females with which to mate. Dads, of course, should have no trouble, but how can cads reproduce, given that females will avoid them? Here are some reproductive options for them:

1. Cads can use deception to secure mates, such as promising to stay loyal during the courtship process and then reneging after a female is impregnated.

2. Cads can intimidate and injure any rival males.

3. Cads can exaggerate their abilities to be a good provider, such as by stealing and cheating others out of resources.

4. Cads can use force to have sex when voluntary methods fail.

Are there cads "out there," and are their actions at least partly genetically programmed, as Rowe (1990, 1996), Mealey (1995), and Ellis (2003, 2004, 2005) have argued? And are cads more involved in crime than are other males? The short answer to these questions is as follows: There is a psychiatric condition known as *psychopathy* or *antisocial personality* that is almost exclusive to males (Cottler, Price, Compton, & Mager, 1995; Mulder, Wells, Joyce, & Bushnell, 1994), and genes appear to contribute to this condition (Crowe, 1974). Furthermore, psychopaths are more likely than males generally to be involved in crime (Ellis & Walsh, 2000, p. 17), and they tend to be extremely deceptive, manipulative, cruel, and violent (Hare, Harpur, Hakstian, Forth, Hart, & Newman, 1990).

Theorizing About Specific Types of Violent Crime

In addition to the broad-ranging evolutionary/genetic theories of criminality just described, there are other theories of a similar nature that have been applied to specific types of violent offenses. The most extensive investigations into the possible evolutionary underpinnings of criminal violence have been conducted by Martin Daly and Margo Wilson (1985, 1988, 1994; Wilson, Daly, & Weghorst, 1980).

One focus of their work has been the study of child abuse by parents, such as the case of Joel Zellmer that we described earlier. In *The Truth about Cinderella*, Daly and Wilson (1999) point to studies that have shown that adults are much more likely to injure stepchildren than they are any biological children they may have. In evolutionary terms, this can be explained by noting that far fewer genes are shared between adults and stepchildren than between adults and their biological children. In other words, from an evolutionary perspective, individuals who harm close genetic relatives are less likely to pass genes on to future generations than are individuals who harm distant relatives or nonrelatives. This is not to assert that violence does not occur between close genetic relatives, and it certainly does not serve to condone any form of child abuse. The work by Daly and Wilson indicates that, given the same opportunities in terms of time spent together, genetically unrelated persons will be substantially more violent to each other than will those who are close relatives (Ellis & Walsh, 1997, p. 242).

In discussing their findings, Daly and Wilson (1999) were quick to note the obvious: Most stepparents do not harm or hurt their stepchildren. Nevertheless, there is a highly elevated probability of their doing so compared to biological parents, and this is quite consistent with predictions derived from evolutionary theory.

Another line of investigation by Daly, Wilson, and Weghorst (1982) involved spouse abuse. Evolutionary reasoning caused them to predict that much spouse abuse is motivated by infidelity (or suspicions of infidelity). Males, in particular, have difficulty knowing which offspring are theirs, except by inferring parenthood if they have maintained exclusive sexual relations with the offspring's mother. Because helping to rear the offspring of another male will be strongly disfavored from an evolutionary standpoint, males should strenuously act to prevent their mates from being sexually involved with other males. Daly and Wilson (1996) believe that this helps to explain why sexual jealousy has been shown to be the single most common "cause" of spousal abuse. Theoretically, violence toward spouses, especially by males, may represent part of an evolved response to male risks of misdirecting their so-called "parental investment" to the offspring of some other male. This explanation does not justify spouse abuse, but it may offer a way to understand why it is so common throughout the world, and it may eventually help to develop preventive strategies.

Another realm of criminological investigation using evolutionary/genetic principles concerns rape (or sexual assault). In the 1980s, various evolutionary thinkers began to entertain the idea that because males, compared to females, make such minimal direct investment in producing offspring, they should be more eager to copulate. Some males may even carry their "eagerness" so far that they sometimes resort to force if they are unsuccessful at securing voluntary compliance (Thornhill & Thornhill, 1983; Ellis, 1991a; Thornhill & Palmer, 2000). From a biological standpoint, these males may stand to father more offspring than males who do not use forceful tactics, and thereby their genes will be better represented in future generations. While any number of social countermeasures may be advanced to combat rape, it has even been suggested that rapists should be imprisoned throughout most of their reproductive years.

In sum, there are strong selective and population genetics reasons to expect that violent behavior, particularly among young men, is part of our evolutionary legacy. But is there more direct evidence of genetic influences on criminal violence?

Show Me the Genes!

If evolutionary theory can help to explain violent criminal behavior, genes *must* be making a significant contribution to the variations in such behavior. In other words, no trait can evolve by natural selection if genes are not at least partly responsible for the trait. This means that some people must be more genetically predisposed to act in ways that are defined as criminal than are other people. In order to explore this possibility, researchers use two different approaches: behavioral genetics and molecular genetics.

Is there evidence for any specific genes contributing to criminality, especially violent criminality? Behavioral genetics research, which is often based on so-called twin studies and adoption studies, has allowed scientists to separate genetic and environmental influences on traits. While the actual percentage estimates vary from 35% (van der Valk et al., 1998) to as much as 80% (Dionne, Tremblay, Boivin, Laplante, & Perusse, 2003), nearly all studies agree that the role of genetics in affecting tendencies toward aggression and violent crime is substantial.

So, what specific genes seem to be involved? In order to address this question, researchers engage in *molecular genetics* studies, which seek to isolate specific genes and identify their effects. Scientists now estimate that the development of each human is guided by approximately 22,000 genes located on our 23 pairs of chromosomes. However, we are a long way away from identifying what each of those genes does in terms of building and regulating our bodies. It is safe to assume that many of these 22,000 genes code for vital structures and processes in our brains, which, in turn, affect how we react to the experiences we have every day. Progress is being made in identifying how these genes work and thereby affect the probability of our behaving in ways that violate criminal statutes.

Four instances of how genes seem to affect our probability of engaging in criminal violence will be briefly described here. You will see that in one way or another, all four examples involve the brain's neurotransmitters, biochemicals that send messages from one nerve cell to another and make it possible for us to think and carry out complex activities.

1. For over a decade, scientists have been intrigued by an unnamed Dutch family, in which some extremely disturbing behavior was found among many of the men (Brunner, Nelen, Breakefield, Ropers, & van Oost, 1993; Brunner, Nelen, van Zandovoot et al., 1993). One of the men attempted to rape his sister and later assaulted a prison warden with a pitchfork. Others in the family had committed arson, assaults on both men and women, and had made numerous threats with weapons. In total, 14 male members of this family over four generations have committed numerous violent acts while also exhibiting mild mental retardation.

What drew scientists to study this family was the discovery that the affected men had an unusual version of a gene controlling an enzyme that helps break down important neurotransmitters, an enzyme known as monoamine oxidase. This family suffered from a particularly rare mutation in this gene that essentially eliminates the production of one form of monoamine oxidase (known as MAO-A). Several other studies have implicated variants of genes regulating monoamine oxidase activity as a contribution to criminal behavior, at least among males (Ellis, 1991b; Sjoberg et al., 2008).

In a recent New Zealand study, a gene coding for low MAO-A activity was found to be associated with violent and antisocial behavior if individuals also suffered substantial maltreatment as children. Individuals with the same genetic variant but who were not abused as children were not unusually prone to antisocial conduct (Caspi, McClay, Moffitt, Mill, Martin, & Craig, 2002). The researchers interpreted this finding as suggesting that both genetic and family environmental factors must often interact to affect criminality. Overall, this line of research on MAO-A suggests that the way genes alter the breakdown of neurotransmitters may help in the understanding of antisocial behavior.

2. Another line of research has pointed to genes regulating *dopamine,* an important neurotransmitter associated with the pleasurable and rewarding experiences that people gain from activities ranging from having sex to using drugs such as cocaine and alcohol. At a genetic level, there are several alleles (i.e., various forms of the same gene) that code for different types of dopamine receptors (i.e., special locations on nerve cells that lock onto dopamine molecules).

In recent years, at least two of these special types of dopamine receptors (DRD2 and DRD4) have been found to be associated with an increased risk of criminality and/or closely related behaviors such as alcoholism, drug abuse, and antisocial personality disorder (Comings, Muhleman, Ahn, Gysin, & Flanagan, 1994; Noble, Ozkaragoz, Ritchie, Belin, & Sparkes, 1998), although not all of the research has been able to replicate these links (Lee, Lee, Kim, Kim, & Lee, 2003). A recent article may help to explain the inconsistencies. It suggested that certain forms of genes for *both* DRD2 and DRD4 may have to be present before these receptors alter dopamine brain activity enough to promote behavioral traits conducive to criminal offending (Beaver et al., 2007).

3. Genes that influence another neurotransmitter—serotonin—have also been found to be related to criminal violence. Elevated levels of serotonin activity in the brain are associated with feelings of calm and contentment; low levels are associated with irritability and gloom. Studies have shown that impulsive violence is more common in persons with low levels of serotonin activity (Blumensohn et al., 1995; Coccaro, 1992; Virkkunen, Eggert, Rawlings, & Linnoila, 1996). While there are many environmental variables involved in regulating how active serotonin is in the brain (including some of the foods we eat), most of the variation appears to be due to genetic factors (Greenberg, Tolliver, Huang, Li, Bengel, & Murphy, 1999; Heinz et al. 2005; Liao, Hong, Shih, & Tsai, 2004). The message from this line of research seems to be that violence can be avoided by somehow keeping serotonin levels in our brains high.

4. The final line of evidence for genetic influences on violent criminality may help criminologists understand sex differences in criminal violence. Males have an entire chromosome that females lack: the Y-chromosome. Located on this chromosome are genes that direct would-be female ovaries

to become male testes instead. The testes have evolved into specialized organs for producing testosterone, a hormone that has been shown in many species to contribute in complex ways to physical aggression (Jasnow, Huhman, Bartness, & Demas, 2000; Sanchez-Martin, Fano, Ahedo, Cardas, Brain, & Azpiroz, 2000). The tendency to behave aggressively is not simply a matter of how much testosterone is present in the body at a given point in time, however. It also depends on how much testosterone gets into the brain even before birth and how many special cell receptors (called *androgen receptors*) are present in the brain to lock onto each testosterone molecule that enters (Lundin, Nordenskjold, Giwercman, & Giwercman, 2006). As with testosterone production itself, the number of androgen receptors individuals possess appears to be under considerable genetic control (Jorm, 2004; Sluyter, Hof, Ellenbroek, Degen, & Cools, 2000).

How does testosterone affect physical aggression tendencies, including those that are considered criminal? The answer is complex, but part of it has been shown to involve the ability of testosterone to influence neurotransmitter functioning, including both dopamine and serotonin (Guo, Roettger, & Shih, 2007; Miczek, Fish, de Bold, & de Almeida, 2002).

Noting that testosterone affects the probability of criminal violence, one can infer that males are going to be more involved in crime, especially violent crime, than are females. Reinforcing the view that evolution is at least partly responsible for this sex difference is evidence that in nearly all mammalian species, males are more prone to violence than are females (Ellis et al., 2008, pp. 705–709).

Conclusion

The ideas outlined in this chapter are part of an approach to criminology known as *biosocial criminology*. According to this approach, both biological and social environmental factors interact to affect people's probabilities of violating criminal statutes. In other words, criminological theories that only stipulate the involvement of environmental factors may be true, but they are incomplete. In fact, environmental factors are dependent upon genes to have their effects. As Matt Ridley (2003) notes,

> [genes] are devices for extracting information from the environment. Every minute, every second, the pattern of genes being expressed in your brain changes, often in direct or indirect response to events outside the body. Genes are the mechanisms of experience. (p. 248)

Ridley here is referring to the role of genes in *development*—the characteristics that are expressed in an organism over the course of its lifetime. In the biosocial approach, characteristics like violence and aggression can only be fully understood by considering the interaction of genes and environment in their production.

However, the genes that are operative in development have been selected for over evolutionary time. In effect, natural selection chooses among alternative developmental pathways, and our evolutionary history has established a species-typical developmental trajectory for humans. Part of that species-typical trajectory involves the capacity to behave in aggressive and violent ways. While genes and environment interact to produce violent behavior in any individual case, it is our evolutionary history that explains the quite stable and predicable patterns of violent and aggressive behavior more generally, that is, the universally higher rates of violence among young men.

While the things that we do not know about how evolution and genes have influenced aggression and criminality are immense, as the literature discussed in this chapter has shown, progress is being made. The ultimate payoff for our knowledge will come when it helps to reduce the number of victims who suffer violent offenses every year.

Discussion Questions

1. Describe the process of natural selection.

2. Discuss the different roles that genes play in evolution and in development. Discuss their relationship to population genetics research as well as behavioral and molecular genetics research.

3. What is "sexual selection" and how is it related to violent behavior?

4. Some specific genes have been identified as being related to violent behavior. In general, how do these specific genes influence violent behavior?

5. Discuss the moral and political issues that are raised by our increasing knowledge of genetic influences on violent behavior.

Internet Resources

British Psychological Society, Forensic Research Update: http://bps-research-digest.blogspot.com/search/label/Forensic

Crime Causation: Biological Theories: http://law.jrank.org/pages/795/Crime-Causation-Biological-Theories.html

Human Genome Project: http://www.ornl.gov/sci/techresources/Human_Genome/home.shtml

References

Bateman, A. J. (1948). Intra-sexual selection in drosophila. *Heredity, 2*, 349–368.

Beaver, K. M., Wright, J. P., DeLisi, M., Walsh, A., Vaughn, M. G., Boisvert, D., et al. (2007). A gene x gene interaction between DRD2 and DRD4 is associated with conduct disorder and antisocial behavior in males. *Behavioral and Brain Functions, 3*, 30.

Blumensohn, R., Ratzoni, G., Weizman, A., Israeli, M., Greuner, N., Apter, A., et al. (1995). Reduction in serotonin 5HT receptor binding on platelets of delinquent adolescents. *Psychopharmacology, 118*, 354–356.

Brunner, H. G., Nelen, M., Breakefield, X. O., Ropers, H. H., & van Oost, B. A. (1993). Abnormal behavior associated with a point mutation in the structural gene for monoamine oxidase a. *Science, 262*, 578–580.

Brunner, H. G., Nelen, M. R., van Zandovoot, P., Abeling, N. G., van Gennip, A. H., Wolters, E. C., et al. (1993). X-linked borderline mental retardation with prominent behavioral disturbance: Phenotype, genetic localization, and evidence for disturbed monoamine metabolism. *American Journal of Human Genetics, 52*, 1032–1039.

Caspi, A., McClay, J., Moffitt, T. E., Mill, J., Martin, J., & Craig, I. W. (2002). Role of genotype in the cycle of violence in maltreated children. *Science, 297*, 851–854.

Coccaro, E. (1992). Impulsive aggression and central serotonergic function in humans: An example of a dimensional brain-behavioral relationship. *International Clinical Psychopharmacology, 16*, 1–12.

Comings, D. E., Muhleman, D., Ahn, C., Gysin, R., & Flanagan, S. D. (1994). The dopamine d2 receptor gene: A genetic risk factor in substance abuse. *Drug and Alcohol Dependence, 34*(3), 175–180.

Cottler, L. B., Price, R. K., Compton, W. M., & Mager, D. E. (1995). Subtypes of adult antisocial behavior among drug abusers. *Journal of Nervous and Mental Disorders, 183*, 154–161.

Crowe, R. R. (1974). An adoption study of antisocial personality. *Archives of General Psychiatry, 31*, 785–791.

Daly, M., & Wilson, M. (1985). Child abuse and other risks of not living with both parents. *Ethology and Sociobiology, 6*, 197–210.

Daly, M., & Wilson, M. (1988). *Homicide*. New York: Aldine de Gruyter.

Daly, M., & Wilson, M. I. (1994). Some differential attributes of lethal assaults on small children by stepfathers versus genetic fathers. *Ethology and Sociobiology, 15*, 207–217.

Daly, M., & Wilson, M. I. (1996). Violence against stepchildren. *Current Direction in Psychological Science, 5*, 77–81.

Daly, M., & Wilson, M. (1999). *The truth about Cinderella: A Darwinian view of parental love*. New Haven, CT: Yale University.

Daly, M., Wilson, M., & Weghorst, S. J. (1982). Male sexual jealousy. *Ethology and Sociobiology, 3*, 11–27.

Darwin, C. (1859). *The origin of species*. New York: Mentor.

Darwin, C. (1871). *The descent of man, and selection in relation to sex*. London: John Murray.

Dionne, G., Tremblay, R. E., Boivin, M., Laplante, D., & Perusse, D. (2003). Physical aggression and expressive vocabulary in 19-month-old twins. *Developmental Psychology, 39*, 261–273.

de Waal, F. (1986). The brutal elimination of a rival among captive male chimpanzees. *Ethology and Sociobiology, 7*, 237–251.

de Waal, F. (1998). *Chimpanzee politics* (Rev. ed.). Baltimore, MD: The Johns Hopkins University Press.

Dobzhansky, T. (1997). Nothing in biology makes sense except in the light of evolution. In M. Ridley (Ed.), *Evolution* (pp. 378–387). New York: Oxford University Press.

Ellis, L. (1990). The evolution of collective counterstrategies to crime: From the primate control role to the criminal justice system. In L. Ellis & H. Hoffman (Eds.), *Crime in biological, social, and moral contexts* (pp. 81–99). New York: Praeger.

Ellis, L. (1991a). A synthesized (biosocial) theory of rape. *Journal of Consulting and Clinical Psychology, 59,* 631–642.

Ellis, L. (1991b). Monoamine oxidase and criminality: Identifying an apparent biological marker for antisocial behavior. *Journal of Research on Crime and Delinquency, 28,* 227–251.

Ellis, L. (2003). Genes, criminality, and the evolutionary neuroandrogenic theory. In A. Walsh & L. Ellis (Eds.), *Biosocial criminology: Challenging environmentalism's supremacy* (pp. 13–34). Hauppauge, NY: Nova Science.

Ellis, L. (2004). Sex, status, and criminality: A theoretical nexus. *Social Biology, 51,* 144–160.

Ellis, L. (2005). A theory explaining biological correlates of criminality. *European Journal of Criminology, 2*(3), 287–315.

Ellis, L., Hershberger, S., Field, E., Wersinger, S., Pellis, S., Geary, D., et al. (2008). Sex *differences: Findings from more than a century of scientific research.* New York: Taylor & Francis Psychology Press.

Ellis, L., & Walsh, A. (1997). Gene-based evolutionary theories in criminology. *Criminology, 35,* 229–276.

Ellis, L., & Walsh, A. (2000). *Criminology: A global perspective.* Boston: Allyn & Bacon.

Greenberg, B. D., Tolliver, T. J., Huang, S.-J., Li, Q., Bengel, D., & Murphy, D. L. (1999). Genetic variation in serotonin transporter promoter region affects serotonin uptake in human blood platelets. *Neuropsychiatric Genetics, 88*(1), 83–87.

Guo, G., Roettger, M. E., & Shih, J. C. (2007). Contributions of the dat1 and the drd2 genes to serious and violent delinquency among adolescents and young adults. *Human Genetics, 121,* 125–136.

Hagey, J. (2007, June 8). Stepfather charged in drowning. *The News Tribune,* p. A1.

Hare, R. D., Harpur, T. J., Hakstian, A. R., Forth, A. E., Hart, S. D., & Newman, J. P. (1990). The revised psychopathy checklist: Reliability and factor structure. *Psychological Assessment: A Journal of Consulting and Clinical Psychology, 2,* 338–341.

Heinz, A., Braus, D. F., Smolka, M. N., Wrase, J., Puls, I., Hermann, D., et al. (2005). Amygdala-prefrontal coupling depends on a genetic variation of the serotonin transporter. *Nature Neuroscience, 8*(1), 20–21.

Jasnow, A. M., Huhman, K. L., Bartness, T. J., & Demas, G. E. (2000). Sort-day increases in aggression are inversely related to circulating testosterone concentrations in male Siberian hamsters (*Phodopus sungorus). Hormones and Behavior, 38,* 102–110.

Johnson, T. (2007, June 7). "Bizarre injuries" trail murder suspect. *Seattle Post-Intelligencer,* p. A1.

Jorm, A. F. (2004). Association of adverse childhood experiences, age of menarche, and adult reproductive behavior: Does the androgen receptor gene play a role? *American Journal of Medical Genetics, 125B,* 105–111.

Kandel, E. R. (2006). *In search of memory.* New York: W. W. Norton & Company.

Kondrashov, A. S. (1982). Selection against harmful mutations in large sexual and asexual populations. *Genetic Research, 40,* 325–332.

Lee, H. J., Lee, H. S., Kim, Y. K., Kim, L., & Lee, M. S. (2003). D2 and d4 dopamine receptor gene polymorphisms and personality traits in a young Korean population. *American Journal of Medical Genetics. Part B, Neuropsychiatric Genetics, 121,* 44–49.

Liao, D. L., Hong, C. J., Shih, H. L., & Tsai, S. J. (2004). Possible association between serotonin transporter promoter region polymorphism and extremely violent crime in Chinese males. *Neuropsychobiology, 50,* 284–287.

Lundin, K. B., Nordenskjold, A., Giwercman, A., & Giwercman, Y. L. (2006). Frequent finding of the androgen receptor a645d variant in normal population. *Journal of Clinical Endocrinology and Metabolism, 91*(8), 3228–3231.

Mealey, L. (1995). The sociobiology of sociopathy: An integrated evolutionary model. *Behavioral and Brain Sciences, 18,* 523–599.

Miczek, K. A., Fish, E. W., de Bold, J. F., & de Almeida, R. M. (2002). Social and neural determinants of aggressive behavior: Pharmacotherapeutic targets at serotonin, dopamine, and gamma-aminobutyric acid systems. *Psychopharmacology, 163*, 434–458.

Mulder, R. T., Wells, J. E., Joyce, P. R., & Bushnell, J. A. (1994). Antisocial women. *Journal of Personality Disorders, 8*, 279–287.

Nachman, M. W. (2004). Haldane and the first estimates of the human mutation rate. *Journal of Genetics, 83*(3), 237–233.

Noble, E. P., Ozkaragoz, T. Z., Ritchie, X. Z., Belin, T. R., & Sparkes, R. S. (1998). D2 and d4 dopamine receptor polymorphisms and personality. *American Journal of Medical Genetics, 81*, 257–267.

Pastore, A., & Maguire, K. (2005). *Sourcebook for criminal justice statistics 2003.* Washington, DC: U.S. Department of Justice.

Ridley, M. (2003). *Nature via nurture.* New York: HarperCollins.

Rowe, D. C. (1990). Inherited dispositions toward learning delinquent and criminal behavior: New evidence. In L. Ellis & H. Hoffman (Eds.), *Crime in biological, social, and moral contexts* (pp. 121–133). New York: Praeger.

Rowe, D. C. (1996). An adaptive strategy theory of crime and delinquency. In J. D. Hawkins (Ed.), *Delinquency and crime: Current theories* (pp. 268–314). Cambridge: Cambridge University Press.

Sanchez-Martin, J. R., Fano, E., Ahedo, L., Cardas, J., Brain, P. F., & Azpiroz, A. (2000). Relating testosterone levels and free play social behavior in male and female preschool children. *Psychoneuroendocrinology, 25*, 773–783.

Sjoberg, R. L., Ducci, F., Barr, C. S., Newman, T. K., Dell'osso, L., Virkkunen, M., et al. (2008). A non-addictive interaction of a functional MAO-A VNTR and testosterone predicts antisocial behavior. *Neuropsychopharmacology, 33*, 425–430.

Sluyter, F., Hof, M. W. P., Ellenbroek, B. A., Degen, S. B., & Cools, A. R. (2000). Genetic, sex, and early environmental effects on the voluntary alcohol intake in Wistar rats. *Pharmacology, Biochemistry and Behavior, 67*(4), 801–808.

Thornhill, R., & Palmer, C. T. (2000). *A natural history of rape: Biological bases of sexual coercion.* Cambridge, MA: The MIT Press.

Thornhill, R., & Thornhill, N. (1983). Human rape: An evolutionary analysis. *Ethology and Sociobiology, 4*, 137–173.

Trivers, R. L. (1972). Parental investment and sexual selection. In B. Campbell (Ed.), *Sexual selection and the descent of man: 1871–1971* (pp. 136–179). New York: Aldine.

Van der Valk, J. C., Verhulst, F. C., Neale, M. C., & Boomsma, D. I. (1998). Longitudinal genetic analysis of problem behaviors in biologically related and unrelated adoptees. *Behavior Genetics, 28*(5), 365–380.

Virkkunen, M., Eggert, M., Rawlings, R., & Linnoila, M. (1996). A prospective follow-up study of alcoholic violent offenders and fire setters. *Archives of General Psychiatry, 53*, 523–529.

Wilson, M. I., Daly, M., & Weghorst, S. J. (1980). Household composition and the risk of child abuse and neglect. *Journal of Biosocial Science, 12*, 333–340.

CHAPTER 5

The Biochemistry of Violent Crime

Kevin M. Beaver

The study of crime and criminals has historically been monopolized by scholars advocating the salience of social factors in the development of antisocial behaviors. Dominant mainstream criminological theories, for example, posit that neighborhoods, families, parents, peers, and other social institutions are causal agents of crime and delinquency. While these perspectives have accrued varying degrees of empirical support, they all are guilty of at least one serious shortcoming: They have pretended that biological factors are unimportant in the genesis of violent behaviors (but see Moffitt, 1993). This is a serious oversight, especially given that there is now a considerable amount of research revealing that biology can—and, indeed, does—have profound effects on physical aggression and violence (Niehoff, 1999; Raine, 1993; Rowe, 2002).

CASE STUDY: THE MAO-A GENE

Some of the earliest evidence revealing that MAO-producing genes may be implicated in the development of antisocial phenotypes came from a Dutch kindred. Within this family pedigree, at least 14 males were inflicted with a disorder that caused borderline mental retardation; the remaining men and all of the women were unaffected. Inflicted males had difficulty functioning in society. For example, only one male with the disorder completed primary education, and he was the only one to secure steady employment (Brunner, Nelen, van Zandvoort et al., 1993). But mental retardation was only one symptom of a larger constellation of problems that were caused by this disorder. Abnormal behaviors, which sometimes included aggression and violence, were widespread among all the affected males. One male was convicted of raping his

(Continued)

(Continued)

sister, and later, while in prison, he stabbed a warden with a pitchfork. Another male forced his sisters, at knifepoint, to undress in front of him. These behaviors were very frequent and, as a consequence, females in this family were often so fearful of the inflicted males that they would sometimes move out of the house at an early age (Brunner, Nelen, van Zandvoort et al., 1993). Other forms of antisocial behaviors, including arson, exhibitionism, voyeurism, impulsive violence, and attempted rape, were also reported to be relatively common in affected males from this family.

Brunner and his colleagues (Brunner, Nelen, Breakefield, Ropers, & van Oost, 1993; Brunner, Nelen, van Zandvoort et al., 1993) were interested in identifying the cause of this disorder. They reasoned that because only males were affected with this syndrome, the gene or genes causing the disorder must be located on the X-chromosome. Why would this be the case? Well, most genes are made up of two copies, but males only have one copy of X-linked genes, whereas females have two copies. Knowing this information, Brunner et al. hypothesized that there might be a problem with a gene on the X-chromosome within this family. If a male inherited this "bad" gene, he would not have a back-up copy to replace it. Females, on the other hand, would have two copies of all X-linked genes, so even one "bad" gene would not necessarily be detrimental because their other copy of the gene could compensate for it. Thus, Brunner and his associates calculated genetic linkage analysis on the X-chromosome to help identify the genes that may be responsible for this disorder.

What their analyses revealed was quite striking: All inflicted family members (and some noninflicted females) had inherited a mutated gene that could not produce MAO-A. Given that MAO-A modulates levels of a number of different neurotransmitters, the fact that affected males had a deficiency of MAO-A meant that their neurotransmitter levels were left unregulated. These aberrant neurotransmitter levels were thought to be the main cause of the antisocial behaviors exhibited by males with this disorder (Brunner, Nelen, & Breakefield et al., 1993). Brunner et al.'s studies revealing that a single gene was responsible for the MAO-A deficiency disorder necessarily raised questions about whether this MAO-A-producing gene may be a major cause of criminal behaviors. Subsequent researchers searched other samples of families to determine the frequency with which this MAO-A deficiency occurs in the population. At present, there are no reported cases of the MAO-A deficiency syndrome outside the single Dutch kindred studied by Brunner and colleagues (Mejia, Ervin, Palmour, & Tremblay, 2001; Murphy et al., 1998; Schuback et al., 1999).

A wealth of biological factors, ranging from hypoglycemia and a low resting heart rate to epilepsy and maternal smoking during pregnancy, have been linked to a range of different antisocial outcomes (Ellis, 2005). Of all the biological risk factors for crime and delinquency, those relating to an individual's biochemistry have been studied the most extensively. Although a diverse array of biochemicals are found throughout the body and brain, this chapter will focus on how two of the most widely examined biochemicals—neurotransmitters and hormones—affect the propensity to engage in violent behaviors. However, before proceeding to a discussion of the effects that these biochemicals have on different forms of physical aggression, three caveats need to be presented.

First, the effects that biochemicals have on antisocial conduct are quite variable and depend, in large part, on the type of behavior being studied and how that behavior is measured. Biological risk factors, for instance, tend to have the strongest and most consistent effects on serious physical violence and impulsive aggression but minimal or no effects on minor forms of delinquency. As a result, and except where noted, this chapter will review only those studies that employ measures of violent behaviors or measures of serious antisocial phenotypes, while studies that examine more mundane forms of misbehavior (e.g., truancy or lying) will be omitted.

Second, biological factors associated with violent behaviors are *risk* factors that confer a greater probability of becoming involved in aggression. Someone who has a particular biological risk factor will not necessarily become violent and someone lacking a particular biological risk factor may become violent. In the parlance of social scientists, the presence of a biological risk factor is neither a necessary nor a sufficient condition to developing a particular antisocial phenotype—it is simply a risk factor. Risk factors work in a probabilistic fashion; as the number of risk factors increases, the odds of developing the phenotype (in this case, aggression/violence) also increase, but even people with a large number of risk factors may never become physically aggressive.

Third, and perhaps most noteworthy, is the growing recognition that biological risk factors and environmental risk factors often *interact* in the etiology of violence and aggression (Raine, 2002). This emerging perspective—known as biosocial criminology—holds particular promise for identifying the mechanisms by which the environment and biology work in combination to produce antisocial behaviors (Walsh, 2002). According to the logic of these perspectives, biological risk factors have the most potent effects when paired with specific environmental risk factors: Remove the environmental risk factor and the biological risk factor will not have as strong an effect; reintroduce the environmental risk factor and the biological risk factor will once again have a powerful effect. Unfortunately, a very limited number of studies have employed a biosocial approach when examining the effects that biochemicals have on violent behaviors (for notable exceptions, see Dabbs & Morris, 1990; Maughan, 2005). As a result, only studies that examine the main effects (i.e., nonbiosocial studies) that neurotransmitters and hormones have on antisocial behaviors will be reviewed.

Neurotransmitters

Neurotransmitters are chemical compounds that allow electrical signals to be passed from one neuron to another. *Neurons* are nerve cells in the brain that consist of a cell nucleus and two types of fibers: axons and dendrites. *Axons* extend away from the cell nucleus and transport information via electrical signals to other neurons. *Dendrites,* in contrast, receive incoming signals from axons and then transmit the information to the cell's nucleus. Thus, when a signal from one neuron needs to be transmitted to another neuron, the message is transported down the neuron's axon and is then delivered to the dendrite of an adjacent neuron. Once received by the dendrite, the signal is processed by the cell and sent down the axon, where it can then be passed along to the dendrite of another neuron. Information continues to move from axon to dendrite to axon to dendrite, until the signal reaches its final target.

As an electrical signal moves down an axon, and before it can pass the message to a dendrite, a small gap, known as a *synapse,* is encountered. The synapse separates axons from dendrites, and thus signals cannot be transmitted directly from axon to dendrite. Instead, neurotransmitters are released from the axon of one neuron (i.e., the presynaptic neuron), move across the synapse, and eventually deliver the message to the dendrite of another neuron (i.e., the postsynaptic neuron). Once neurotransmitters have transmitted the signal to the postsynaptic neuron, they need to be removed from the synapse. There are two main processes by which neurotransmitters are eliminated from the synaptic cleft: reuptake and enzymatic degradation. In reuptake, transporter proteins are released into the synapse, where they capture neurotransmitters and eventually return them to the presynaptic neuron. In the process of enzymatic degradation, enzymes are released into the synapse, where they metabolize neurotransmitters into inactive particles. Both of these processes are important because they work to modulate levels of neurotransmitters.

Levels of neurotransmitters are determined by a combination of genetic and environmental factors. Genetic factors are largely responsible for controlling the processes of reuptake and enzymatic degradation. Each person's unique suite of genes, for instance, dictates how quickly and how effectively neurotransmitters are cleansed from the synapse. The efficiency with which neurotransmitters are removed from the synaptic gap helps to modulate levels of neurotransmitters. But neurotransmitter levels also wax and wane in response to environmental conditions. Almost every imaginable social stimulus, including eating, sexual intercourse, watching a sad movie, and sleeping, alters concentrations of certain neurotransmitters.

Levels of neurotransmitters are important because different concentrations of certain neurotransmitters have been linked to a number of maladaptive outcomes. Research has revealed, for example, that aberrant neurotransmitter levels are associated with depression, schizophrenia, bulimia, and anorexia (Clark & Grunstein, 2000; Hamer & Copeland, 1998). Most important to this chapter, however, is that even violence, aggression, and other antisocial phenotypes have been tied to neurotransmitter levels. Some research has revealed that *high* dosages of certain neurotransmitters are associated with an increased risk of violence, whereas other studies have revealed that *low* concentrations of certain neurotransmitters are related to an increased risk of violence.

What accounts for these seemingly paradoxical findings? To shed some light on this question, it is first necessary to point out that neurotransmitters can roughly be divided into two groups: One group is known as inhibitory neurotransmitters and the other group is known as excitatory neurotransmitters. Without going into technical details, *inhibitory neurotransmitters* decrease postsynaptic neuronal activity (i.e., decrease the rate at which neurons fire), whereas *excitatory neurotransmitters* increase postsynaptic neuronal activity (i.e., increase the rate at which neurons fire). Broadly speaking, and with the qualification that important exceptions exist, inhibitory neurotransmitters are thought to dampen antisocial propensities, whereas excitatory neurotransmitters are thought to increase violent and aggressive tendencies (Anderson, 2007; Raine, 1993; Rowe, 2002). So whether neurotransmitter levels are positively or negatively associated with antisocial behaviors depends, in part, on whether the neurotransmitter is inhibitory or excitatory. In the following sections, I will discuss the association between antisocial behaviors and five neurotransmitters: serotonin, dopamine, norepinephrine, gamma-aminobutyric acid, and monoamine oxidase.[1]

Serotonin and Antisocial Behaviors

Serotonin (5-HT) is a neurotransmitter that has inhibitory properties that act as the body's natural brake system. It is manufactured by serotonin-producing neurons that extend to areas of the brain that have been found to be associated with violence and aggression (e.g., the amygdala). This is particularly important because the release of 5-HT into the brain serves to modulate behaviors, curtail impulses, and dampen innate drives. But the precise effect that is generated from the production of 5-HT depends, in part, on where 5-HT is released (Manuck, Kaplan, & Lotrich, 2006). Serotonin that is found in the hippocampus, for example, may have one effect on the body, whereas 5-HT in the hypothalamus may have a very different impact. So the most reliable way to examine the influence that 5-HT may have on antisocial behaviors would be to measure quantities of 5-HT in specific regions of the brain. Serotonin, however, cannot pass the blood-brain barrier, making it impossible to measure 5-HT directly in the brain without risking permanent injury. Instead, indirect methods have been developed to assay overall levels of 5-HT. These techniques rely on measuring certain substances found outside the brain that are known to correlate with 5-HT. Two of the most widely used techniques will be reviewed here.

The first indirect way to gauge 5-HT levels is by measuring the 5-HT metabolite, 5-hydroxindoleacetic acid (5-HIAA). Remember that after neurotransmitters have transferred a signal from the presynaptic neuron to the postsynaptic neuron, enzymes are needed to eliminate neurotransmitters from the synapse. In the brain, 5-HT is broken down by the enzyme monoamine oxidase (MAO). As MAO metabolizes 5-HT, residual particles known collectively as 5-HIAA are formed. After being produced, 5-HIAA then travels into the spinal cord, where it can be measured by taking a sample of cerebrospinal fluid (CSF) via a lumbar puncture. Given that 5-HIAA is a direct descendant of 5-HT, levels of 5-HIAA provide a proxy measure of the concentration of 5-HT in the central nervous system.

The second technique employed to quantify 5-HT levels involves directly measuring the concentration of 5-HT found in the peripheral nervous system. In this method, blood samples are drawn and assayed for levels of 5-HT in blood cells. Blood 5-HT, however, cannot pass the blood-brain barrier, and unlike brain 5-HT, blood 5-HT is produced by cells in the gastrointestinal system, not by neurons. Although there are some connections between blood 5-HT and brain 5-HT, they are largely independent of each other. Perhaps as a consequence, the relationship between brain 5-HT and antisocial behavior differs from the relationship between blood 5-HT and antisocial behavior. More specifically, and for reasons that are not well understood, *low* brain 5-HT levels have been found to be associated with greater involvement in crime and aggression, while some evidence has shown that *high* blood 5-HT levels are associated with greater involvement in crime and aggression.

RECAP 5.1   Serotonin (5-HT) and Aggression

Serotonin Marker	Location	Hypothesized Association With Aggression
5-HIAA	Brain (cerebral spinal fluid)	Low levels = aggression
5-HT	Gastrointestinal tract (blood)	High levels = aggression

This is a somewhat perplexing finding given that serotonin is an inhibitory neurotransmitter and, thus, high levels should reduce antisocial behaviors. Rowe (2002), however, provides a plausible explanation for why these two types of 5-HT may have opposite effects on antisocial behavior:

> The studies of spinal fluid measure the amount of metabolite after serotonin has been released into the synapse between nerve cells and then used. If the metabolite is low, it means that less serotonin has been available for communicating between nerve cells. The platelet serotonin studies measure the amount of serotonin still stored inside the platelet—the amount that has not yet been released for communication. Thus, if communication between cells is poor, this effect would theoretically result in *high* concentrations of serotonin stored (in neurons or platelet cells) and *low* concentrations released to be converted into a serotonin metabolite (by synapse or muscle), conceptually resolving the opposite direction of the associations found with the two assays. (p. 77)

Regardless of the reason(s) for these divergent effects, there is a body of research revealing that levels of 5-HT are linked to antisocial behaviors. Table 5.1 provides a summary of the outcomes that have been tied to 5-HT and to other neurotransmitters that will be discussed later. However, in light of the opposite effects of brain 5-HT and blood 5-HT, the remaining discussion of 5-HT will be divided into two halves. The first half will be confined to studies assaying 5-HT through 5-HIAA, and the second half will focus only on studies that measure 5-HT through blood cells.

Evidence revealing that low levels of 5-HIAA are associated with increased levels of aggressive behaviors dates back to the mid-1970s when Asberg, Traskman, and Thoren (1976) discovered an inverse relationship between suicidal behavior and 5-HIAA among a sample of depressed patients (i.e., low levels of 5-HIAA were related to increased suicidal behavior). Perhaps even more revealing was that all of the patients who attempted to commit suicide violently, and all patients who eventually committed suicide, had low levels of 5-HIAA. While suicide is not the same as criminal conduct, it is a form of impulsive aggression, albeit self-directed aggression. Subsequent researchers drew from Asberg et al.'s work and reasoned that low 5-HIAA may also have effects that extend beyond suicide to other forms of non-self-directed aggressive behaviors.

In the late 1970s and early 1980s, Brown and associates (Brown, Goodwin, Ballenger, Goyer, & Major, 1979; Brown et al. 1982) conducted

Table 5.1 Neurotransmitters Associated With Antisocial Outcomes

Neurotransmitter	Abbreviation	Type of Neurotransmitter	Antisocial Outcomes
Serotonin	5-HT	Inhibitory neurotransmitter	Aggression, antisocial behavior, antisocial personality disorder, behavioral disinhibition, overt conduct problems, cruelty to animals, homicide, suicidal behaviors
Dopamine	DA	Excitatory neurotransmitter	Aggression, physical violence
Norepinephrine	NE	Excitatory neurotransmitter	Aggression, agitation, alcohol abuse, impulsive behaviors, risk-taking, violence
Gamma-aminobutyric acid	GABA	Inhibitory neurotransmitter	Aggression, physical violence
Monoamine oxidase	MAO	Metabolic enzyme	Aggression, crime, drug use, hyperactivity, impulsivity, psychopathy, risky behaviors, violence

two of the first studies revealing a link between low 5-HIAA and violence. In a small sample of males with personality disorders, Brown et al. (1979) reported that subjects with lower 5-HIAA engaged in more aggressive incidents. The results were confirmed in a follow-up study in which an inverse relationship between 5-HIAA and aggression was found in a different sample of males (Brown et al., 1982). These initial reports of a moderately strong and consistent effect of 5-HIAA on antisocial behaviors set the stage for a wave of researchers to examine the 5-HIAA-aggression nexus.

Studies bearing on the relationship between 5-HIAA and antisocial phenotypes have produced mixed results. Findings from some research groups, for instance, have reinforced the importance of 5-HIAA in the development of aggression and violence in adults (Limson et al., 1991) and in the development of disruptive behavior in young children (Kruesi, Rapoport, Hamburger, Hibbs, & Potter, 1990). One of the more fascinating studies to emerge out of this work was conducted by Constantino, Morris, and Murphy (1997). They were interested in examining whether 5-HIAA levels in 193 newborns varied as a function of their family's history of psychopathology. The analysis revealed that 5-HIAA was lower in infants whose biological parents scored high on an assessment of antisocial personality disorder (see also Halperin et al., 1997). It should be noted, however, that support for the effect of 5-HIAA on antisocial behaviors is not clear cut; some studies, for example, have failed to detect a statistically significant effect of 5-HIAA on aggressive behaviors (Gardner, Lucas, & Cowdry, 1990; Simeon, Stanley, Frances, Mann, Winchel, & Stanley, 1992) such as murder (Lidberg, Tuck, Asberg, Scalia-Tomba, & Bertilsson, 1985).

What accounts for these divergent findings, where 5-HIAA has effects in some studies, but not in others? Part of the explanation centers on the type of violence examined. There is some evidence to indicate that low 5-HIAA may only have effects on impulsive forms of violent behaviors. In support of this view, Linnoila, Virkkunen, Schwannian, Nuutila, Rimon, and Goodwin (1983) reported that 5-HIAA was significantly lower in offenders who committed an impulsive crime versus offenders who committed a premeditated crime. "Low 5-HIAA concentration in the CSF of violent offenders," according to Linnoila and colleagues, is "more of a marker of impulsivity than violence per se" (p. 2610). Subsequent studies have produced additional evidence revealing that the effects of low 5-HIAA are confined only to impulsive forms of violence (Virkkunen, Nuutila, Goodwin, & Linnoila, 1987; Virkkunen et al., 1994).

The hypothesis that 5-HIAA only relates to impulsive aggression was investigated in a recent meta-analysis by Moore, Scarpa, and Raine (2002). Moore et al. identified 20 studies that had examined the association between 5-HIAA and antisocial behavior. The results of their analysis indicated a statistically significant inverse relationship between 5-HIAA and violence. Additional statistical tests revealed that the effect of 5-HIAA was not moderated by type of crime; that is, 5-HIAA had consistent effects on all types of violent behaviors, not just impulsive violent behaviors.

Even though the meta-analysis by Moore and colleagues (2002) did not confirm the hypothesis that 5-HIAA is linked only to impulsive violence, it did confirm a significant and negative association between 5-HIAA levels and antisocial behaviors in general. So how do these results stack up against the findings from studies assessing the association between antisocial behavior and blood 5-HT? Comparatively less research has employed measures of blood 5-HT to examine the association between 5-HT and aggressive violence. The research that does exist, however, is far from conclusive. Most studies have reported a positive association between blood 5-HT and antisocial behaviors (Mann, McBride, Anderson, & Mieczkowski, 1992; Pliszka, Rogeness, Renner, Sherman, & Broussard, 1988; Unis et al., 1997), but some studies have failed to detect any relationship (Stoff, Ieni, Friedman, Bridger, Pollock, & Vitiello, 1991) and some studies have even reported a negative association between blood 5-HT and antisocial behavior (Greenberg & Coleman, 1976; Twitchell, Hanna, Cook, Fitzgerald, Little, & Zucker, 1998).

The inconsistent effects of blood 5-HT are probably partially attributable to methodological differences among the studies. Of particular importance is that most of the studies have analyzed nonrepresentative samples that comprise mentally handicapped patients, juvenile inmates, or other clinically based samples. The use of such heterogeneous samples makes it difficult to compare the effects across studies. For example, if a relationship between blood 5-HT and aggression is found in a sample of adolescent offenders, does that mean that this same relationship would be observed for the general population? Perhaps, but this is an empirical question that can only be answered by examining the effect that blood 5-HT has on violence in a representative sample. In the first study of its kind, Moffitt and her colleagues (1998) employed an epidemiological sample to determine the relationship between blood 5-HT and antisocial behavior. The results suggested that violence was more common among respondents with higher blood 5-HT concentrations, thereby revealing strong evidence of a positive correlation between blood 5-HT and antisocial behavior. Collectively, the results of 5-HIAA studies and blood 5-HT studies provide reason to believe that 5-HT plays a role in the development of antisocial behaviors.

Dopamine and Antisocial Behaviors

Like serotonin (5-HT), dopamine (DA) is a common neurotransmitter found throughout the body and brain, but unlike 5-HT, DA is an excitatory neurotransmitter, not an inhibitory neurotransmitter. Dopamine is a major player in the body's reward/pleasure system, and the release of DA is accompanied by intense euphoric feelings. Engaging in certain acts, such as eating, sleeping, and sexual intercourse, stimulates the release of DA. Once released, DA acts as a type of natural reinforcement and is partially the reason why certain behaviors, even if harmful, are repeated time and again.

The "highs" associated with the use of certain types of psychoactive drugs and with the consumption of alcohol are also due to alterations in DA (Volkow, Fowler, & Wang, 2003). Most drugs, especially highly addictive drugs, target DA and the dopaminergic system. Take, for example, cocaine. When cocaine is ingested, it blocks dopamine transporter proteins (see discussion above) from sweeping the synapses of DA. The result is that more DA piles up in the synapses, and this excess of DA causes the user to feel "high." Consider this: Sexual intercourse increases DA by a factor of about two (Fiorino, Coury, & Phillips, 1997), but by comparison, there is a staggering ten-fold increase in DA when amphetamines enter the body and more than a three-fold increase in DA when cocaine enters the body (Di Chiara & Imperato, 1988). It takes no stretch of the imagination to realize that these rapid influxes in DA are largely the reason certain drugs are addictive.

But are DA levels associated with antisocial behaviors other than drug use? Much of what is known about the effects of DA comes from nonhuman animal studies. Researchers, for example, have manipulated DA levels in rodents and observed the behavioral patterns in high-DA rodents versus low-DA rodents. In general, high-DA rodents are more likely to fight and to displays signs of physical aggression than are low-DA rodents or rodents with normal levels of DA (Eichelman, 1990; Niehoff, 1999). Of particular interest is that engaging in violence also brings about a surge in DA (Modigh, 1973). As a consequence, high DA levels may be a predisposing factor to violence, and the use of physical aggression may be reinforced by increases in DA.

The importance of the bidirectional effect between DA and violence should not be overlooked. One of the most consistent criminological findings is that antisocial behaviors are relatively stable over long periods of the life course (Loeber, 1982; Olweus, 1979). Although a number of explanations have been advanced, much remains unknown about the causes of behavioral stability, but it is quite possible that DA plays a role. Remember that the release of DA serves as a powerful reinforcement, and any actions that stimulate the production of DA (e.g., drug use and sexual intercourse) are likely to be repeated. Thus, if DA is released when an individual uses violence or aggression, then future criminal acts will likely be repeated because DA is discharged into the brain.

Unfortunately, studies using samples composed of humans have not investigated the ebb and flow of DA in response to serious violence. There is a limited body of research, however, examining the effects that antipsychotic drugs have on aggression. Antipsychotic drugs reduce DA and thus should also reduce violence. Studies have demonstrated that patients taking antipsychotic drugs are less involved in multiple forms of aggressive behaviors (Anderson, 2007; Brizer, 1988; Yudofsky, Silver, & Schneider, 1987). Other drugs that reduce DA have been shown to reduce aggressiveness in conduct-disordered children and in patients with Attention Deficit/Hyperactivity Disorder (Eichelman, 1990). On the other hand, researchers have not reported a consistent link between levels of DA metabolites and involvement in aggression (Raine, 1993). The effect of DA on violence, therefore, appears to be isolated to studies that have investigated whether antipsychotic drugs and other medications affect aggressive impulses. Given these contradictory findings, the verdict is still out on whether levels of DA correlate with antisocial behaviors.

Norepinephrine and Antisocial Behaviors

Norepinephrine (NE) is an excitatory neurotransmitter that is found throughout the sympathetic nervous system and is prevalent in the brain. The release of NE increases arousal and underlies the *fight or flight* response that often surfaces when stressful situations are encountered. Thus, NE may prime animals for resorting to aggression, especially in retaliation to life-threatening stimuli (Berman & Coccaro, 1998). But whether NE actually relates to violent behaviors in humans remains an open empirical question. Much of the early research exploring the effect of NE on aggression was conducted using rodents. This line of research provided some support in favor of the hypothesis that NE plays a facilitative role in aggression. Increased NE activity in the brains of rodents, for example, has been linked with shock-induced fighting (Eichelman & Barchas, 1975; Stolk, Connor, Levine, & Barchas, 1974). Higher NE has also been shown to correlate with aggression in primates (Higley et al., 1992; Kaplan, Manuck, Fontenot, & Mann, 2002), pointing to the possibility that NE may have effects on antisocial behaviors that extend to humans.

Clinical researchers have reported decreases in aggression among samples of human subjects who were administered NE-reducing drugs (Sorgi, Ratey, & Polakoff, 1986; Yudofsky, Williams, & Gorman, 1981), while NE-increasing drugs have been shown to promote aggression (Rampling, 1978), which is consistent with findings from animal studies. The findings garnered from these studies thus suggest that high levels of NE in humans would be linked to higher rates of violence. But the research results are far from unequivocal. In line with expectations, there is some evidence showing a positive association between the main NE metabolite, 3-methoxy-4-hydroxyphenylglycol (MHPG), and aggressive behaviors and impulsivity (Roy, Pickar, De Jong, & Karoum, 1989). Other studies have produced opposite findings showing that low levels of MHPG actually increase antisocial behaviors (Coccaro, Kavoussi, Hauger, Cooper, & Ferris, 1998;

Virkkunen et al., 1987) and still other studies have reported no association between NE and aggression (Linnoila et al., 1983).

So, how should these findings be interpreted? Should we conclude that NE increases antisocial behaviors, decreases antisocial behaviors, or has no effect on antisocial behaviors? Given the disparate findings it is difficult to say, but a meta-analysis conducted by Raine (1993) helps to clarify this question. This meta-analysis revealed that CSF NE was lower in alcoholic antisocials, in antisocials with borderline personality disorder, and in antisocials with depression. Conversely, urinary NE was higher in nonaggressive offenders, in antisocials with a history of alcohol abuse, and in antisocials with depression. Clearly, the way in which NE is measured—whether by CSF or by urine—determines whether the effect of NE is negative or positive. In light of these findings, much more research is needed to elucidate whether NE has an effect on antisocial behaviors and, if so, whether low or high levels of NE predispose to violence (Anderson, 2007). In all likelihood, though, the relationship between NE and aggression is complex and depends partially on where in the brain NE is expressed.

Gamma-Aminobutyric Acid and Antisocial Behaviors

Gamma-aminobutyric acid (GABA) is the major inhibitory neurotransmitter in the central nervous system. According to Collins (2004), "GABA regulates essentially every behavioral function of the brain, including the autonomic nervous system, sexual function, growth function, ingestive behaviors, motor functions, as well as the behavioral functions of anxiety, fear, and aggression" (p. 7). As a result of its inhibitory effect on behaviors and impulses, higher levels of GABA should reduce aggression, whereas a deficiency in GABA should instigate violence (Eichelman, 1990). Unfortunately, there is a scarcity of research testing this hypothesis.

The research that does exist, however, tends to come from nonhuman animal studies and from studies examining the effects that GABA-altering medications have on aggression. Findings from animal studies have indicated that rodents injected with GABA display a decrease in fighting and killing behaviors (Eichelman, 1990; Paredes & Agmo, 1992). Moreover, a group of drugs known as benzodiazepines enhance GABA activity. Experimental studies have revealed that when rodents are administered benzodiazepines, aggression is often reduced. Even here, though, benzodiazepines have been shown to actually increase aggression in some mice (Fox, Tuckosh, & Wilcox, 1970).

Research conducted with human subjects is not any more conclusive. For example, although there is some evidence to indicate that benzodiazepines reduce aggression in violent patients, there is also evidence to the contrary revealing that benzodiazepines facilitate aggression in some patients

(Eichelman, 1990; Miczek & Fish, 2006). The one study that directly measured GABA levels via blood samples reported an inverse relationship between GABA and aggressiveness (Bjork et al., 2001). Even so, the small number of studies investigating the connection between GABA and violence makes it difficult to draw any firm conclusions about whether or not GABA has effects on antisocial behaviors. At the same time, the overwhelming majority of research that has been conducted has not directly measured GABA levels, but instead has examined how GABA-altering drugs relate to aggression. To understand with any degree of certainty the role that GABA plays in the development of violence, more research is needed.

Monoamine Oxidase and Antisocial Behaviors

Unlike the other neurochemicals discussed thus far, monoamine oxidase (MAO) is not a neurotransmitter per se, but rather an enzyme that metabolizes neurotransmitters. In the brain, MAO is the major metabolic enzyme; it is primarily responsible for "mopping up" neurotransmitters from the synapse once they have transferred a signal to the postsynaptic neuron (i.e., the process of enzymatic degradation). Levels of serotonin, dopamine, norepinephrine, and other neurotransmitters are partly controlled by MAO activity. If something impedes the activity of MAO, then neurotransmitter levels may be altered accordingly. And, as was discussed previously, changes in concentrations of neurotransmitters may have some influence over the likelihood of engaging in aggression (Raine, 1993).

Low levels of MAO and low MAO activity are thought to be inversely related to a host of antisocial phenotypes. Some of the earliest studies testing this hypothesis directly assayed MAO levels and reported that individuals with the lowest levels of MAO were also, on average, the most at risk for becoming involved in crime, delinquency, and other forms of antisocial conduct. The inverse relationship between MAO and criminal behaviors was also upheld in a large review of the MAO literature. In this review, Ellis (1991) concluded that the extant literature showed that low MAO was tied to the development of criminality, impulsivity, hyperactivity, sensation seeking, drug and alcohol use, and psychopathy. In comparison with the influence of other biochemicals, MAO appears to have one of the strongest and most consistent effects on a range of different antisocial outcomes.

Variations in MAO levels are important contributors to criminal behaviors, and levels of MAO are determined, in large part, by genetic factors. What this means is that some genotypes produce MAO that is not efficient at eradicating neurotransmitters from the synapse, whereas other genotypes produce MAO that is highly proficient at metabolizing neurotransmitters. In extremely rare cases, a gene responsible for the production of MAO can even malfunction, resulting in the inability to manufacture MAO (see Case Study:

The MAO-A Gene). Geneticists have thus begun examining whether variants (i.e., alleles) of these MAO-producing genes are linked to aggressive and violent phenotypes. Results garnered from this pool of genetic research have revealed that alleles corresponding to low MAO activity confer a greater risk of developing various forms of psychopathology, including criminal and violent behaviors (Caspi et al., 2002; Kim-Cohen et al., 2006; Volavka, Bilder, & Nolan, 2004). Of all the candidate genes ever examined by geneticists and biosocial criminologists, the MAO-producing genes have had some of the most consistent effects (Kim-Cohen et al., 2006). Taken together, there is strong evidence indicating that MAO levels and MAO genes play a role in a range of different antisocial outcomes (Anderson, 2007).

RECAP 5.2   Neurotransmitters and Violence

Neurotransmitter	Function	Hypothesized Relationship With Violence
Serotonin (5-HT)	Inhibitory	Low brain levels = increased violence
Dopamine (DA)	Excitatory	High DA associated with violence
Norepinephrine (NE)	Excitatory	Presently unclear
GABA	Inhibitory	Presently unclear
Monoamine Oxidase (MOA)	Enzyme	Low levels = increased violence

Hormones

Hormones are a group of molecules that are responsible for carrying messages to cells throughout the body. Hormones are produced by cells in the endocrine system and by certain nerve cells, called *neurosecretory cells*. Once produced, hormones either can be released directly into the bloodstream or can be stored in glands (e.g., ovaries and testes), where they will eventually be discharged into the body. After entering the bloodstream, hormones make contact with each and every cell, but only a select category of cells, known as target cells, are affected by the hormone. All other cells (i.e., non-target cells) ignore the hormone and thus do not respond to it. Whether or not a cell is a target cell depends on the specific hormone released. One cell, for example, may be a target cell for the hormone testosterone but not a target cell for another type of hormone, such as insulin (Anderson, 2007).

Hormones are responsible for a host of duties in the human body. They regulate metabolism, they play a role in growth and development, and they are important to the immune system. Hormones, however, can have more visible effects as well. When hormonal levels are aberrant, or when certain hormones are released, mood swings can occur, personality can be altered, and behavioral patterns may change. Most relevant to this chapter is that different types of violent and aggressive phenotypes have also been linked to levels of certain hormones. Not all hormones have such salient effects, and whether hormones affect specific phenotypes, such as antisocial behaviors, depends in large part on what hormone is produced and the level of that hormone. Although there are more than 50 hormones found throughout the human body, our discussion will be restricted to how antisocial behaviors are influenced by two different hormones: testosterone and cortisol.

Testosterone and Antisocial Behaviors

One of the best-known criminological findings is that males, in comparison with females, are much more likely to engage in acts of serious physical violence. The common perception is that the social environment causes males to act violently and females to act passively. But if this explanation is true, then the male-female gap in aggression should be quite variable across cultures, and in some societies females should be more violent than males. This simply is not the case. Males have been found to be more physically violent than females in every culture studied, at every time period in history, and in every sample ever examined (Archer, 2004; Ellis, 1988), suggesting that biological factors are important in explaining the gender gap in criminality (Boyd, 2000; Ghiglieri, 1999). Of course, not all biological risk factors are able to account for gender differences in antisocial behaviors. Only those biological risk factors that are known to correlate with violence and that are known to be more prevalent in males have the potential to explain the gender disparity in aggression. One biochemical meeting these two requirements is testosterone (Mazur & Booth, 1998).

Testosterone is a steroid hormone produced by the testes and adrenal glands in males and by the ovaries and adrenal glands in females. The secretion of testosterone is responsible for an array of different bodily functions ranging from building muscle mass and producing sperm to making red blood cells and stimulating the release of neurotransmitters (Dabbs & Dabbs, 2000). The development of secondary-sex characteristics is also a function of testosterone. Although testosterone is found in both genders, postpubertal adolescent males have 8 to 10 times more testosterone than do females. Perhaps as a result, when most people think of testosterone, they think of maleness, aggression, and violence. After all, testosterone is *the* male hormone that causes males to act, well, like males, right? Well, it is not quite that straightforward, but there is a considerable amount of research examining the association between levels of testosterone and different forms of aggressive and dominant behaviors.[2]

As with neurotransmitters, it is the *level* of testosterone that is linked to violence and aggression. Thus, it is important to understand what causes variation in testosterone levels. Baseline testosterone is under substantial genetic control, with heritability estimates ranging somewhere between 50% and 70% (Booth, Granger, Mazur, & Kivlighan, 2006). Genes clearly play a major role in structuring and determining the amount of testosterone produced by the body. But testosterone levels also rise and fall in response to environmental conditions. Winners of chess matches and other competitions, for example, have been found to have a spike in their testosterone levels (Booth et al., 2006; Dabbs & Dabbs, 2000; Mazur, Booth, & Dabbs, 1992). In addition, testosterone levels decrease in men when they are married but increase around the time of a divorce (Mazur & Michalek, 1998). A host of other social stimuli have also been found to be associated with changing testosterone levels (Dabbs & Dabbs, 2000). Both genetic and environmental factors, in short, bring about variation in concentrations of testosterone.

High levels of testosterone are thought to be related to greater involvement in certain types of antisocial behaviors. There are a vast number of studies testing this hypothesis using different samples, different ways of measuring testosterone, and different measures of antisocial behaviors (Dabbs & Dabbs, 2000; Harris, 1999). Consequently, the effect that testosterone has on violent behaviors is variable. Some researchers have reported a weak effect of testosterone on antisocial outcomes (Gladue, 1991; Meyer-Bahlburg, Boon, Sharma, & Edwards, 1974) and some studies have failed to detect any association (Halpern, Udry, Campbell, & Suchindran, 1994). Still, there is evidence indicating that testosterone levels do have effects on a range of behavioral phenotypes, especially aggression (Harris, 1999). A recent meta-analysis indicated that there is a statistically significant relationship between testosterone and antisocial behaviors, but this association, as indexed by the mean weighted correlation ($r = .14$), is relatively small (Book, Starzyk, & Quinsey, 2001).

Some testosterone researchers, however, have pointed out that testosterone levels should be associated with dominance-related behaviors but not with nondominance-related behaviors (Mazur & Booth, 1998). The problem is that extant studies often confound these two very different types of behaviors and assume that testosterone has equal effects on both. The most accurate way to examine how testosterone relates to aggression would be to divide behaviors into two groups—dominance behaviors and nondominance behaviors—and investigate how testosterone levels affect each of them separately. So what is the difference between dominance and closely related nondominance behaviors, such as aggression? According to Mazur and Booth (1998),

An individual [is] said to act *aggressively* if its apparent intent is to inflict physical injury on a member of its species. An individual [is] said to act *dominantly* if its apparent intent is to achieve or maintain high status—that is, to obtain power, influence, or valued prerogatives—over a conspecific [i.e., a member of the same species]. (p. 353)

When this distinction is made, researchers have reported that testosterone has relatively strong and consistent effects on dominance-related behaviors, but not necessarily on other types of antisocial behaviors (Mazur & Booth, 1998). In a classic study, Ehrenkranz, Bliss, and Sheard (1974) examined testosterone levels in three groups of prisoners. The first group consisted of prisoners who were chronically aggressive, the second group consisted of prisoners who were dominant but not physically aggressive, and the third group consisted of prisoners who were not dominant and not aggressive. The results of their analysis revealed that testosterone levels were significantly lower in prisoners who were neither dominant nor aggressive when compared to prisoners in the other two categories. Additional studies have also found that testosterone levels correlate positively with measures of dominance.

The effect of testosterone on dominance is not a one-way relationship; there are reciprocal effects where testosterone levels actually change as a direct result of competitive events, including physically aggressive combat. For example, Mazur and Booth (1998), two of the foremost experts on the testosterone-dominance link, have noted that

there is strong correlational and experimental evidence that T [testosterone] responds in predictable ways both before and after competitions for status. First, T rises shortly before a competitive event, as if anticipating the challenge. Second, after the conclusion of competition, T in winners rises relative to that of losers. T also rises after status elevations, and it falls after status demotions . . . [H]igh or rising T, by encouraging dominant behavior, induces men to compete for high status. The experience of winning or successfully defending high rank boosts T, which in turn encourages more dominant behavior. The experience of losing depresses T, encouraging a switch from dominant to deferential treatment. (p. 362)

This is a particularly important observation, and one that has direct application to the study of crime over the life course. For example, dominant and aggressive men already have high levels of testosterone. After winning a dominance contest, these men's levels of testosterone increase even more, making it even more likely that they will resort to aggression again in the future. At the same time, decreases in testosterone in the losers of dominance contests could begin to explain why some men are repeatedly victimized; their lower levels of testosterone make it likely that they will not retaliate when victimized. That is to say, they will engage in acts of deference while being dominated (Mazur, 2005). Unfortunately, there is no evidence directly bearing on either of these two propositions, and for now all that the extant literature is able to reveal is that high levels of testosterone are associated with increased involvement in acts of dominance (Dabbs & Dabbs, 2000; Harris, 1999; Mazur, 2005; Mazur & Booth, 1998).

Cortisol and Antisocial Behaviors

Cortisol is a stress hormone that is secreted by the adrenal cortex in response to stressful stimuli. When cortisol is released into the bloodstream, it sets in motion a chain of physiological responses that prepare the body for fighting or for fleeing threatening situations. High cortisol levels correspond to elevated levels of fear, anxiety, and arousal in general, whereas low cortisol levels correspond to an absence of these physiological responses and indicate that the individual is underaroused. Underarousal also appears to be a predisposing factor to antisocial behaviors (Hare, 1993; Raine, 1993). Criminal offenders and serious violent predators, for example, are relatively fearless, are sensation seekers, are risk takers, have a low resting heart rate, and lack empathy—all of which are symptoms of underarousal (Ellis, 2005; Raine, 1996). What this means is that low levels of cortisol should increase the odds of engaging in antisocial behaviors (Raine, 1993).

In comparison with the testosterone literature, much less research has examined the association between cortisol and aggression. Of the studies that have been conducted, most have analyzed clinical samples, not representative samples, making it impossible to generalize the findings to the larger population. For example, Virkkunen (1985) found that cortisol levels were low in habitually violent prison inmates. Additional research has also reported low cortisol levels in aggressive children (Tennes & Kreye, 1985;

RECAP 5.3 Hormones and Violence

Hormone	Production Location	Hypothesized Relationship With Violence
Testosterone	Testes/Ovaries/Adrenals	Associated with dominance-related behaviors
Cortisol	Adrenal Cortex	Low levels = increased violence

Tennes, Kreye, Avitable, & Wells, 1986) and in conduct-disordered adolescents (McBurnett, Lahey, Rathouz, & Loeber, 2000; Pajer, Gardner, Rubin, Perel, & Neal, 2001). Although exceptions exist, the available evidence seems to support the cortisol-antisocial conduct link, especially in samples of adult respondents (Van Goozen, 2005).

Conclusion

This chapter reviewed the biochemical underpinnings to serious violent crime and revealed how five neurotransmitters and two hormones affect the propensity to engage in antisocial behaviors. As was discussed throughout this chapter, some of these biochemicals, under certain conditions, have effects on myriad criminal and delinquent behaviors. Even so, much remains unknown about the association between biochemicals and aggressive behaviors. One of the keys to advancing our understanding of the complex relationship between an individual's biochemistry and his or her involvement in antisocial behaviors is to unpack the ways in which biochemicals interact with the environment to produce violence and aggression.

Notes

1. Monoamine oxidase (MAO) is not actually a neurotransmitter, but rather an enzyme that breaks down neurotransmitters. However, given that MAO is closely interconnected with neurotransmitters, and given that MAO affects neurotransmitter levels, MAO will be presented in the section discussing neurotransmitters.

2. In utero, testosterone is largely responsible for masculinizing the brain, and aberrant levels of prenatal/perinatal testosterone have been linked with a number of different psychosocial outcomes. In consideration of space limitations, this chapter will only focus on testosterone levels in adolescents and young adults. For a cogent discussion of the link between prenatal/perinatal testosterone and later-life antisocial behaviors, see Ellis (2005).

Discussion Questions

1. What are neurotransmitters? How are they affected by environmental stimuli?

2. Describe the process of reuptake.

3. Choose two neurotransmitters and explain their association with violent behaviors.

4. What is the function of monoamine oxidase (MAO)?

5. Name two hormones and describe how they affect the propensity to engage in aggression.

Internet Resources

National Institute of Drug Abuse, "Drugs, Brains, and Behavior": http://www.drugabuse.gov/scienceofaddiction/

National Institute of Health, "How Neurotransmission Works": http://science-education.nih.gov/supplements/nih2/addiction/activities/lesson2_neurotransmission.htm

National Institute of Mental Health: http://www.nimh.nih.gov

References

Anderson, G. S. (2007). *Biological influences on criminal behavior*. Boca Raton, FL: CRC Press.

Archer, J. (2004). Sex differences in aggression in real-world settings: A meta-analytic review. *Review of General Psychology, 8,* 291–322.

Asberg, M., Traskman, L., & Thoren, P. (1976). 5-HIAA in the cerebrospinal fluid: A biochemical suicide predictor? *Archives of General Psychiatry, 33,* 1193–1197.

Berman, M. E., & Coccaro, E. F. (1998). Neurobiologic correlates of violence: Relevance to criminal responsibility. *Behavioral Sciences and the Law, 16,* 303–318.

Bjork, J. M., Moeller, F. G., Kramer, G. L., Kram, M., Suris, A., Rush, A. J., et al. (2001). Plasma GABA levels correlate with aggressiveness in relatives of patients with unipolar depressive disorder. *Psychiatry Research, 101,* 131–136.

Book, A. S., Starzyk, K. B., & Quinsey, V. L. (2001). The relationship between testosterone and aggression: A meta-analysis. *Aggression and Violent Behavior, 6,* 579–599.

Booth, A., Granger, D. A., Mazur, A., & Kivlighan, K. T. (2006). Testosterone and social behavior. *Social Forces, 85,* 167–191.

Boyd, N. (2000). *The beast within: Why men are violent.* Vancouver: Greystone Books.

Brizer, D. A. (1988). Psychopharmacology and the management of violent patients. *Psychiatric Clinics of North America, 11,* 551–568.

Brown, G. L., Ebert, M. H., Goyer, P. F., Jimerson, D. C., Klein, W. J., Bunney, W. E., et al. (1982). Aggression, suicide, and serotonin: Relationships to CSF amine metabolites. *American Journal of Psychiatry, 139,* 741–746.

Brown, G. L., Goodwin, F. K., Ballenger, J. C., Goyer, P. F., & Major, L. F. (1979). Aggression in humans correlates with cerebrospinal fluid amine metabolites. *Psychiatry Research, 1,* 131–139.

Brunner, H. G., Nelen, M., Breakefield, X. O., Ropers, H. H., & van Oost, B. A. (1993). Abnormal behavior associated with a point mutation in the structural gene for monoamine oxidase A. *Science, 262,* 578–580.

Brunner, H. G., Nelen, M. R., van Zandvoort, P., Abeling, N. G. G. M., van Gennip, A. H., Wolters, E. C., et al. (1993). X-linked borderline mental retardation with prominent behavioral disturbance: Phenotype, genetic localization, and evidence for disturbed monoamine metabolism. *American Journal of Human Genetics, 52,* 1032–1039.

Caspi, A., McClay, J., Moffitt, T. E., Mill, J., Martin, J., Craig, I. W., et al. (2002). Role of genotype in the cycle of violence in maltreated children. *Science, 297,* 851–854.

Clark, W. R., & Grunstein, M. (2000). *Are we hardwired? The role of genes in human behavior.* New York: Oxford University Press.

Coccaro, E. F., Kavoussi, R. J., Hauger, R. L., Cooper, T. B., & Ferris, C. F. (1998). Cerebrospinal fluid vasopressin levels correlate with aggression and serotonin function in personality disordered subjects. *Archives of General Psychiatry, 55,* 708–714.

Collins, R. E. (2004). Onset and desistance in criminal careers: Neurobiology and the age-crime relationship. *Journal of Offender Rehabilitation, 39,* 1–19.

Constantino, J. N., Morris, J. A., & Murphy, D. L. (1997). CSF 5-HIAA and family history of antisocial personality disorder in newborns. *American Journal of Psychiatry, 154,* 1771–1773.

Dabbs, J. M., & Dabbs, M. G. (2000). *Heroes, rogues, and lovers: Testosterone and behavior.* New York: McGraw-Hill.

Dabbs, J. M., & Morris, R. (1990). Testosterone, social class, and antisocial behavior in a sample of 4,462 men. *Psychological Science, 1,* 209–211.

Di Chiara, G., & Imperato, A. (1988). Drugs abused by humans preferentially increase synaptic dopamine concentrations in the mesolimbic system of freely moving rats. *Proceedings of the National Academy of Sciences, 85,* 5274–5278.

Ehrenkranz, J., Bliss, E., & Sheard, M. (1974). Plasma testosterone: Correlation with aggressive behavior and social dominance in men. *Psychosomatic Medicine, 36,* 469–475.

Eichelman, B. S. (1990). Neurochemical and psychopharmacologic aspects of aggressive behavior. *Annual Review of Medicine, 41,* 149–158.

Eichelman, B., & Barchas, J. D. (1975). Facilitated shock-induced aggression following antidepressant medication in the rat. *Pharmacology, Biochemistry, and Behavior, 3,* 601–604.

Ellis, L. (1988). The victimful-victimless crime distinction and seven universal demographic correlates of victimful criminal behavior. *Personality and Individual Differences, 9,* 525–548.

Ellis, L. (1991). Monoamine oxidase and criminality: Identifying an apparent biological marker for antisocial behavior. *Journal of Research in Crime and Delinquency, 28,* 227–251.

Ellis, L. (2005). A theory explaining biological correlates of criminality. *European Journal of Criminology, 2,* 287–315.

Fiorino, D. F., Coury, A., & Phillips, A. G. (1997). Dynamic changes in nucleus accumbens dopamine efflux during the Coolidge effect in male rats. *The Journal of Neuroscience, 17,* 4849–4855.

Fox, K. A., Tuckosh, J. R., & Wilcox, A. A. (1970). Increased aggression among grouped male mice fed chlordiazepoxide. *European Journal of Pharmacology, 11,* 119–121.

Gardner, D. L., Lucas, P. B, & Cowdry, R. W. (1990). CSF metabolites in borderline personality disorder compared with normal controls. *Biological Psychiatry, 28,* 247–254.

Ghiglieri, M. P. (1999). *The dark side of man: Tracing the origins of male violence.* Reading, MA: Perseus.

Gladue, B. A. (1991). Aggressive behavioral characteristics, hormones, and sexual orientation in men and women. *Aggressive Behavior, 17,* 313–326.

Granger, D. A., Shwartz, E. B., Booth, A., & Arentz, M. (1999). Salivary testosterone determination in studies of child health and development. *Hormones and Behavior, 35,* 18–27.

Greenberg, A. S., & Coleman, M. (1976). Depressed 5-hydroxyindole levels associated with hyperactive and aggressive behavior. *Archives of General Psychiatry, 46,* 237–241.

Halperin, J. M., Newcorn, J. H., Kopstein, I., McKay, K. E., Schwartz, S. T., Siever, L. J., et al. (1997). Serotonin, aggression, and parental psychopathology in children with attention-deficit hyperactivity disorder. *Journal of the American Academy of Child and Adolescent Psychiatry, 36,* 1391–1398.

Halpern, C. T., Udry, R., Campbell, B., & Suchindran, C. (1994). Relationships between aggression and pubertal increases in testosterone: A panel analysis of adolescent males. *Social Biology, 40,* 8–24.

Hamer, D., & Copeland, P. (1998). *Living with our genes: Why they matter more than you think.* New York: Doubleday.

Hare, R. D. (1993). *Without conscience: The disturbing world of psychopaths among us.* New York: The Guilford Press.

Harris, J. A. (1999). Review and methodological considerations in research on testosterone and aggression. *Aggression and Violent Behavior, 4,* 273–291.

Higley, J. D., Mehlman, P. T., Taub, D. M., Higley, S. B., Suomi, S. J., Linnoila, M., et al. (1992). Cerebrospinal fluid monoamine and adrenal correlates of aggression in free-ranging rhesus monkeys. *Archives of General Psychiatry, 49,* 436–441.

Kaplan, J. R., Manuck, S. B., Fontenot, M. B., & Mann, J. J. (2002). Central nervous system monoamine correlates of social dominance in cynomolgus monkeys (*Macaca fascicularis*). *Neuropsychopharmacology, 26,* 431–443.

Kim-Cohen, J., Caspi, A., Taylor, A., Williams, B., Newcombe, R., Craig, I. W., et al. (2006). MAOA, maltreatment, and gene-environment interaction predicting children's mental health: New evidence and a meta-analysis. *Molecular Psychiatry, 11,* 903–913.

Kruesi, M. J., Rapoport, J. L., Hamburger, S., Hibbs, E., & Potter, W. Z. (1990). Cerebrospinal fluid monoamine metabolites, aggression and impulsivity in disruptive behavior disorders of children and adolescents. *Archives of General Psychiatry, 47,* 419–426.

Lidberg, L., Tuck, J. R., Asberg, M., Scalia-Tomba, G. P., & Bertilsson, L. (1985). Homicide, suicide, and CSF 5-HIAA. *Acta Psychiatrica Scandinavica, 71,* 230–236.

Limson, R., Goldman, D., Roy, A., Lamparski, D., Ravitz, B., Adinoff, B., et al. (1991). Personality and cerebrospinal fluid monoamine metabolites in alcoholics and controls. *Archives of General Psychiatry, 48,* 437–441.

Linnoila, M., Virkkunen, M., Schwannian, M., Nuutila, A., Rimon, R., & Goodwin, F. K. (1983). Low cerebrospinal fluid 5-hydroxyindoleacetic acid concentration differentiates impulsive from non-impulsive violent behavior. *Life Sciences, 33,* 2609–2614.

Loeber, R. (1982). The stability of antisocial and delinquent child behavior: A review. *Child Development, 53,* 1431–1446.

Mann, J. J., McBride, P. A., Anderson, G. M., & Mieczkowski, T. A. (1992). Platelet and whole blood serotonin content in depressed inpatients: Correlations with acute and life-time psychopathology. *Biological Psychiatry, 32,* 243–257.

Manuck, S. B., Kaplan, J. R., & Lotrich, F. E. (2006). Brain serotonin and aggressive disposition in humans and nonhuman primates. In R. J. Nelson (Ed.), *Biology of Aggression* (pp. 65–113). New York: Oxford University Press.

Maughan, B. (2005). Developmental trajectory modeling: A view from developmental psychopathology. *The Annals of the American Academy of Political and Social Science, 602,* 118–1130.

Mazur, A. (2005). *Biosociology of dominance and deference.* Lanham, MD: Rowman and Littlefield.

Mazur, A., & Booth, A. (1998). Testosterone and dominance in men. *Behavioral and Brain Sciences, 21,* 353–397.

Mazur, A., Booth, A., & Dabbs, J. (1992). Testosterone and chess competition. *Social Psychology Quarterly, 55,* 70–77.

Mazur, A., & Michalek, J. (1998). Marriage, divorce, and male testosterone. *Social Forces, 77,* 315–330.

McBurnett, K., Lahey, B. B., Rathouz, P. J., & Loeber, R. (2000). Low salivary cortisol and persistent aggression in boys referred for disruptive behavior. *Archives of General Psychiatry, 57,* 38–43.

Mejia, J. M., Ervin, F. R., Palmour, R. M., & Tremblay, R. E. (2001). Aggressive behavior and Brunner syndrome: No evidence for the C936T mutation in a population sample. *American Journal of Medical Genetics B: Neuropsychiatric Genetics, 105,* 396–397.

Meyer-Bahlburg, H. F. L., Boon, D. A., Sharma, M., & Edwards, J. A. (1974). Aggressiveness and testosterone measures in man. *Psychosomatic Medicine, 36,* 269–274.

Miczek, K. A., & Fish, E. W. (2006). Monoamines, GABA, glutamate, and aggression. In R. J. Nelson (Ed.), *Biology of aggression* (pp. 114–149). New York: Oxford University Press.

Modigh, K. (1973). Effects of isolation and fighting in mice on the rate of synthesis of noradrenaline, dopamine, and 5-hydroxytryptamine in the brain. *Psychopharmacology, 33,* 1–17.

Moffitt, T. E. (1993). Adolescence-limited and life-course-persistent antisocial behavior: A developmental taxonomy. *Psychological Review, 100,* 674–701.

Moffitt, T. E., Brammer, G. L., Caspi, A., Fawcett, J. P., Raleigh, M., Yuwiler, A., et al. (1998). Whole blood serotonin relates to violence in an epidemiological study. *Biological Psychiatry, 43,* 446–457.

Moore, T. M., Scarpa, A., & Raine, A. (2002). A meta-analysis of serotonin metabolite 5-HIAA and antisocial behavior. *Aggressive Behavior, 28,* 299–316.

Murphy, D. L., Sims, K., Eisenhofer, G., Greenberg, B. D., George, T., Berlin, F., et al. (1998). Are MAO-A deficiency states in the general population and in putative high-risk populations highly uncommon? *Journal of Neural Transmission, 52*(Supp.), 29–38.

Niehoff, D. (1999). *The biology of violence: How understanding the brain, behavior, and environment can break the vicious circle of aggression.* New York: The Free Press.

Olweus, D. (1979). Stability of aggressive reaction patterns in males: A review. *Psychological Bulletin, 86,* 852–875.

Pajer, K., Gardner, W., Rubin, R. T., Perel, J., & Neal, S. (2001). Decreased cortisol levels in adolescent girls with conduct disorder. *Archives of General Psychiatry, 58,* 297–302.

Paredes, R. G., & Agmo, A. (1992). GABA and behavior: The role of receptor subtypes. *Neuroscience and Biobehavioral Reviews, 16,* 145–170.

Pliszka, S. R., Rogeness, G. A., Renner, P., Sherman, J., & Broussard, T. (1988). Plasma neurochemistry in juvenile offenders. *Journal of the American Academy of Child and Adolescent Psychiatry, 27,* 588–594.

Raine, A. (1993). *The psychopathology of crime: Criminal behavior as a clinical disorder.* San Diego, CA: Academic Press.

Raine, A. (1996). Autonomic nervous system activity and violence. In D. M. Stoff & R. B. Cairns (Eds.), *Aggression and violence: Genetic, neurobiological, and biosocial perspectives* (pp. 145–168.). Mahwah, NJ: Erlbaum.

Raine, A. (2002). Biosocial studies of antisocial and violent behavior in children and adults: A review. *Journal of Abnormal Child Psychology, 30,* 311–326.

Rampling, D. (1978). Aggression: A paradoxical response to tricyclic antidepressants. *American Journal of Psychiatry, 135,* 117–118.

Rowe, D. C. (2002). *Biology and crime.* Los Angeles: Roxbury.

Roy, A., Pickar, D., De Jong, J., & Karoum, F. (1989). Suicidal behavior in depression: Relationship to noradrenergic function. *Biological Psychiatry, 25,* 341–350.

Schuback, D. E., Mulligan, E. L., Sims, K. B., Tivol, E. A., Greenberg, B. D., Chang, S. F., et al. (1999). Screen for MAO-A mutations in target human groups. *American Journal of Medical Genetics B: Neuropsychiatric Genetics, 88,* 25–28.

Simeon, D., Stanley, B., Frances, A., Mann, J. J., Winchel, R., & Stanley, M. (1992). Self-mutilation in personality disorders: Psychological and biological correlates. *American Journal of Psychiatry, 149,* 221–226.

Sorgi, P. J., Ratey, J. J., & Polakoff, S. (1986). Beta-adrenergic blockers for the control of aggressive behaviors in patients with chronic schizophrenia. *American Journal of Psychiatry, 143,* 775–776.

Stoff, D. M., Ieni, J., Friedman, E., Bridger, W. H., Pollock, L., & Vitiello, B. (1991). Platelet 3H-imipramine binding, serotonin uptake, and plasma alpha 1 acid glycoprotein in disruptive behavior disorders. *Biological Psychiatry, 29,* 494–498.

Stolk, J. M., Connor, R. L., Levine, S., & Barchas, J. D. (1974). Brain norepinephrine metabolism and shock induced fighting behavior in rats: Differential effects of shock and fighting on the neurochemical response to a common footshock stimulus. *Journal of Pharmacology and Experimental Therapeutics, 190,* 193–209.

Tennes, K., & Kreye, M. (1985). Children's adrenocortical responses to classroom activities and tests in elementary school. *Psychosomatic Medicine, 47,* 451–460.

Tennes, K., Kreye, M., Avitable, N., & Wells, R. (1986). Behavioral correlates of excreted catecholamines and cortisol in second-grade children. *Journal of the American Academy of Child and Adolescent Psychiatry, 25,* 764–770.

Twitchell, G. R., Hanna, G. L., Cook, E. H., Fitzgerald, H. E., Little, K. Y., & Zucker, R. A. (1998). Overt behavior problems and serotonergic function in middle childhood among male and female offspring of alcoholic fathers. *Alcoholism, Clinical and Experimental Research, 22,* 1340–1348.

Unis, A. S., Cook, E. H., Vincent, J. G., Gjerde, D. K., Perry, B. D., Mason, C., et al. (1997).

Platelet serotonin measures in adolescents with conduct disorder. *Biological Psychiatry, 42,* 553–559.

Van Goozen, S. H. M. (2005). Hormones and the developmental origins of aggression. In R. E. Tremblay, W. W. Hartup, & J. Archer (Eds.), *Developmental origins of aggression* (pp. 281–306). New York: Guilford Press.

Virkkunen, M. (1985). Urinary free cortisol secretion in habitually violent offenders. *Acta Psychiatrica Scandinavica, 72,* 40–44.

Virkkunen, M., Nuutila, A., Goodwin, F. K., & Linnoila, M. (1987). Cerebrospinal fluid monoamine metabolite levels in male arsonists. *Archives of General Psychiatry, 44,* 241–247.

Virkkunen, M., Rawlings, R., Tokola, R., Poland, R. E., Guidotti, A., Nemeroff, C., et al. (1994). CSF biochemistries, glucose metabolism, and diurnal activity rhythms in alcoholic, violent offenders, fire setters, and healthy volunteers. *Archives of General Psychiatry, 51,* 20–27.

Volavka, J., Bilder, R., & Nolan, K. (2004). Catecholamines and aggression: The role of COMT and MAO polymorphisms. *Annals of the New York Academy of Sciences, 1036,* 393–398.

Volkow, N. D., Fowler, J. S., & Wang, G-J. (2003). Positron emission tomography and single-photon emission computed tomography in substance abuse research. *Seminars in Nuclear Medicine, 33,* 114–128.

Walsh, A. (2002). *Biosocial criminology: Introduction and integration.* Cincinnati, OH: Anderson.

Yudofsky, S. C., Silver, J. M., & Schneider, S. E. (1987). Pharmacologic treatment of aggression. *Psychiatric Annals, 17,* 397–407.

Yudofsky, S., Williams, D., & Gorman, J. (1981). Propranolol in the treatment of rage and violent behavior in patients with chronic brain syndromes. *American Journal of Psychiatry, 138,* 218–220.

CHAPTER 6

Brain Injuries and Violent Crime

José León-Carrión and Francisco Javier Chacartegui-Ramos

The neurobiological basis for violence in humans is beginning to be understood, yet violent behavior (to self or others) is multicomponential, with at least three components working together: neurobiological, developmental, and sociobehavioral. An overview of neuroimaging and psychophysiological and psychosocial findings provides support for this notion.

Cerebral Dysfunction and Violent Behavior

Traumatic Brain Injury

The hypothesis that cerebral dysfunction or dysregulation is behind violent conduct has been reported by different authors (Gorenstein & Newman, 1980). Recently, León-Carrión and Chacartegui (2003) examined a group of extremely violent convicted prisoners, noting that criminal behavior and violence may also be a consequence of traumatic brain injuries (TBI) acquired during childhood and youth as a result of gang fights, domestic violence, small blows to the head while driving, falls, and so forth. In the United States, approximately half a million children aged 0 to 14 are hospitalized each year due to TBI. In Europe, recent data from reunified Germany shows the yearly incidence of head injuries to be 337 per 100,000, with serious head injury at 33.5 per 100,000. Fortunately, the majority of hospitalized patients suffer minor head injury (Steudel, Cortbus, & Schwerdtfeger, 2005). We should also note that acts of violence, abuse, or neglect are also experienced by people with TBI (Reichard, Langlois, Sample, Wald, & Pickelsimer, 2007).

Other studies have found brain injury in the inmate population in a county jail. The findings of Slaughter, Fann, and Ehde (2003) showed that 87% of the inmates had suffered some kind of TBI during their lives and that 36.2% had suffered the injury in the year prior to their imprisonment. Interestingly, this latter group showed greater aggressiveness and irritability, yielded the worst cognitive test scores, and had more psychiatric disorders than those who had not sustained brain injuries the previous year.

Similarly, Schofield, Butler, Hollis, Smith, Lee, and Kelso (2006) explored the relationship between TBI and demographic, neuropsychiatric, and criminal aspects of individuals who had recently been incarcerated. Among the 200 prisoners studied, 82% had suffered TBI that same year. TBI was associated with sports-related accidents, expulsion from school, drug abuse, depression, and psychosis. The authors concluded that it was commonplace to find that prisoners had previously suffered some kind of brain injury and, moreover, that those with TBI had a high number of mental disorders.

Individuals with TBI normally develop cognitive, emotional, behavioral, and social disorders that place them at increased risk of committing violence. Aggressiveness and lack of inhibition frequently lead to misconduct by these individuals. Any psychosocial event can trigger this type of behavior. Individuals with TBI may be more easily provoked to aggression by ambiguous stimuli than individuals without TBI. The cognitive disorders of these patients limit their behavioral responses, which limits their ability to maintain appropriate social behavior. Due to cognitive restrictions caused by organic damage to the brain, many of these patients opt for, or are unable to control, aggressive responses to obtain what they want. Neurobiologically, it is easier to give an aggressive and uncontrolled motor response than it is to respond with more elaborate behavior.

Some authors have reported that patients with brain injury who show aggressive behavior are those with deep depression, frontal lesions, poor premorbid (i.e., pre-injury) social functioning, drug abuse problems, and lack of social support (Tateno, Jorge, & Robinson, 2003).

In recent decades, studies have examined the relationship between violence, crime, and brain injury. A study by León-Carrión and Chacartegui (2003) compared violent and nonviolent convicted prisoners' education and history of head injury. The authors found that while both groups had a history of academic difficulties, only the violent group had a history of untreated head injuries. Problems at school alone do not predict violent behavior. According to these authors, a history of discrete neurological damage as a consequence of blows received to the head must also be present. Their results suggest that treatment of the cognitive, behavioral, and emotional consequences of brain injury could be a means to prevent crime.

Similar findings were obtained by Martell (1992) in a descriptive study of 50 randomly selected male patients from a maximum-security state hospital for offenders with mental disorders. He found that at least one indicator of potential damage to the brain was present in 84% of the subjects, including diagnosis of any organic brain disorder, a history of severe head injury with loss of consciousness, a history of seizure activity, evidence of cognitive impairment, abnormal neurological findings, and other relevant neurodiagnostic or historical findings. According to their data, subjects with a diagnosis or history suggesting brain dysfunction were significantly more likely to have been indicted for violent crimes. In another study, Timonen et al. (2002) examined whether suffering a TBI during childhood or adolescence leads to criminal offences in adulthood. They analyzed a general population birth cohort of 10,934 people in Northern Finland, following them prospectively to the age of 31. They found that suffering TBI during childhood or adolescence was significantly related to later mental disorder, with coexisting criminality in male members of cohort.

Organic Brain Syndrome

Other authors have found similar evidence of brain damage in violent criminals. Tardiff and Sweillam (1980) analyzed the records of 9,365 patients admitted to public hospitals in 1974 and found higher rates of assault behavior among patients with a diagnosis of organic brain syndrome (i.e., impaired mental function resulting from a physical, rather than psychiatric, disorder). A network of abnormal cortical and subcortical brain processes that may predispose to violence was found in murderers by Raine, Buchsbaum, and LaCasse (1997). In a psychiatric consultation service, Travin, Lee, and Bluestone (1990) found that half the violent patients were diagnosed with organic brain syndrome. Amen, Stubblefield, Carmichael, and Thisted (1996) used brain Single Photon Emission Computer Tomography (SPECT) to map and evaluate the brains of 40 adolescents and adults who had attacked another person or destroyed property. These data were compared to those of a control group of psychiatric patients who had never been reported to exhibit aggressive behavior. The authors found that the violent individuals showed significant differences from the control group in several areas of the brain. Martell (1992) and Convit, Isay, Otis, and Volavka (1990) found higher rates of organic brain syndrome among indicted criminals and violent recidivists. Volkow et al. (1995) also found that psychiatric patients with a history of repetitive violent behavior showed widespread areas of low brain metabolism. A group of 166 sexual murderers, some with notable signs of brain abnormalities ($N = 50$) and others without ($N = 116$), was studied by Briken, Habermann, Berner, and Hill (2005). They found that sexual murderers with brain abnormalities suffered more from early behavior problems, were less likely to have cohabited with the victim at the time of the homicide, and had more young child victims. Also, transvestic fetishism and paraphilias were more frequent in offenders with brain abnormalities.[1]

CASE STUDY: KORSAKOFF'S SYNDROME

Philip, age 45, worked as an electrical engineer until he was arrested for stalking and physically assaulting his ex-wife. With regard to his early development, Philip's childhood and early adulthood were fairly normal. He achieved well in school and had no problems with aggression or delinquency. He graduated from college at age 21 and remained gainfully employed until his arrest and subsequent incarceration. He married his wife at age 34, and they had no children.

Philip's problems began due to a long-standing alcohol dependency. He began drinking heavily, particularly during social events, while in college, and this pattern of drinking continued past graduation. Although most of his drinking was "social," he found many excuses for social drinking, and every day he consumed enough alcohol to become intoxicated, usually after work. He was unaware of any decline in functioning during this period.

When he was 43, his marriage began to disintegrate, in part due to his drinking problems. He frequently argued with his wife over trivial matters, and he often flew into rages, punched the walls, and damaged furniture. He also began to exhibit paranoid behavior, accusing his wife of infidelity despite no evidence to support such concerns. Ultimately, during one heated argument, he punched his wife in the face. She immediately left him and filed for divorce.

Philip remained obsessed with his wife during the divorce process and after. He remained paranoid that she was "cheating" on him, and following their divorce she did establish a long-term relationship with another man. Philip became increasingly depressed, suicidal, and obsessed with reestablishing the relationship with his ex-wife. He began to follow her, particularly at night, and steal her mail. He admitted to hiding in the bushes near her new house, sometimes peering through her windows in an attempt to catch her in sexual relations with her new boyfriend. Ultimately, Philip forced himself through his ex-wife's door one evening and threatened to strangle her to death. This action appears to have been impulsive rather than planned, provoked by the belief that she was talking to her new boyfriend on the phone. He hit his wife several times, breaking her left arm, but she succeeded in barricading herself in a bathroom and called the police. Philip was arrested on the scene and immediately confessed to stalking and assaulting his wife.

Philip's lawyer noticed that Philip appeared to have significant problems with memory. Specifically, Philip introduced himself to his lawyer several times, each time forgetting that they had already met. Once, this occurred after a one-hour gap between two lengthy meetings. Philip's lawyer requested a competency evaluation. Neuroimaging revealed significant atrophy to the frontal lobes, cerebellum, and hippocampus as well as other areas. Neuropsychological testing revealed considerable impairments to memory, psychomotor control, and executive functioning. Philip was ultimately diagnosed with Korsakoff's Syndrome, a form of brain damage typically brought on by long-term alcohol abuse. Philip was found to be not competent to proceed to trial and was forensically committed to a state mental health hospital pending potential return to competency. Given the permanent damage to his brain due to alcohol consumption, it is unlikely that Philip will be allowed to leave the forensic hospital at any point during the remainder of his life.

Another interesting study, carried out by Grekin, Brennan, Hodgins, and Mednick (2001), examined the crime and hospital records of 565 male criminals diagnosed with organic brain syndrome and 565 male criminals without this diagnosis. All subjects were drawn from a total birth cohort of male individuals born between 1944 and 1947 in Denmark. They found that organic brain syndrome offenders could be divided into two distinct groups, based on age at first arrest: early starters, who were arrested for a criminal offence by age 18, and late starters, who were arrested at age 19 or older. Early starters were more likely to be arrested before the onset of organic brain syndrome and accumulated more arrests per year before onset; they were also more likely to be criminal and/or violent recidivists, to develop antisocial personality disorder, and to have drug abuse problems. According to these findings, early starters with organic brain syndrome committed a far higher number of crimes than early starters without this disorder. The authors concluded that early starters who engage in reckless behavior are more likely to show organic brain syndrome than those who do not.

The Role of the Prefrontal Cortex and Executive Functions

Functional and structural neuroimaging techniques have contributed considerably to knowledge about the cerebral basis for violent conduct. Structural neuroimaging techniques played a key role in obtaining information on damaged structures in violent and condemned individuals, as well as in inmates charged with murder or other violent crimes. Functional neuroimaging techniques have had special relevance in locating the cerebral zones and circuits involved in carrying out violent crimes in individuals without any clinical symptomatology. In a general sense, neuroimaging studies indicate that impulsive violent or aggressive behavior is caused by deteriorated or limited prefrontal functioning, whereas premeditated violent or aggressive behavior does not appear to be linked to prefrontal deterioration.

The majority of neuroimaging studies regarding criminal activity are on the prefrontal zones of the brain. It is generally accepted that the prefrontal cortex is responsible for executive functioning in the human brain (see Figure 6.1). *Executive functions* are those that coherently organize human behavior and make it possible for humans to give a socially appropriate

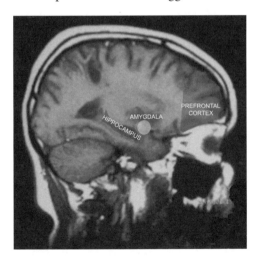

Figure 6.1   Most Relevant Brain Structures Associated With Criminal Violent Antisocial Behavior

response in accordance with time and place and to understand the likely consequences of their actions. Executive function tasks include planning, organization, selective attention, inhibitory control, problem solving, decision making, and prospective thinking, among others (León-Carrión & Barroso y Martín, 1997; León-Carrión, Damas-López, Martín-Rodriguez et al., 2008; León-Carrión, Martín-Rodriguez, Damas-López et al., 2007a; Lezak, 1995; Stuss & Benson, 1986). Disorganized behavior or inadequate social responses are often due to poor prefrontal organization or to an injury in this cerebral zone.

Although violent sex offenders and violent non-sex offenders are not a homogeneous group, due to different background characteristics and criminal profiles (van Wijk, Mali, Bullens, & Vermeiren, 2007), executive and frontal disorders have been commonly found in a particular type of violent subject: the sexual delinquent (Graber, Hartmann, Coffman, Huey, & Golden, 1982; Kelly, Richardson, Hunter, & Knapp, 2002; Veneziano, Veneziano, LeGrand, & Richards, 2004). In a review of the literature, Joyal, Black, and Dassylva (2007) found a profile of verbal deficits and lower-order executive dysfunctions among sexual offenders (e.g., dysfunctions associated with sustained attention and inhibition), with intact or good capacities for higher-order executive functioning (e.g., reasoning and cognitive flexibility; see León-Carrión & Chacartegui, 2005). They also observed visuospatial processing that suggested basal frontotemporal anomalies in pedophiles that were more consistently and severely impaired than in rapists of adults. The authors indicated that this basal frontotemporal profile is also associated with delinquency and criminality in general.

Langevin (2006) reported that in a sample of 476 male sexual offenders who underwent forensic assessment, 49.3% had sustained head injuries that left them unconscious, and, of these, 22.5% sustained significant neurological insults. A major cause was motor vehicle accidents, but lifestyle variables including alcohol and drug abuse and history of violence also contributed. Graber et al. (1982) found that 50% of the sexual offenders they tested showed brain dysfunction, as demonstrated by decreased density measures, decreased blood flow, and poor performance in neuropsychological assessments. According to Briken et al. (2005), sexual murderers with brain abnormalities suffered more from early behavior problems. In addition, these murderers were less likely to have cohabited with the victim at the time of the homicide and had more victims aged 6 or younger. They also found more paraphilias, such as transvestic fetishism and paraphilias not otherwise specified, among these offenders. Similarly, people with paraphilias and paraphilia-related disorders (PRD) were found by Briken, Habermann, Kafka, Berner, and Hill (2006) to have the most cumulative sexual impulsivity disorders in their lifetime as well as more developmental problems, the highest frequency of sexual activity and previous sexual offences, more sexual sadism, and a higher incidence of compulsive masturbation. They also found that men with PRD had suffered more from childhood sexual abuse and showed more promiscuity, psychopathic behavior, and alcohol problems.

The hypothesis that emotionally violent offenders have lower prefrontal activity, higher subcortical activity, and reduced prefrontal/subcortical ratios, while predatory violent offenders show relatively normal brain functioning, was tested by Raine, Meloy, Bihrle, Stoddard, LaCasse, and Buchsbaum (1998). They found that emotional murderers had lower left and right prefrontal functioning, higher right hemisphere subcortical functioning, and lower right hemisphere prefrontal/subcortical ratios, whereas predatory murderers had regular prefrontal functioning and excessively high right subcortical activity. Their results suggest that emotional, impulsive murderers have problems regulating and controlling aggressive impulses generated from subcortical structures, due to deficient prefrontal regulation. Put another way, emotional murderers lack the executive functioning necessary to contain aggressive impulses. Raine et al. concluded that while it has been hypothesized that excessive subcortical activity predisposes to aggressive behavior, predatory murderers have sufficiently good prefrontal functioning to regulate these aggressive impulses, whereas emotional murderers lack such prefrontal control over emotion regulation.

Raine, Lencz, Bihrle, LaCasse, and Colletti (2000) studied whether people with antisocial personality disorder (APD) who do not have discernable brain trauma also have subtle prefrontal deficits. They found that an APD group showed an 11.0% reduction in prefrontal gray matter volume in the absence of ostensible brain lesions and reduced autonomic activity during a stress task. These frontal-lobe deficits predicted group membership (APD or not), independent of psychosocial risk factors. According to these authors, this prefrontal structural deficit may underlie the low arousal, poor fear conditioning, lack of conscience, and decision-making deficits that have been found to characterize antisocial, psychopathic behavior. Among the principal difficulties encountered by individuals with prefrontal lesions are self-control and inhibiting inappropriate social behavior. In a brain imaging study on a group of criminal violent men, Bergvall, Wessely, Forsman, and Hansen (2001) examined aspects of prefrontally guided executive functions. They found that violent offenders have a double impairment in inhibitory cognitive control: They have problems shifting attention from one category to another, and their capacity to change behavior in response to fluctuations in the emotional significance of stimuli is compromised.

The three main divisions of the prefrontal cortex pertinent to our topic are the *orbitofrontal*, the *ventromedial*, and the *dorsolateral*. The internal organization of these divisions and the networks they belong to mark the differences between individuals. Although we are all born with a prefrontal cortex, its level of organization is not the same for everyone. Just as certain individuals are blond while others are brunette, or some are shorter than others, not everyone has the same level of organizational development of the prefrontal cortex.

The Orbitofrontal Cortex

Poor organization in, or lesions to, the orbitofrontal cortex will lead an individual to abnormally impulsive behavior and a lack of any control or inhibition. These individuals tend to do whatever they wish at any given moment, without considering whether it is appropriate, permitted, the correct moment, or socially acceptable. Their capacity for inhibiting socially unacceptable behavior is limited by the level of the prefrontal injury suffered or by their level of prefrontal functional organization. An injury to the orbitofrontal cortex, together with high right subcortical activity, are what most easily lead an individual to commit violent or criminal acts. Evidently, carrying out these criminal and violent acts will depend, in great part, on the integrity and physical capacity of the aggressor, along with the rest of the individual's cognitive capacities. For example, many patients with TBI suffer multiple injuries to their entire body, leaving them incapacitated to carry out specific physical activities. Obviously, TBI patients with these limitations would not find it easy to carry out violent acts against other individuals or objects, and they could easily be physically subdued. Individuals with frontal lesions or poor orbitofrontal organization, but with the physical capacity to carry out violent or criminal acts, commonly manifest other cognitive disorders that complicate their social relationships and the execution of their actions. Unplanned rapes and crimes of passion are usually committed by these individuals. Our experience shows that aggressors who are awkward individuals are easily identified by police, given that their clumsiness makes them more harshly violent and disorganized.

Different studies have shown that murderers have reduced activity in the orbitofrontal cortex (Raine, Buchsbaum, Stanley, Lottenberg, Abel, & Stoddard, 1994; Raine, Meloy, et al., 1998). A study by Horn, Dolan, Elliott, Deakin, and Woodruff (2003) used functional magnetic resonance imaging to examine the neural correlates of response inhibition. The study showed that neural response during response inhibition was most prominent in the right lateral orbitofrontal cortex and that greater engagement of the right orbitofrontal cortex was needed to maintain behavioral inhibition in impulsive individuals. There are patients who developed manic syndromes after brain injury, especially in the right hemisphere (Leon-Carrion et al., 2001), that can lead to violence against self or others. In a study by Altshuler et al. (2005), manic subjects had significantly increased activation in the left amygdala and reduced bilateral activation in the lateral orbitofrontal cortex relative to the comparison subjects.

CASE STUDY: ORBITOFRONTAL CORTEX INJURY

Alfred, aged 20, worked as a delivery person at a pizza bar. He was a normal boy with a high school education who grew up in a working class neighborhood. He was well adapted to his environment, had no history of violence or aggressiveness, and had never had problems with the police. He was mindful of his parents and treated women and girls with respect. One afternoon, he had a traffic accident at an intersection. At the hospital, he was diagnosed as having a TBI that caused diffused brain damage, particularly in the parietal and orbitofrontal cortex. He was discharged from the hospital with minor physical and behavioral impairments.

Shortly after his return home, Alfred's parents noticed that their son was impulsive, impatient, and unreasonable. For example, stray cats had always lived in the area around his house. Now, when he spotted one, he would pursue it and strangle it to death. Sometimes he would accompany his parents to the market or the shopping center. When he fancied something, he would take it with him, refusing to take "no" for an answer. On occasion, he would act violently in the store in order to get what he wanted, often destroying merchandise, which his parents would have to pay for later. Relatives, friends, and neighbors who visited Alfred's family complained of his verbal and physical aggression toward female visitors. The mere presence of a woman provoked his sexual overtures. He masturbated in front of house guests without any inhibition. Although he was reported to the police on certain occasions, charges were never laid. In the end, everyone understood that he was ill due to his brain injury. There were repeated attempts at rape, with one victim in particular. Every time his father left him alone in the house with his mother, she became the target of his sexual aggression. Alfred attempted to rape his mother on several occasions, and in the end, he could not be left alone with her. There were also episodes of violence against his father. The severity of Alfred's cognitive impairments made it impossible to reason with him. He was under the constant supervision of individuals who could control him physically. In the end, his parents decided to send him to a center specializing in the rehabilitation of persons with brain injury.

At admission, Alfred was diagnosed as having severe neurocognitive deficits. He suffered from temporal disorientation, but his sense of space and self were intact. Neuropsychological assessment showed a typical orbitofrontal cortical lesion. He also showed signs of cognitive fatigue, abandoning tasks with any degree of difficulty. When Alfred first began rehabilitation, his behavior was completely uninhibited. He would act impulsively, playing the fool and telling irreverent, often sexual, jokes, and he would often break out into fits of uncontrolled laughter. He verbally and physically threatened anyone who did not satisfy his wishes and desires. In general, his conduct was infantile, impulsive, and undisciplined. He was quite intolerant of his own frustration, and in social situations his behavior was inappropriate. There were episodes of physical aggression against male therapists and verbal sexual abuse against female therapists.

Alfred's rehabilitation was intensive and multidisciplinary. Within four months of treatment, his sexual aggression toward his mother was totally eliminated. After six months of treatment, his aggression in general was noticeably reduced. Discharged from rehabilitation after 20 months of treatment, Alfred no longer showed signs of aggressive or sexual behavior, which made living with his parents possible once again. He continued to have residual dysexecutive problems, with certain childish behavior and certain problem-solving difficulties. Six years later, he continues to live with his parents, works with supervision, and leads a quiet life in his community.

The Ventromedial Prefrontal Cortex

The *ventromedial prefrontal cortex* (VMPFC) is connected to the sensory areas of the brain and to the amygdala, thereby exerting cortical control over the amygdala. When this cortical control is damaged, behavior associated with fear is affected. Commonly, adaptive fear responses are reduced or eliminated. Injury to, or poor organization in, the VMPFC leads individuals to risky behavior that they are incapable of inhibiting, even if it results in significant legal problems. It is almost as though they are insensitive to the possible consequences of their actions (Anderson, Bechara, Damasio, Tranel, & Damasio, 1999). The behavior of these patients is primarily guided by stimuli present at the precise moment of their actions.

The Dorsolateral Prefrontal Cortex

When the *dorsolateral prefrontal cortex* (DLPFC) is injured or poorly organized, the subject will have difficulty making decisions: Decisions will be made fortuitously or will be inhibited completely. Recent neuroimaging studies have found that the DLPFC is actively involved when processing visual stimuli with strong emotional significance (especially unpleasant and highly arousing stimuli; León-Carrión et al., 2006, 2007a, 2007b). León-Carrión et al. suggest that the role of this area in emotional processing is to maintain the stimuli representation in working memory in order to prepare an adequate response and, thus, make a decision. If the DLPFC is damaged, individuals will tend to be apathetic and have socially inverse behavior; their actions will be morally and socially inappropriate rather than violent or criminal in nature. Individuals who are aggressive show functional deterioration in the bilateral DLPFC, as opposed to individuals with dementia, who do not (Hirono, Mega, Dinov, Mishkin, & Cummings, 2000). In a study assessing DLPFC and VMPFC function in individuals with APD, Dolan and Park (2002) found that subjects with APD displayed impairments in DLPFC executive function tasks on planning ability and set shifting.[2] The results showed that APD was associated not only with a broad range of deficits in DLPFC, but with deficits in VMPFC as well.

A Possible Role for the Amygdaloid Complex in Criminality

Another important area of the brain, the amygdala, is involved in controlling emotions and, thus, has been linked to violent behavior and criminality.

The *amygdala* is a subcortical structure localized in the medial margins of the temporal lobes (see Figure 6.1). This cerebral zone appears to play an important role in confronting fear, in giving emotional significance to what occurs in the environment, and in the regulation of negative emotions. Thus, individuals with brain injury to this cerebral zone tend to have problems controlling negative feelings toward others, which could lead to violent conduct or to viewing any interaction with another individual as a potential challenge. Moreover, these patients may not fear the possible negative effects that this violent behavior may cause them. An intact prefrontal cortex may be one of the best guarantees for inhibiting outbreaks of impulsive behavior, given its connections to the amygdala. Individuals with a damaged prefrontal-amygdala circuit tend to misinterpret basic emotional clues to what is going on around them or to interrelating with other individuals, such as the meaning of a facial expression. Misinterpreting a facial expression as threatening could lead the subject to impulsive violent behavior. Hence, although subcortical structures supply the affective information, what really matters is the role of the prefrontal cortex in the response behavior.

The prefrontal cortex and amygdalo-hippocampal complex (AHC) in violent patients has been studied by Critchley et al. (2000) using (1)H-magnetic resonance spectroscopy. They found that violent patients have reduced neuronal density and abnormal phosphate metabolism in the prefrontal lobe and AHC, compared to nonviolent control subjects. According to Blair, Mitchell, and Blair (2005), an injury to the amygdala causes representations of negative feelings that deteriorate more markedly than those of positive feelings. This is why responses from violent subjects to stimulus-punishment associations are more impaired than responses to associations of stimulus-reinforcement. Different studies have found that violent patients commonly have tissue loss or anomalies in their hippocampus-amygdala circuit (Sakuta & Fukushima, 1998; Tonkonogy, 1991; van Elst, Woermann, Lemieux, Thompson, & Trimble, 2000).

It has also been found that pedophilic perpetrators show structural impairments in brain regions critical to sexual development, such as the amygdala. Subtle defects in the right amygdala and in closely related structures may be implicated in the pathogenesis of pedophilia and might reflect developmental disturbances or environmental insults at critical periods (Schiltz et al., 2007).

RECAP 6.1   Brain Injuries and Violence

Region	Subregion	Primary Function	Hypothesized Effects of Damage Related to Violence
Prefrontal Cortex		Executive functioning	Sex offenses, emotional violence, antisocial personality disorder
	orbitofrontal	Impulse control	Impulsive violence
	ventromedial	Emotional regulation	Fear inhibition
	dorsolateral	Decision making	Inappropriate social responses, antisocial personality disorder
Amygdala		Emotional regulation, fear	Impulsive violence, low concern with consequences

Neurobehavioral Genetics and Violent Behavior

Although social resistance to accepting a genetic basis for violent, aggressive, or murderous behavior exists, there is growing scientific evidence that genetics contributes to this type of behavior. Some authors have found hereditary factors that influence violent conduct (Lesch & Merschdorf, 2000; Moffitt, 2005). Studies on adoption and twins have established that variation in violent, aggressive, and antisocial behavior has a significant genetic component (Rhee & Waldman, 2002). However, aggressive, violent behavior and criminality are not solely determined by genetic factors. Environment also plays an important role in genetic expression, and it may be the trigger for violent acts in persons with genes predisposed to violence. In non-Mendelian inheritance, some genes need to interact with an adequate environment or find an environmental trigger in order to be expressed.

According to Prichard, Jorm, Mackinnon, and Easteal (2007), the most likely candidate genes are those involved in brain development, differentiation, and function. These authors investigated genes involved in development of dopamine neurons (Lim Homeobox transcription factor 1B, LMX1B), dopamine synthesis (dopamine-[beta]-hydroxylase, DBH), dopamine neurotransmission (dopamine receptor D2, DRD2), dopamine metabolism (monoamine oxidase A, MAO-A), and transcriptional regulation of dopamine-related genes (nuclear receptor 4A2, NR4A2 and transcription factor AP2B, TFAP2B). The aim of the study was to establish the role of insecure attachment in antisocial behavioral outcomes and the preponderance of antisocial traits in men. Polymorphisms in genes involved in steroid hormone regulation (androgen receptor, AR and estrogen receptor [alpha], ESR1) and social or attachment-related behaviors (vasopressin receptor, AVPR1A and oxytocin receptor, OXTR) were also tested for association with antisocial traits. They found significant associations for antisocial traits with AR and ESR1 polymorphisms in men and with polymorphisms within NR4A2 and TFAP2B in women. The association with TFAP2B remained significant after correction for multiple testing. Prichard et al. suggest that genetic variation within transcription factors may, in part, explain the variation observed in the population for antisocial behavioral phenotypes.

In a study exploring genetic and environmental influences on aggressive and nonaggressive antisocial behavior (ASB) using over 1,000 twin pairs at the age of 8–9 and again at 13–14, Eley, Lichtenstein, and Moffitt (2003) found that aggressive ASB was highly hereditary, with little influence from shared environment, such as family environment during childhood and adolescence, whereas nonaggressive ASB was significantly influenced both by genes and shared environment. Eley et al. interpreted their data as being in agreement with the hypothesis that aggressive ASB is a stable hereditary trait as compared to nonaggressive behavior, which is more strongly influenced by the environment and shows less genetic stability over time. This data highlights the expression of genes associated with aggressiveness and violent conduct.

A clear relationship has been found to exist between genetic variations and aggressiveness, particularly with regard to monoamine oxidase A (MAO-A), an essential enzyme for the serotonin system. According to Craig (2007), reaction to stress appears to be an important factor in precipitating aggressive episodes, and individuals may vary in their ability to cope with stressful environments depending on their genetic makeup. In reviewing the literature, Craig found that evidence from humans and primates indicates that adverse rearing conditions may interact with variants in stress and neurotransmitter pathway genes, leading to antisocial and/or violent behavior. He stresses that examination of the interaction between the alleles of MAO-A and environmental stressors may provide protection against, or increase sensitivity to, an abusive upbringing, an observation that may explain part of the variability in developmental outcomes associated with maltreatment.

Other studies have shown that a functional polymorphism in the promoter region of the MAO-A gene moderates the impact of adverse childhood events on the risk of developing antisocial behavior. Meyer-Lindenberg et al. (2006), by means of a multimodal imaging study, identified differences in limbic circuitry for emotion regulation and cognitive control that may be involved in the association between MAO-A and impulsive aggression. The authors found functional and structural differences in the prefrontal-amygdala-hippocampal system for emotional regulation, memory, and cognitive control, suggesting the existence of neural mechanisms for a genetic bias toward impulsive violence. They concluded that their data implicate neural systems in social adaptation and cognition under partial genetic control and suggest adverse consequences for increased serotonergic tone during brain development in humans. Their review led them to claim that there is a deficiency in the neural systems that regulate emotion and memory that is related to observed gene-environment interaction. This is in agreement with current proposals linking brain structures involved in emotional control, such as the amygdala and medial prefrontal and orbitofrontal cortices, to the emergence of violent behavior.

In a very interesting study, Reif et al. (2007) investigated 184 adult male volunteers to note whether aggressive behavior is influenced by variation in serotonergic circuitry genes and early life experiences. They found that high environmental adversity during childhood was associated significantly with violent behavior. Forty-five percent of violent individuals, and only 30% of nonviolent individuals, carried the low-activity, short MAO-A allele. An interaction between childhood environment and 5HTT genotype affecting violent behavior was found, in that high adversity during childhood only impacted later-life violence if the short promoter alleles were present. According to Reif et al., these findings indicate complex interactions between genetic variation of the serotonergic circuitry and environmental factors, arguing against simplistic, monocausal explanations of violent behavior. Liao, Hong, Shih, and Tsai (2004) studied the 5-HTTLPR genetic polymorphism in a group of Chinese males convicted of extremely violent crime ($N = 135$) and in a normal control group ($N = 111$). They found that carriage of the low-activity S allele is associated with extremely violent criminal behavior in Chinese males, and they suggested that the 5-HTT may be implicated in mechanisms underlying violent behaviors.

In a search for biological predictors of adolescent criminal behavior, Nilsson et al. (2006) found that carrying the 3-repeat allele of the MAO-A gene promoter increases the risk of male adolescent criminal behavior when it interacts with psychosocial factors. No effects of the MAO-A genotype were found on adolescent criminal activity when the MAO-A genotype was considered alone (i.e., without its psychosocial context). According to Nilsson et al., these findings support the notion that genotype and psychosocial factors interact to precipitate male adolescent criminal behavior.

RECAP 6.2   Genes Related to Violence

Name	Abbreviatio	Primary Function	Hypothesized Relationship With Violence
Lim Homeobox transcription factor 1B	LMX1B	Development of dopamine neurons	None found
Dopamine-[beta]-hydroxylase	DBH	Dopamine synthesis	None found
Dopamine receptor D2	DRD2	Dopamine transcription	None found
Monoamine oxidase A	MAO-A	Metabolism of dopamine	Deficiency interacts with stress to lead to violence
Nuclear receptor 4A2	NR4A2	Transcriptional regulation of dopamine-related genes	Related to antisocial traits in women
Transcription factor AP2B	TFAP2B	Transcriptional regulation of dopamine-related genes	Related to antisocial traits in women
Androgen receptor	AR	Steroid-hormone regulation	Related to antisocial traits in men
Estrogen receptor [alpha]	ESR1	Steroid-hormone regulation	Related to antisocial traits in men
Vasopressin receptor	AVPR1A	Social/ Attachment behaviors	None found
Oxytocin receptor	OXTR	Social/ Attachment behaviors	None found
Serotonergic circuitry genes	5-HTT	Serotonin regulation	Deficiency interacts with childhood stress to lead to violence

Conclusion

The origin of violent behavior in humans must be considered multicomponential, with neurobiological, developmental, and sociobehavioral factors each playing an important role. None of these factors alone can explain why a person becomes violent at a particular moment. However, most studies on the subject, including our own experience, seem to indicate that acquired brain injury has a very important role in the genesis of violent behavior. Apart from individuals suffering from a known brain injury, currently there are many people, apparently without cerebral damage, who during their youth and infancy suffered significant blows to the head (from gang fights, domestic violence, small blows to the head while driving, falls, etc.). The result of these blows is considered a mild, or even a moderate, brain injury, but the injured were never taken to a hospital to be treated. This means that they suffered from a hidden brain injury. As we have seen, the probability of violent and criminal people suffering from moderate or severe brain injury (especially abnormalities in, or damage to, the frontal lobe and limbic system) is very high. In general, it appears that there are two types of violent criminals: those who commit impulsive crimes and assaults and those who plan them beforehand. The former suffered injuries to the prefrontal cortex; the latter have subcortical lesions, particularly limbic lesions. The genetic factor associated with brain injury in the same individual complicates the scenario and means of violent expression, but these elements should receive further study nonetheless.

What does seem evident is that violent behavior appears when several factors exist simultaneously. The presence of brain injury is a factor that considerably increases the probability of violent behavior, particularly if the appropriate environmental triggers are in place. One trigger is the inability to satisfy one's desires or appetites through dialogue, negotiation, or argument. Another trigger is executive dysfunction, which impedes an individual's ability to delay immediate satisfaction of his or her will and desires.

Notes

1. Transvestic fetishism is recurrent and intense sexually arousing fantasies, sexual urges, or sexual behavior involving cross-dressing. Paraphilia, which usually affects heterosexual males, is a disorder of sexual preference or a repeated, intense sexual arousal to unconventional and socially deviant stimuli involving inanimate objects, children or nonconsenting adults, or suffering or humiliation of oneself or the partner.

2. *Set shifting* is the ability to switch between cognitive categories, or *sets*, and flexibly adapt to changing environments.

Discussion Questions

1. What is executive functioning and what role might it play in violent behavior?

2. What areas of the brain are involved in executive functioning?

3. What role may the amygdala play in violent behavior?

4. How would the course of violence in an individual's behavior differ between individuals with TBI and antisocial individuals without TBI?

Internet Resources

Federal Bureau of Investigation National Center for the Analysis of Violent Crime: http://www.fbi.gov/hq/isd/cirg/ncavc.htm

International Brain Injury Association: http://www.internationalbrain.org

National Association of State Mental Health Program Directors: http://www.nasmhpd.org/general_files/position_statement/sexpred.htm

References

Altshuler, L. L., Bookheimer, S. Y., Townsend, J., Proenza, M. A., Eisenberger, N., Sabb, F., et al. (2005). Blunted activation in orbitofrontal cortex during mania: A functional magnetic resonance imaging study. *Biological Psychiatry, 58*(10), 763–769.

Amen, D. G., Stubblefield, M., Carmichael, B., & Thisted, R. (1996). Brain SPECT findings and aggressiveness. *Annals of clinical psychiatry, 8*(3), 129–137.

Anderson, S. W., Bechara, A., Damasio, H., Tranel, D., & Damasio, A. R. (1999). Impairment of social and moral behavior related to early damage in human prefrontal cortex. *Nature Neuroscience, 2*(11), 1032–1037.

Bergvall, A. H., Wessely, H., Forsman, A., & Hansen, S. (2001). A deficit in attentional set-shifting of violent offenders. *Psychological Medicine, 31*(6), 1095–1105.

Blair, J., Mitchell, D., & Blair, K. (2005). *The psychopath: Emotion and the brain.* Oxford: Blackwell.

Briken, P., Habermann, N., Berner, W., & Hill, A. (2005). The influence of brain abnormalities on psychosocial development, criminal history and paraphilias in sexual murderers. *Journal of Forensic Science, 50*(5), 1204–1208.

Briken, P., Habermann, N., Kafka, M. P., Berner, W., & Hill, A. (2006). The paraphilia-related disorders: An investigation of the relevance of the concept in sexual murderers. *Journal of Forensic Science, 51*(3), 683–688.

Convit, A., Isay, D., Otis, D., & Volavka, J. (1990). Characteristics of repeatedly assaultive psychiatric inpatients. *Hospital & community psychiatry, 41*(10), 1112–1115.

Craig, I. W. (2007). The importance of stress and genetic variation in human aggression. *Bioessays, 29*(3), 227–236.

Critchley, H. D., Simmons, A., Daly, E. M., Russell, A., van Amelsvoort, T., Robertson, D. M., et al. (2000). Prefrontal and medial temporal correlates of repetitive violence to self and others. *Biological Psychiatry, 47*(10), 928–934.

Dolan, M., & Park, I. (2002). The neuropsychology of antisocial personality disorder. *Psychological Medicine, 32*(3), 417–427.

Eley, T. C., Lichtenstein, P., & Moffitt, T. E. (2003). A longitudinal behavioral genetic analysis of the etiology of aggressive and nonaggressive antisocial behavior. *Development and Psychopathology, 15*(2), 383–402.

Gorenstein, E. E., & Newman, J. P. (1980). Disinhibitory psychopathology: A new perspective and a model for research. *Psychological Review, 87,* 301–315.

Graber, B., Hartmann, K., Coffman, J. A., Huey, C. J., & Golden, C. J. (1982). Brain damage among mentally disordered sex offenders. *Journal of Forensic Sciences, 27*(1), 125–134.

Grekin, E. R., Brennan, P. S., Hodgins, D., & Mednick, D. S. (2001). Male criminals with organic brain syndrome: Two distinct types based on age at first arrest. *The American Journal of Psychiatry, 158,* 1099–1104.

Hirono, N., Mega, M. S., Dinov, I. D., Mishkin, F., & Cummings, J. L. (2000). Left frontotemporal hypoperfusion is associated with aggression in patients with dementia. *Archives of Neurology, 57*(6), 861–866.

Horn, N. R., Dolan, M., Elliott, R., Deakin, J. F., & Woodruff, P. W. (2003). Response inhibition and impulsivity: An fMRI study. *Neuropsychologia, 41*(14), 1959–1966.

Joyal, C. C., Black, D. N., & Dassylva, B. (2007). The neuropsychology and neurology of sexual deviance: A review and pilot study. *Sex Abuse, 19*(2), 155–173.

Kelly, T., Richardson, G., Hunter, R., & Knapp, M. (2002). Attention and executive function deficits in adolescent sex offenders. *Child Neuropsychology, 8*(2), 138–143.

Langevin, R. (2006). Sexual offenses and traumatic brain injury. *Brain and Cognition, 60*(2), 206–207.

León-Carrión, J., & Barroso y Martín, J. M. (1997). *Neuropsicología del pensamiento: Control ejecutivo y lóbulo frontal.* Sevilla: Kronos, Colección Neuropsicológica.

León-Carrión, J., & Chacartegui, F. J. (2003). Blows to the head during development can predispose to violent criminal behavior: Rehabilitation of consequences of brain injury is a measure for crime prevention. *Brain Injury, 17*(3), 207–216.

León-Carrión, J., & Chacartegui, F. J. (2005). Desorganización perceptiva, déficit contructivos y memoria visual en sujetos con delitos violentos. *Revista Española de Neuropsicología, 7*(2–4), 117–134.

León-Carrión, J., Damas, J., Izzetoglu, K., Pourrezai, K., Martín-Rodríguez, J. F., Barroso y Martín, J. M., et al. (2006). Differential time course and intensity of PFC activation for men and women in response to emotional stimuli: A functional near-infrared spectroscopy (fNIRS) study. *Neuroscience Letters, 403*(1–2), 90–95.

León-Carrión, J., Damas-López, J., Martín-Rodríguez, J. F., Domínguez-Roldán, J. M., Murillo-Cabezas, F., Barroso Y Martin, J. M., et al. (2008). The hemodynamics of cognitive control: The level of concentration of oxygenated hemoglobin in the superior prefrontal cortex varies as a function of performance in a modified Stroop task. *Behavioural Brain Research, 193*(2), 248–256.

León-Carrión, J., De Serdio-Arias, M. L., Cabezas, F. M., Roldán, J. M., Domínguez-Morales, R., Martín, J. M., et al. (2001).

Neurobehavioural and cognitive profile of traumatic brain injury patients at risk for depression and suicide. *Brain Injury, 15*(2), 175–181.

León-Carrión, J., Martín-Rodríguez, J. F., Damas-López, J., Pourrezai, K., Izzetoglu, K., Barroso y Martín, J. M., et al. (2007a). A lasting post-stimulus activation on dorsolateral prefrontal cortex is produced when processing valence and arousal in visual affective stimuli. *Neuroscience Letters, 422*(3), 147–152.

León-Carrión, J., Martín-Rodríguez, J. F., Damas-López, J., Pourrezai, K., Izzetoglu, K., Barroso y Martín, J. M., et al. (2007b). Does dorsolateral prefrontal cortex (DLPFC) activation return to baseline when sexual stimuli cease? The role of DLPFC in visual sexual stimulation. *Neuroscience Letters, 416*(1), 55–60.

Lesch, K. P., & Merschdorf, U. (2000). Impulsivity, aggression, and serotonin: A molecular psychobiological perspective. *Behavioral Sciences & the Law, 18*(5), 581–604.

Lezak, M. D. (1995). *Neuropsychological assessment* (3rd ed.). New York: Oxford University Press.

Liao, D. L., Hong, C. J., Shih, H. L., & Tsai, S. J. (2004). Possible association between serotonin transporter promoter region polymorphism and extremely violent crime in Chinese males. *Neuropsychobiology, 50*(4), 284–287.

Martell, D. A. (1992). Estimating the prevalence of organic brain dysfunction in maximum-security forensic psychiatric patients. *Journal of Forensic Sciences, 37*(3), 878–893.

Meyer-Lindenberg, A., Buckholtz, J. W., Kolachana, B. R., Hariri, A., Pezawas, L., Blasi, G., et al. (2006). Neural mechanisms of genetic risk for impulsivity and violence in humans. *Proceedings of the National Academy of Sciences of the United States of America, 103*(16), 6269–6274.

Moffitt, T. E. (2005). The new look of behavioral genetics in developmental psychopathology: Gene-environment interplay in antisocial behaviors. *Psychological Bulletin, 131*(4), 533–554.

Nilsson, K. W., Sjoberg, R. L., Damberg, M., Leppert, J., Ohrvik, J., Alm, P. O., et al. (2006). Role of monoamine oxidase A genotype and psychosocial factors in male adolescent criminal activity. *Biological Psychiatry, 59*(2), 121–127.

Prichard, Z. M., Jorm, A. F., Mackinnon, A., & Easteal, S. (2007). Association analysis of 15 polymorphisms within 10 candidate genes for antisocial behavioral traits. *Psychiatric Genetics, 17*(5), 299–303.

Raine, A., Buchsbaum, M., & LaCasse, L. (1997). Brain abnormalities in murderers indicated by positron emission tomography. *Biological Psychiatry, 42*(6), 495–508.

Raine, A., Buchsbaum, M. S., Stanley, J., Lottenberg, S., Abel, L., & Stoddard, J. (1994). Selective reductions in prefrontal glucose metabolism in murderers. *Biological Psychiatry, 36*(6), 365–373.

Raine, A., Lencz, T., Bihrle, S., LaCasse, L., & Colletti, P. (2000). Reduced prefrontal gray matter volume and reduced autonomic activity in antisocial personality disorder. *Annals of General Psychiatry, 57*(2), 119–127.

Raine, A., Meloy, J. R., Bihrle, S., Stoddard, J., LaCasse, L., & Buchsbaum, M. S. (1998). Reduced prefrontal and increased subcortical brain functioning assessed using positron emission tomography in predatory and affective murderers. *Behavioral Sciences & the Law, 16*(3), 319–332.

Raine, A., Phil, D., Stoddard, J., Bihrle, S., & Buchsbaum, M. (1998). Prefrontal glucose deficits in murderers lacking psychosocial deprivation. *Neuropsychiatry, Neuropsychology, and Behavioral Neurology, 11*(1), 1–7.

Reichard, A. A., Langlois, J. A., Sample, P. L., Wald, M. M., & Pickelsimer, E. E. (2007 Nov/Dec). Violence, abuse, and neglect among people with traumatic brain injuries. *Journal of Head Trauma Rehabilitation, 22*(6), 390–402.

Reif, A., Rosler, M., Freitag, C. M., Schneider, M., Eujen, A., Kissling, C., et al. (2007). Nature and nurture predispose to violent behavior: Serotonergic genes and adverse childhood environment. *Neuropsychopharmacology, 32,* 2375–2383.

Rhee, S. H., & Waldman, I. D. (2002). Genetic and environmental influences on antisocial behavior: A meta-analysis of twin and adoption studies. *Psychological Bulletin, 128*(3), 490–529.

Sakuta, A., & Fukushima, A. (1998). A study of abnormal findings pertaining to brain in criminals. *International Medical Journal, 5,* 283–292.

Schiltz, K., Witzel, J., Northoff, G., Zierhut, K., Gubka, U., Fellmann, H., et al. (2007). Brain pathology in pedophilic offenders: Evidence of volume reduction in the right amygdala and related diencephalic structures. *Archives of General Psychiatry, 64*(6), 737–746.

Schofield, P. S., Butler, T. G., Hollis, S. J., Smith, N. E., Lee, S. J., & Kelso, W. M. (2006). Traumatic brain injury among Australian prisoners: Rates, recurrence, and sequelae. *Brain Injury, 20,* 499–506.

Slaughter, B., Fann, J. R., & Ehde, D. (2003). Traumatic brain injury in a county jail population: Prevalence, neuropsychological functioning and psychiatric disorders. *Brain Injury, 17*(3), 731–741.

Steudel, W. I., Cortbus, F., & Schwerdtfeger, K. (2005). Epidemiology and prevention of fatal head injuries in Germany: Trends and the impact of the reunification. *Annals of Emergency Medicine, 45,* 37–42.

Stuss, D. T., & Benson, D. F. (1986). *The frontal lobes.* New York: Raven Press.

Tardiff, K., & Sweillam, A. (1980). Assault, suicide and mental illness. *Archives of General Psychiatry, 37,* 164–169.

Tateno, A., Jorge, R. E., & Robinson, R. G. (2003). Clinical correlates of aggressive behavior after traumatic brain injury. *The Journal of Neuropsychiatry and Clinical Neurosciences, 15,* 155–160.

Timonen, M., Miettunen, J., Hakko, H., Zitting, P., Veijola, J., von Wendt, L., et al. (2002). The association of preceding traumatic brain injury with mental disorders, alcoholism and criminality: The Northern Finland 1966 Birth Cohort Study. *Psychiatry Research, 113*(3), 217–226.

Tonkonogy, T. M. (1991). Violence and temporal lobes lesion: Head CT and MRI data. *Journal of Neuropsychiatry and Clinical Neuroscience, 3,* 189–196.

Travin, S., Lee, H. K., & Bluestone, H. (1990). Prevalence and characteristics of violent patients in a general hospital. *New York State Journal of Medicine, 90*(12), 591–595.

van Elst, L. T., Woermann, F. G., Lemieux, L., Thompson, P. J., & Trimble, M. R. (2000). Affective aggression in patients in patients with temporal lobe epilepsy. *Brain, 123,* 234.

van Wijk, A. P., Mali, B. R., Bullens, R. A., & Vermeiren, R. R. (2007). Criminal profiles of violent juvenile sex and violent juvenile non sex offenders: An explorative longitudinal study. *Journal of Interpersonal Violence, 22*(10), 1340–1355.

Veneziano, C., Veneziano, L., LeGrand, S., & Richards, L. (2004). Neuropsychological executive functions of adolescent sex offenders and nonsex offenders. *Perceptual and Motor Skills, 98*(2), 661–674.

Volkow, N. D., Tancredi, L. R., Grant, C., Gillespie, H., Valentine, A., Mullani, N., et al. (1995). Brain glucose metabolism in violent psychiatric patients: A preliminary study. *Psychiatry Research, 61*(4), 243–253.

PART II

The Offenders

CHAPTER 7

Violence Among School-Aged Youth

An Examination of School, Gang, Dating, and Sexual Violence

Cricket Meehan and Patricia Kerig

This chapter provides an overview of three major components of violence among school-aged youths: (1) historical trends, (2) general information about the types of youth violence, and (3) evidence-based prevention and intervention strategies to combat youth violence. First, we discuss historical prevalence rates, general patterns of violence, developmental etiology, risk factors, and protective factors for perpetrators and victims. We then describe types of youth violence, including school, gang, dating, and sexual violence. A case study of school bullying is provided. Finally, we present evidence-based prevention and intervention strategies designed to combat specific types of youth violence.

Historical Trends of Youth Violence

Prevalence rates of youth violence historically have been calculated based on youths' arrest records, which began to be systematically recorded in the 1930s. Prior to 1983, the number of youths arrested remained at a very constant and relatively low level. However, during the decade between 1983 and 1993, a surge in arrests of youths for violent crimes marked an epidemic in youth violence (U.S. Department of Health and Human Services, 2001, 2002), highlighted by media coverage of school shootings across the country. By the turn of the 21st century, the number of youths arrested for violent crimes, including homicide, rape, and robbery, had dropped to pre-1983 levels. Results from youth self-report surveys indicate that self-reported levels of victimization also returned to their pre-1983 levels by the end of the 1990s, while self-reported levels of perpetrating serious violent acts remained constant from 1983 to the present (U.S. Department of Health and Human Services, 2002). The discrepancies in these data point to the complexities of interpreting arrest and self-report crime rates, although the general trends suggest a current decline in youth violence.

General Patterns of Violence

Developmental Etiology of Perpetrators

Two developmental patterns have emerged in the study of youth violence (U.S. Department of Health and Human Services, 2001, 2002). In the *early-onset* pattern, some at-risk youth begin to engage in antisocial behaviors, gradually culminating in serious violence such as aggravated assault, robbery, gang fights, and rape, prior to their adolescence. This group has higher rates of offending and more serious offenses throughout their adolescence, and their pattern of behavior generally persists into adulthood (as compared to the late-onset pattern group). In the *late-onset* group, youths do not engage in violent behavior until their adolescence, and they generally cease to engage in violent acts after a period of a year or so. Overall, the late-onset trajectory is more prevalent among youths than the early-onset pattern. This trend is consistent with the American Psychiatric Association's (APA) data on the etiology of Conduct Disorder, the symptoms of which mirror the above-mentioned pattern of violence (APA, 2000).

Sampson and Laub (2005) describe the development of violent behavior through the lens of a *life-course perspective.* Specifically, they theorize that violence develops through the interaction of the individual's unique characteristics and the environmental factors surrounding that individual. Therefore, they argue, delinquency is more likely when an individual's bond to society is weakened.

Moffitt (1993) views the development of violent behavior through a dual taxonomy, to explain two seemingly incongruous statistics: that violent behavior is consistent over time and that the prevalence of violent behavior spikes in adolescence. She argues that there are two (dual) groups of individuals: those who are engaging in violent acts at every stage of their lives, and those who are engaging in violence only during adolescence.

Taken together, these theories of the developmental etiology of perpetrators appear to demonstrate that early-onset youths perpetrate aggressive behavior in a relatively consistent pattern over the course of their lives, while late-onset youths perpetrate aggressive behavior primarily during their adolescence. The difference between these two groups likely emerges because of the interplay of individual characteristics and environmental factors facing those youths, with early-onset youths experiencing more consistently negative factors compared to late-onset youths. In the following section, we describe general risk and protective factors for perpetrators of youth violence.

Risk Factors for Perpetrators

Several risk factors predictive of violence among youths have been identified (Hawkins & Catalano, 1992; U.S. Department of Health and Human Services, 2001, 2002). Individual risk factors include alienation and rebelliousness; favorable attitudes toward violence; prior criminal offenses; substance use; being male; prior aggression; low intelligence levels; and antisocial behaviors, attitudes, and beliefs. Familial risk factors include family history of violence, family conflict, low socioeconomic status/poverty, antisocial parents, poor parent-child relations, poor parental discipline, separation from one or more parents, and abusive parents. School risk factors, including poor attitude, poor performance, lack of commitment to school, and academic failure, and peer group risk factors, including weak social ties and antisocial peers, also increase the likelihood of youth engagement in violence. Among early-onset youths, additional risk factors have been identified, both individual (e.g., hyperactivity, medical/physical problems, and dishonesty) and familial (e.g., separation from parents and parental neglect). Among late-onset youths, the Surgeon General's *Youth Violence* report (U.S. Department of Health and Human Services, 2002) identified additional risk factors related to the individual (e.g., restlessness, difficulty concentrating, risk-taking behavior, and exposure to physical violence), the family (e.g., poor parental monitoring and supervision, low parental involvement, and family conflict), the school (e.g., academic failure), the peer group (e.g., delinquent friends, gang membership), and the community (e.g., neighborhood crime, access to drugs, neighborhood disorganization). Many of these risk factors, however, are prevalent in the general population and may have only marginal value in predicting violent behavior in youths.

Protective Factors for At-Risk Youth

Similarly, several protective factors decreasing the probability of violence among youth have been identified (Hawkins & Catalano, 1992; U.S. Department of Health and Human Services, 2001, 2002). Individual protective factors include an intolerant attitude toward violence, high intelligence, being female, positive social skills, outgoing personality, and expectation of punishment for antisocial behaviors. Familial protective factors include warm and supportive relationships with parents/adults, parental approval of peers, and positive parental monitoring. School protective factors include commitment to school and recognition for involvement in activities. Peer group protective factors include having friends who engage in socially acceptable behaviors. With regard to school violence, factors that appear to protect students from perpetrating violence at school include positive feelings about/connection to their school (Resnick et al., 1997), positive self-esteem, social support, coping strategies, and participation in social activities (Flaherty, 2001).

Developmental Etiology of Victims

As with perpetrators, youths who experience victimization tend to fall within identifiable developmental trajectories (Goldbaum, Craig, Pepler, & Connolly, 2003). In the *stable victimization* trajectory, youths experience victimization throughout their lives, often beginning when they are quite young. In the *late-onset* group, youths do not experience violent behavior until they reach adolescence. In the *early-onset* trajectory, youths experience high levels of victimization at an early age, but their levels of victimization gradually decline over time. In the following section, we describe general risk and protective factors for victims of youth violence.

Risk Factors for Victims

Among youth, several risk factors related to the probability of becoming the victim of violence have been identified. Children who are quiet, sensitive, passive, anxious, depressed, and lonely and who have low levels of self-worth/self-esteem are at greatest risk of victimization (Bendtro, 2001; Goldbaum et al., 2003; Grills & Ollendick, 2002; Hawker & Boulton, 2000; Hodges & Perry, 1999; Roecker-Phelps, 2001). In peer situations, children who lack social skills, are socially withdrawn, lack close friends, are uncomfortable in social situations, are socially incompetent, exhibit high levels of social anxiety, feel abandoned by their peers, and are unaccepted/rejected by their peers are more likely to become victims of violence (Bendtro, 2001; Goldbaum et al., 2003; Hawker & Boulton, 2000; Hodges & Perry, 1999; Roecker-Phelps, 2001). In addition, children who associate with other victimized children increase their own susceptibility to violence from others (Hodges & Perry, 1999).

Protective Factors for Potential Victims

Protective factors that lower the probability of becoming the victim of violence include having high-quality friendships that are characterized by high levels of warmth, intimacy, and trust; experiencing low levels of anxiety; and engaging in fewer aggressive behaviors (Goldbaum et al., 2003). Factors that appear to protect students against experiencing victimization at school include positive feelings about/connection to their school (Resnick et al., 1997), positive self-esteem, social support, coping strategies, and participation in social activities (Flaherty, 2001).

Following our discussion of the general development of youth violence among perpetrators and victims, we define and delineate several specific types of violence faced by youths today, including school violence, gang violence, dating/sexual violence, and juvenile sexual offenses. Additionally, we include a discussion of prevention and intervention strategies for the reduction of youth violence.

School Violence

The Center for the Prevention of School Violence (2008) defines school violence as "any behavior that violates a school's educational mission or climate of respect or jeopardizes the intent of the school to be free of aggression against persons or property, drugs, weapons, disruptions, or disorder." In this chapter, we include examples of school violence such as classroom violence, bullying, harassment, and fighting and assaults.

Types of School Violence

Classroom Violence. School-aged children spend many hours of their day in the classroom. Classroom violence is often associated with behavioral/psychological disorders and/or lack of age-appropriate social skills (Evans & Evans, 1985). This challenges teachers to manage a variety of nonacademic barriers in the classroom (Osher, Van Acker, Morrison, Gable, Dwyer, & Quinn, 2004). Unfortunately, many teachers do not receive adequate training to identify these nonacademic "warning signs" for unsafe classrooms, leaving them ill-equipped to counter risk factors for violence in their classrooms (Farmer, Farmer, & Gut, 1999; Osher et al., 2004; Reinke & Herman, 2002). Along with smaller class sizes, well-trained teachers equipped with effective classroom management techniques appear to be protective factors against classroom violence, enhancing academic achievement (Pritchard, 1999).

School Bullying. Bullying is a common form of violence in the classroom and other areas of the school. A student is the victim of bullying when he or she is repeatedly exposed to hurtful actions (physical or psychological) by one or more youths (Olweus, 1991, 1993). Prevalence studies have found that approximately 15% of students report bullying others (Kaltiala-Heino,

Rimpela, Marttunen, Rimpela, & Rantanen, 1999). Of those students who report engaging in bullying behaviors, approximately 50% come from abusive homes. Students who bully also misbehave more at school, blame others for their misbehavior, and lie to avoid consequences (Kaltiala-Heino et al., 1999). Victims of bullies who have no support from others to stop the bullying may retaliate against the perpetrators (DeBernardo & McGee, 1999), perpetuating the cycle of violence. Alternatively, victims may turn to suicidal thoughts and behaviors following chronic exposure to bullying that is not addressed by adults in their lives (see Kerby's story in the case study).

CASE STUDY: CONSEQUENCES OF CHRONIC BULLYING IN MIDDLE SCHOOL

In September, 1999, Kerby Casey Guerra began her eighth-grade year at Eagleview Middle School, nestled in an affluent neighborhood in the foothills of Colorado Springs, Colorado. Kerby, who had many friends, enjoyed music, literature, and learning at school. However, going to school for Kerby and her friends meant being subjected to name calling; taunting; teasing; physical attacks such as being kicked, pushed, and knocked down; and threats against their lives by the "populars" at school. Kerby reportedly hid in the bathrooms during the classes she had with the "populars," in an effort to avoid them. This treatment continued for years, despite Kerby and her friends telling the principal and the school counselor about their torment. The principal reportedly said that Kerby "is too sensitive, and she complains too much. She needs to get a backbone."

In January, 1999, Kerby felt she had no other option but to write a suicide note that read, "I know my death will shock you, but I had to do it. All my life I've been teased, harassed and pushed around. I just couldn't stand it anymore." She then took all the pills she could find in her parents' medicine cabinet. Kerby's suicide attempt failed and she was admitted to an inpatient psychiatric unit. This was her parents' first indication that something was seriously wrong at school. After completing inpatient treatment, Kerby returned to school with a prescription for antidepressant medication. Unfortunately, the bullying did not end, and Kerby was once again admitted to inpatient treatment in March, 1998. Shortly after, Kerby, her parents, her friends, and her friends' parents attended a meeting with school officials to discuss the bullying and the possibility of starting a support group for children who were bullied. Unfortunately, the school officials did not implement their suggestions, and Kerby's parents made the decision to withdraw her from the school.

On March 19, 1999 (the day after the meeting at school), Kerby's parents were hopeful that a change of schools would be a positive influence in Kerby's life. That evening, her parents and sister went out for the evening to celebrate her sister's 30th birthday while Kerby watched her young niece and nephew. Kerby insisted to her parents that everything was fine and that she was doing much better. After putting her niece and nephew to bed and leaving presents for them, 13-year-old Kerby Casey Guerra killed herself with a deer rifle. Her suicide note read, "I'm very sorry I lied to you all. I love you all. Kerby."

SOURCE: Eastburn (1999).

Repeated verbal and psychological harassment is a form of bullying behavior, the effects of which can profoundly impact the victim (Olweus, 1993). Verbal and psychological harassment can include threatening, taunting, teasing, calling others names, making faces or dirty gestures, and refusing to comply with someone else's wishes. Relational aggression, a form of harassment more often seen in girls, involves intentionally excluding others from activities, spreading rumors, or threatening to end a friendship in order to hurt another child (Crick & Grotpeter, 1995).

Fighting and Assaults. Fighting and assaults are often precipitated by interpersonal disputes between students and usually escalate into punching, shoving, and hitting events (Flaherty, 2001). Less frequently, the fight or assault involves a weapon, such as a gun, knife, or club; approximately 8% of students report being threatened or injured by a weapon on school property (Centers for Disease Control and Prevention, 2005). Violent deaths among school-aged children are rare events; less than 1% of homicides of children between the ages of 5 and 19 occur on school property (Centers for Disease Control and Prevention, 2005).

School-Based Prevention Efforts

Prevention of Youth Aggression. Fast Track (Conduct Problems Prevention Research Group, 1992) is based on the developmental research that identifies the early signs of youth aggression and the ways in which parents, teachers, and peers contribute to its maintenance. The target population is first graders evidencing early disruptive behaviors such as noncompliance, aggression, impulsivity, and immaturity. The techniques used are multifaceted, including teaching parents more effective disciplinary practices and increasing children's social skills, but they also extend to decreasing the likelihood of other risks that have been shown to predict the acceleration of an aggressive trajectory, such as school failure. For example, sessions with the family focus on setting up a structured learning environment in the home and encouraging parental involvement in the child's learning as well as increasing communication and positive relationships with the child's teacher. In addition, Fast Track clinicians work directly with teachers to foster strategies for effective management of disruptive behaviors in the classroom, such as establishing clear rules, rewarding positive behavior, and ignoring inappropriate behavior. Teachers also implement classroom-based programs designed to strengthen children's self-control, to build and maintain friendships, and to enhance problem-solving abilities. Practical assistance is also provided to children at high risk; for example, children with poor reading ability would receive tutoring. The Fast Track program's effect sizes for outcomes ranged from .14 to .27.

Prevention of School Violence. Of increasing urgency is the need for effective prevention of school violence, not only to prevent rare but horrific massacres such as the Virginia Tech and Columbine tragedies, but also to eliminate much more common bullying behaviors (U.S. Department of Education, 2002). By the end of the 1990s, nation-wide antibullying campaigns had been implemented in many countries, including Norway, Finland, England, Ireland, and the Netherlands (Smith & Brain, 2000), while in the U.S. efforts remain on a smaller scale.

One best practices program that has received extensive empirical support and international recognition is the Olweus Bullying Prevention Program (OBPP; Olweus, Limber, & Mihalic, 1999). What sets OBPP apart from the other initiatives to end youth violence is that the program does not focus on changing the individual child or family; rather, it focuses on transforming the school climate in order to create an environment that fosters prosocial behavior and discourages bullying. The first step involves actively engaging teachers, parents, administrators, and youths in a process designed to enhance their recognition of the problem of bullying in their school and to reduce attitudes that tolerate bullying or dismiss it as merely a matter of "kids being kids." To accomplish this, an anonymous survey about bullying and victimization is administered and the results are communicated back to the school community, often to the surprise of adults who were not aware of the extent to which children were experiencing violence and harassment or of the "hot spots" where bullies are able to perpetrate without detection. Motivated by this new knowledge, a Bullying Prevention Coordinating Committee is formed and charged with the task of creatively adapting the principles of the OBPP program to their unique circumstances and needs, including developing school policies against bullying, consequences for bullying behavior, staff training, and options for parent involvement. Classroom interventions for children are designed to help them to label bullying and understand its consequences, to speak up and seek help if they see bullying or are victimized by it, and to withdraw reinforcement from bullies by refraining from providing them with an audience or social approval. In addition, an essential part of the program is the introduction of "class meetings," in which teachers and children are encouraged to foster better connection and communication with one another, thus making the school a source of emotional safety, social support, and positive attachment for youths. Bullying reduction effect size estimates from the original outcome studies conducted in Norway ranged from −.10 to −.50. Other effective school-based violence prevention programs being implemented in the U.S. include PeaceBuilders (Flannery et al., 2003) and Resolving Conflicts Creatively (Aber, Brown, & Jones, 2003).

Following this discussion of school violence, we turn our attention to another type of violence impacting our youths today: gang violence.

Gang Violence

Definition of Gang Violence

The following is a common definition of a youth gang:

A self-formed association of peers having the following characteristics: three or more members, generally ages 12 to 24; a name and some sense of identity, generally indicated by such symbols as style of clothing, graffiti, and hand signals; some degree of permanence and organization; and an elevated level of involvement in delinquent or criminal activity. (Institute for Intergovernmental Research, 2007)

Typically, gang members engage in delinquent and criminal activities, including school truancy/dropping out, loitering, aggravated assault, robbery, burglary, motor vehicle theft, larceny/theft, use of firearms, and drug trafficking. In 1999, there were over 840,500 active youth gang members in the United States (Egley, 2000), and gang members committed the majority of serious youth violence and criminal offenses (U.S. Department of Health and Human Services, 2001). According to the National Youth Gang Survey, there were more than 26,000 active youth gangs in schools and communities in 1999 (Egley, 2000). Gang members tend to be predominantly male (92%), with gang membership forming around ethnic and racial boundaries (U.S. Department of Health and Human Services, 2001). Approximately 49% of gang members are Hispanic, 34% are African American, 10% are non-Hispanic white, and 6% are Asian (Egley & Ritz, 2006).

Patterns of Gang Violence

Youth gangs tend to form when adolescents experience four community conditions: (1) families and schools are ineffective in socializing the youth in a conventional manner and adult supervision is largely absent from the youths' lives; (2) the adolescents have a great deal of free time that is not spent in other prosocial activities; (3) there are limited opportunities for the youths to obtain positive adult careers/jobs; and (4) the youths have a well-defined place to congregate (Institute for Intergovernmental Research, 2007). In the following section, we describe risk and protective factors for youth becoming involved in gang activity.

Risk Factors for Gang Involvement

Youths join gangs for a variety of reasons, including neighborhood, family, school, peer, and individual factors (Hill, Howell, Hawkins, & Battin-Pearson, 1999); youths experiencing multiple risk factors are at the highest risk of joining a gang. Three prominent risk factors that increase the likelihood of gang involvement are the need and/or desire for money, protection, and recreation (Stone, 1999). Individuals involved in gangs tend to have greater access to marijuana, engage in more violent acts, have more difficulties achieving academically, are more likely to be identified as learning disabled (Hill et al., 1999), and display more antisocial characteristics (Stone, 1999) than their peers.

Protective Factors Against Gang Involvement

Youths who reside in communities with adequate opportunities to make money, that are perceived to be safe environments, and that offer positive social and recreational activities are less likely to become involved in gang activity (Stone, 1999).

Gang Recruitment

The impact of risk and protective factors must be viewed in light of youths' exposure to gang recruitment. Gangs use a variety of methods to recruit new members, including peer pressure; fear and intimidation; and the promise of money, power, prestige, and recognition (Rees, 1996). Gangs often target schoolchildren for recruitment because they are a more vulnerable and easily swayed group. Youths may join gangs to obtain a sense of identity that includes specific clothing styles, hand signals, language, and graffiti. Too often, however, identification with gangs also leads to criminal activity and delinquency, which may lead to involvement in the juvenile justice system.

The Juvenile Justice System

All too often, society's response to the problem of youth criminal activity and delinquency is punishment rather than treatment or prevention. Juveniles are involved in 12% of all violent crimes committed in the U.S., and each year approximately 2.2 million youths are arrested (Snyder, 2005). As a result, on any given day approximately 109,000 youths are incarcerated in juvenile detention facilities (Sickmund, 2004). Furthermore, societal concerns about youth violence have led to calls to increase the severity of legal punishments, such as lowering the age at which adolescents can be tried as adults in criminal court and even allowing them to face the death penalty for their actions. According to the U.S. Department of Justice, 200,000 youth under the age of 18 are tried as adults each year. Recently, a number of developmental psychologists have expressed concern about adolescents' abilities to participate in the legal process in the same capacity as adults. For example, Steinberg and Scott (2003) found significant difficulties in young offenders' abilities to comprehend their rights, understand courtroom procedures, and reason about information relevant to their legal rights. The investigators concluded that many adolescents' capacity to participate in legal proceedings was diminished by virtue of their deficient decision-making skills, heightened vulnerability to coercion, and reactivity to their environments. Thus, many young offenders are not able participate effectively in their own defense.

The need for intervention for juveniles in detention is highlighted by the fact that as many as 54% of males and 78% of females in the juvenile justice system had major depressive episodes, manic episodes, and/or psychosis within the past 6 months (Teplin, Elkington, McClelland, Abram, Mericle, & Washburn, 2005). Many of these youths had not been identified and had received no services in their communities prior to their arrests (Wasserman, McReynolds, Fisher, & Lucas, 2003). Left untreated, these youths' unmet mental health needs contribute to further delinquency and repeated reentries into the legal system (Thornberry, Huizinga, & Loeber, 2004). Consequently, efforts have been made to integrate mental health treatment into the juvenile justice system. The goals are to reduce the risk factors that increase the likelihood of future delinquent behavior and to enhance protective factors that will help the defender to make a successful transition to the community (Kelly, Thornberry, & Smith, 1997). Evidence suggests that the most efficacious interventions for juvenile offenders are those that are focused on developing and practicing specific competencies, such as social skills, substance abuse resistance, anger management, and interpersonal problem solving (McMackin, Leisen, Sattler, Krinsey, & Riggs, 2002). In addition, new model treatments have been developed that attend specifically to symptoms of underlying trauma in the lives of detained youths, which are alarmingly high (Ford, Courtois, Steele, van der Hart, & Nijenhuis, 2005) and disproportionately so for females (Leve & Chamberlain, 2004).

Following this overview of gang violence, we present an interpersonal type of violence impacting our youths' romantic relationships: dating violence.

Dating Violence

Definition of Dating Violence

The term dating violence refers to "any attempt to control or dominate another person physically, sexually, or psychologically, resulting in harm"

(Wolfe & Feiring, 2000, p. 360). From this definition, dating violence can take many forms, including physical abuse, such as slapping or hitting a partner; sexual abuse, such as forcing a partner into unwanted sexual activity; psychological abuse, such as degrading, insulting, or ridiculing a partner; relational abuse, such as spreading rumors, excluding someone, or attempting to turn a partner's friends against him or her; and coercive/domineering behaviors, such as attempting to control how one's partner dresses or behaves, refusing to allow a partner to spend time with friends or family, and threatening or terrifying a partner into submitting to one's wishes.

Prevalence of Youth Dating Violence

Adolescent dating violence is increasingly recognized as a public health problem of considerable concern in the United States (Centers for Disease Control, 2004). However, prevalence rates range widely, depending on the age of the samples studied and the definitions of violence used. Data from one study of nearly 2,000 eighth and ninth graders found that 25% had been victims of nonsexual dating violence and 8% had been victims of sexual abuse by dating partners (Foshee, Bauman, Arriaga, Helms, & Linder, 1998). Other studies show that between 28% and 45% of middle school children report having experienced some form of sexual harassment at school (Cascardi & Avery-Leaf, 2000). By the time youths reach high school, as many as 45% of girls and 43% of boys report that they have been victims of physical aggression in a dating relationship, and 17% of girls and 9% of boys have been coerced by their partners to perform a sex act (O'Keefe & Triester, 1998). In the most recent Youth Risk Behavior Survey, a large nationally representative sampling of U.S. youths (which did not ask about psychological or sexual violence), 9.5% of high school students reported being physically hurt by a dating partner in the preceding 12 months, with state-specific prevalence rates ranging from 6% to 18% (Centers for Disease Control, 2004). Finally, it is important to note that these forms of dating violence tend to co-occur; for example, physical violence most often occurs in a relationship in which there is psychological abuse, and sexual violence most often occurs in a relationship in which there is physical abuse (Jouriles, Wolfe, Garrido, & McCarthy, 2006).

Consequences of Dating Violence

Dating violence has been shown to negatively impact adolescent victims' physical and mental health in many ways, including increasing depression, substance abuse, eating disorders, anxiety, antisocial behavior, self-harm, suicidality, risky sexual behavior, and teenage pregnancy (Roberts, Klein, & Fisher, 2003; Silverman, Raj, Mucci, & Hathaway, 2001; Thompson, Wonderlich, Crosby, &

Mitchell, 2001). Furthermore, experiencing dating violence in adolescence can act as a catalyst for a pattern of violence and victimization that extends into adult intimate relationships with partners and children (Ball, Kerig, & Rosenbluth, in press; Wolfe, Wekerle, Scott, Straatman, Grasley, & Reitzel-Jaffe, 2003). For example, youths who experience dating violence in high school are at risk for engaging in violent dating relationships in college (Smith, White, & Holland, 2003), which, in turn, is associated with increased risk for violence in marriage (O'Leary, Barling, Arias, Rosenbaum, Malone, & Tyree, 1989).

Risk Factors for Dating Violence

Intriguingly, very similar risk factors predict dating violence perpetration and victimization (Wolfe, Scott, & Crooks, 2005). Among the key variables that increase the likelihood of involvement in a violent dating relationship are having been a victim of child abuse (Wolfe, Jaffe, Wilson, & Zak, 1988) and being exposed to interparental violence in the home (Kerig, 1999; Wolfe & Jaffe, 2001). Symptoms of trauma resulting from family violence have been found to be a powerful predictor of involvement in violent dating relationships for both boys and girls (Wolfe, Wekerle, Scott, Straatman, & Grasley, 2004) but especially female victims (Messman-Moore & Long, 2000). Further, youths who have grown up in abusive homes, in which their closest attachments have been marked by harshness and rejection, develop negative expectations and distorted appraisals of relationships. One such negative cognition is rejection sensitivity, the cognitive disposition to "anxiously expect, readily perceive, and intensely react to rejection" by others (Downey, Khouri, & Feldman, 1997, p. 85). Research has shown that rejection sensitivity predicts boys' controlling and violent behavior toward dating partners and predicts girls' relational insecurity and willingness to take desperate measures in order to maintain a relationship (Downey, Bonica, & Rincon, 1999; Purdie & Downey, 2001). Further, youths with negative schemas of relationships and aggressive conflict resolution styles tend to associate with and exacerbate one another, thereby increasing the risk for dating violence (Gray & Foshee, 1997). For example, O'Leary and Slep (2003) found that both boys and girls who were relationally aggressive associated with partners who became increasingly physically violent over time.

Perpetrators

Perpetrators of dating violence also tend to hold beliefs that the use of violence in intimate relationships is normative and justified and will result in desirable outcomes (Brengden, Vitaro, Tremblay, & Wanner, 2002; Foshee, Linder, MacDougall, & Bangdiwala, 2001; Grych, Kinsfogel, Hart, Klockow, & Robbins, 2003). Youths who demonstrate these attitudes early on are likely to engage in sexual harassment of both same- and other-sex peers, which, in turn, predicts later aggression toward dating partners (Pepler, Craig, Connolly, & Henderson, 2002). Not surprisingly, such attitudes are predicted by youths having grown up in a violent family where such behaviors were modeled and normalized (Foshee, Bauman, & Linder, 1999). Yet another risk factor for dating violence perpetration that co-occurs with family violence is youth antisocial behavior, including fighting in general, substance abuse, and delinquency (Capaldi, Dishion, Stoolmiller, & Yoerger, 2001; Coker, McKeown, Sanderson, Davis, Valois, & Huebner, 2000).

Youths also are influenced by social norms that model and justify the use of violence in intimate relationships, whether these are evidenced in the peer group, the school environment, or the culture at large (Pellegrini, 2002; Stein, 1995). Research suggests that friends play a particularly important role in influencing one another's behavior: Boys whose friends engage in dating violence or express approving attitudes toward it are likely to go on to victimize their own partners (Brendgen et al., 2002; Capaldi et al., 2001; Jouriles et al., 2006).

Victims

Female victims of dating violence also tend to engage in delinquent behaviors, including substance abuse and risky sexual activity (Silverman et al., 2001). In particular, girls who mature early engage in a number of problem behaviors, including dating early, dating older boys, and dating boys who are antisocial (Stattin & Magnusson, 1990), perhaps in these ways associating themselves with unhealthy choices of romantic partners.

Prevention of Adolescent Dating Violence

Recognition of adolescent dating violence has led to the development of a number of prevention programs. Many of these programs are school based and are provided universally as part of the curriculum of an existing health class. For example, the Safe Dates program (Foshee, Bauman, Greene, Koch, Linder, & MacDougall, 2000) involves 10 classroom sessions designed to change beliefs that intimate partner violence is normative and acceptable, to increase constructive conflict resolution skills as alternatives to physical aggression, and to help youths to learn where to go and how to seek help if they are abused. In studies involving over 1,500 middle school and high school youths, the intervention was found to be effective, with the benefits being retained over a year later (Foshee et al., 2000).

Other empirically supported interventions focus specifically on youths who are identified as being at high risk for dating violence, such as those who have been exposed to family violence or child maltreatment, and provide intensive small group interventions either at schools (Rosenbluth, 2004) or in community settings (Wolfe et al., 2003). For example, in addition to working to change the larger school climate and decrease acceptance of gendered violence, the Expect Respect program (Ball et al., in press) includes a support group curriculum for at-risk youths designed to assist participants in healing from past abuse, to increase expectations for equality and respect in current and future relationships, to develop healthy communication and conflict resolution skills, and to encourage taking social action to end violence in their schools, homes, and communities.

Improper sexual contact can occur not only in romantic relationships, but also when youths perpetrate sexual offenses/molestation against other children.

Juvenile Sexual Offenders

Teenage offenders are responsible for up to 40% of child sexual abuse (Berliner & Elliott, 2002). In contrast to perpetrators of adolescent dating violence, who generally abuse agemates, the majority of juvenile sex offenders perpetrate against younger children. Approximately 43% of molestations of children under the age of 6 are perpetrated by adolescents (National Center for Juvenile Justice, 1999). Frequently, the victim is a sibling or other relation and the majority of victims are female. In turn, the typical juvenile sex offender is male; the male-to-female ratio is about 20 to 1.

Predictors of Sexual Offending

A consistent finding is that a dysfunctional family environment increases the risk for juvenile sexual offending, particularly an environment characterized by domestic violence, severe maltreatment, early sexual victimization (Vizard, Monch, & Misch, 1995), and caregiver instability (Schwartz, Cavanaugh, Pimental, & Prentky, 2006). These effects are especially pronounced for the small proportion of juvenile sexual offenders who are females. In comparison to male perpetrators, female offenders have experienced child sexual abuse that was longer lasting and more severe and involved a larger number of perpetrators, and they have witnessed more domestic violence and sexual deviance in the home (Schwartz et al., 2006).

It is important to note, moreover, that some youths are equal opportunity or "versatile" offenders. For example, Butler and Seto (2002) compared non-sex offenders, sex-only offenders, and sex-plus-other-crime offenders and found that youths who commit *only* sexual offenses evidenced fewer childhood conduct problems, fewer antisocial attitudes, better current behavioral adjustment, and less likelihood of future delinquency than either of the other groups. Therefore, it appears that for some youths, sexual offending is part of a larger and ever-increasing repertoire of antisocial behaviors, whereas for others it is a specific and time-limited behavior (van Wijk, Mali, & Bullens, 2007). Indeed, the developmental course of juvenile sexual offending suggests that, for many youths, the behavior may be limited to the adolescent period. For example, Vandiver (2006) followed a sample of 300 male juvenile sex offenders into adulthood and found that only 13 were rearrested for a sexual offense, although more than half were arrested at least once for some other kind of crime. Similarly, Waite, Keller, McGarvey, Wieckowski, Pinkerton, and Brown (2005) found that only 5% of a sample of 261 males were rearrested for a sexual offense over a 10-year period, whereas more than one-third were rearrested for a nonsexual offense.

Another important distinction appears to be whether the offender perpetrates against a young child as opposed to an adult or agemate (van Wijk, Vermeiren, Loeber, Hart-Kerkhoffs, Doreleijers, & Bullens, 2006). For example, Hunter, Figueredo, Malamuth, and Becker (2003) found that, when compared to those whose victims were teenagers or adults, adolescent males who molested prepubescent girls demonstrated greater psychosocial deficits, including depression, anxiety, poor self-esteem, immaturity, and peer rejection. Those who molested children also used less aggression during the act and were more likely to offend against siblings.

Interventions for Sexual Offenders

The majority of treatments for juvenile sex offenders are downward extensions of those developed for adults. Whether offered in residential or community settings, they typically involve identifying deviant sexual interests and triggers for arousal, increasing impulse control, increasing social skills and empathy for victims, and changing cognitions that justify the use of sexual violence. However, neither the appropriateness nor the effectiveness of these models for treating adolescent sex offenders has yet been demonstrated (Hunter & Longo, 2004). More empirically sound evidence comes from two small clinical trials of family treatment utilizing multisystemic therapy (MST), with research and a 10-year follow-up suggesting the effectiveness of MST with teenage sexual offenders (Bourdin, Henggeler, Blaske, & Stein, 1990; Henggeler, Schoenwald, Rowland, & Cunningham, 2002).

Recently, Letourneau and Miner (2005) have issued a criticism of the movement toward increasingly harsh legal sanctions and lengthy restrictive treatments for juvenile sex offenders. The authors point out that these trends are based on three assumptions: (1) there is an epidemic of juvenile sexual offending (the data indicate no such rise in prevalence); (2) juvenile sex offenders are unlike other delinquents (as we have described, the research shows few clear patterns of difference); and (3) the risk of reoffending is extremely high without intervention (in fact, rearrest rates among juvenile sex offenders appear to be lower than is commonly assumed). Moreover, the authors argue that the prevailing legal and clinical approaches do not take into account the unique developmental features of adolescence, making them likely ineffectual and even perhaps harmful to the offender.

Additional Violence Prevention and Intervention Strategies

In this chapter, we have presented evidence that youths who commit acts of violence early in life are highly likely to remain on a negative developmental trajectory characterized by escalating behavioral, emotional, interpersonal, and legal problems. In addition, individual victims and society at large pay a high price, both in terms of personal suffering and financial costs associated with youth violence. In addition to the prevention and intervention strategies already presented, child and family intervention efforts have received empirical support.

Child-Focused Interventions

Individual Therapy

Cognitive-behavioral interventions for aggressive children focus on helping them to develop more accurate interpretations of interpersonal events and more effective strategies for resolving social problems. Shure and Spivack (1988) focus on building competence in five skills found to be deficient in aggressive children. For example, one of the most significant predictors of disruptive, defiant, and disrespectful behavior in preschool settings is children's inability to come up with a variety of solutions to common interpersonal problems, such as wanting to play with a toy that another child is playing with. Therefore, the first target of treatment is to help children to generate alternative solutions to problems. The therapist encourages children to brainstorm and explore a variety of different ideas, no matter how unrealistic or "silly" those might be, in order to help children to develop the habit of thinking before acting, to increase self-confidence in their ability to arrive at solutions on their own, and to begin to develop a repertoire of interpersonal problem-solving strategies to draw on.

Second, because aggressive children generally are impulsive and do not think beyond the present to consider the possible costs associated with their misbehavior, they are coached to consider the consequences of social acts.

The third goal is to develop means-ends thinking, to help aggressive children to think through the step-by-step process needed to carry out a particular solution. The fourth step involves the development of social-causal thinking, to help children understand how others feel and what motivates them to act the way they do—for example, recognizing the fact that one's aggression may anger other children and cause them to retaliate. Fifth, children are helped to develop sensitivity to interpersonal problems. Aggressive children often lack sensitivity to the cues that would alert them to the fact that there is a relational problem between them and another person. Finally, at the highest level of ICPS skills training, children develop a dynamic orientation, which refers to the ability to recognize that underneath the surface of people's behavior are their own concerns, motivations, and unique perspectives. For example, a youth with a dynamic orientation would be able to recognize that the bully who provokes him may be a mean boy who likes to hurt others, one who is insecure and trying to prove his worth, or one who is mistreated at home and is taking his frustrations out on others—understanding these underlying dynamics might guide the youth to a more effective response.

Group Therapy

Other cognitive-behavioral interventions take place with groups of children. For example, the Anger Coping Program (Larson & Lochman, 2002) involves school-aged children in groups that are designed to address core issues such as anger management, perspective taking, social problem solving, awareness of emotions, relaxation training, social skills, dealing with peer pressure, and self-regulation. For example, children learn self-control techniques, such as calming self-talk, and practice them in vivo while other children in the group attempt to taunt and tease them into losing their cool. The intervention takes place in the school setting and also involves teachers and parents so that they can reinforce children's use of these new skills outside the groups. Follow-up studies show that the intervention is effective in reducing aggression and disruptive behavior at both home and school, and gains have been maintained for as long as three years after the groups ended (Lochman, Wells, & Murray, in press).

Family Interventions

Parent Management Training

In contrast to interventions that focus on the individual child, Patterson (see Forgatch and Patterson, 1998) developed Parent Management Training (PMT) to address what he saw as the chief training ground for the development of youth aggression—maladaptive parent-child interactions. Using the principles of operant conditioning, PMT focuses on altering the interactions between parent and child so that prosocial behavior is reinforced and negative behavior is extinguished. First, therapists help parents learn how to think about their childrearing problems in behavioral terms, such as identifying what precipitates them and what consequences follow (e.g., acting up may be the only way the child of a stressed and busy parent can elicit attention). In this way, parents are better able to perceive their role in perpetuating child misbehavior and can abandon such unhelpful attributions as personalizing the problem ("I'm a lousy parent") or pathologizing the child ("He's a bad seed"). Second, parents are coached in behavior modification techniques, including the use of positive reinforcements such as praise and rewards, and mild punishments such as time out from reinforcement or loss of privileges. As children's behavior improves, parents learn higher-level skills such as negotiation and mutual problem solving, which help the overall tone of family relationships to become more positive and collaborative as well as support children's increasing self-control. Many outcome studies conducted over the past two decades attest to the effectiveness of PMT (Kazdin, 1997; Webster-Stratton & Reid, 2004).

Multisystemic Therapy

Multisystemic therapy (MST) is recognized as the one of the most well-supported interventions for youth aggression and has produced an impressive rate of success with some of the most seriously antisocial youth (Henggeler et al., 2002). MST takes to heart the lesson learned by previous investigators: There are multiple roots of antisocial behavior. While focused on the family system, the treatment is individualized and flexible, offering a variety of interventions depending on the special needs of the particular youth. Thus, treatment may focus on family disharmony and school underachievement in one case and lack of social skills and parental unemployment in another. Empirical studies show the efficacy of the multisystemic approach with severely disordered youth, including chronically violent adolescents and sex offenders (Bourdin et al., 1995). Follow-up studies have shown that, for as long as five years following treatment, youths who receive MST have lower arrest rates than those who receive other forms of treatment.

Culturally Sensitive Approaches

An example of a culturally sensitive approach to family therapy is Familias Unidas, which was developed to reduce the risk for problem behavior among Hispanic immigrant youth (Coatsworth, Pantin, & Szapocznik, 2002). The intervention is focused on engaging parents and helping them to overcome the stresses of immigration and acculturation to a new society, to increase their understanding of risk and protective factors in their child's social world, and to develop skills needed to cope effectively with their new cultural environment. In order to address feelings of marginalization and to empower parents, the intervention includes a number of small, supportive multi-parent support groups. One of the goals for these groups is Bicultural Effectiveness Training, which promotes and honors the home culture's strengths while educating parents about mainstream culture, in order to help them better understand and cope with the social contexts their children will encounter. In working with the family as a whole, the therapists strive to reduce parent-youth conflict, increase cohesion, and increase both structure and warmth in the parent-child relationships. Parents are encouraged to become actively involved in their youth's school, to monitor peer activities, and to model prosocial skills for their children. Initial investigations of the intervention's effectiveness are promising, with increased parental involvement and decreased behavior problems over a one-year period.

Conclusion

Today's youth face violence in myriad settings, including school, home, community, and interpersonal relationships. Throughout this chapter, we presented information about the patterns, prevalence rates, developmental etiology, and risk factors associated with youth violence. Fortunately, protective factors, prevention strategies, and intervention techniques exist to combat the effects violence has on youths. With the appropriate awareness, education, skills, and support, youths can overcome the challenges of exposure to violence.

Discussion Questions

1. What methods are used to try to treat youth who are at high risk for violence? How effective do you think such treatments are likely to be?

2. How big a problem is bullying in American schools? How can bullying be effectively prevented?

3. How prevalent is violence among youth? Why do you think that violence among youth declined during the 1990s and 2000s?

4. In what ways is dating violence among teens similar to dating violence among adults? In what ways is it different?

Internet Resources

Centers for Disease Control, "Youth Risk Behavior Surveillance–United States, 2005": http://www.cdc.gov/mmwr/PDF/SS/SS5505.pdf

National Youth Gang Center: http://www.iir.com/nygc/

References

Aber, J. L., Brown, J., & Jones, S. (2003). Developmental trajectories toward violence in middle childhood: Course, demographic differences, and response to school-based intervention. *Developmental Psychology, 39,* 324–348.

American Psychiatric Association. (2000). *Diagnostic and statistical manual of mental disorders* (Text rev.). Washington, DC: Author.

Ball, B., Kerig, P. K., & Rosenbluth, B. (in press). "Like a family except better because you can trust each other:" The Expect Respect dating violence prevention program. *American Journal of Health Promotion.*

Bendtro, L. K. (2001). Worse than sticks and stones: Lessons from research on ridicule. *Reclaiming Children and Youth, 10*(1), 47–53.

Berliner, L., & Elliott, D. M. (2002). Sexual abuse of children. In J. E. B. Myers, L. Berliner, J. Briere, C. T. Hendrix, C. Jenny, & T. A. Reid (Eds.), *The APSAC handbook on child maltreatment* (2nd ed., pp. 55–78). Thousand Oaks, CA: Sage.

Bourdin, C. M., Henggeler, S. W., Blaske, D. M., & Stein, R. (1990). Multisystemic treatment of adolescent sex offenders. *International Journal of Offender Therapy and Comparative Criminology, 33,* 161–172.

Bourdin, C. M., Mann, B. J., Cone, L. T., Henggeler, S. W., Fucci, B. R., Blaske, D. M., et al. (1995). Multisystemic treatment of serious juvenile offenders: Long-term prevention of criminality and violence. *Journal of Consulting and Clinical Psychology, 63,* 569–578.

Brendgen, M., Vitaro, F., Tremblay, R. E., & Wanner, B. (2002). Parent- and peer-related efforts on delinquency-related violence and dating violence: A test of two mediational models. *Social Development, 11,* 225–244.

Butler, S. M., & Seto, M. C. (2002). Distinguishing two types of adolescent sex offenders. *Journal of the American Academy of Child and Adolescent Psychiatry, 41,* 83–90.

Capaldi, D. M., Dishion, T. J., Stoolmiller, M., & Yoerger, K. (2001). Aggression toward female partners by at-risk young men: The contribution of male adolescent friendships. *Developmental Psychology, 37,* 61–73.

Cascardi, M., & Avery-Leaf, S. (2000). *Violence against women: Synthesis of research for secondary school officials* [Pamphlet]. Washington, DC: U.S. Department of Justice.

Centers for Disease Control. (2004). Youth risk behavior surveillance—United States, 2003. *Morbidity and Mortality Weekly Report, 2,* 1–98.

Centers for Disease Control and Prevention. (2005). Youth risk behavior surveillance—United States. *Morbidity and Mortality Weekly Report, 55,* No. SS-5. Retrieved July 24, 2007, from http://www.cdc.gov/mmwr/PDF/SS/SS5505.pdf.

Center for the Prevention of School Violence. (2008). The North Carolina Department of Juvenile Justice and Delinquency Prevention. Retrieved July 24, 2007, from http://www.ncdjjdp.org/cpsv/.

Coatsworth, D. J., Pantin, H., & Szapocznik, J. (2002). Familias Unidas: A family-centered ecodevelopmental intervention to reduce risk for problem behavior among Hispanic adolescents. *Clinical Child and Family Psychology Review, 5,* 113–132.

Coker, A. L., McKeown, R. E., Sanderson, M., Davis, K. E., Valois, R. F., & Huebner, E. S. (2000). Severe dating violence and quality of life among South Carolina high school students. *American Journal of Preventive Medicine, 19,* 220–227.

Conduct Problems Prevention Research Group. (1992). A developmental and clinical model for the prevention of conduct disorder: The FAST Track Program. *Development and Psychopathology, 4,* 509–528.

Crick, N. R., & Grotpeter, J. K. (1995). Relational aggression, gender, and social-psychological adjustment. *Child Development, 66*(3), 710–722.

DeBernardo, C. R., & McGee, J. P. (1999). Preventing the classroom avenger's next attack: Safeguarding against school shootings. *The Forensic Examiner, 8,* 16–18.

Downey, G., Bonica, C., & Rincon, C. (1999). Rejection sensitivity and adolescent romantic relationships. In W. Furman, B. B. Brown, & C. Feiring (Eds.), *The development of romantic relationships in adolescence* (pp. 148–174). New York: Cambridge University Press.

Downey, G., Khouri, H., & Feldman, S. I. (1997). Early interpersonal trauma and later adjustment: The mediational role of rejection sensitivity. In D. Cicchetti & S. L. Toth (Eds.), *Developmental perspectives on trauma: Theory, research, and intervention* (pp. 85–114). Rochester, NY: University of Rochester Press.

Eastburn, K. (1999, September 16). No way out. *Colorado Spring Independent.* Retrieved from http://csindy.com/csindy/1999-09-16/cover.html.

Egley, A., Jr. (2000). *Highlights of the 1999 National Youth Gang Survey* (OJJDP Fact Sheet #20). Washington, DC: U.S. Department of Justice, Office of Justice Programs, Office of Juvenile Justice and Delinquency Prevention.

Egley, A., Jr., & Ritz, C. E. (2006). *Highlights of the 2004 National Youth Gang Survey* (Fact Sheet #2006-01). Washington, DC: U.S. Department of Justice, Office of Juvenile Justice and Delinquency Prevention.

Evans, W. H., & Evans, S. S. (1985). The assessment of school violence. *Pointer, 29*(2), 18–21.

Farmer, T. W., Farmer, E. M. Z., & Gut, D. W. (1999). Implications for social development research for school-based interventions for aggressive youth with EBD. *Journal of Emotional and Behavioral Disorders, 7,* 130–136.

Flaherty, L. T. (2001). School violence and the school environment. In M. Shafii & S. L. Shafii (Eds.), *School violence: Assessment, management, prevention* (pp. 25–51). Washington, DC: American Psychiatric.

Flannery, D. J., Vazsonyi, A. T., Liau, A. K., Guo, M. S., Powell, K. E., Atha, H., et al. (2003). Initial behavior outcomes for the Peace-Builders Universal School-Based Violence Prevention Program. *Developmental Psychology, 39,* 292–308.

Ford, J. D., Courtois, C. A., Steele, K., van der Hart, O., & Nijenhuis, E. R. S. (2005). Treatment of complex posttraumatic self-dysregulation. *Journal of Traumatic Stress, 18,* 437–447.

Forgatch, M. S., & Patterson, G. R. (1998). Behavioral family therapy. In F. M. Dattilio (Ed.), *Case studies in couple and family therapy: Systemic and cognitive perspectives* (pp. 85–107). New York: Guilford Press.

Foshee, V. A., Bauman, K. E., Arriaga, X. B., Helms, R. W., & Linder, G. F. (1998). An evaluation of Safe Dates, an adolescent dating violence prevention program. *American Journal of Public Health, 88,* 45–50.

Foshee, V. A., Bauman, K. E., Greene, W. F., Koch, G. G., Linder, G. F., & MacDougall, J. E. (2000). The Safe Dates program: 1-year follow-up results. *American Journal of Public Health, 90,* 1619–1622.

Foshee, V. A., Bauman, K. E., & Linder, G. F. (1999). Family violence and the perpetration of adolescent dating violence: Examining social learning and social control processes. *Journal of Marriage and the Family, 61,* 331–343.

Foshee, V. A., Linder, F., MacDougall, J. E., & Bangdiwala, S. (2001). Gender differences in the longitudinal predictors of adolescent dating violence. *Preventive Medicine: An International Journal Devoted to Practice and Theory, 32,* 128–141.

Goldbaum, S., Craig, W. M., Pepler, D., & Connolly, J. (2003). Developmental trajectories of victimization: Identifying risk and protective factors. *Journal of Applied School Psychology, 19*(2), 139–156.

Gray, H. M., & Foshee, V. (1997). Adolescent dating violence: Differences between one-sided and mutually violent profiles. *Journal of Interpersonal Violence, 12,* 141.

Grills, A. E., & Ollendick, T. H. (2002). Peer victimization, self-worth, and anxiety in middle school children. *Journal of Clinical Child and Adolescent Psychology, 31*(1), 59–68.

Grych, J. H., Kinsfogel, K., Hart, N., Klockow, L. L., & Robbins, D. (2003, April). *Investigating links between family relationships and abuse in adolescent dating relationships: Cognitive, affective, and attachment processes.* Paper presented at the meeting of the Society for Research in Child Development, Tampa, FL.

Hawker, O. S. J., & Boulton, M. J. (2000). Twenty years' research on peer victimization and psychosocial maladjustment: A meta-analytical review of cross-sectional studies. In *Annual Progress in Child Psychiatry and Child Development* (pp. 505–534). New York: Brunner-Routledge.

Hawkins, J. D., & Catalano, R. F. (1992). *Communities that care: Action for drug abuse prevention.* San Francisco: Jossey-Bass.

Henggeler, S. W., Schoenwald, S. K., Rowland, M. D., & Cunningham, P. B. (2002). *Serious emotional disturbance in children and adolescents: Multisystemic therapy.* New York: Guilford Press.

Hill, K. G., Howell, J. C., Hawkins, J. D., & Battin-Pearson, S. R. (1999). Childhood risk factors for adolescent gang membership: Results from the Seattle Social Development Project. *Journal of Research in Crime and Delinquency, 36*(3), 300–322.

Hodges, E. V., & Perry, D. G. (1999). Personal and interpersonal antecedents and consequences of victimization by peers. *Journal of Personality and Social Psychology, 76*(4), 677–685.

Hunter, J. A., Figueredo, A. J., Malamuth, N. M., & Becker, J. V. (2003). Juvenile sex offenders: Toward the development of a typology. *Sexual Abuse: Journal of Research and Treatment, 15,* 27–48.

Hunter, J., & Longo, R. E. (2004) Relapse prevention with juvenile sexual abusers: A holistic and integrated approach. In G. O'Reilly, W. Marshall, A. Carr, & R. C. Beckett (Eds.), *The handbook of clinical intervention with young people who sexually abuse* (pp. 297–314). New York: Brunner-Routledge.

Institute for Intergovernmental Research. (2007). *National Youth Gang Center.* Retrieved from http://www.iir.com/nygc/.

Jouriles, E. N., Wolfe, D. A., Garrido, E., & McCarthy, A. (2006). Relationship violence. In D. A. Wolfe & E. J. Mash (Eds.), *Behavioral and emotional disorders in adolescents* (pp. 621–641). New York: Guilford Press.

Kaltiala-Heino, R., Rimpela, M., Marttunen, M., Rimpela, A., & Rantanen, P. (1999). Bullying, depression and suicidal ideation in Finnish adolescents: School surveys. *British Medical Journal, 329,* 348–351.

Kazdin, A. E. (1997). Problem solving and parent management in treating aggressive and antisocial behavior. In E. D. Hibbs & P. S. Jensen (Eds.), *Psychosocial treatments for child and adolescent disorders: Empirically based strategies for clinical practice* (pp. 377–408). Washington, DC: American Psychological Association.

Kelly, B. T., Thornberry, T. P., & Smith, C. A. (1997). *In the wake of childhood maltreatment* [Pamphlet]. Washington, DC: U.S. Department of Justice.

Kerig, P. K. (1999). Gender issues in the effects of exposure to violence on children. *Journal of Emotional Abuse, 1,* 87–105.

Larson, J., & Lochman, J. E. (2002). *Helping school-children cope with anger: A cognitive-behavioral intervention.* New York: Guilford Press.

Letourneau, E. J., & Miner, M. H. (2005). Juvenile sex offenders: A case against the legal and clinical status quo. *Sexual Abuse: Journal of Research and Treatment, 17,* 293–312.

Leve, L. D., & Chamberlain, P. (2004). Female juvenile offenders: Defining an early-onset pathway for delinquency. *Journal of Child and Family Studies, 13,* 439–452.

Lochman, J. E., Wells, K. C., & Murray, M. (in press). The Coping Power program: Preventive intervention at the middle school transition. In P. Tolan, J. Szapocznik, & S. Sambrano (Eds.), *Preventing substance abuse: 3 to 14.* Washington, DC: American Psychological Association.

McMackin, R. A., Leisen, M. B., Sattler, L., Krinsley, K, & Riggs, D. S. (2002). Preliminary development of trauma-focused treatment groups for incarcerated juvenile offenders. *Journal of Aggression, Maltreatment, and Trauma, 6,* 175–199.

Messman-Moore, T. L., & Long, P. J. (2000). Child sexual abuse and revictimization in the form of adult sexual abuse, adult physical abuse, and adult psychological maltreatment. *Journal of Interpersonal Violence, 15,* 489–502.

Moffitt, T. E. (1993). Adolescence-limited and life-course persistent anti-social behavior: A developmental taxonomy. *Psychological Review, 100,* 674–701.

National Center for Juvenile Justice. (1999). *Juvenile offenders and their victims: 1999 national report.* Washington, DC: Office of Juvenile Justice and Delinquency Prevention

O'Keefe, M., & Treister, L. (1998). Victims of dating violence among high school students: Are the predictors different for males and females? *Violence Against Women, 4,* 195–223.

O'Leary, K. D., Barling, J., Arias, I., Rosenbaum, A., Malone, J., & Tyree, A. (1989). Prevalence and stability of physical aggression between spouses: A longitudinal analysis. *Journal of Consulting and Clinical Psychology, 57,* 263–268.

O'Leary, K. D., & Slep, A. M. (2003). A dyadic longitudinal model of adolescent dating aggression. *Journal of Clinical Child and Adolescent Psychology, 32,* 314–327.

Olweus, D. (1991). Bully/victim problems among schoolchildren: Basic facts and effects of a school-based intervention program. In D. Pepler & K. Rubin (Eds.), *The development and treatment of childhood aggression* (pp. 411–438). Hillsdale, NJ: Lawrence Erlbaum.

Olweus, D. (1993). *Bullying in schools: What we know and what we can do.* Cambridge, MA: Blackwell.

Olweus, D., Limber, S., & Mihalic, S. (1999). *The bullying prevention program: Blueprints for violence prevention.* Boulder, CO: Center for the Study and Prevention of Violence.

Osher, D., Van Acker, R., Morrison, G., Gable, R., Dwyer, K., & Quinn, M. M. (2004). Warning signs of problems in schools: Ecological perspectives and effective practices for combating school aggression and violence. *Journal of School Violence, 3,* 13–37.

Pellegrini, A. D. (2002). Bullying, victimization, and sexual harassment during the transition to middle school. *Educational Psychologist, 37,* 151–163.

Pepler, D. J., Craig, W. M., Connolly, J., & Henderson, K. (2002). Bullying, sexual harassment, dating violence, and substance use among adolescents. In C. Wekerle & A. M. Wall (Eds.), *Violence and addiction equation: Theoretical and clinical issues in substance use and relationship violence* (pp. 153–168). New York: Brunner-Routledge.

Pritchard, I. (1999). *Reducing class size: What do we know?* Washington, DC: U.S. Department of Education.

Purdie, V., & Downey, G. (2001). Rejection sensitivity and adolescent girls' vulnerability to relationship-centered difficulties. *Child Maltreatment, 5,* 338–350.

Rees, T. A. (1996). Joining the gang: A look at youth gang recruitment. *Journal of Gang Research, 4*(1), 19–25.

Reinke, W. M., & Herman, K. C. (2002). Creating school environments that deter antisocial behaviors in youth. *Psychology in the Schools, 39,* 549–560.

Resnick, M. D., Bearman, P. S., Blum, R. W., Bauman, K. E., Harris, K. M., Jones, J., et al. (1997). Protecting adolescents from harm: Findings from the National Longitudinal Study of Adolescent Health. *Journal of the American Medical Association, 278,* 823–832.

Roberts, T. A., Klein, J. D., & Fisher S. (2003). Longitudinal effect of intimate partner abuse on high-risk behavior among adolescents. *Archives of Pediatric Adolescent Medicine, 157,* 875–881.

Roecker-Phelps, C. E. (2001). Children's responses to overt and relational aggression. *Journal of Clinical Child Psychology, 30*(2), 240–252.

Rosenbluth, B. (2004). *Expect Respect: A support group curriculum for safe and healthy relationships.* Austin, TX: SafePlace.

Sampson, R. J., & Laub, J. H. (2005). A general age-graded theory of crime: Lessons learned and the future of life-course criminology. In D. Farrington (Ed.), *Advances in criminological theory: Testing integrated developmental/life course theories of offending* (Vol. 13, pp. 165–181). New Brunswick, NJ: Transaction.

Schwartz, B. K., Cavanaugh, D., Pimental, A., & Prentky, R. (2006). Descriptive study of precursors to sex offending among 813 boys and girls: Antecedent life experiences. *Victims and Offenders, 1,* 61–77.

Shure, M. B., & Spivack, G. (1988). Interpersonal cognitive problem-solving. In R. H. Price, E. L. Cowen, R. P. Lorion, & J. Ramos-McKay (Eds.), *Fourteen ounces of prevention: A casebook for practitioners* (pp. 69–82). Washington, DC: American Psychological Association.

Sickmund, M. (2004). *Juveniles in corrections* [Pamphlet]. Washington, DC: U.S. Department of Justice.

Silverman, J. G., Raj, A., Mucci, L., & Hathaway, M. J. (2001). Dating violence against adolescent girls and associated substance use, unhealthy weight control, sexual risk behavior, pregnancy, and suicidality. *Journal of the American Medical Association, 286,* 572–579.

Smith, P. H., White, J. W., & Holland, L. J. (2003). A longitudinal perspective on dating violence among adolescent and college-age women. *American Journal of Public Health, 93,* 1104–1109.

Smith, P. K., & Brain, P. (2000). Bullying in schools: Lessons from two decades of research. *Aggressive Behavior, 26,* 1–9.

Snyder, H. N. (2005). *Juvenile arrests 2003* [Pamphlet]. Washington, DC: U.S. Department of Justice.

Stattin, H., & Magnusson, D. (1990). *Pubertal maturation in female development.* Hillsdale, NJ: Lawrence Erlbaum.

Stein, N. (1995). Sexual harassment in school: The public performance of gendered violence. *Harvard Educational Review, 65,* 145–162.

Steinberg, L., & Scott, E. S. (2003). Less guilty by reason of adolescence: Developmental immaturity, diminished responsibility, and the juvenile death penalty. *American Psychologist, 58,* 1009–1018.

Stone, S. S. (1999). Risk factors associated with gang joining among youth. *Journal of Gang Research, 6*(2), 1–18.

Teplin, L. A., Elkington, K. S., McClelland, G. M., Abram, K. M., Mericle, A. A., & Washburn, J. J. (2005). Major mental disorders, substance use disorders, comorbidity, and HIV-AIDS risk behaviors in juvenile detainees. *Psychiatric Services, 56,* 823–828.

Thompson, K. M., Wonderlich, S. A., Crosby, R. D., & Mitchell, J. (2001). Sexual violence and weight control techniques among adolescent girls. *International Journal of Eating Disorders, 29,* 166–176.

Thornberry, T. P., Huizinga, D., & Loeber, R. (2004). *The causes and correlates study: Findings and policy implications* [Pamphlet]. Washington, DC: U.S. Department of Justice.

U.S. Department of Education. (2002). *Exemplary and promising school-based programs that promote safe, disciplined and drug-free schools.* Washington, DC: Author.

U.S. Department of Health and Human Services. (2001). *Youth violence: A report of the Surgeon General.* Washington, DC: Government Printing Office.

U.S. Department of Health and Human Services. (2002). *What you need to know about youth violence prevention.* Rockville, MD: U.S. Department of Health and Human Services, Substance Abuse and Mental Health Services Administration, Center for Mental Health Services.

Vandiver, D. M. (2006). A prospective analysis of juvenile male sex offenders. *Journal of Interpersonal Violence, 21,* 673–688.

van Wijk, A. P., Mali, S. R. F., & Bullens, R. A. R. (2007). Juvenile sex-only and sex-plus offenders. *International Journal of Offender Therapy and Comparative Criminology, 51,* 407–419.

van Wijk, A., Vermeiren, R., Loeber, R., Hart-Kerkhoffs, L., Doreleijers, T. & Bullens, R. (2006). Juvenile sex offenders compared to non-sex offenders: A review of the literature 1995–2005. *Trauma, Violence, & Abuse, 7,* 227–243.

Vizard, E., Monch, E., & Misch, P. (1995). Child and adolescent sex abuse perpetrators: A review of the research literature. *Journal of Child Psychology and Psychiatry, 36,* 731–756.

Waite, D., Keller, A., McGarvey, E. L., Wieckowski, E., Pinkerton, R., & Brown, G. L. (2005). Juvenile sex offender re-arrest rates for sexual, violent nonsexual and property crimes: A 10-year follow-up. *Sexual Abuse: Journal of Research and Treatment, 17,* 313–331.

Wasserman, G. A., McReynolds, L. S., Fisher, P., & Lucas, C. (2003). Psychiatric disorders in incarcerated youths. *Journal of the American Academy of Child and Adolescent Psychiatry, 42,* 1011–1021.

Webster-Stratton, C., & Reid, M. J. (2004). The Incredible Years parents, teachers, and children training series: A multifaceted treatment approach for young children with conduct problems. In A. E. Kazdin & J. R. Weisz (Eds.), *Evidence-based psychotherapies for children and adolescents* (pp. 224–240). New York: Guilford Press.

Wolfe, D. A., & Feiring, C. (2000). Dating violence through the lens of adolescent romantic relationships. *Child Maltreatment, 5,* 360–363.

Wolfe, D. A., & Jaffe, P. (2001). Prevention of domestic violence: Emerging initiatives. In S. Graham-Bermann & J. Edleson, (Eds.), *Domestic violence in the lives of children: The future of research, intervention, and social policy* (pp. 283–298). Washington, DC: American Psychological Association.

Wolfe, D. A., Jaffe, P., Wilson, S. K., & Zak, L. (1988). A multivariate investigation of children's adjustment to family violence. In G. Hotaling, D. Finkelhor, J. Kilpatrick, & M. Straus (Eds.), *Family abuse and its consequences: New directions in research* (pp. 228–241). Thousand Oaks, CA: Sage.

Wolfe, D. A., Scott, K., & Crooks, C. V. (2005). Abuse and violence in adolescent girls' dating relationships. In D. Bell, S. Foster, & E. Mash (Eds.), *Handbook of behavioral and emotional problems in girls* (pp. 381–414). New York: Plenum.

Wolfe, D. A., Wekerle, C., Scott, K., Straatman, A., & Grasley, C. (2004). Predicting abuse in adolescent dating relationships over 1 year: The role of child maltreatment and trauma. *Journal of Abnormal Psychology, 113,* 406–415.

Wolfe, D. A., Wekerle, C., Scott, K., Straatman, sA. L., Grasley, C., & Reitzel-Jaffe, D. (2003). Dating violence prevention with at-risk youth: A controlled outcome evaluation. *Journal of Consulting and Clinical Psychology, 71,* 279–291.

CHAPTER 8

Violence and the Elderly

Jeanette M. Daly

Violence against the elderly includes acts of aggression or abuse that intentionally or unintentionally cause injury to a person. *Elder mistreatment* is a form of violence against the elderly that usually involves abuse, neglect, or exploitation. Although an intent to cause harm is central to the concept of violence, it is sometimes absent from certain cases of elder mistreatment, such as when an older person is left alone, isolated, or forgotten.

Although we now recognize violence against the elderly as a crime, historically, elder abuse was viewed as a social problem. With the legislation of adult protective services statutes, mandatory reporting, and penalties for not reporting, elder abuse has been criminalized (Payne, Berg, & Toussaint, 2001). This criminalization requires law enforcement to intervene in elder abuse allegation investigations and to prevent further incidents (Blakely & Dolon, 2001; Davis & Medina-Ariza, 2001; Wolf, 1996).

CASE STUDY: MARY

A nurse aide, Mary, who was also a second-year nursing student, approached the nursing home Director of Nursing. She reported witnessing another nurse aide hitting a resident three times.

The resident, Herman, was a 68-year-old white male. He'd been a resident of the nursing home for two years. He was physically dependent on others for all his activities of daily living and had Alzheimer's disease. He was 5'8" tall and weighed 178 lbs. Herman had a habit of pinching and spitting on his caregivers.

(Continued)

(Continued)

Mary reported she and Melissa had been providing routine before-bed care, changing a soiled pad, washing Herman's perineal area, and putting on his nightgown. Herman pinched Melissa on her arm two times and spit on her face. Melissa hit him three times on his thigh and yelled at him with profanity to stop pinching and spitting.

Mary said she was scared of retaliation from Melissa for reporting her. The Director of Nursing had Mary put her story in writing. She informed Mary she was required by law to report this allegation to the State Department of Inspections and Appeals.

Prior to making the report, the Director of Nursing conducted her own investigation. She immediately went to Herman's room. She talked to him, but he was unable to answer any questions. She took his vital signs and performed a full assessment of his body, looking for any indications of his having been hit. There were no discolorations on his thighs. The Director of Nursing then called Herman's physician and daughter to report the allegation. All was documented in the medical record.

Melissa was scheduled to work the evening shift. When she came on duty, the Director of Nursing called Melissa into her office and explained the allegation. Melissa described how upset she was by being pinched and spit on. She didn't deny the incident. The Director of Nursing asked her to write down the experience as best she could recall it. Melissa did so. She then told Melissa she could continue working but could not care for Herman. She also explained to Melissa this report had to be filed with the Department of Inspections and Appeals.

At the conclusion of their meeting, the Director of Nursing placed her call to the state agency. In addition, she prepared a written report to the state and mailed it within 24 hours of the report.

State investigators were required to investigate the allegation within 21 days of receiving the report. After the investigation, there was a court hearing and Melissa lost her nurse aide certificate. The allegation of physical abuse was founded.

Definitions of Elder Abuse

Elder mistreatment can be categorized as domestic or institutional elder abuse. Elder mistreatment refers to

> (a) intentional actions that cause harm or create a serious risk of harm (whether or not harm is intended) to a vulnerable elder by a caregiver of other person who stands in a trust relationship to the elder or (b) failure by a caregiver to satisfy the elder's basic needs or to protect the elder from harm. (National Research Council, 2003, p. 1)

Maltreatment may be in the form of abandonment, emotional/psychological abuse, financial/material exploitation, neglect, physical abuse, sexual abuse, or verbal abuse. *Institutional abuse* consists of the same maltreatments but affects elders in care facilities and includes additional types of abuse, such as involuntary seclusion and resident-to-resident abuse. *Self-neglect* implies that the elderly are not caring for their own needs and are causing a threat to their own health or safety; it can include behaviors such as hoarding, failure to take essential medications or refusal to seek medical treatment for serious illness, leaving a burning stove unattended, poor hygiene, and inability to attend to housekeeping (National Research Council, 2003).

For the purposes of this chapter, the term *elder abuse* will be used to encompass all forms of abuse, neglect, and exploitation. The National Center on Elder Abuse (2006) provides definitions of different types of abuse: physical, emotional, and sexual abuse; exploitation; neglect; and abandonment (see Table 8.1).

In an institutional setting, abuse and neglect take on different meanings than in a domestic setting. Resident-to-resident abuse can involve any of the types of abuse described above. "Whenever people live and work together—and especially when one group is dependent on another for basics of everyday life—there is the potential for abuse" (Livengood, 1980, p. 29). Situations that have been reported include elopement from an institution, involuntary seclusion, bathing residents in whirlpool baths in which bedpans are cleaned (Thompson, 1997), manual evacuation of fecal impactions without consent (Castledine, 2000), and undertreating pain (Greene, 2001). Consequences of institutional neglect are poor hygiene, skin lesions, dehydration, malnutrition, pressure ulcers, urine burns and excoriation, contractures, delirium, vermin infestation, and accelerated functional decline (Aziz & Campbell-Taylor, 1999; Fulmer & Ashley, 1989; Glendenning, 1999; Gold, 2000; Hawes, 2003; Kimsey, Tarbox, & Bragg, 1981; MacLean, 1995; Tammelleo, 1999).

Table 8.1 Definitions of Elder Abuse

- *Physical Abuse:* Inflicting, or threatening to inflict, physical pain or injury on a vulnerable elder or depriving him or her of a basic need.
- *Emotional Abuse:* Inflicting mental pain, anguish, or distress on an elder person through verbal or nonverbal acts.
- *Sexual Abuse:* Nonconsensual sexual contact of any kind.
- *Exploitation:* Illegal taking, misuse, or concealment of funds, property, or assets of a vulnerable elder.
- *Neglect:* Refusal or failure by those responsible to provide food, shelter, health care, or protection for a vulnerable elder.
- *Abandonment:* The desertion of a vulnerable elder by anyone who has assumed the responsibility for care or custody of that person.

Incidence and Prevalence

Estimates of abuse prevalence in domestic and institutional settings have been calculated in an attempt to define the extent of elder abuse. Most studies are based on local data and cannot reliably be extrapolated to the entire U.S. To some extent, the wide variations in the findings of prevalence studies on elder abuse reflect major differences in the research methods employed by the studies. Variations include differences in operational definition and measurement of elder abuse, types of abuse, definition of incidence or prevalence, sample size and sampling method, location and method of data collection, and patient population.

Incidence is the number of new occurrences of elder abuse in a population over a period of time. Incidence rates use new cases in the numerator, and individuals with a history of elder abuse are not included. The denominator for incidence rates is the population at risk. For domestic elder abuse incidence rates, the population at risk is persons 60 years and older.

Prevalence is the measure of elder abuse in a population at a given point in time, usually referred to as *point prevalence.* Prevalence can also be measured over a period of time, such as a year, in which case it is referred to as *period prevalence.* Period prevalence is a common measure of prevalence used in epidemiological studies and often is expressed as a percentage. Prevalence of elder abuse and incidence of elder abuse are neither identical nor equivalent measures. The measures refer to the rate at which people suffer elder abuse (incidence) versus the total number actually being abused at any given time (prevalence).

Community Prevalence

To identify the incidence or prevalence of elder abuse, data from various sources, such as adult protective service/human services agencies' reports (Hajjar & Duthie, 2001; Jogerst, Daly, Brinig, Dawson, Schmuch, & Ingram, 2003), probability samples of elderly in a community (Comijs, Pot, Smit, Bouter, & Jonker, 1998; Ogg & Bennett, 1992; Pillemer & Finkelhor, 1988), and surveys of healthcare personnel working with the elderly, have been used (Kivela, Kongas-Saviaro, Kesti, Pahkala, & Ijas, 1992; National Center on Elder Abuse, 1998; Ockleford et al., 2003; Saveman & Sandvide, 2001; Yan & Tang, 2001).

A major epidemiological study on the prevalence of elder abuse was conducted with a random sample survey of all elders in the Boston metropolitan area. Through a two-stage interview process, 2,020 interviews were conducted; only those identified as abuse victims in the first interview were interviewed a second time (Pillemer & Finkelhor, 1988). Physical abuse was measured as period prevalence for victims who had suffered one act of physical violence since they had turned 65 years of age. Neglect was measured as period prevalence for victims who, in the past year, had been deprived 10 or more times of some assistance that they needed for important activities of daily living. Psychological abuse was measured as period prevalence for victims who, in the past year, had suffered verbal aggression 10 or more times. For this sample, reported domestic elder abuse (excluding self-neglect and financial exploitation) was 32 per 1,000 elders; physical aggression was 20 per 1,000; verbal aggression 11 per 1,000; and neglect 4 per 1,000.

Investigators in other countries have attempted to replicate Pillemer and Finkelhor's (1988) epidemiological study on the prevalence of elder abuse. Comijs and colleagues (1998) replicated this study in Amsterdam using similar definitions of abuse and period prevalence; they added financial mistreatment and considered a category of "other familiar and trusted people" as possible victims. The one-year prevalence of overall abuse and types of abuse are reported in Table 8.2. For comparison purposes, the prevalence for the period since the respondent reached 65 years of age was 3.9% for physical aggression and 4.8% for financial mistreatment. Physical aggression was almost twice as prevalent as that reported by Pillemer and Finkelhor (1988). However, Comijs and colleagues (1998) note they did not limit responses on the Conflict Tactics Scale to a spouse, one co-resident child, and one member of the elder's social network, as did Pillemer and Finkelhor. Ogg and Bennett (1992) reported a higher percentage of verbal abuse compared to the other two studies using the same instruments (see Table 8.2).

Using APS agency reports, percentage prevalence of elder abuse has been calculated for specific states and the entire U.S. Hajjar and Duthie (2001) analyzed the Wisconsin APS dataset for 1996, reporting an overall abuse

Table 8.2 Percentage Prevalence of Abuse Categorized by Type of Study

	Overall Abuse	Physical Abuse	Verbal Abuse	Financial Abuse	Neglect
Probability Samples					
Comijs et al. (1998)	5.6	1.2	3.2	1.4	0.2
Ogg and Bennett (1992)	8.8	1.7	5.6	1.5	
Pillemer and Finkelhor (1988)	3.2	2	1.1		.04
APS Agency Reports					
Jogerst, Daly, Brinig et al. (2003)	2.7				
Hajjar and Duthie (2001)	.02				
Pavlik et al. (2001)	1.3				

percentage of .02 for physical, emotional, and financial abuse; neglect by others; and self-neglect. Results by type of abuse were not available. Pavlik, Hyman, Festa, and Dyer (2001) reported on Texas reports that indicated an overall prevalence of elder abuse of 1.3%. In 1995, the number of elder abuse reports was 274,550, with a substantiation at 63% (Tatara & Kuzmeskus, 1997). Jogerst, Daly, Brinig, and colleagues (2003) collected APS reports for one year, eliminated adult reports from APS data, and found 242,430 recorded investigations of domestic elder abuse in 47 states for 1999, that is, 5.5 investigations per 1,000 elders. They also reported 102,879 substantiations in 35 states, or 2.7 substantiations per 1,000 elders (see Table 8.2).

Institutional Prevalence

In 2004, the U.S. had 16,100 nursing homes with approximately 1.5 million residents (Centers for Disease Control and Prevention, 2007). Sparse research has been conducted on the prevalence of institutional elder/dependent adult abuse. Prevalence figures have been provided by researchers, the National Ombudsman Reporting System (NORS), and the Centers for Medicare and Medicaid Services (CMS).

Nursing home prevalence has been documented by gathering opinions of health care professionals, rather than by gathering information directly from elders. In a random sample survey of 577 nursing home nurses and nurse aides, 36% of the respondents had witnessed an incident of physical abuse in the preceding year, 81% had observed an incident of psychological abuse, and 10% of the respondents admitted to committing one or more abusive acts (Pillemer & Moore, 1989). In another study, 27 randomly selected nurse aides from 3 nursing homes were interviewed and 93% of the aides had seen or heard of residents being abused and neglected (Mercer, Heacock, & Beck, 1993). More than half of Pennsylvania nursing home administrators and ombudsmen perceived that about 60% of institutional elder abuse cases are unreported (Peduzzi, Watzlaf, Rohrer, & Rubinstein, 1997). With 90% of the nursing homes in Iowa responding to a mailed questionnaire, the annual rate of abusive events was 20.7 per 1,000 nursing home residents, with a rate of 18.4 reported events and 5.2 substantiated events (Jogerst, Daly, Dawson, Peek-Asa, & Schmuch, 2006).

Yearly, states are required to collect the NORS data from ombudsmen and report it to the Administration on Aging (AOA). One reporting category concerning residents' rights is "abuse, gross neglect, and exploitation," which is a sum of the following specific categories of abuse: physical abuse, sexual abuse, verbal/psychological abuse, financial exploitation, gross neglect, resident-to-resident sexual abuse, and other (AOA, 2002). In 2005, there were 15,814 complaints of abuse, gross neglect, and exploitation (AOA, 2006).

CMS implemented a federal complaint/incident system in 2004 with the stated purpose of helping to promote and protect the health, safety, and welfare of residents receiving health care services. The number of incidents and complaints that had been reported, investigated, and substantiated in 2004 was obtained through a Freedom of Information Act request (#CO6FO10249W) to CMS. There were 8,022 reported complaints from 48 states and the District of Columbia, a rate of 7.5 per 1,000 nursing home residents. There were 7,547 complaint investigations (6.5 per 1,000 nursing home residents) and 1,239 complaint substantiations (1.5 per 1,000 nursing home residents).

Who Abuses and Who Is Abused

Elder abuse perpetrators are nonfamily members as well as family members, may be in a position of control or authority, or may be anyone who establishes a relationship of trust with an older person. In domestic settings, the perpetrator in almost 90% of incidents of elder mistreatment is a family member, most commonly adult children (Boldy, Horner, Crouchley, & Davey, 2005; Brozowski & Hall, 2004). Caregivers are also at risk for inflicting elder abuse, and those who suffer from psychological impairment or substance abuse or have a history of child abuse may be at higher risk for inflicting abuse (Barker & Himchak, 2006; Ramsey-Klawsnik, 2003). These statistics reflect the unfortunate fact that vulnerable elders sometimes need protection from their own caregivers. Older persons in a shared living situation face a higher risk of abuse than those living alone (Lachs, Williams, O'Brien, Hurst, & Horwitz, 1997; Pillemer & Finkelhor, 1988; Pillemer & Suitor, 1992). In the institutional setting, the main perpetrators are professional caregivers unrelated to the victim (Payne & Cikovic, 1995).

Substance abuse by the perpetrator or victim is one of the leading causes of all types of abuse. Persons with alcohol or substance abuse problems may have difficulty holding jobs or have no source of income, and thus need to live with someone and seek support for their dependency. Households then may become the base of operation for drug use or trafficking. Violence is more apt to occur when the perpetrator is under the influence. The typical perpetrator is a family member or caregiver who has substance abuse or mental health problems, has a controlling personality, and is under financial or emotional distress (Clarke & Ogg, 1994; Greenberg, McKibben, & Raymond, 1990; Powell & Berman, 2006).

Victims of elder abuse share common characteristics, particularly the vulnerability of an older person who is dependent on others for care because of physical or cognitive impairment. In addition to common characteristics of the victim, there are common characteristics of perpetrators, such as stress or psychopathology in the abuser that causes him or her to be abusive. These similarities may provide caseworkers and investigators with predictive information about likely perpetrators as well as likely victims. Collectively, this information is referred to as *victimology,* the study of victims (see Chapter 15). It is possible that through an in-depth examination of the victims—that is, taking an accurate and thorough history, conducting a physical examination of the victim and an in-home assessment— the perpetrator may be discovered.

Certain demographic characteristics of victims have been noted to be predictors of elder abuse. Victims are more likely to be older (Lachs, Berkman, Fulmer, & Horwitz, 1994; Lachs, Williams, O'Brien, Hurst, & Horwitz, 1996; Pillemer & Finkelhor, 1988); persons 75 years and older are abused and neglected two to three times more often than the overall elderly population (Lachs et al., 1994; Wolf & Pillemer, 1989). In addition, victims are more likely to be female (National Center on Elder Abuse, 1998), be married (Pillemer & Finkelhor, 1988; Podnieks, 1992), have low educational attainment, have low income, be socially isolated, have poor social networks, and be persons of color (Lachs et al., 1994, 1996, 1997; Shugarman, Fries, Wolf, & Morris, 2003; Wolf & Li, 1999).

Recent evidence indicates that elder abuse is associated with a range of adverse health outcomes. Substantiated reports of elder abuse have been linked to increased dementia and depression (Coyne, Reichman, & Berbig, 1993; Dyer, Pavlik, Murphy, & Hyman, 2000; Pillemer & Suitor, 1992), stroke (Homer & Gilleard, 1990), and shorter life span, after adjusting for other factors related to increased mortality in older adults (Lachs, Williams, O'Brien, Pillemer, & Charlson, 1998). Other findings indicate that older women who experience abuse are likely to consult practitioners with conditions such as physical injuries, gynecological complaints, gastrointestinal disorders, fatigue, headache, myalgias, depression, and anxiety (Mouton & Espino, 1999). Dementia sufferers are also more likely to experience abuse (Coyne et al., 1993; Dyer et al., 2000; Paveza et al., 1992).

Treatment, Intervention, and Legislation

Prevention of elder abuse requires the involvement of multiple sectors of society. Interventions for prevention of elder abuse have been suggested but have not been tested. The National Research Council (2003) notes, "no efforts have yet been made to develop, implement, and evaluate interventions based on scientifically grounded hypotheses about the cases of elder mistreatment, and no systematic research has been conducted to measure and evaluate the effects of existing interventions" (p. 121). Appropriate interventions for preventing elder abuse could include legislation, respite care, social support, and money management programs. Education and dissemination of information are other vital interventions both for health care professionals and the general public.

Legislation

All 50 states and the District of Columbia have enacted state laws governing domestic elder abuse and institutional abuse. State laws for domestic elder abuse are typically administered by the state adult protective services programs. Currently, no federal legislation governs domestic elder abuse, but the Federal Nursing Home Reform Act or the Omnibus Budget Reconciliation Act of 1987 (OBRA 1987) governs institutional abuse and the long-term care ombudsman programs. In addition to federal law, states have enacted legislation on institutional care and services, some of which have more requirements than the federal law. Other state laws pertaining to the function of long-term care ombudsman programs, the Medicaid Fraud Control Unit, and prosecution of certain types of abuse may contain some elder abuse components, although providing elderly people with protective services is not their primary purpose.

Adult Protective Services Legislation

Most states have adult protective service laws and some states have specific elder abuse laws (Tatara, 1995). In 1965, the Older Americans Act was passed and established programs that offer services and opportunities for older Americans. In 1973, Area Agencies on Aging were established by amendments to the Act and, in 1974, Congress mandated protective services programs for adults under Title XX of the Social Security Act (Administration on Aging, 2004). These adult protective services programs provide a system of preventive, supportive, and surrogate services for the elderly living in the community, to enable them to maintain independent living and avoid abuse and exploitation. The primary intent in most jurisdictions has been to implement a reporting and investigative mechanism to identify victims or potential victims of abuse and make available community services for the well-being of citizens.

In the United States, a basic legal foundation has been established to protect the elderly from various forms of maltreatment. Some laws are more comprehensive than others, and their content varies widely in scope of coverage and types of provisions. For example, in their APS-related statutes, all states except Maryland and New York have a comprehensive definition of elder/dependent adult abuse, but Indiana has no definition of abuse (Daly & Jogerst, 2001). Reviews of the APS-related statutes have been conducted (Loue, 2001; Roby & Sullivan, 2000; Tatara, 1995), but understanding the association between the law and elder abuse reports and investigations provides a different viewpoint.

To evaluate the impact of state APS legislation on the rates of investigated and substantiated domestic elder abuse, elder abuse data were collected from APS administrators for one year in all states and the District of Columbia, and APS legislation was reviewed and coded. In this study, a *report* meant an allegation of abuse was received by APS and an *investigation* was conducted to evaluate the potential victim. *Substantiation* meant that the evaluation found that abuse had occurred, according to state law. Higher investigation rates were associated with mandatory reporting requirements and the presence of a clause in the statute imposing penalties for failure to report elder abuse (Jogerst, Daly, Brinig, Dawson, Schmuch, & Ingram, 2003). Six states (Colorado, New Jersey, New York, North Dakota, South Dakota, and Wisconsin) do not require mandatory reporters. The statutes' terminology regarding mandatory reporters, whether it listed all types of mandatory reporters or just said "any person," was not significantly associated with higher rates of abuse reports, investigations, or substantiations (Daly, Jogerst, Brinig, & Dawson, 2003).

Substantiation ratios (substantiated rates divided by investigation rates) were higher in states that have more abuse definitions in the regulations and in states that have separate caseworkers for child and elder abuse investigations. Eleven states have caseworkers who investigate child, adult, and elder abuse allegations. The 16 states that track or record reports of abuse prior to investigation had higher rates of investigations, substantiations, and substantiation ratios. This relationship with tracking reports remained significant at the $p < 0.05$ level after controlling for total expenditures on APS agency services per capita (Jogerst, Daly, Brinig et al., 2003).

Health care providers and other professionals dealing with elder abuse should be familiar with their state's legislation, the local APS agency, community resources, and police and sheriff's departments. The APS organizational structure, APS Web site, hotline telephone number for reporting domestic abuse, and Web site for each state's legislation are provided in Appendix A.

Nursing Home Legislation

Each state and the District of Columbia have established licensing and recertification legislation that provides for the development, establishment, and enforcement of basic standards for the health, care, and treatment of persons in nursing homes and for the maintenance and operation of such institutions to ensure the safe, adequate, and appropriate care, treatment, and health of persons in those facilities. Nursing home complaint investigation procedures are established by each state's legislation, and minimum standards have been set by the Federal Nursing Home

Reform Act to ensure that residents of nursing homes receive quality care that will result in their achieving or maintaining their physical, mental, and psychosocial well-being (National Long Term Care Ombudsman Resource Center, 2001). Included in this legislation is the requirement that a nursing home be licensed in order to operate, as well as requirements for annual unannounced inspections, a procedure for handling complaints, prohibition of discrimination, sanctions for violation, and provisions for licensure suspension and revocation. Any reports of alleged abuse or violations are investigated by the state regulatory agency.

When a suspicious injury or outright abuse has been observed or suspected concerning persons residing in nursing homes, the facility administrator or health care providers must report it. The state's licensing authority must inspect the complaint, which may or may not be substantiated. Investigation for Medicaid fraud, a malpractice suit for personal injury, or criminal charges may be the end result of an investigation (MacLean, 2000).

Jurisdiction regarding nursing home laws is inconsistent across states; some are merged with hospital licensure and some are independent. These laws contain specific sections regarding annual surveys for re-licensure, civil and criminal penalties, deficiencies, discharge and transfer of residents, end-of-life treatment, inspection, licensure, nurse aide registry, reporting abuse, residents' rights, and more. Fourteen of these licensure and recertification of nursing home state statutes have text specifically addressing the topic of abuse reports and investigation in the nursing homes (Daly & Jogerst, 2007). The main issues addressed in those sections are reporting requirements, mandatory reporting, and definitions.

Abuse reports are classified as complaints or incidents. A *complaint* is a report made to the state agency or regional office by anyone other than the administrator or authorized official for a provider or supplier that alleges noncompliance with Federal and/or state laws and regulations. An *incident* is an official notification to the state agency or regional office from a self-reporting provider or supplier (i.e., the administrator or authorized official for the provider or supplier) that results in an onsite survey (U.S. Department of Health and Human Services, 2005). A report of an allegation of abuse is either an incident or a complaint, not both.

Few reviews of the licensure and recertification statutes (Daly & Jogerst, 2006; Daly & Jogerst, 2007) have been conducted, but understanding the association between these laws and nursing home abuse reports and investigations provides insight into the role of the law. When evaluating the effect of state legislation (adult protective service, nursing home licensure and recertification, and long-term care ombudsman), census demographics, nursing home characteristics, staffing and deficiencies, and nursing home resident characteristics on the rates of reported, investigated, and substantiated nursing home mistreatment, investigators found that the enactment of nursing home statutes that require the facility to report abuse and contain abuse definitions different from APS definitions is associated with lower incident outcomes (Jogerst, Daly, & Hartz, in press).

Health care providers and other professionals dealing with elder abuse should be familiar with their state's licensure and recertification legislation. Fifteen licensure and recertification statutes require health care professionals to be mandatory reporters of abuse allegations in the nursing home. Six licensure and recertification statutes require the facility to report abuse allegations. Appendix B lists the licensure and recertification agencies, by state.

Respite Care

Respite care is temporary or short-term care that provides relief for caregivers and families from their daily routine and stress of caregiving. The term *respite care* can describe a very diverse set of services. Respite care can be provided in different settings that are convenient for the situation, such as the person's home, an institution, or adult day care (Townsend & Kosloski, 2002) and by trained or untrained or licensed staff or volunteers. Respite care may involve one day or many days and may be overnight or just through the day. "Respite is one way that the strain of caregiving may be relieved" (Nicoll, Ashworh, McNally, & Newman, 2002), and it could be considered a method of preventing elder abuse.

The stress of caring for someone 24 hours a day impacts the caregiver's psychological well-being. Through in-depth qualitative interviews with caregivers, researchers identified the need to support the caregiver's role (Lane, McKenna, Ryan, & Fleming, 2003). In-home respite was suggested as a means to relieve the burden without causing additional problems for the dependent person by relocating him or her. Factors related to client satisfaction have been identified and indicate that caregivers who were able to dress the dependent person and transport him or her to adult day care services were more satisfied than those caregivers who were unable to do so (Montgomery, Marquis, Schaefer, & Kosloski, 2002; Townsend & Kosloski, 2002). A pilot weekend respite program found that caregivers need to be reassured that their loved ones are safe in a respite program and that both the caregiver and the dependent person benefit from the experience (Perry & Bontinen, 2001). In addition, social support is an important factor in a caregiver's satisfaction with respite care (Nicoll et al., 2002), and family support relieves caregiver burden (Lane et al., 2003).

A meta-analysis of respite interventions was planned to determine its effect on caregivers (McNally, Ben-Shlomo, & Newman, 1999). Twenty-nine studies were usable for analysis, but because of the variety of respite interventions offered, a true meta-analysis was not able to test for moderator effects by treatment type. Results indicated that "although caregivers often exhibit improvements in well-being during respite periods, these gains are short-lived" (p. 13), suggesting the respite does not provide a long-term social support system. Evidence from a more recent meta-analysis has similar findings that respite has a small effect upon caregiver burden and mental and physical health (Mason et al., 2007).

Social Support

Social support is the physical and emotional comfort given to a person by his or her family, friends, coworkers, and others. Social support can be very diverse; it can be formal or informal, a single person or a network of people, and continuous or intermittent. It is the knowledge that one is part of a community of people who love and care for one.

Caregivers have identified a need for social support, which varies with an individual's stage of life, length of time as a caregiver, and the acuity and intensity of the caregiving situation (Norbeck, Chaftez, Skodol-Wilson, & Weiss, 1991). For example, care for persons who have total hip replacements is dramatically different from care for persons with dementia. A meta-analysis of 18 studies providing interventions for caregiver distress demonstrated respite services and individual psychosocial interventions (effect .41 for burden and effect .58 for emotional dysphoria) were moderately effective, and group psychosocial interventions had a .31 effect size for emotional dysphoria and .15 effect for burden, thus being slightly effective (Knight, Lutzky, & Macofsky-Urban, 1993). In another literature review, the effectiveness of mental health interventions for long-term caregivers of highly dependent persons concluded that psychosocial interventions promoting support and coping help reduce caregiver stress (Tilford, Delaney, & Vogels, 1997).

In a qualitative study, four themes of caregiver support were identified: need for a social life, need for instrumental support, need for informational support, and need for emotional support (Ploeg, Biehler, Willison, Hutchison, & Blythe, 2001). It was recommended that telephone support services have the potential to provide informational, emotional, and social support. Caregiver support groups can help alleviate the stress and strain of caregiving. The research literature provides a wealth of information on social support and its measurement, but it has not been tested as an intervention to prevent elder abuse.

Money Management Programs

Intervention trials to prevent exploitation have not been completed, but daily money management (DMM) programs have emerged as a result of professionals in diverse settings observing their clients having exploitation problems. DMM programs assist people who have difficulty managing their personal financial affairs, which includes preparing checks, making bank deposits, dispensing cash, negotiating with creditors, maintaining home payroll for attendants, and calculating federal and state taxes. Educators, client advocates, debt managers, bill payers, paying agents, representative payees, attorneys-in-fact, trustees, and guardians are all professionals who have roles in DMM programs (Nerenberg, 2003).

Wilber (1991) examined whether DMM services would divert vulnerable older persons from conservatorship (a legal arrangement under which an individual is appointed by the court to manage the affairs of an adult). Sixty-three community residents, aged 60 to 96, were assigned to customary screening or to money management groups. After 12 months of intervention, there were no significant differences in rates of conservatorship between the groups, suggesting DMM programs do not divert persons from conservatorships.

Education

Elder mistreatment education for health care professionals and the public is a component of most agencies involved in investigating and providing services for persons at risk and actual victims of elder abuse. A Cochrane review was conducted to assess the effects of printed educational materials in improving the behavior of health care professionals and patient outcomes; the review compared printed material with either no intervention or educational packages. Findings indicated the printed educational materials had uncertain clinical significance and that audit and feedback and conferences/workshops did not appear to substantially change practices (Freemantle, Harvey, Wolf, Grimshaw, Grilli, & Bero, 2000).

Community Setting

Iowa is the only state that requires education for mandatory reporters of elder abuse. Other states require education for reporters of child abuse. In Iowa, a person required to report allegations of dependent adult abuse has to complete two hours of training within six months of initial employment and every five years thereafter (Iowa Code § 235B.1). The dependent adult abuse may occur in a community or institutional setting. A comparison of the investigation and substantiation rates for elder abuse allegations before and after July, 1988, when the Iowa statute was revised to ensure training of mandatory reporters, revealed that elder abuse investigation and substantiation rates did not change (Jogerst, Daly, Dawson, Brinig, & Schmuch,

2003). If the desired outcome of required training for mandatory reporters is to increase the number of reports of elder abuse, it has not been evidenced in Iowa.

Institutional Setting

In an institutional setting, Pillemer and Hudson (1993) developed and implemented a model abuse prevention curriculum for nursing assistants. The eight-module curriculum included video, lectures, problem solving, role-playing, and group support (Hudson, 1992). Using a pretest/posttest design following the intervention, they found the number of conflicts with residents had declined and a reduction in resident aggression was reported; no effect size was reported. Another educational intervention consisting of a video, booklet, and interactive workshop was conducted with nursing assistants in nursing facilities in Hawaii. The pretest/posttest design after the intervention indicated improved job satisfaction by a mean of 1 (Braun, Suzuki, Cusick, & Howard-Carhart, 1997).

In a randomized controlled trial, investigators measured whether attendance at an educational course was superior to duplicate printed material on elder abuse alone. Final group sizes were 31 and 33, and findings revealed the knowledge instrument was reliable and valid; knowledge was increased significantly for the group who took the educational course (OR 6.8), but learning was not associated with attitude change or the burnout score (Richardson, Kitchen, & Livingston, 2002). Suitably targeted educational courses/seminars tailored to the participants' pre-existing knowledge are recommended. Educational interventions conducted have been varied by setting, participants, content, and instructional method. These interventions have demonstrated some utility in prevention or reduction of elder abuse.

Conclusion

Actual prevalence of elder abuse is unknown in any setting. Estimates of overall abuse range from 3.2% to 8.8%. The typical elder abuse victim is a socially isolated married female, 75 years or older, with low socioeconomic status and poor education. It is evident that legislation and public policy have an impact on elder abuse rates, but there are other interventions that may also be beneficial. Differentiating the types of elder abuse and knowing the prevalence of each type may provide useful information for the development and testing of interventions to prevent elder abuse.

Appendix A Organizational Structure of State Agencies With Adult Protective Services

State	Organizational Structure	APS Website	Hotline	State Law Website
Alabama	Department of Human Resources: Adult Protective Services Division	http://www.dhr.state.al.us/page.asp?pageid=274	1-800-458-7214	http://www.legislature.state.al.us/ALISHome.html
Alaska	Department of Health and Social Services: Division of Senior and Disabilities Services: APS	http://www.hss.state.ak.us/dsds/aps.htm	1-800-478-9996 (in state), 1-907-269-3666 (outside of Alaska)	http://www.legis.state.ak.us/folhome.htm
Arizona	Department of Economic Security: Division of Aging & Adult Services: APS	https://www.azdes.gov/aaa/programs/aps/	1-877-767-2385	http://www.azleg.state.az.us/ArizonaRevisedStatutes.asp
Arkansas	Department of Human Services: Division of Aging and Adult Services: APS; Adult Protective Services	http://www.aradultprotection.com/	1-800-482-8049	http://170.94.58.9/data/ar_code.asp
California	Health and Human Services Agency: Department of Social Services: Disability and Adult Programs Division: Adult Programs Branch: APS	http://www.cdss.ca.gov/agedblinddisabled/PG1298.htm	1-888-436-3600	http://www.leginfo.ca.gov/callaw.html

State	Organizational Structure	APS Website	Hotline	State Law Website
Colorado	Department of Human Services: Division of Aging and Adult Services: APS	http://www.cdhs.state.co.us/aas/adultprotection_index.htm	1-800-773-1366	http://www.leg.state.co.us/
Connecticut	Department of Social Services: Bureau of Aging, Community, and Social Work Services: Protective Services Unit: Protective Services for the Elderly (PSE)	http://www.ct.gov/dss/cwp/view.asp?a=2353&q=305232	1-888-385-4225 (in state), 1-800-203-1234 (out of state)	http://www.cga.ct.gov/asp/menu/Statutes.asp
Delaware	Department of Health and Social Services: Division of Services for Aging and Adults with Physical Disabilities: Adult Protective Services Program	http://www.dhss.delaware.gov/dhss/dsaapd/aps.html	1-800-223-9074	http://delcode.delaware.gov/index.shtml
Florida	Department of Children & Families: Adult Services: Adult Protective Services Program	http://www.dcf.state.fl.us/as/	1-800-962-2873	https://www.flrules.org/default.asp
Georgia	Department of Human Resources: Division of Aging Services: APS	http://aging.dhr.georgia.gov/portal/site/DHR-DAS/menuitem.9e91405d0e4	1-888-774-0152	http://www.legis.state.ga.us/cgi-bin/gl_codes_detail.pl?code=1-1-1

(Continued)

State	Organizational Structure	APS Website	Hotline	State Law Website
		24e248e738510 da1010a0/?vgnextoid=01826 7b27edb0010VgnVCM10000 0bf01010aRCRD		
Hawaii	Department of Human Services: Social Services Division: Adult and Community Care Services Branch	http://hawaii.gov/health/eoa/	Oahu: 1-808-832-5115, Hilo/Hamakua/Puna: 1-808-933-8820, Kona/Kohala/Kamuela/Kau: 1-808-327-280, Kauai: 1-808-241-3432, Molokai/Maui: 1-808-243-5151, Lanai: 1-808-565-7104	http://www.capitol.hawaii.gov /site1/docs/docs.asp?press1= docs
Idaho	Idaho Commission on Aging: Area Agencies on Aging: APS	http://www.idahoaging.com/ programs/ps_adultprotect .htm	1-877-471-2777	http://www.legislature.idaho .gov/statutesrules.htm
Illinois	Department on Aging: Division of Older American Services: Bureau of Elder Rights: Elder Abuse and Neglect Program (in conjunction with Area Agencies on Aging)	http://www.state.il.us/aging/ 1abuselegal/abuse.htm	1-866-800-1409	http://www.illinois.gov/govern ment/gov_legislature.cfm

State	Organizational Structure	APS Website	Hotline	State Law Website
Indiana	Family and Social Services Administration: Division of Aging: APS	http://www.in.gov/fssa/da/2652.htm	1-800-992-6978	http://www.in.gov/legislative/ic/code/
Iowa	Department of Human Services: Division of Children and Family Services: APS	http://www.dhs.state.ia.us/Consumers/Safety_and_Protection/Abuse_Reporting/Dependent AdultAbuse.html	1-800-362-2178	http://www.legis.state.ia.us/
Kansas	Department of Social and Rehabilitation Services: APS	http://www.srskansas.org/ISD/ees/adult.htm	1-800-922-5330 (in state), 1-785-296-0044 (outside of Kansas)	http://www.kslegislature.org/legsrv-legisportal/index.do
Kentucky	Cabinet for Families and Children: Department for Community Based Services: Division for Protection and Permanency: Adult Protective Services Branch	http://chfs.ky.gov/dcbs/dpp/facs.htm	1-800-752-6200	http://www.lrc.ky.gov/Statrev/frontpg.htm
Louisiana	Department of Health and Hospitals: Office of Aging and Adult Services: APS	http://goea.louisiana.gov/eps.htm	1-800-259-4990	http://www.legis.state.la.us/

(Continued)

Appendix A (Continued)

State	Organizational Structure	APS Website	Hotline	State Law Website
Maine	Department of Health and Human Services: Office of Elder Services: APS	http://www.maine.gov/dhhs/beas/aps.htm	1-800-624-8404	http://janus.state.me.us/legis/
Maryland	Department of Human Resources: Community Services Administration: Office of Adult Services: APS	http://www.dhr.state.md.us/how/srvadult/protect.htm	1-800-917-7383	http://mlis.state.md.us/
Massachusetts	Executive Office of Elder Affairs: Aging Services Access Points: Protective Services Program	http://www.mass.gov/?pageID=eldershomepage&L=1&L0=Home&sid=Eelders	1-800-922-2275	http://www.mass.gov/legis/laws/mgl/
Michigan	Department of Human Services: Individual and Family Services: Adult Programs: APS	http://www.michigan.gov/dhs/0,1607,7-124-5452_7122_15663_,00.html	1-800-996-6228	http://www.legislature.mi.gov/
Minnesota	Department of Human Services: Aging & Adult Services Division: Adult Protective Services Unit	http://www.dhs.state.mn.us/main/idcplg?IdcService=GET_DYNAMIC_CONVERSION&RevisionSelectionMethod=LatestReleased&dDocName=id_005710	1-800-333-2433	http://www.leg.state.mn.us/leg/statutes.asp

State	Organizational Structure	APS Website	Hotline	State Law Website
Mississippi	Department of Human Services: Division of Family and Children's Services: APS	http://www.mdhs.state.ms.us/fcs_aps.html	1-800-222-8000 (in state), 1-601-359-4991 (outside of Mississippi)	http://www.sos.state.ms.us/ed_pubs/mscode/
Missouri	Department of Health and Senior Services: Division of Senior and Disability Services: APS	http://www.dhss.mo.gov/ProtectiveServices/	1-800-392-0210	http://www.moga.mo.gov/statutesearch/
Montana	Department of Public Health and Human Services: Senior Long-Term Care Division: Adult Protective Services Program	http://www.dphhs.mt.gov/sltc/services/APS/index.shtml	1-800-551-3191 (in state)	http://data.opi.state.mt.us/bills/mca_toc/index.htm
Nebraska	Health and Human Service System: Department of Services: Aging Services: APS	http://www.hhs.state.ne.us/HCS/Programs/APS.htm	1-800-652-1999 (in state), 1-402-595-1324 (outside of Nebraska)	http://law.justia.com/nebraska/codes/
Nevada	Department of Health and Human Resources: Division for Aging Services: Elder Protective Services	http://www.nvaging.net/protective_svc.htm	No hotline, call for Carson City, 775-687-4210, Reno 775-688-2964, Elko 775-738-1966, Las Vegas 702-486-3545	http://leg.state.nv.us/law1.cfm

(Continued)

Appendix A (Continued)

State	Organizational Structure	APS Website	Hotline	State Law Website
New Hampshire	Department of Health and Human Services: Bureau of Elderly & Adult Services: Adult Protection Program	http://www.dhhs.state.nh.us/DHHS/BEAS/adult-protection.htm	1-800-949-0470	http://www.gencourt.state.nh.us/rsa/html/indexes/default.html
New Jersey	Department of Health and Senior Services: Division of Aging and Community Services: APS	http://www.state.nj.us/health/senior/aps.shtml	1-800-792-8820	http://www.njleg.state.nj.us
New Mexico	Aging and Long-Term Services Department: Adult Protective Services Division	http://www.nmaging.state.nm.us/Adult_Protective_Services_Division.html	1-866-654-3219	http://www.conwaygreene.com/NewMexico.htm
New York	Office of Children & Family Services: Bureau of Adult Services: Protective Services for Adults	http://www.ocfs.state.ny.us/main/psa/	1-800-342-3009, Press Option 6 (within New York State only); outside New York contact the local county Department of Social Services APS	A free on-line official version of New York statutes is not available; see http://law.justia.com/newyork/codes/
North Carolina	Department of Health and Human Services: Division of Aging and Adult Services: APS	http://www.dhhs.state.nc.us/aging/adultsvcs/afs_aps.htm	No hotline, should call county Department of Social Service office	http://www.ncleg.net/gascripts/Statutes/Statutes.asp

State	Organizational Structure	APS Website	Hotline	State Law Website
North Dakota	Department of Human Services: Aging Services Division: Vulnerable Adult Protective Services	http://www.nd.gov/dhs/services/adultsaging/vulnerable.html	1-800-451-8693	http://www.legis.nd.gov/information/statutes/cent-code.html
Ohio	Department of Aging: County Departments of Job and Family Services: Adult Protective Services Program	http://www.goldenbuckeye.com/families/aps.html	866-886-3537	http://ohio.gov/GovState.stm#ohjud
Oklahoma	Department of Human Services: Family Support Services Division: Adult Protective Services Unit	http://204.87.68.21/aps/	1-800-522-3511	http://www.lsb.state.ok.us/
Oregon	Department of Human Resources: Seniors and People with Disabilities Division: APS	http://www.oregon.gov/DHS/spwpd/abuse/aps.shtml#report	1-800-232-3020	http://www.leg.state.or.us/ors/
Pennsylvania	Department of Aging: Area Agencies on Aging: Protective Services for Older Adults Program	http://www.aging.state.pa.us/aging/cwp/view.asp?A=2848&Q=173897	1-800-490-8505	http://www.pacode.com/; a free on-line official version of Pennsylvania statutes is not available

(Continued)

Appendix A (Continued)

State	Organizational Structure	APS Website	Hotline	State Law Website
Rhode Island	Department of Elderly Affairs: Protective Services	http://www.dea.ri.gov/programs/protective_services.php	1-401-462-0550	http://www.rilin.state.ri.us/Statutes/Statutes.html
South Carolina	Department of Social Services: Division of Adult Protective Services	http://www.state.sc.us/dss/aps/index.html	Contact local Adult Protective Services in county person lives in	http://www.scstatehouse.net/code/statmast.htm
South Dakota	Department of Social Services: Division of Adult Services and Aging: Adult Protective Services Program	http://dss.sd.gov/elderlyservices/services/adultprotective.asp	1-866-854-5465	http://legis.state.sd.us/statutes/index.aspx
Tennessee	Department of Human Services: Division of Adult and Family Services: APS	http://www.state.tn.us/humanserv/adfam/afs_aps.htm	1-888-277-8366	http://www.legislature.state.tn.us/
Texas	Health and Human Services Commission: Department of Family and Protective Services: APS	http://www.dfps.state.tx.us/Adult_Protection/About_Adult_Protective_Services/	1-800-252-5400	http://www.legis.state.tx.us/
Utah	Department of Human Services: Division of Aging and Adult Services: APS	http://www.hsdaas.utah.gov/ap_referral.htm	1-800-371-7897	http://www.utah.gov/government/utahlaws.html

State	Organizational Structure	APS Website	Hotline	State Law Website
Vermont	Agency of Human Services: Department of Disabilities, Aging, & Independent Living: Division of Licensing and Protection: Adult Protective Services Program	http://www.dad.state.vt.us/lp/aps.htm	1-800-564-1612	http://www.leg.state.vt.us
Virginia	Department of Social Services: Division of Family Services: APS	http://www.dss.virginia.gov/family/as/aps.cgi	1-888-832-3858	http://www.virginia.gov/cmsportal/government_881/virginia_1048/index.html
Washington	Department of Social and Health Services: Aging and Disability Services Administration: APS	http://www.aasa.dshs.wa.gov/	1-866-363-4276	http://www1.leg.wa.gov/LawsAndAgencyRules
West Virginia	Department of Health and Human Resources: Bureau for Children and Families: Office of Social Services: APS	http://www.wvdhhr.org/bcf/children_adult/aps/report.asp	1-800-352-6513	http://www.legis.state.wv.us

(Continued)

Appendix A (Continued)

State	Organizational Structure	APS Website	Hotline	State Law Website
Wisconsin	Department of Health and Family Services: Division of Supportive Living: Bureau of Aging and Long Term Care Resources: County Adult-at-Risk Agency	http://dhfs.wisconsin.gov/aps/index.htm	1-608-261-4400	http://www.legis.state.wi.us/rsb/stats.html
Wyoming	Department of Family Services: Protective Services	http://dfsweb.state.wy.us/aps.htm	1-307-777-3602	http://legisweb.state.wy.us
District of Columbia	Department of Human Services: Family Services Administration: APS	http://www.dhs.dc.gov/dhs/cwp/view,a,3,q,492691.asp	1-202-541-3950	http://government.westlaw.com/linkedslice/default.asp?SP=DCC-1000

Appendix B Licensure and Recertification Agencies, by State

State	Agency	Website	Hotline
		Report Nursing Home Abuse to:	
Alabama	Alabama Department of Senior Services	http://www.adss.state.al.us/	1-800-458-7214
Alaska	Alaska Health Facilities Licensing and Certification	http://www.hss.state.ak.us/dph/CL/HFLC/about.htm	1-800-730-6393 (in state), 1-907-334-4483 (outside of Alaska)
Arizona	Arizona Division of Licensing Services	http://www.azdhs.gov/als/index.htm	1-602-364-2677
Arkansas	Arkansas Office of Long Term Care	http://www.medicaid.state.ar.us/Internet Solution/General/units/oltc/complaint.aspx	1-800-582-4887
California	Licensing and Certification Division, Department of Health Services	http://www.dhs.ca.gov/lnc/	1-800-236-9747 (in state), 1-916-552-8700 (outside of California)
Colorado	Health Facilities Division, Department of Public Health & Environment	http://www.cdphe.state.co.us/hf/	303-692-2800 or 1-800-886-7689 ext, 2800
Connecticut	Facility Licensing and Investigation Section, Department of Public Health	http://www.dph.state.ct.us/hcquality/complts/complts.HTM	1-860-509-7400
Delaware	Division of Long Term Care Residents Protection, Health and Social Services	http://www.dhss.delaware.gov/dhss/dltcrp/contact.html	1-302-577-7295
Florida	Division of Health Quality Assurance, Agency for Health Care Administration	http://www.fdhc.state.fl.us/Contact/call_center.shtml	1-888-419-3456

(Continued)

173

Appendix B (Continued)

State	Agency	Report Nursing Home Abuse to:	
		Website	Hotline
Georgia	Office of Regulatory Services, Department of Human Resources	http://dhr.georgia.gov/portal/site/DHR/me nuitem.2425948422 1d3c0b50c8798dd0 3036a0/?vgnextoid=7d79e1d09cb4ff00V gnVCM100000bf01010aRCRD	1-404-657-1453
Hawaii	State Department of Health, Office of Health Care Assurance	http://www.hawaii.gov/health/elder-care/health-assurance/licensing/index.html	1-808-692-7400
Idaho	Bureau of Facility Standards, Department of Health and Welfare	http://www.healthandwelfare.idaho.gov/site/3628/default.aspx	1-208-334-6626
Illinois	Office of Health Care Regulation, Department of Public Health	http://www.idph.state.il.us/about/ohcr.htm	1-800-252-4343
Indiana	Health Care Regulatory Services Commission, State Department of Health	http://www.in.gov/isdh/regsvcs/ltc/complai nts/index.htm	1-800-246-8909
Iowa	Iowa Department of Inspections and Appeals	https://dia-hfd.iowa.gov/DIA_HFD/Process.do	1-877-686-0027
Kansas	Bureau of Health Facility Regulation, Department of Health and Environment	http://www.kdheks.gov/bhfr/elder_abuse_hotlines.html	1-800-842-0078

Report Nursing Home Abuse to:

State	Agency	Website	Hotline
Kentucky	Division of Health Care Facilities and Services	http://chfs.ky.gov/oig/dhcfscomplaintinfo.htm	Western Enforcement Branch: 1-270-889-6052; Northern Enforcement Branch: 1-502-595-4079; Southern Enforcement Branch: 1-606-878-7827; Eastern Enforcement Branch: 1-859-246-2301
Louisiana	Health Standards, Management & Finance-Health Services Financing	http://www.dhh.louisiana.gov/offices/?ID=112	1-888-810-1819
Maine	Division of Licensing and Certification, Department of Health and Human Services	http://www.state.me.us/dhhs/bms/contacts/contacts_topnav.shtml	1-800-383-2441 (in state free), 1-207-287-9308 (outside of Maine)
Maryland	Office of Health Care Quality, Department of Health and Mental Hygiene	http://www.dhmh.state.md.us/ohcq/complaint/complaint.htm	1-877-402-8218
Minnesota	Facility and Provider Compliance Division, Department of Health	http://www.health.state.mn.us/divs/fpc/ohfcinfo/contohfc.htm	1-800-369-7994
Mississippi	Mississippi Department of Health, Health Facilities Licensure & Certification	http://www.msdh.state.ms.us/	1-800-227-7308
Missouri	Division of Health and Senior Services, Division of Senior and Disability Services	http://www.dhss.mo.gov/ElderAbuse/	1-800-392-0210 (in state), 1-753-751-4842 (outside of Missouri)

(Continued)

Appendix B (Continued)

State	Agency	Website	Hotline
		Report Nursing Home Abuse to:	
Montana	Montana Department of Public Health and Human Services, Quality Assurance Division	http://www.dphhs.mt.gov/qad/index.shtml	1-406-444-1518
Nebraska	Regulation & Licensure, Department of Health and Human Services	http://www.hhs.state.ne.us/crl/invest/invest.htm	1-402-471-0316
New Hampshire	Office of Program Support, Licensing & Regulation Services, Department of Health & Human Services	http://www.dhhs.nh.gov/DHHS/OPS/default.htm	1-603-271-0853
New Jersey	Long Term Care Systems, Department of Health & Senior Services	http://www.state.nj.us/health/ltc/index.shtml	1-800-367-6543 (in state), 1-609-292-7837 (outside of New Jersey)
New Mexico	Bureau of Health Facility Licensing & Certification, Department of Health	http://dhi.health.state.nm.us/hflc/index.php	1-800-752-8649 (in state), 1-505-476-9028 (outside of New Mexico)
New York	Health Care Standards and Surveillance, Department of Health	http://www.health.state.ny.us/facilities/nursing/index.htm	1-888-201-4563
North Carolina	Licensure and Certification Section, Division of Facility Services, Department of Health and Human Services	http://facility-services.state.nc.us/mlicpage.htm	1-800-624-3004 (in state), 1-919-855-4500

Report Nursing Home Abuse to:

State	Agency	Website	Hotline
North Dakota	Health Facilities, Health Resources Section, Department of Health	http://www.health.state.nd.us/hf/North_Dakota_Basic_Care_Facilities.htm	1-701-328-2352
Ohio	Nursing Homes/Facilities, Division of Quality Assurance, Department of Health	http://www.odh.ohio.gov/odhprograms/ltc/nurhome/nurhome1.aspx	1-614-466-7857
Oregon	Health Care Licensure & Certification, Department of Human Services	http://www.oregon.gov/DHS/ph/hclc/index.shtml'	1-971-673-0540
Pennsylvania	Bureau of Facility Licensure and Certification, Bureau of Quality Assurance, Department of Health	http://www.dsf.health.state.pa.us/health/cwp/browse.asp?a=188&bc=0&c=35675	1-800-254-5164
Rhode Island	Division of Health Services Regulation, Department of Health	http://www.health.ri.gov/hsr/regulations/index.php	1-401-222-6015
South Carolina	Bureau of Certification, Department of Health & Environmental Control	http://www.scdhe.net/hr/cert/hrcomp.htm	1-800-922-6735
South Dakota	South Dakota Department of Health, Health Care Facility Complaints	http://www.state.sd.us/doh/Facility/complain.htm	1-800-738-2301
Tennessee	Division of Health Care Facilities, Department of Health	http://www2.state.tn.us/health/HCF/complaints.htm	1-877-287-0010

(Continued)

Appendix B (Continued)

State	Agency	Report Nursing Home Abuse to:	
		Website	Hotline
Texas	Bureau of Licensing and Compliance, Department of State Health Services	http://www.dshs.state.tx.us/hfp/complain.shtm	1-512-834-6646
Vermont	Division of Licensing and Protection, Department of Aging and Disabilities	http://www.dad.state.vt.us/lp/	1-800-564-1612 (in state), 1-802-241-2345 (outside of Vermont)
Virginia	Office of Licensure & Certification, Department of Health	http://www.vdh.virginia.gov/OLC/Complaint/	1-800-955-1819
Washington	Facilities and Services Licensing, Department of Health	http://www.doh.wa.gov/hsqa/fsl/default.htm	1-800-633-6828
West Virginia	Office of Health Facility Licensure & Certification, Department of Health & Human Resources	http://www.wvdhhr.org/ohflac/Default.htm	1-304-558-0050
Wisconsin	Bureau of Quality Assurance, Department of Health & Family Services	http://dhfs.wisconsin.gov/bqaconsumer/HealthCareComplaints.htm	1-608-226-8481
Wyoming	Wyoming Office of Health Licensing and Survey	http://wdh.state.wy.us/ohls/complaint.asp	1-800-548-1367
District of Columbia	Health Regulation Administration, Department of Health	http://doh.dc.gov/doh/cwp/view,a,1374,q,577097,dohNav_GID,1806.asp	1-202-442-5888

Discussion Questions

1. Could a randomized control trial be conducted to test an intervention for the prevention of elder abuse? Describe how it could be conducted.

2. Review your state's APS-related statute for elder abuse. Are the definitions of abuse limiting or inclusive of all types of abuse? Are there qualifications for the victim to meet before an investigation can be conducted?

3. How could a prevalence study be conducted without using expensive resources (i.e., without using direct interviews with respondents or potential victims)?

Internet Resources

Administration on Aging: http://www.aoa.gov/eldfam/eldfam.aspx

American Bar Association Commission on Law and Aging: http://www.abanet.org/aging/

Clearinghouse on Abuse and Neglect of the Elderly (CANE): http://www.cane.udel.edu/

International Network for the Prevention of Elder Abuse: http://www.inpea.net/

National Association of State Units on Aging: http://www.nasua.org/

National Center on Elder Abuse: http://www.ncea.aoa.gov

National Long-Term Care Ombudsman Resource Center: http://www.ltcombudsman.org/default.cfm

References

Administration on Aging. (2002). *Long-term care ombudsman program complaint codes.* Retrieved October 9, 2002, from http://www.aoa.dhhs.gov/.

Administration on Aging. (2004). *Historical evolution of programs for older Americans.* Retrieved from http://www.aoa.gov/about/over/over_history.aspx

Administration on Aging. (2006). *Elder rights: LTC ombudsman: LTC ombudsman reporting system data tables.* Retrieved August 13, 2007, from http://www.aoa.gov/prof/aoaprog/elder_rights/

LTCombudsman/ National _and_State_Data/ national_and_state_data.aspx.

Aziz, S. J., & Campbell-Taylor, I. (1999). Neglect and abuse associated with undernutrition in long-term care in North America: Causes and solutions. *Journal of Elder Abuse & Neglect, 10*(1/2), 91–117.

Barker, N. N., & Himchak, M. V. (2006). Environmental issues affecting elder abuse victims in their reception of community based services. *Journal of Gerontological Social Work, 48*(1/2), 233–255.

Blakely, B. E., & Dolon, R. (2001). Another look at the helpfulness of occupational groups in the discovery of elder abuse and neglect. *Journal of Elder Abuse & Neglect, 13*(3), 1–23.

Boldy, D., Horner, B., Crouchley, K., & Davey, M. (2005). Addressing elder abuse: Western Australian case study. *Australasian Journal on Ageing, 24*(1), 3–8.

Braun, K. L., Suzuki, K. M., Cusick, C. E., & Howard-Carhart, K. (1997). Developing and testing training materials on elder abuse and neglect for nurse aides. *Journal of Elder Abuse & Neglect, 9*(1), 1–15.

Brozowski, K., & Hall, D. R. (2004). Growing old in a risk society: Elder abuse in Canada. *Journal of Elder Abuse & Neglect, 16*(3), 65–81.

Castledine, G. (2000). Nurse who carried out manual evacuations without consent. *British Journal of Nursing, 9*(17), 1123.

Centers for Disease Control and Prevention. (2007). National nursing home survey (NNHA). Retrieved January 3, 2007, from http://www.cdc.gov/nchs/about/major/nnhsd/Trendsnurse.htm.

Clarke, M., & Ogg, J. (1994). Identifying the elderly at risk. *Journal of Community Nursing, 8*(3), 4, 6, 9.

Comijs, H. C., Pot, A. M., Smit, J. H., Bouter, L. M., & Jonker, C. (1998). Elder abuse in the community: Prevalence and consequences. *Journal of the American Geriatrics Society, 46*(7), 885–888.

Coyne, A. C., Reichman, W. E., & Berbig, L. J. (1993). The relationship between dementia and abuse. *American Journal of Psychiatry, 150*(4), 643–646.

Daly, J. M., & Jogerst, G. J. (2001). Statute definitions of elder abuse. *Journal of Elder Abuse & Neglect, 13*(4), 39–57.

Daly, J. M., & Jogerst, G. J. (2006). Nursing home statute: Mistreatment definitions. *Journal of Elder Abuse & Neglect, 18*(1), 19–39.

Daly, J. M., & Jogerst, G. J. (2007). Nursing home abuse report and investigation legislation. *Journal of Elder Abuse & Neglect, 19(3/4),* 119–131.

Daly, J. M., Jogerst, G. J., Brinig, M., & Dawson, J. (2003). Mandatory reporting: Relationship of APS statute language on state reported elder abuse. *Journal of Elder Abuse & Neglect, 15*(2), 1–21.

Davis, R. C., & Medina-Ariza, J. (2001). *Results from an elder abuse prevention experiment in New York City.* National Institute of Justice. Retrieved November 1, 2002, from http://www.ojp.usdoj.gov/nij.

Dyer, C. B., Pavlik, V. N., Murphy, K. P., & Hyman, D. J. (2000). The high prevalence of depression and dementia in elder abuse or neglect. *Journal of the American Geriatrics Society, 48,* 205–208.

Freemantle, N., Harvey, E. L., Wolf, F., Grimshaw, J. M., Grilli, R., & Bero, L. A. (2000). Printed educational materials: Effects on professional practice and health care outcomes. *Cochrane Database Systematic Reviews, 2,* CD000172.

Fulmer, T., & Ashley, J. (1989). Clinical indicators of elder neglect. *Applied Nursing Research, 2,* 161–167.

Glendenning, F. (1999). Elder abuse and neglect in residential settings: The need for inclusiveness in elder abuse research. *Journal of Elder Abuse & Neglect, 10*(1/2), 1–11.

Gold, M. F. (2000). Regulators crack down on abuse. *Provider, 26*(4), 24–37.

Greenberg, J. R., McKibben, M., & Raymond, J. A. (1990). Dependent adult children and elder abuse. *Journal of Elder Abuse & Neglect, 2*(1/2), 73–86.

Greene, J. (2001). When not treating pain equals abuse. *Hospitals and Health Networks, 3,* 34.

Hajjar, I., & Duthie, E. (2001). Prevalence of elder abuse in the United States: A comparative report between the national and Wisconsin data. *Wisconsin Medical Journal, 100*(6), 22–26.

Hawes, C. (2003). Elder abuse in residential long-term care settings: What is known and what information is needed. In R. J. Bonnie & R. B. Wallace (Eds.), *Elder mistreatment, abuse, neglect, and exploitation in an aging America* (pp. 446–500). Washington, DC: National Research Council of the National Academies.

Homer, A. C., & Gilleard, C. (1990). Abuse of elderly people by their carers. *British Medical Journal, 301,* 1359–1362.

Hudson, B. (1992). Ensuring an abuse-free environment: A learning program for nursing home staff. *Journal of Elder Abuse & Neglect, 4*(4), 25–36.

Jogerst, G., Daly, J. M., Brinig, M., Dawson, J., Schmuch, G., & Ingram, J. (2003). Domestic elder abuse and the law. *American Journal of Public Health, 93*(12), 2131–2136.

Jogerst, G. J., Daly, J. M., Dawson, J., Brinig, M., & Schmuch, G. (2003). Required education for Iowa mandatory reporters of elder abuse. *Journal of Elder Abuse & Neglect, 15*(1), 59–73.

Jogerst, G. J., Daly, J. M., Dawson, J. D., Peek-Asa, C., & Schmuch, G. A. (2006). Iowa nursing home characteristics associated with reported abuse. *Journal of the American Medical Directors Association, 7*(4), 203–207.

Jogerst, G. J., Daly, J. M., & Hartz, A. J. (in press). State policies and nursing home characteristics associated with rates of resident mistreatment. *Journal of the American Medical Directors Association.*

Kimsey, L. R., Tarbox, A. R., & Bragg, D. F. (1981). Abuse of the elderly: The hidden agenda. The caretaker and the categories of abuse. *American Geriatrics Society Journal, 29,* 465–472.

Kivela, S., Kongas-Saviaro, P., Kesti, E., Pahkala, K., & Ijas, M. (1992). Abuse in old age: Epidemiological data from Finland. *Journal of Elder Abuse & Neglect, 4*(3), 1–18.

Knight, B. G., Lutsky, S. M., & Macofsky-Urban, F. (1993). A meta-analytic review of interventions for caregiver distress: Recommendations for future research. *Gerontologist, 33,* 240–248.

Lachs, M. S., Berkman, L., Fulmer, T., & Horwitz, F. (1994). A prospective community-based pilot study of risk factors for the investigation of elder mistreatment. *Journal of the American Geriatrics Society, 42*(2), 169–173.

Lachs, M. S., Williams, C., O'Brien, S., Hurst, L., & Horwitz, R. (1996). An 11-year longitudinal study of adult protective service use. *Archives of Internal Medicine, 156,* 449–453.

Lachs, M. S., Williams, C., O'Brien, D., Hurst, L., & Horwitz, R. I. (1997). Risk factors for reported elder abuse and neglect: A nine-year observational cohort study. *Gerontologist, 37*(4), 469–474.

Lachs, M. S., Williams, C. S., O'Brien, S., Pillemer, K. A., & Charlson, M. E. (1998). The mortality of elder mistreatment. *JAMA, 280,* 428–432.

Lane, P., McKenna, H., Ryan, A., & Fleming, P. (2003). The experience of the family caregivers' role: A qualitative study. *Research and Theory for Nursing Practice: An International Journal, 17*(2), 137–151.

Livengood, M. (1980). A group-process approach to resident and staff abuse. *American Health Care Association Journal, 6*(1), 29–30, 35.

Loue, S. (2001). Elder abuse and neglect in medicine and law. *The Journal of Legal Medicine, 22,* 159–209.

MacLean, D. S. (1995). Abuse and neglect of elderly persons. *New England Journal of Medicine, 333,* 70.

MacLean, D. S. (2000). Preventing abuse and neglect in long-term care Part II: Clinical and administrative aspects. *Annals of Long-Term Care, 8*(1), 65–70.

Mason, A., Weatherly, H., Spilsbury, K., Golder, S., Arksey, H., Adamson, J., et al. (2007). The effectiveness and cost-effectiveness of respite for caregivers of frail older people.

Journal of the American Geriatrics Society,
55, 290–299.

McNally, S., Ben-Shlomo, Y., & Newman, S.
(1999). The effects of respite care on informal carers' well-being: A systematic review.
Journal of Disability and Rehabilitation,
21(1), 1–14.

Mercer, S. O., Heacock, P., & Beck, C. (1993).
Nurse's aides in nursing homes: Perceptions
of training, work loads, racism, and abuse
issues. *Journal of Gerontological Social Work,*
21(1/2), 95–112.

Montgomery, R. J. V., Marquis, J., Schaefer, J. P.,
& Kosloski, K. (2002). Profiles of respite use.
Home Health Care Services Quarterly,
21(3/4), 33–63.

Mouton, C. P., & Espino, D. V. (1999). Health
screening in older women. *American Family*
Physician, 59(7), 1835–1842.

National Center on Elder Abuse. (1998). *The*
National Elder Abuse Incidence Study.
Washington, DC: American Public Human
Services Association. Retrieved June 5, 2001,
from http://www.aoa.gov/eldfam/Elder_
Rights/Elder_Abuse/ABuseReport_Full.pdf

National Center on Elder Abuse. (2006). *What is*
elder abuse? Retrieved May 18, 2007, from
http://www.ncea.aoa.gov/

National Long Term Care Ombudsman
Resource Center. (2001). *OBRA '87.*
Retrieved February 27, 2007, from http://
www.ltcombudsman.org/ombpublic/
49_346_1023.cfm.

National Research Council. (2003). *Elder mistreat-*
ment: Abuse, neglect, and exploitation in an
aging America. Washington, DC: The National
Academies Press.

Nerenberg, L. (2003). *Daily money management*
programs: A protection against elder abuse.
Washington, DC: National Center on Elder
Abuse.

Nicoll, M., Ashworh, M., McNally, L., &
Newman, S. (2002). Satisfaction with
respite care: A pilot study. *Health and Social*
Care in the Community, 10(6), 479–484.

Norbeck, J. S., Chaftez, L., Skodol-Wilson, H., &
Weiss, S. J. (1991). Social support needs of
family caregivers of psychiatric patients
from three age groups. *Nursing Research, 40,*
208–213.

Ockleford, E., Barnes-Holmes, Y., Morichelli, R.,
Morjaria, A., Scocchera, F., Furniss, F., et al.
(2003). Mistreatment of older women in
three European countries. *Violence Against*
Women, 9(12), 1453–1464.

Ogg, J., & Bennett, G. (1992). Elder abuse
in Britain. *British Medical Journal, 305,*
998–999.

Paveza, F., Cohen, D., Eisdorfer, C., Freels, S.,
Semla, T., Ashford, J. W., et al. (1992). Severe
family violence and Alzheimer's disease:
Prevalence and risk factors. *Gerontologist,*
32(4), 493–497.

Pavlik, V. N., Hyman, D. J., Festa, N. A., & Dyer,
C. B. (2001). Quantifying the problem of
abuse and neglect in adults—Analysis of a
statewide database. *Journal of the American*
Geriatrics Society, 49, 45–48.

Payne, B. K., Berg, B. L., & Toussaint, J. (2001).
The police response to the criminalization
of elder abuse: An exploratory study.
Policing: An International Journal of Police
Strategies & Management, 24(4), 605–625.

Payne, B., & Cikovic, R. (1995). An empirical examination of the characteristics, consequences,
and causes of elder abuse in nursing homes.
Journal of Elder Abuse & Neglect, 7, 61–74.

Peduzzi, J. J., Watzlaf, V. J. M., Rohrer, W. M., &
Rubinstein, E. N. (1997). A survey of nursing home administrator's and ombudsmen's perception of elderly abuse in
Pennsylvania. *Top Health Inform Manage,*
18(1), 68–76.

Perry, J., & Bontinen, K. (2001). Evaluation of a
weekend respite program for persons with
Alzheimer Disease. *Canadian Journal of*
Nursing Research, 33(1), 81–95.

Pillemer, K., & Finkelhor, D. (1988). The prevalence of elder abuse: A random sample survey. *The Gerontologist, 28*(1), 51–57.

Pillemer, K., & Hudson, B. (1993). A model abuse prevention program for nursing assistants. *Gerontologist, 33*(1), 128–131.

Pillemer, K., & Moore, D. W. (1989). Abuse of patients in nursing homes: Findings from a survey of staff. *The Gerontologist, 29*(3), 314–320.

Pillemer, K. A., & Suitor, J. J. (1992). Violence and violent feelings: What causes them among family caregivers? *Journal of Gerontological Nursing, 47*(4), S165–S172.

Ploeg, J., Biehler, L., Willison, K., Hutchison, B., & Blythe, J. (2001). Perceived support needs of family caregivers and implications for a telephone support service. *Canadian Journal of Nursing Research, 33*(2), 43–61.

Podnieks, E. (1992). National survey on abuse of the elderly in Canada. *Journal of Elder Abuse & Neglect, 4,* 5–58.

Powell, M. E., & Berman, J. (2006). Effects of dependency on compliance rates among elder abuse victims at the New York City Department for the aging, elderly crime victim's unit. *Journal of Gerontological Social Work, 46*(3/4), 229–247.

Ramsey-Klawsnik, H. (2003). Elder sexual abuse within the family. *Journal of Elder Abuse & Neglect, 15*(1), 43–58.

Richardson, B., Kitchen, G., & Livingston, G. (2002). The effect of education on knowledge and management of elder abuse: a randomized controlled trial. *Age and Ageing, 31,* 335–341.

Roby, J. L., & Sullivan, R. (2000). Adult protection service laws: A comparison of state statutes from definition to case closure. *Journal of Elder Abuse & Neglect, 12*(3/4), 17–51.

Saveman, B., & Sandvide, A. (2001). Swedish general practitioners' awareness of elderly patients at risk of or actually suffering from elder abuse. *Scandinavian Journal of Caring Science, 15,* 244–249.

Shugarman, L. R., Fries, B. E., Wolf, R. S., & Morris, J. N. (2003). Identifying older people at risk of abuse during routine screening practices. *Journal of the American Geriatrics Society, 51*(1), 24–31.

Tammelleo, A. D. (1999). "Reckless" neglect of elders violates elder abuse act. *The Regan Report on Nursing Law, 39*(11), 1.

Tatara, T. (1995). *An analysis of state laws addressing elder abuse, neglect, and exploitation.* Washington, DC: National Center on Elder Abuse.

Tatara, T., & Kuzmeskus, L. B. (1997). *Summaries of the statistical data on elder abuse in domestic settings for FY 95 and FY 96.* Washington, DC: National Center on Elder Abuse.

Thompson, M. (1997). Fatal neglect. *Time, 150*(17), 34–38.

Tilford, S., Delaney, F., & Vogels, M. (1997). Mental health promotion in high risk groups. *Effective Health Care, 3*(3), 1–12.

Townsend, D., & Kosloski, K. (2002). Factors related to client satisfaction with community-based respite services. *Home Health Care Services Quarterly, 21*(3/4), 89–106.

U.S. Department of Health and Human Services. (2005). *State operations manual: Complaint procedures.* Retrieved November 30, 2006, from http://www.cms.hhs.gov/manuals.

Wilber, K. H. (1991). Alternatives to conservatorship: The role of daily money management services. *Gerontologist, 31*(2), 150–155.

Wolf, R. S. (1996). Understanding elder abuse and neglect. *Aging, 367,* 4–9.

Wolf, R. S., & Li, D. (1999). Factors affecting the rate of elder abuse reporting to a state protective services program. *Gerontologist, 39*(2), 222–228.

Wolf, R. S., & Pillemer, K. (1989). *Helping elderly victims: The reality of elder abuse.* New York: Columbia University Press.

Yan, E., & Tang, C. S. (2001). Prevalence and psychological impact of Chinese elder abuse. *Journal of Interpersonal Violence, 16*(11), 1158–1174.

CHAPTER 9

Beyond Violence Against Women

Gender Inclusiveness in Domestic Violence Research, Policy, and Practice

Sarah L. Desmarais, Andrea Gibas, and Tonia L. Nicholls

D omestic violence in the form of violence against women is a well-established global, social problem. The sheer prevalence; associated personal, social, and economic costs; and repetitive nature of domestic violence set it apart from other criminal acts. Based on a review of 48 population-based studies, the World Health Organization (WHO; Krug, Dahlberg, Mercy, Zwi, & Lozano, 2002) found that between 10% and 69% of women surveyed had been physically abused by an intimate male partner at some point in their lives. Surveys in the United States suggest approximately one-quarter of women will experience physical violence at the hands of an intimate partner during their lifetime (Tjaden & Thoennes, 2000).

The issue of female-perpetrated domestic violence against men has received considerably less attention despite evidence that perpetration prevalence rates are fairly comparable across gender (Dutton & Nicholls, 2005). Although assaults by men are more likely to result in physical injury, there are now more than 150 studies demonstrating approximately equal rates of physical assault by women against their male partners as by men against their female partners (Straus, 2006). Further, there is now evidence to suggest that domestic violence is not unilateral within relationships; that is, both partners may engage in abusive behaviors (Archer, 2000; Whitaker, Haileyesus, Swahn, & Saltzman, 2007). Accordingly, in this chapter we take a gender-inclusive approach to domestic violence, first defining the phenomenon generally. Second, we present the costs of domestic violence, including its impact on the victims and society. Third, we discuss factors that may increase the risk for domestic violence victimization and perpetration. Fourth, we consider theories regarding the causes of domestic violence. Fifth, we review what can be done to reduce rates of domestic violence, focusing on assessment, intervention, and treatment. Last, we present a domestic violence case study that illustrates key themes of the chapter.

Definition

Merriam-Webster's Collegiate Dictionary (2003) defines domestic violence as "the inflicting of physical injury by one family or household member on another; *also:* a repeated or habitual pattern of such behavior" (p. 371). This dictionary definition masks the complexity of domestic violence in the real world. The terms *abusive* or *violent* can be used to define the nature of the behaviors (e.g., domestic *abuse* versus domestic *violence*). However, *abuse* implies less severe acts (i.e., not resulting in victim injury), whereas *violence* implies more severe acts (Johnson & Sigler, 2000; Nicholls & Dutton, 2001). Such inconsistencies may have important implications for law enforcement, service delivery, and policy (Holtzworth-Munroe, Clements, & Farris, 2005). For instance, if there is violence in the relationship, mediation between separated partners may not be used, whereas abusive behaviors may not preclude such intervention (Beck & Frost, 2006).

Definitions and terminology differ between criminal justice and health care systems, as well. On the one hand, the United States Department of Justice (n.d.) defines *domestic violence* as "a pattern of abusive behavior in any relationship that is used by one partner to gain or maintain power and control over another intimate partner." The WHO, on the other hand, defines *intimate partner violence* as "any behavior within an intimate relationship that causes physical, psychological, or sexual harm to those in the relationship" (Krug et al., 2002, p. 89). In this chapter, we aggregate and expand these definitions to define domestic violence as *any behavior within a current or past intimate relationship that involves "actual, attempted, or threatened harm"* (Webster, Douglas, Eaves, & Hart, 1997, p. 24) *that may impact or detract from the victim's physical, psychological, sexual, economic, or spiritual well-being.*

Types of Domestic Violence

As evidenced by our definition, domestic violence is a multidimensional phenomenon. The different types of domestic violence are not mutually exclusive (Coker et al., 2002) and may occur in public as well as in private (Hegarty, Hindmarsh, & Gilles, 2000).

Physical Violence

Physical violence is defined as any physical act that is intended to injure, harm, or disable an intimate partner (Flinck, Paavilainen, & Åstedt-Kurki, 2005). Resulting harm can range from slight pain to severe injury (Garcia-Morena, Jansen, Ellsberg, & Watts, 2006). At its most severe, physical violence can result in death (Campbell, Glass, Sharps, Laughon, & Bloom, 2007). Preventing a partner's access to sleep, warmth, or nutrition also is considered physical abuse (Hegarty et al., 2000).

Psychological Violence

Psychological abuse (also called emotional or verbal abuse) is defined as threats or coercive acts that seek to overpower and control the victim (e.g., isolation from friends and family; Coker et al., 2002; Flinck et al., 2005). Verbal abuse includes ridiculing, shouting, swearing, and name-calling. Psychological abuse is often minimized by researchers and service agencies when physical violence is present in the relationship (O'Leary, 1999). Studies suggest, however, that this form of abuse may have a greater negative impact on victims than physical abuse (O'Leary, 1999).

Sexual Violence

Although specific definitions may vary state by state, a general legal guideline for defining sexual assault is two-fold: (1) any genital, oral, or anal penetration by force by the accused that (2) occurs without the victim's consent (American Medical Association, 1995; Coker et al., 2002). Sexual abuse also may include nonassaultive controlling acts, such as forcing the victim to perform sexual acts, sexual degradation or humiliation (e.g., dictating what clothes to wear, withholding sex to frustrate or humiliate the partner), and refusing to use contraception (Campbell, 2002; Garcia-Morena et al., 2006).

Financial Abuse

Financial abuse is defined as controlling finances without the knowledge, consent, or input from a partner (Lambert & Firestone, 2000). The perpetrator may, for example, prevent the victim from earning an independent income or pursuing further education, exclude the victim from participating in financial decisions, provide only a strict "allowance," force the victim to beg for money (Professional Education Taskforce on Family Violence, 1991), or neglect his or her financial responsibilities (Flinck et al., 2005).

Spiritual Abuse

Less recognized than other types of domestic violence, spiritual abuse includes preventing participation in spiritual activities (e.g., not allowing the victim to attend church service or read spiritual literature; Flinck et al., 2005), ridiculing spiritual beliefs, or using these beliefs to manipulate the victim (e.g., interpreting the Bible in a manner that supports dominance by the abusive partner, sanctions entrapment in a marital union, or demands that the victim "forgive" the abuse; Bent-Goodley & Fowler, 2006).

Stalking

Stalking, in the context of intimate relationships, generally occurs once an intimate relationship has ended (Zona, Sharma, & Lane, 1993). Under United States law, stalking is the willful, repeated, and malicious following of another individual (Coleman, 1997). Common stalking behaviors include attempting to "win" the partner back (e.g., leaving notes or flowers, making unwanted phone calls), following or observing the partner, and threatening the partner. Stalking is found in the majority of relationships marked by domestic violence (Melton, 2007).

Consequences of Domestic Violence

All types of domestic violence are associated with adverse (Coker et al., 2002) and predictable victim outcomes (Plichta, 2004). Domestic violence has both an immediate and a continued negative impact on victims, even after the abuse has ceased (Campbell, 2002; Plichta, 2004).

Physical trauma is an obvious direct health effect of domestic violence, and although physical violence may be perpetrated by either partner, women may be at greater risk than men for serious injury (Statistics Canada, 2005). An indirect impact of repeated physical assaults is the increase in the risk of developing chronic diseases (e.g., chronic pain; Coker et al., 2002). Victims experience significantly greater than average symptoms of neurological (e.g., fainting), cardiopulmonary (e.g., hypertension), and gastrointestinal disorders (e.g., loss of appetite). Fear and stress of victimization may contribute to chronic health problems and/or to increased lifestyle risk behaviors (e.g., smoking, substance misuse; Campbell, 2002).

In women, domestic violence may lead to gynecological and reproductive problems (e.g., STDs, preterm labor; Janssen, Holt, Sugg, Emanuel, Critchlow, & Henderson, 2003).

Domestic violence also can contribute to impaired psychological functioning. Victims of domestic violence are more likely to meet diagnostic criteria for major psychiatric disorders (e.g., depression, posttraumatic stress disorder; Coker et al., 2002; Kernic, Wolf, & Holt, 2000). Psychological distress can indirectly exacerbate acute and chronic physical health conditions, as well (McNutt, Carlson, Persaud, & Postmus, 2002). Of substantive concern, victimization may be a significant risk factor for self-harm and suicide (Campbell, 2002).

In addition to health consequences, domestic violence may result in deteriorating occupational and economic functioning. Victims of domestic violence may have difficulty seeking or maintaining employment (e.g., are fired due to repeated "personal" phone calls, quit for safety reasons; Lloyd, 1997). Research further demonstrates that economic hardship, welfare receipt, poverty, and homelessness are associated with victim vulnerability to domestic violence, although the direction of the relationship has not been determined (i.e., whether domestic violence is a risk factor for financial difficulty or financial difficulty is a risk factor for domestic violence; Tolman & Rosen, 2001).

The effects of domestic violence extend beyond adult victims. Children and adolescents are adversely affected by witnessing domestic violence (English, Marshall, & Stewart, 2003). These children may demonstrate increased psychological symptoms (e.g., depression, posttraumatic stress disorder) and behavioral problems (e.g., Conduct Disorder, problems at school; Wolak & Finkelhor, 1998). That they are at increased risk of perpetrating domestic violence in adulthood (e.g., Langhinrichsen-Rohling, Neidig, & Thorn, 1995) has long-term societal implications as well.

The cost of domestic violence victimization to our communities and society is significant. Annually, domestic violence victims add $19.3 million to United States healthcare expenses (Rivara et al., 2007) and account for 10% to 20% increased expenditure (Campbell, 2002; see also Arias & Corso, 2005). Significant indirect costs associated with victims' impaired occupational functioning include absenteeism, tardiness, decreased productivity, turnover, greater security costs, and medical expenses. Organizational costs of domestic violence are estimated to be as much as $5 billion per year (Johnson & Indvik, 1999). Additional societal costs include expenditures for social services as well as criminal justice and legal services (Stanko, Crisp, Hale, & Lucraft, 1998).

The above review demonstrates the wide-reaching devastating effects of domestic violence. In the next section, we narrow our focus and examine risk factors for domestic violence victimization and perpetration.

Victims and Perpetrators of Domestic Violence

Research demonstrates that victims and perpetrators of domestic violence are a heterogeneous group (Holtzworth-Munroe & Meehan, 2004; Rhodes & McKenzie, 1998). In the following two sections, we review characteristics that may increase the risk for domestic violence victimization and perpetration.

Risk Factors for Victimization

Individuals who are educated, employed, and highly competent as well as individuals who struggle due to marginalization (e.g., as a result of age, physical disability, financial limitations, or ethnic minority status) are victims of domestic violence. Mental and physical health problems, economic concerns, and substance abuse, however, have been shown to increase the likelihood of victimization (Foshee, Benefield, Ennett, Bauman, & Suchindran, 2004). Because many of these same characteristics are consequences of domestic violence, as reviewed above, they may be both effects of and risk factors for domestic violence. Mental disorders, for example, may predate the onset of domestic violence, but the association, although significant, is inconsistent across diagnoses. For example, results of the National Comorbidity Survey demonstrate only two significant associations between DSM-III-R mental disorder diagnoses and subsequent victimization: Social phobia was associated with increased risk of severe violence victimization, whereas substance dependence was associated with a decreased risk (Kessler, Molnar, Feurer, & Appelbaum, 2001).

Traditional sex role beliefs and trauma history have been shown to increase vulnerability to domestic violence. For example, some studies have found that women who endorse traditional sex role or relationship beliefs (e.g., the man is the dominant partner and the woman should tend to his needs) are more likely to condone violence and remain with a violent partner (Foa, Cascardi, Zoellner, & Feeny, 2000). Exposure to prior traumas, including witnessing interparental violence or being abused as a child, may predict victimization in that it increases the likelihood that relationship violence will be seen as a normal means of resolving conflict (Stith, Rosen, Middleton, Busch, Lundenberg, & Carlton, 2000). In addition, such experiences may contribute to the development of mental health problems, which, as reviewed above, increase vulnerability (Foa et al., 2000).

Social and community factors also may increase vulnerability to domestic violence victimization. Social isolation (e.g., living in a rural community, being an immigrant) may contribute to a failure to identify experiences as "violent" and prevent reporting (e.g., Phillips, Torres de Ardon, & Briones,

2000). Victims of domestic violence may be socially isolated as a result of perpetrator attempts to prevent contact with others. Even when victims are not isolated, family or friends may not support attempts to seek help or end the relationship due to cultural, religious, or generational beliefs regarding normative spousal behaviors, the sanctity of marriage, and the responsibility of the victim to maintain the family unit (e.g., Klevens et al., 2007; Ramsey-Klawsnick, 2003).

Risk Factors for Perpetration

Considerable effort has been directed to identifying predictors of domestic violence perpetration. These efforts have explored a range of biological, social, and psychological correlates (Holtzworth-Munroe, Bates, Smutzler, & Sandin, 1997). The extent and nature of the heterogeneity among domestic violence perpetrators, as among domestic violence victims, has become increasingly obvious as research progresses (Dutton, 2006). Individual, community, and societal factors can increase the risk for perpetrating domestic violence (Krug et al., 2002).

Individual factors include age, substance abuse, mental health problems (e.g., personality disorders or depression), dependency, and witnessing or experiencing violence as a child (Krug et al., 2002). For example, research demonstrates that substance use increases the likelihood of domestic violence perpetration (Thompson & Kingree, 2006) because it can reduce perpetrator inhibitions and aid in the rationalization of the behavior (Fals-Stewart & Kennedy, 2005). Although often framed as a risk factor for victimization, attachment to or dependency on an intimate partner (financially, emotionally, or otherwise) may increase risk for perpetration: In response to feeling helpless, a dependent partner may become aggressive to gain power and control in the relationship (Johnson, 2001; Kernsmith, 2005a). The above review draws attention to the considerable overlap between risk factors for domestic violence victimization and perpetration.

There are a number of community factors (e.g., poverty, low social capital, and inadequate sanctions) and social factors (e.g., traditional gender and social norms) associated with increased risk for domestic violence perpetration (Krug et al., 2002). These factors may increase tolerance or acceptance of domestic violence, reducing the likelihood that an individual will be prevented from engaging in such behaviors (e.g., Levinson, 1989). We review community and legal sanctions in more detail later in this chapter.

Gender Issues

In contrast to the extensive literature on male-perpetrated domestic violence against a female intimate partner, significantly less has been written about female perpetrators (Babcock, Miller, & Siard, 2003; Nicholls & Dutton, 2001). Research examining female inmates, offenders, and psychiatric patients suggests that many risk factors are common to general violence perpetrated by both men and women, such as a history of violence (Cale & Lilienfeld, 2002; Nicholls, Ogloff, & Douglas, 2004). Substance abuse has been shown to increase risk for domestic violence perpetration among both men and women (Stuart, Moore, Ramsey, & Kahler, 2003). Women's motives for perpetrating domestic violence can be highly similar to those of men (Dutton & Nicholls, 2005). However, some risk factors may be gender specific (e.g., gang membership) or may impact women uniquely or differentially (e.g., sexual abuse, mental disorder, intellectual deficits; Babcock et al., 2003). As a result, models predicting male-perpetrated domestic violence may not predict female-perpetrated domestic violence (e.g., Kernsmith, 2005b). Because there is a dearth of research on female-perpetrated domestic violence, much more work is needed in this area.

Theories and Causes of Domestic Violence

Theories shape prevention, management, and intervention strategies. Our understanding of the causes and correlates of violence and crime determines *who* or *what* is targeted by treatment and guides policy changes in the criminal justice system (Hollin, 1999). In this section, we turn our attention to theories of domestic violence and look at their strengths and limitations.

Feminist or Gender-Based Theories

Proponents of the feminist or gender-based perspective maintain that domestic violence is primarily perpetrated by men against women and that it is reinforced by social-structural conditions and male assumptions of privilege and domination over women (Dobash & Dobash, 1978). Domestic violence is considered to be distinct from other forms of aggression because it is not an isolated act but rather is *a pattern of coercive control.* Critics of this perspective note (1) the theory's failure to explain abuse in homosexual relationships, (2) the research demonstrating that the majority of men do not condone violence against women, and (3) the predominance of mutual couple aggression, as well as female-only aggression against nonoffending men (Dutton & Nicholls, 2005; Straus, 2006).

Psychiatric Theories

Diagnosable psychiatric disorders are viewed as central to the causes and treatment of domestic violence (Faulk, 1974). This perspective suggests that only people with mental illness abuse their partners and implies that domestic violence is quite rare in the general population. In contrast, many individuals who perpetrate domestic violence do not have a diagnosable mental illness (Kessler et al., 2001).

Sociological Theories

Sociological theories focus on factors that put groups of people at risk of domestic violence; individual differences are de-emphasized. Sociological theories explain domestic violence as a result of social or cultural factors that are external to the individual and exist prior to the abuse. From this perspective, male dominance is viewed as being generated and perpetuated by the larger culture, society, and gender roles (Straus, 1976). Such sociological explanations help to reduce the myth that domestic violence is rare, but they do not explain the fact that domestic violence knows no sociocultural boundaries.

Psychological Theories

Psychological theories of domestic violence emphasize individual differences. Subtle personality differences or extreme dysfunction (e.g., personality disorders) are believed to be the causes and correlates of domestic violence (Dutton, 1998).

Social-Psychological Theories

Social-psychological explanations presume that domestic violence is learned through social interactions (Widom, 1989). Control theories, learning theories, social learning theory, and social labeling are examples of social-psychological explanations of violence.

Nested Ecological Theories

Many of the leading scholars in the domestic violence field have moved from a focus on single-factor explanations to multifactor models (Stith, Smith, Penn, Ward, & Tritt, 2004). Nested ecological theories have a long history in developmental psychology and ethology (see Dutton, 1995) and were introduced to the domestic violence field more than 20 years ago by two of the field's most influential and prolific scholars: Murray Straus (1973) and Donald Dutton (1985). This theory of domestic violence suggests that individual characteristics occur against a backdrop of the family system, the circumstances in which the abuse occurs, and the larger social context of cultural values. Specifically, individual characteristics (e.g., psychological dysfunction, psychiatric disorders) interact with situational determinants

Table 9.1 Definitions and Examples of the Levels of Characteristics in the Nested Ecological Theory of Domestic Violence

Level	Definition	Examples
Macrosystem	• Broadest • Includes *cultural values and beliefs* that influence the development of the individual (ontogenetic) and the social (exosystem) and familial systems • They shape an individual's expectations of his or her partner and how a family "should" function	• Patriarchal beliefs • Traditional gender-role expectations • Women's socioeconomic and political power and influence
Exosystem	• Formal and informal *social structures* that influence the individual	• Friendships • Workplace • Education • Income
Microsystem	• Includes the *circumstances leading up to and surrounding the abusive incident* (i.e., the "couple's conflict pattern" [Dutton, 2006, p. 22] or "the immediate setting" in which abuse occurs [Stith et al., 2004, p. 68])	• Jealousy • Marital separation • Stress
Ontogenetic	• *Individual characteristics of the abuser.* The development and maintenance of these risk factors are believed to be influenced by the other levels and to interact with them.	• Personality dysfunction • Poor coping • Substance abuse • Anger • Cognition

(e.g., intoxication, stress) to create violent outcomes (Dutton, 2006). Factors contributing to domestic violence are categorized into four levels: (1) macrosystem, (2) exosystem, (3) microsystem, and (4) ontogenetic. Table 9.1 provides definitions and examples of each of these levels.

In summary, violence is a complex phenomenon (Hart, 1998) and domestic violence is particularly complex. A review of the various theoretical perspectives demonstrates that most theories are complementary, not competitive (Dutton, 2006). Sociology, psychiatry, psychiatry, sociobiology, criminology—virtually every scholarly field—have made important contributions to our understanding of abuse in intimate relationships. Any single-factor explanation is incapable of explaining the complex dynamics of domestic violence. Thus, a theoretical framework that can account for these findings, such as nested ecological theory, is required. Adopted by agencies such as the WHO (Krug et al., 2002), the nested ecological theory of domestic violence holds considerable promise, but much more research is needed (Dutton, 2006; Stith et al., 2004).

Strategies for Reducing Domestic Violence

"Virtually every policy or action taken regarding crime is based on some underlying theory or theories of crime" (Akers & Sellers, 2004, p. 2). In this section, we review policy and actions aimed at reducing the occurrence of domestic violence, including assessment, intervention, and treatment.

Assessment

Risk assessment is "the process of understanding hazards to minimize their negative consequences" (McNiel et al., 2002, p. 147). It anchors intervention and treatment strategies, providing a transparent and scientifically based means of ensuring that scarce services are delivered to those with the greatest need. There is, however, a longstanding debate regarding the extent to which professionals can forecast violence risk (Monahan & Steadman, 1994).

Early approaches relied primarily on *unguided* or *unaided clinical judgment,* which generally forecast violence at rates no better than chance (Ennis & Litwack, 1974; Monahan, 1981). Actuarial methods were developed to improve risk assessment accuracy. The *actuarial approach* estimates an individual's propensity for the undesired outcome (e.g., domestic violence perpetration) based on statistical formulas or decision-making trees. The Ontario Domestic Assault Risk Assessment (ODARA; Hilton, Harris, Rice, Lang, Cormier, & Lines, 2004) is an example of an actuarial approach to domestic violence risk assessment. Actuarial measures consistently outperform unaided clinical judgment (e.g., Monahan et al., 2001), but they have been critiqued for their failure to inform decision making about a specific individual (Hart, Michie, & Cooke, 2007). Because they rely primarily on static or unchangeable variables (e.g., gender, prior offending), their capacity to shape risk management plans also is limited (Nicholls, Desmarais, Douglas, & Kropp, 2007). By focusing on risk factors that, by definition, we cannot change (e.g., being male vs. female, having a history of violence, age), actuarial measures may still identify as "high" risk those individuals who change their behavior over time (see Douglas & Skeem, 2005).

Structured professional judgment (SPJ) combines empirical evidence and clinical knowledge. SPJ measures, such as the Spousal Assault Risk Assessment Guide (SARA; Kropp, Hart, Webster, & Eaves, 1999), guide assessors to consider a minimum number of variables. The assessment is sufficiently structured to be transparent and replicable, yet it allows for professional discretion. For example, after coding each of the 20 items on the SARA, assessors form an overall judgment of low, moderate, or high risk for future abuse, rather than simply total the item scores. In this way, assessors can take into consideration factors that may be particularly important in a given case. Emphasis is placed on the value of clinically relevant or treatment-friendly factors that inform risk management in the individual case.

Although the debate regarding the most appropriate method for conducting risk assessments persists, there is widespread agreement that evaluations structured by research-informed measures outperform unaided clinical assessments (Webster & Hucker, 2007). Domestic violence risk assessment should consider information gathered through multiple methods and from multiple sources, including official records (e.g., police reports, criminal history), self-reports of the couple (both perpetrator and victim), and collateral informants (e.g., family, children, friends, neighbors). A small number of well-designed studies of female victims of male abusers suggest that victims' perceptions contribute significantly to the accuracy of risk judgments (e.g., Heckert & Gondolf, 2004). Current and historical information should be considered, as well as projections for the future (Webster et al., 1997). Beyond the scope of this chapter, readers are referred to Dutton and Kropp (2000), Kropp (2007), and Nicholls et al. (2007) for reviews of domestic violence risk assessment measures.

Intervention and Treatment

There are three levels of violence prevention: primary, secondary, and tertiary (see Table 9.2). Most intervention and treatment strategies are at the tertiary level (Gunderson, 2002).

Perpetrator-Targeted Strategies

In the criminal justice system, mandatory (or pro-) arrest policies have been implemented as intervention strategies. In the United States, all states authorize warrantless arrests of perpetrators based on the arresting police officer's determination that a domestic violence offence has occurred and that the person arrested has committed this offence (Dutton & Corvo, 2006). In 21 states and the District of Columbia, arrest is mandatory (Miller, 2004). Some research suggests that pro-arrest policies can have a deterrent effect for perpetrators (e.g., a 30% reduction in aggression following arrest; Barnett, 2000). However, other research suggests that pro-arrest policies have a deterrent effect only for those individuals most likely to socially conform (e.g., married, educated, employed) and may aggravate rates of domestic violence in other groups (e.g., unmarried, uneducated, unemployed; for a review, see Gelles, 1993). For example, one study found that domestic violence recidivism occurred 20% earlier following arrest compared to following warning (Sherman et al., 1992).

Table 9.2   Definitions and Examples of the Three Levels of Domestic Violence Prevention

Level	Definition	Examples
Primary	• Prevents the *onset* of violence • Broad, public-based, *targets everyone* • Typically educational	• Media messages (e.g., posters in public places) • Elementary school education
Secondary	• Early detection and treatment • Targets *at-risk* populations • Prevents violence from becoming an entrenched pattern	• First-time offender programming • Victim safety planning
Tertiary	• Takes place *after* violence has occurred • Targets *victims and perpetrators* • "Damage control"	• Batterer intervention programs • Victim shelter services

Pro-prosecution policies, or the mandatory ("no-drop") prosecution of domestic violence perpetrators, are parallel intervention strategies (Dutton & Corvo, 2006). Some victims do not pursue criminal charges against their abusive partners (Drumbl, 1994); thus, pro-prosecution policies were introduced to shift the onus from the victim to the criminal justice system. Some argue that pro-prosecution and pro-arrest policies disempower the victim by duplicating the power-control differential present in abusive relationships (e.g., Hoyle & Sanders, 2000; Mills, 2003; Young, Cook, Smith, Turteltaub, & Hazlewood, 2007). These strategies also may conflict with victims' desires to reunite with their partners (Ursel & Brickey, 1996).

Other criminal justice interventions include post-conviction sanctions against domestic violence perpetrators, such as probation. For domestic violence perpetrators, enforceable probation conditions may include orders to refrain from contacting ("no-contact" order) or from being in the vicinity of the victim ("no-go" order), also known as protection orders. Such conditions are intended to ensure that the perpetrator cannot continue to be abusive toward the victim, either directly or indirectly. However, protection orders may give victims a false sense of security because these orders may be easily, and frequently are, breached by the abusive partner (Mills, 2003). Another condition of probation may be mandated treatment, in which the court directs a perpetrator to participate in treatment for domestic violence (Babcock & Steiner, 1999).

Mandated treatments, often called Batterer Intervention Programs (BIPs), combine punishment and rehabilitation (Babcock, Green, & Robie,

2004). There are three approaches to treatment: psychoeducational (i.e., re-education, skill building), group therapy, and couples therapy (Healey, Smith, & O'Sullivan, 1998). The first BIP, a psychoeducational program, was developed in the 1980s by the Domestic Abuse Intervention Project in Duluth, Minnesota. Widely known as the Duluth Model, this program takes a pro-feminist approach and is based on the theory that society's explicit sanctioning of men's use of power and control over women is the primary cause of domestic violence (Dutton & Corvo, 2007; Babcock et al., 2004). The goal of the program is to shift domestic violence perpetrators' thinking from power and control to equality in intimate relationships.

The Duluth Model has formed the basis for other BIPs. The two largest and most recognized BIPs in the United States are the EMERGE (Quincy, Massachusetts) and AMEND (Denver, Colorado) programs (for a review, see Healey et al., 1998). These programs incorporate some of the tenets of the Duluth Model (e.g., skills building, re-education), but diverge by including more in-depth group therapy requiring the perpetrators to accept responsibility for their aggressive behavior. EMERGE focuses on the abusive relationship and the emotional consequences of the domestic violence for the victim (known as *accountability-focused group therapy*). AMEND focuses on the perpetrator's maladaptive moral development that may be the origin of the abusive behavior. Overall, analyses of the effectiveness of BIPs have found modest, but significant, reductions in domestic violence recidivism (treatment effect sizes ranged from $r = .06$ to .17; Babcock et al., 2004). The majority of this research, however, has been conducted with male BIP participants only.

Victim-Targeted Strategies

There also are a number of interventions tailored specifically to assist victims' escapes and efforts to recuperate from their domestic violence victimization. For example, victims may access shelters and crisis centers, which provide housing for victims leaving an abusive partner. The shelters and crisis centers may also facilitate access to other services that may aid in reducing revictimization (e.g., advocacy, legal services; Mears, 2003). Recognizing that domestic violence has no boundaries, services are responsive to the diversity of female victims affected (Denham & Gillespie, 1998); however, there exist few services for male victims (Dutton & Corvo, 2006).

For serious and recurring domestic violence cases, shelters and crisis centers may not afford sufficient protection. In such cases, victim relocation services are available. Similar to the Federal Witness Protection program, these services provide a victim (and dependents) with legal documentation to establish a new identity (e.g., name, Social Security number, birth certificates; Haberman, 2005). The location and identity of the victim cannot be disclosed, unless it can be shown that the perpetrator is no longer a threat.

For all victims, safety planning is a critical tool in ensuring their well-being. A safety plan is an individualized plan that is developed to help a victim cope with and/or anticipate violence without holding the victim responsible for the violence (Davies, Lyon, & Monti-Catania, 1998). Safety planning strategies include having a password with relatives that indicates that violence is occurring or hiding a small bag with necessities (e.g., cash, identification, passport, car keys, a change of clothes) in case an urgent escape is necessary.

Despite a wealth of research on intervention and treatment methods, there is little consensus about what is *consistently* and *significantly* (i.e., contributing to substantial changes in behavior) effective in reducing domestic violence (Mears, 2003). In contrast to the significant body of literature evaluating screening and assessment strategies, there is a dearth of research evaluating interventions (Krug et al., 2002).

A Case Study: Joseph and Millie

The following case study illustrates the major concepts reviewed in this chapter. Although based on an actual police case, identifying information has been altered to protect the privacy of individuals involved.

Background

Joseph Whipple is a 52-year-old man recently convicted of spousal assault causing bodily harm of his partner, Millie Johnston (age 59). Joseph and Millie have lived in a common law relationship for 17 years.

Both Joseph and Millie are currently unemployed and on disability benefits. Joseph has been on disability benefits since his mid-thirties, due to chronic back pain from a car accident. Millie has just recently begun receiving disability benefits for chronic depression. Both have an extensive history of alcohol abuse. Joseph is a recovering alcoholic who recently "fell off the wagon." Millie also drinks quite heavily (approximately one bottle of rum every three days), but she insists that it is not a problem. In addition, Joseph has battled an addiction to methamphetamine and admitted to recently using heroin and cocaine. Millie does not tolerate drug use, which has exacerbated problems in their relationship. Joseph has been attempting to access community mental health services for his addiction problems. Millie receives ongoing out-patient treatment for chronic depression.

Intimate Relationship

The 17 years of Joseph and Millie's relationship has been tumultuous, especially when one or both partners are intoxicated. The couple is known as the "fighting couple" in the townhouse complex where they live, due to their constant and loud arguments.

On occasion, Joseph and Millie have been seen pushing each other. On several occasions, Millie has locked Joseph out of their house and thrown items at him from the upstairs window. Neighbors have reported hearing Joseph verbally and physically assault Millie, although no police action was taken. Millie recently informed Joseph that she wanted to relocate to Florida and intended to leave with or without him. A number of verbal arguments ensued.

Current Incident

On the night of the incident that led to Joseph's arrest, police were called to the residence by a neighbor. Intoxicated, Joseph had gone to the neighbor's door and stated that he had "killed the love of his life." Police arrived on the scene to find Millie in the living room, lying on the floor in a pool of blood. She was unconscious, but alive. She had several knife wounds along the back of her legs, arms, and shoulders. Her forehead was swollen and purple. Joseph was found in a local pub drinking beer; he stated, "Oh my poor Millie! Is she hurt real bad?" and "I wasn't going to kill her; I needed her to make me dinner." In addition, Joseph indicated that he had a stroke and could not remember how the incident occurred.

Further investigation revealed that on the evening of the incident, both were intoxicated. Millie had been pinching Joseph in the arm, a common habit of hers to get his attention, which upset him. At one point, he shoved her away from him, and she fell and hit her forehead on the coffee table, which knocked her unconscious. Joseph stated he then "snapped" and grabbed a box-cutter knife and began to cut her. He stated in the interview, "She didn't say anything, just laid there and took it, just like all women, like pieces of sh-t." When the phone rang, disturbing him, he stumbled over to his neighbor's townhouse.

Police Actions and Case Outcome

Joseph was arrested, charged, and convicted of assault causing bodily harm. He was sentenced to prison for less than a year, in conjunction with a no-contact order. Joseph, however, contacted Millie via multiple letters, expressing remorse for his actions and intent to reunite with her. Millie refused to participate in victim counseling and did not relocate to Florida.

Summary

This case study highlights a number of key features of domestic violence. It is evident that Joseph and Millie's intimate relationship is mutually abusive. In this case, it is difficult to concretely label one partner as the "perpetrator" and one as the "victim" over the course of their relationship. Both show many risk factors for domestic violence, including substance abuse, financial problems, history of abuse, and attitudes that condone violence. Aside from the obvious physical injuries, there is evidence that Millie's mental health has been adversely affected over the years of abuse (e.g., chronic depression, alcohol use). Joseph may be similarly impacted by the ongoing domestic strife (e.g., substance use). It is not clear whether their current life circumstances are the result of or the precursor to abuse.

The Case Study also demonstrates the potential for domestic violence to be repetitive and processional in nature (i.e., severity and/or frequency of domestic violence may increase over time; Lempert, 1996). Despite intervention, victims do not necessarily end the relationship and often are battered repeatedly before they seek assistance (Anderson & Saunders, 2003). Research suggests that, on average, victims make five attempts to leave before they actually terminate the relationship (Okun, 1986). Terminating domestic violence is a very complex process (Anderson & Saunders, 2003).

Conclusion

The lack of research on domestic violence perpetrated by women against men has been a recurring theme in this chapter. With gender-*exclusive* policies the norm, we are disregarding the detrimental effects of female perpetration and male victimization and essentially preventing the delivery of effective treatment intervention to high-risk groups (Dutton & Corvo, 2006; Dutton & Nicholls, 2005). Domestic violence in varying relationship contexts, such as among elderly intimate partners (Desmarais & Reeves, 2007) and in homosexual relationships (Cruz & Firestone, 1998), also has largely been ignored. Despite important advances in research, policy, and practice over the last 30 years, domestic violence remains a serious social problem and more gender-*inclusive* work is needed.

There has been very little examination of the role of protective factors (e.g., social support, intelligence, occupational success), and we know little about desisters (i.e., people who were abusive but who no longer engage in domestic violence). It also generally seems to be overlooked that one-third of domestically violent relationships resolve without intervention (Dutton, 2006). A better understanding of protective factors that reduce the risk of domestic violence would greatly benefit current theories and intervention strategies.

Discussion Questions

1. Should measures developed for assessing the risk for male-perpetrated domestic violence against a female intimate partner be used to assess the risk for female-perpetrated domestic violence against a male intimate partner? Does treatment designed for a male perpetrator need to be modified when applied to a female perpetrator?

2. What factors might protect against domestic violence? Why or how?

3. At the individual, community, and societal levels, what can be done to prevent domestic violence?

Internet Resources

American Bar Association Commission on Domestic Violence: http://www.abanet.org/domviol/home.html

Centers for Disease Control and Prevention, Intimate Partner Violence Overview: http://www.cdc.gov/ncipc/factsheets/ipvfacts.htm

National Coalition Against Domestic Violence: http://www.ncadv.org

United States Department of Justice, Domestic Violence: http://www.usdoj.gov/ovw/domviolence.htm

References

Akers, R. L., & Sellers, C. S. (2004). *Criminological theories: Introduction, evaluation, and application* (4th ed.). Los Angeles: Roxbury.

American Medical Association. (1995). *Strategies for the treatment and prevention of sexual assault.* Chicago: Author.

Anderson, D. K., & Saunders, D. G. (2003). Leaving an abusive partner: An empirical review of predictors, the process of leaving, and psychological well-being. *Trauma, Violence, & Abuse, 4,* 163–191.

Archer, J. (2000). Sex differences in aggression between heterosexual partners: A meta-analytic review. *Psychological Bulletin, 126,* 651–680.

Arias, I., & Corso, P. (2005). Average cost per person victimized by an intimate partner of the opposite gender: A comparison of men and women. *Violence and Victims, 20,* 379–391.

Babcock, J. C., Green, C. E., & Robie, C. (2004). Does batterers' treatment work? A meta-analytic review of domestic violence treatment. *Clinical Psychology Review, 23,* 1023–1053.

Babcock, J. C., Miller, S. A., & Siard, C. (2003). Toward a typology of abusive women: Differences between partner-only and generally violent women in the use of violence. *Psychology of Women Quarterly, 27,* 153–161.

Babcock, J. C., & Steiner, R. (1999). The relationship between treatment, incarceration, and recidivism of battering: A program evaluation of Seattle's coordinated community response to domestic violence. *Journal of Family Psychology, 13,* 46–59.

Barnett, O. W. (2000). Why battered women do not leave, part 1: External inhibiting factors within society. *Trauma, Violence, & Abuse, 1,* 343–372.

Beck, C. J. A., & Frost, L. E. (2006). Defining a threshold for client competence to participate in divorce mediation. *Psychology, Public Policy, and Law, 12,* 1–35.

Bent-Goodley, T., & Fowler, B. (2006). Spiritual and religious abuse: Expanding what is known about domestic violence. *Affilia, 21,* 282–295.

Cale, E. M., & Lilienfeld, S. O. (2002). Histrionic personality disorder and antisocial personality disorder: Sex-differentiated manifestations of psychopathy? *Journal of Personality Disorders, 16,* 52–72.

Campbell, J. C. (2002). Health consequences of intimate partner violence. *The Lancet, 369,* 1331–1336.

Campbell, J. C., Glass, N., Sharps, P. W., Laughon, K., & Bloom, T. (2007). Intimate partner homicide: Review and implications of research and policy. *Trauma, Violence, & Abuse, 8,* 246–269.

Coker, A. L., Davis, K. E., Arias, I., Desai, S., Sanderson, M., Brandt, H. M., et al. (2002). Physical and mental health effects of intimate partner violence for men and women. *American Journal of Preventative Medicine, 23,* 260–268.

Coleman, F. L. (1997). Stalking behaviour and the cycle of domestic violence. *Journal of Interpersonal Violence, 12,* 420–432.

Cruz, J. M., & Firestone, J. M. (1998). Exploring violence and abuse in gay male relationships. *Violence and Victims, 13,* 159–173.

Davies, J., Lyon, E., & Monti-Catania, D. (1998). *Safety planning with battered women: Complex lives/difficult choices.* Thousand Oaks, CA: Sage.

Denham, D., & Gillespie, J. (1998). Two steps forward . . . one step back: An overview of Canadian initiatives and resources to end woman abuse, 1989–1997. Ottawa, ON: Health Canada, Family Violence Prevention Unit.

Desmarais, S. L., & Reeves, K. A. (2007). Gray, black, & blue: The state of research and intervention for intimate partner abuse among elders. *Behavioral Sciences & the Law, 25,* 377–391.

Dobash, R. E., & Dobash, R. P. (1978). Wives: The appropriate victims of marital assault. *Victimology, 2,* 426–442.

Douglas, K. S., & Skeem, J. (2005). Violence risk assessment: Getting specific about being dynamic. *Psychology, Public Policy, and Law, 11,* 347–383.

Drumbl, M. (1994). Civil, constitutional, and criminal justice responses to female partner abuse: Proposal for reform. *Canadian Journal of Family Law, 12,* 115.

Dutton, D. G. (1985). An ecologically nested theory of male violence toward intimates. *International Journal of Women's Studies, 8,* 404–413.

Dutton, D. G. (1995). *The domestic assault of women: Psychological and criminological perspectives.* Vancouver, BC: UBC Press.

Dutton, D. G. (1998). *The abusive personality: Violence and control in intimate relationships.* New York: Guilford Press.

Dutton, D. G. (2006). *Re-thinking domestic violence.* Vancouver, BC: UBC Press.

Dutton, D. G., & Corvo, K. (2006). Transforming a flawed policy: A call to revive psychology and science in domestic violence research and practice. *Aggression and Violent Behavior, 11,* 457–483.

Dutton, D. G., & Corvo, K. (2007). The Duluth model: A data-impervious paradigm and a failed strategy. *Aggression and Violent Behavior, 12,* 658–667.

Dutton, D. G., & Kropp, P. R. (2000). A review of domestic violence risk instruments. *Trauma, Violence and Abuse, 1,* 171–182.

Dutton, D. G., & Nicholls, T. L. (2005). The gender paradigm in domestic violence research and theory: Part 1—The conflict of theory and data. *Aggression and Violent Behavior, 10,* 680–714.

English, D., Marshall, D., & Stewart, A. (2003). Effects of family violence on child behavior and health during early childhood. *Journal of Family Violence, 18,* 43–57.

Ennis, B. J., & Litwack, T. R. (1974). Psychiatry and the presumption of expertise: Flipping coins in the courtroom. *California Law Review, 62,* 693–752.

Fals-Stewart, W., & Kennedy, C. (2005). Addressing intimate partner violence in substance-abuse treatment. *Journal of Substance Abuse Treatment, 29,* 5–17.

Faulk, M. (1974). Men who assault their wives. *Medicine, Science and the Law, 14,* 180–183.

Flinck, A., Paavilainen, E., & Åstedt-Kurki, P. (2005). Survival of intimate partner violence as experienced by women. *Journal of Clinical Nursing, 14,* 383–393.

Foa, E. B., Cascardi, M., Zoellner, L. A., & Feeny, N. C. (2000). Psychological and environmental factors associated with partner violence. *Trauma, Violence, & Abuse, 1,* 67–91.

Foshee, V. A., Benefield, T. S., Ennett, S. T., Bauman, K. E., & Suchindran, C. (2004). Longitudinal predictors of serious physical and sexual dating violence victimization during adolescence. *Preventive Medicine, 39,* 1007–1016.

Garcia-Morena, C., Jansen, H. A. F. M, Ellsberg, M., & Watts, C. H. (2006). Prevalence of intimate partner violence: Findings from the WHO multi-country study on women's health and domestic violence. *The Lancet, 368,* 1260–1269.

Gelles, R. J. (1993). Constraints against family violence: How well do they work? *American Behavioral Scientist, 36,* 575–586.

Gunderson, L. (2002). Intimate-partner violence: The need for primary prevention in the community. *Current Clinical Issues, 136,* 637–640.

Haberman, P. S. (2005). Before death we must part: Relocation and protection for domestic violence victims in volatile divorce and custody situations. *Family Court Review, 43,* 149–163.

Hart, S. D. (1998). The role of psychopathy in assessing risk for violence: Conceptual and methodological issues. *Legal and Criminological Psychology, 3,* 121–137.

Hart, S. D., Michie, C., & Cooke, D. J. (2007). Precision of actuarial risk assessment instruments: Evaluating the "margins of error" of group v. individual predictions of violence. *British Journal of Psychiatry, 190,* s60–s65.

Healey, K., Smith, C., & O'Sullivan, C. (1998). *Batterer intervention: Program approaches and criminal justice strategies.* Washington, DC: U.S. Department of Justice.

Heckert, D. A., & Gondolf, E. W. (2004). Battered women's perceptions of risk versus risk factors and instruments in predicting repeat reassault. *Journal of Interpersonal Violence, 19,* 778–800.

Hegarty, K., Hindmarsh, E. D., & Gilles, M. T. (2000). Domestic violence in Australia: Definition, prevalence and nature of presentation in clinical practice. *Medicine and the Community, 173,* 363–367.

Hilton, N. Z., Harris, G. T., Rice, M. E., Lang, C., Cormier, C. A., & Lines, K. J. (2004). A brief actuarial assessment for the prediction of wife assault recidivism: The Ontario Domestic Assault Risk Assessment. *Psychological Assessment, 16,* 267–275.

Hollin, C. R. (1999). Treatment programs for offenders: Meta-analysis, "What works," and beyond. *International Journal of Law and Psychiatry, 22,* 361–372.

Holtzworth-Munroe, A., Bates, L., Smutzler, N., & Sandin, E. (1997). A brief review of the research on husband violence: I. Maritally violent versus non-violent men. *Aggression and Violent Behavior, 2,* 65–99.

Holtzworth-Munroe, A., Clements, K., & Farris, C. (2005). Working with couples who have experienced physical aggression. In M. Harway (Ed.), *Handbook of couples therapy* (pp. 289–312). Hoboken, NJ: John Wiley & Sons.

Holtzworth-Munroe, A., & Meehan, J. C. (2004). Typologies of men who are maritally violent: Scientific and clinical implications. *Journal of Interpersonal Violence, 19,* 1369–1389.

Hoyle, C., & Sanders, A. (2000). Police response to domestic violence: From victim choice to victim empowerment? *British Journal of Criminology, 40,* 14–36.

Janssen, P. A., Holt, V. L., Sugg, N. K., Emanuel, I., Critchlow, C. M., & Henderson, A. D. (2003). Intimate partner violence and adverse pregnancy outcomes: A population-based study. *American Journal of Obstetrics and Gynecology, 188,* 1341–1347.

Johnson, I. M., & Sigler, R. T. (2000). Public perceptions: The stability of the public's endorsement of the definition and criminalization of the abuse of women. *Journal of Criminal Justice, 28,* 165–179.

Johnson, J., & Indvik, P. R. (1999). The organizational benefits of assisting domestically abused employees. *Public Personnel Management, 28,* 365–374.

Johnson, M. P. (2001). Conflict and control: Symmetry and asymmetry in domestic violence. In A. Booth & A. C. Crouter (Eds.), *Couples in conflict* (pp. 94–104). Mahwah, NJ: Lawrence Erlbaum Associates.

Kernic, M. A., Wolf, M. E., & Holt, V. L. (2000). Rates and relative risk of hospital admission among women in violent intimate partner relationships. *American Journal of Public Health, 90,* 1416–1420.

Kernsmith, P. (2005a). Exerting power or striking back: A gendered comparison of motivations for domestic violence perpetration. *Violence and Victims, 20,* 173–185.

Kernsmith, P. (2005b). Treating perpetrators of domestic violence: Gender differences in the applicability of the theory of planned behaviour. *Sex Roles, 52,* 757–770.

Kessler, R. C., Molnar, B. E., Feurer, I. D., & Appelbaum, M. (2001). Patterns and mental health predictors of domestic violence in the United States: Results from the National Comorbidity Survey. *International Journal of Law and Psychiatry, 24,* 487–508.

Klevens, J., Shelley, G., Clavel-Arcas, C., Barney, D. D., Tobar, C., Duran, E. X., et al. (2007). Latinos' perspectives and experiences with intimate partner violence. *Violence Against Women, 13,* 141–158.

Kropp, P. R. (2007). Spousal assaulters. In C. D. Webster & S. J. Hucker (Eds.), *Violence risk assessment and management* (pp. 123–131). West Sussex, England: John Wiley & Sons.

Kropp, P. R., Hart, S. D., Webster, C. D., & Eaves, D. (1999). *Manual for the Spousal Assault Risk Assessment Guide* (3rd ed.). Toronto, ON: Multi-Health Systems.

Krug, E., Dahlberg, L. L., Mercy, J. A., Zwi, A. B., & Lozano, R. (Eds.). (2002). *World report on violence and health.* Geneva: World Health Organization.

Lambert, L., & Firestone, J. M. (2000). Economic context and multiple abuse techniques. *Violence Against Women, 6,* 49–67.

Langhinrichsen-Rohling, J., Neidig, P., & Thorn, G. (1995). Violent marriages: Gender differences in levels of current violence and past abuse. *Journal of Family Violence, 10,* 159–175.

Lempert, L. B. (1996). Women's strategies for survival: Developing agency in abusive relationships. *Journal of Family Violence, 11,* 269–289.

Levinson, D. (1989). *Family violence in cross-cultural perspective.* Thousand Oaks, CA: Sage.

Lloyd, S. (1997). The effects of domestic violence on women's employment. *Law & Policy, 19,* 139–167.

McNiel, D. E., Borum, R., Douglas, K. S., Hart, S. D., Lyon, D. R., Sullivan, L. E., et al. (2002). In J. R. P. Ogloff (Ed.), *Taking psychology and law into the twenty-first century* (pp. 147–170). New York: Kluwer Academic.

McNutt, L. A., Carlson, B. E., Persaud, M., & Postmus, J. (2002). Cumulative abuse experiences, physical health and health behaviors. *Annals of Epidemiology, 12,* 123–130.

Mears, D. P. (2003). Research and interventions to reduce domestic violence revictimization. *Trauma, Violence, & Abuse, 4,* 127–147.

Melton, H. C. (2007). Predicting the occurrence of stalking in relationships characterized by domestic violence. *Journal of Interpersonal Violence, 22,* 3–25.

Merriam-Webster's collegiate dictionary (11th ed.). (2003). Springfield, MA: Merriam-Webster.

Miller, N. (2004). *Domestic violence legislation.* Retrieved August 28, 2005, from www.ilj.org/dv/Papers/DV_Legislation3 .pdf

Mills, L. (2003). *Insult to injury: Rethinking our responses to intimate abuse.* Princeton, NJ: Princeton University Press.

Monahan, J. (1981). *Predicting violent behavior: An assessment of clinical techniques.* Beverly Hills, CA: Sage.

Monahan, J., & Steadman, H. (1994). *Violence and mental disorder: Developments in risk assessment.* Chicago: Chicago Press.

Monahan, J., Steadman, H. J., Silver, E., Appelbaum, P. S., Robbins, P. C., Mulvey,

E. P., et al. (2001). *Rethinking risk assessment: The MacArthur study of mental disorder and violence.* New York: Oxford University Press.

Nicholls, T. L., Desmarais, S. L., Douglas, K. S., & Kropp, P. R. (2007). Assessment of high risk perpetrators of intimate partner abuse. In J. Hamel & T. L. Nicholls (Eds.), *Family therapy for domestic violence: A practitioner's guide to gender-inclusive research and treatment* (pp. 275–301). London: Springer.

Nicholls, T. L., & Dutton, D. G. (2001). Abuse committed by women against male intimates. *Journal of Couples Therapy, 10,* 41–57.

Nicholls, T. L., Ogloff, J. R. P., & Douglas, K. S. (2004). Assessing risk for violence among male and female civil psychiatric patients: The HCR-20, PCL:SV, and VSC. *Behavioral Sciences & the Law, 22,* 127–158.

Okun, L. (1986). *Women abuse: Facts replacing myths.* New York: State University of New York Press.

O'Leary, K. D. (1999). Psychological abuse: A variable deserving critical attention in domestic violence. *Violence & Victims, 14,* 3–23.

Phillips, L., Torres de Ardon, E., & Briones, G. (2000). Abuse of female caregivers by care recipients: Another form of elder abuse. *Journal of Elder Abuse & Neglect, 12,* 123–144.

Plichta, S. (2004). Intimate partner violence and physical health consequences: Policy and practice implications. *Journal of Interpersonal Violence, 19,* 1296–1323.

Professional Education Taskforce on Family Violence. (1991). *Family violence: Everybody's business, somebody's life.* Sydney, Australia: Federation Press.

Ramsey-Klawsnik, H. (2003). Elder sexual abuse within the family. *Journal of Elder Abuse & Neglect, 15,* 43–58.

Rhodes, N. R., & McKenzie, E. B. (1998). Why do battered women stay? Three decades of research. *Aggression and Violent Behavior, 3,* 391–406.

Rivara, F. P., Anderson, M. L., Fishman, P., Bonomi, A. E., Reid, R. J., Carrell, D., et al. (2007). Healthcare utilization and costs for women with a history of intimate partner violence. *American Journal of Preventive Medicine, 32,* 89–96.

Sherman, L. W., Schmidt, J. D., Rogan, D. P., Smith, D. A., Gartin, P. R., & Cohn, E. G., et al. (1992). The variable effects of arrest on criminal careers: The Milwaukee domestic violence experiment. *Journal of Criminal Law and Criminology, 83,* 137–169.

Stanko, E. A., Crisp, D., Hale, C., & Lucraft, H. (1998). *Counting the costs: Estimating the impact of domestic violence in the London borough of Hackney.* Swindon, UK: Crime Concern. Retrieved August 31, 2007, from http://www.met.police.uk/dv/files/estimate_impact.pdf

Statistics Canada. (2005). *Family violence in Canada: A statistical profile.* Ottawa, ON: Author.

Stith, S. M., Rosen, K. H., Middleton, K. A., Busch, A. L., Lundenberg, K., & Carlton, R. P. (2000). The intergenerational transmission of spouse abuse: A meta-analysis. *Journal of Marriage & the Family, 62,* 640–654.

Stith, S. M., Smith, D. B., Penn, C. E., Ward, D. B., & Tritt, D. (2004). Intimate partner physical abuse perpetration and victimization risk factors: A meta-analysis review. *Aggression and Violent Behavior, 10,* 65–98.

Straus, M. A. (1973). A general systems theory approach to a theory of violence between family members. *Social Science Information, 12,* 105–125.

Straus, M. A. (1976). Sexual inequality, cultural norm and wife beating. *Victimology, 2,* 443–459.

Straus, M. A. (2006). Future research on gender symmetry in physical assaults on partners. *Violence Against Women, 12,* 1086–1097.

Stuart, G. L., Moore, T. M., Ramsey, S. E., & Kahler, C. W. (2003). Relationship aggression and substance use among women court-referred to domestic violence intervention programs. *Addictive Behaviors, 28,* 1603–1610.

Thompson, M. P., & Kingree, J. B. (2006). The roles of victim and perpetrator alcohol use in intimate partner violence outcomes. *Journal of Interpersonal Violence, 21,* 163–177.

Tjaden, P., & Thoennes, N. (2000). *Extent, nature, and consequences of intimate partner violence: Findings from the National Violence Against Women Survey.* Washington, DC: U.S. Department of Justice, National Institute of Justice.

Tolman, R. M., & Rosen, D. (2001). Domestic violence in the lives of women receiving welfare. *Violence Against Women, 7,* 141–158.

Ursel, J. E., & Brickey, S. (1996). The potential of legal reform reconsidered: An examination of Manitoba's zero-tolerance policy on family violence. In T. O'Reilly-Fleming (Ed.), *Post-critical criminology* (pp. 56–77). Scarborough, ON: Prentice-Hall.

U.S. Department of Justice. (n.d.). *Domestic violence.* Retrieved July 8, 2007, from http://www.usdoj.gov/ovw/domviolence.htm.

Webster, C. D., Douglas, K. S., Eaves, D. & Hart, S. D. (1997). *HCR-20: Assessing risk for violence (Version 2).* Burnaby, BC: Simon Fraser University, Mental Health Law and Policy Institute.

Webster, C. D., & Hucker, S. J. (2007). *Violence risk assessment and management.* West Sussex, England: John Wiley & Sons.

Whitaker, D. J., Haileyesus, T., Swahn, M. H., & Saltzman, L. S. (2007). Differences in frequency of violence and reported injury between relationships with reciprocal and nonreciprocal intimate partner violence. *American Journal of Public Health, 97,* 941–947.

Widom, C. (1989). Does violence beget violence? A critical examination of the literature. *Psychological Bulletin, 106,* 13–28.

Wolak, J., & Finkelhor, D. (1998). Children exposed to partner violence. In J. Jasinski & L. Williams (Eds.), *Partner violence: A comprehensive review of 20 years of research* (pp. 184–209). Thousand Oaks, CA: Sage.

Young, C., Cook, P., Smith, S., Turteltaub, J., & Hazlewood, L. (2007). Domestic violence: New visions, new solutions. In J. Hamel & T. L. Nicholls (Eds.), *Family therapy for domestic violence: A practitioner's guide to gender-inclusive research and treatment* (pp. 601–619). London: Springer.

Zona, M. A., Sharma, K. K, & Lane, J. L. (1993). A comparative study of erotomania and obsessional subjects in a forensic sample. *Journal of Forensic Sciences, 65,* 894–903.

CHAPTER 10

Physical Child Abuse

Mary E. Haskett, Sharon G. Portwood,
and Kristen M. Lewis

Background

Although rates of physical child abuse in the U.S. have been declining since the mid-1990s (Finkelhor & Jones, 2006), many children are physically abused every year. According to *Child Maltreatment 2005* (Children's Bureau, 2005), the most recent report of data from the National Child Abuse and Neglect Data System, approximately 899,000 U.S. children were victims of child abuse or neglect in 2005. Of this number, 16.6% were physically abused. Physical abuse occurs across all ethnic and racial groups; in 2005, 10.3% of victims were Hispanic, 14% were African American, 16.6% were Asian, 11.5% were Pacific Islander, and 10% were white. The remainder were self-reported as other ethnic minorities or multiple races or were of unknown race. In 2005, the largest group of perpetrators of physical abuse was parents (76.5%), including birth parents, adoptive parents, and stepparents. Recent nationwide surveys in the U.S. indicate that the prevalence rate of physical abuse is approximately 4% of the population (Finkelhor, Ormrod, Turner, & Hamby, 2005; Straus, Hamby, Finkelhor, Moore, & Runyan, 1998).

CASE STUDY: DANA

When Dana, a pregnant 23-year-old African American woman, entered our treatment program, she had been married to Doug for six years. Doug was the father of her four children. The oldest child, Brian, was highly aggressive and noncompliant in both home and school settings.

(Continued)

(Continued)

Developmentally delayed twin daughters were 5 years of age. The 10-month-old baby was underweight and malnourished. Dana was unable to work due to complications associated with her pregnancy; thus, the family income was limited to Doug's salary as a cook at a nearby restaurant and financial assistance from Temporary Aid to Needy Families (TANF). Doug worked long hours in an effort to earn overtime pay. Although he was committed to his family, he was rarely home to help with parenting responsibilities. Dana's mother lived next door to the family and Dana was very involved in her church, which provided emotional and social support. The family lived in a public housing complex characterized by a high level of community violence; Dana insisted that her children stay in the house for their safety. The home was kept clean and neat, but there were only two bedrooms and the housing complex had failed to repair a broken air conditioner. The heat in the summer months was nearly unbearable.

Dana had a lifetime history of depression and was experiencing severe depression at the time the family was referred for treatment. She felt trapped by her children and did not look forward to the baby's arrival. Because she did not allow her children to go outside, they had few forms of entertainment and limited social contact. Brian, recently diagnosed with Attention Deficit/Hyperactivity Disorder, was expected to take care of his baby brother. He most often ignored the baby and fought constantly with his sisters. On one occasion, Brian left the house and Dana was charged with child neglect when he was found unsupervised at the neighborhood pool. Several months later, Brian attempted to leave the house again and the twins ran to get their mother. Dana grabbed Brian as he tried to leave the house, pushed him against the apartment wall, which resulted in a laceration on his forehead, and slapped him hard across the face. When Brian went to school the next day, the teacher noticed the marks on his face and made a report to child protective services. Dana was charged with physical abuse. Following that incident, the family was referred to a multifamily group intervention to address their multiple needs. The family was characterized by many risk factors, including Dana's elevated level of parenting stress and her depression, community violence, poverty and inadequate housing, and children with special needs. However, there also were some protective factors in place, including a supportive family member nearby, a loving husband and father, and a supportive church community. In addition, the family lived in a city rich with family support services. Many services were mobilized to help Dana's family, including mental health treatment for Dana, afterschool care and child care for the children, home visiting services for Dana after the birth of her child, and assistance from the local food bank.

Outcomes of abuse vary widely, but for many children, physical abuse has a devastating and lasting impact. Physical injuries are obvious manifestations of abuse and may include mild injuries, such as bruises and lacerations, as well as more serious injuries such as subdural hemorrhages, burns, or bone fractures. Delayed growth, permanent physical disabilities, and, in the most extreme cases, death are also possible. In addition to the physical manifestations of abuse, physical child abuse is associated with disturbances in cognitive, social, and emotional development (Lansford, Dodge, Pettit, Bates, Crozier, & Kaplow, 2002). Specifically, children who experience physical abuse tend to perform more poorly in school than do children without a history of abuse. Many physically abused children demonstrate aggression and other externalizing problems, including later involvement in criminal activity. Finally, some physically abused children experience depression, low self-esteem, and increased risk for suicide ideation and attempts. The degree to which abused children will experience these negative outcomes is dependent upon the "protective factors" or "buffers" available in their lives, which may serve to mitigate the negative outcome of traumatic life experiences. Although research on resilience among physically abused children is in its early stages, it appears that factors such as close friendships, the availability of a nurturing parent, and strong self-regulatory skills might provide some degree of protection against the negative impact of physical abuse (Haskett, Nears, Ward, & McPherson, 2006).

To develop effective responses to physical child abuse, consensus is needed on the definition of abuse. Unfortunately, there is no definition of physical child abuse that is applied consistently across the many disciplines and stakeholders involved in responding to child maltreatment (see Feerick, Knutson, Trickett, & Flanzer, 2006). Instead, research has shown that definitions vary based on both professional and social values (Haugaard, 2006; Portwood, 1998, 1999). Moreover, formal definitions differ across state and federal legislative bodies, child protection agency officials, researchers, and mental health clinicians. Typically, state laws define physical abuse as injury caused by nonaccidental means that harms or creates substantial risk of serious physical harm to the child; however, these laws vary considerably in regard to the specific acts listed as constituting physical abuse (Myers, 1992). Similarly, researchers use a wide variety of methods to define abuse, including parents' self-reports of parenting and discipline practices, official child protective services reports, retrospective self-reports of abuse, and observations of parent-child interaction. For purposes of this chapter, the definition of physical abuse endorsed by the Centers for Disease Control and Prevention will be used: Physical abuse is defined as the intentional use of physical force against a child that results in, or has the potential to result in, physical injury (Leeb, Paulozzi, Melanson, Simon, & Arias, 2008).

The process of determining whether or not physical abuse has occurred, particularly when resulting injuries are relatively minor, is complicated by the fact that there is debate concerning what constitutes appropriate and inappropriate parenting. For example, some cultural practices are generally not defined as physical abuse but, nonetheless, result in physical harm. "Coining," or *cao gio*, for example, is a practice used by Southeast Asians to treat various illnesses by rubbing the body forcefully with a coin until blood appears under the skin. In the U.S., the practice of spanking continues to receive considerable attention. Today, corporal punishment is not sanctioned in most school districts, but there is not a clear consensus on whether parents' use of corporal punishment in the home constitutes abuse; although estimates vary based on sampling methods, definitions of corporal punishment, and measurement approaches, Straus and Stewart (1999) found that 90% of American parents report using corporal punishment as a form of discipline.

Risk and Protective Factors for Physical Abuse

Understanding factors that increase risk for physical abuse aids professionals in identifying maltreatment and other high-risk situations. Although researchers have identified a number of factors commonly associated with physical abuse, the presence of these factors, while indicating an elevated risk for experiencing abuse, does not conclusively indicate maltreatment. Moreover, factors that contribute to abuse in one family may not result in abuse in another family (e.g., due to protective factors in the family or community). For example, although teen parenthood is a risk factor for abuse, a teenaged mother who has support from her family and is enrolled in school is likely at lower risk than is a teen mother who has dropped out of school and is homeless and without family support.

Consistent with Bronfenbrenner's (1986) ecological model of family functioning, risk and protective factors fall into four domains of influence on children: (a) individual child and parent characteristics, (b) family influences and parent-child relationship factors, (c) features of the neighborhood and community, and (d) broader societal factors. Physical abuse is best explained through a complex interaction of factors at all of these levels (Belsky, 1993). It is not clear, however, whether these various risk factors precede and contribute to maltreatment or whether they are a consequence of the dynamics of maltreatment. It is also not clear whether these factors are direct causes or simply indicators of maltreatment risk. For example, poverty is associated with abuse, but it is possible that poverty is only an indirect cause of abuse and another factor associated with poverty (e.g., stress, depression) contributes more directly to abusive parenting.

Individual Child Characteristics

Research suggests that children who are viewed as difficult by their parents or who have special needs, a difficult temperament, psychiatric symptoms, or behavioral problems are at increased risk of physical abuse (Brown, Cohen, Johnson, & Salzinger, 1998). Children with certain psychiatric diagnoses, especially disruptive behavior disorders, might also be at elevated risk for harsh physical discipline and physical abuse (e.g., Alizadeh, Applequist, & Coolidge, 2007; Briscoe-Smith & Hinshaw, 2006). For example, children with Attention Deficit/Hyperactivity Disorder have difficulty paying attention, controlling impulses, and regulating their activity level; irritability and defiance are features of children with Oppositional Defiant Disorder; and children with Conduct Disorder disobey rules and can be aggressive. These behaviors are incredibly challenging for caregivers, so it is not surprising that parents of children with disruptive behaviors experience elevated levels of childrearing stress (Mash & Johnston, 1990). Difficult child behavior has also been associated with increased parental alcohol consumption (another risk factor for abusive parenting) as adults attempt to cope with such behavior (Pelham & Lang, 1993). Again, it is important to note that associations between childhood disruptive disorders and physical abuse are highly complex, and it is not clear whether difficult child behavior occurs before or following abuse experiences (Endo, Sugiyama, & Someya, 2006). In addition, child behavior may contribute indirectly to abuse when it interacts with certain parent characteristics, such as poor coping skills, substance use, or difficulty controlling emotions.

Parent Characteristics

Taken as a whole, studies of mothers' demographic characteristics, which have been much more common than studies of fathers' characteristics, do not establish clear associations between physical child abuse and maternal age, education, or marital status (Black, Heyman, & Slep, 2001). Research by Murray Straus and colleagues indicated that mothers who were younger at the birth of their child exhibited higher rates of child abuse than did older mothers (Connelly & Straus, 1992; Straus et al., 1998). However, any link between mother's age and physical child abuse may be a function of the relationship between age and other factors that increase risk of abuse, including lower socioeconomic status and lack of social support. Investigations of racial characteristics have also produced mixed results, such that the role of race in the perpetration of physical abuse is unclear (Black et al., 2001). Minority-race children are consistently overrepresented in child welfare reports (Cappalleri, Eckenrode, & Powers, 1993); however, in one study, the increased risk for physical abuse by African American mothers disappeared when the researchers controlled for socioeconomic status (Berger & Brooks-Gunn, 2005).

Serious mental disorders are not common among abusive parents, but these parents often experience elevated stress related to their role as parents

(Haskett, Ahern, Ward, & Allaire, 2006). In addition, controlled studies indicate that physically abusive parents tend to experience low self-esteem, low parenting efficacy, poor impulse control and anger management, a low threshold for frustration, and poor stress management (Wolfe, 1999). There is, however, wide variability in mental health functioning of abusive parents, with some abusive parents experiencing relatively low levels of distress.

Parental substance abuse is a factor contributing to physical abuse for a significant proportion of maltreated children in the child welfare system (Young, Gardner, & Dennis, 1998). The mechanism by which substance abuse is associated with abuse is not well understood, however. Clearly, alcohol and drugs can interfere with a parent's mental functioning, judgment, inhibitions, and protective capacity. Moreover, substance abuse often co-occurs with other risk factors for abuse, including mental illness, HIV/AIDS, other health problems, domestic violence, and poverty. The number and complexity of co-occurring family problems makes it difficult to understand the unique impact of substance abuse on child abuse.

The *intergenerational transmission hypothesis* (also referred to as the *cycle of abuse*) states that maltreatment in parents' own childhood places parents at risk for abusing their children, perhaps because those with poor parental role models may find it very difficult to meet the needs of their children. However, this hypothesis has been hotly debated, and the precise strength of the relationship between abuse history and risk for child abuse remains in question. Although a history of maltreatment does appear to increase one's risk of abusing one's children, the majority of individuals abused as children (about 70%) *do not* grow up to be abusers (Kaufman & Zigler, 1987; Miller-Perrin & Perrin, 1999). It is not known why some parents or caregivers who were maltreated as children abuse or neglect their own children while others do not, but the presence of emotionally supportive relationships may help lessen the risk of perpetuating the intergenerational cycle of abuse (deGruyter, Zuravin, McMillen, DePanfilis, & Risley-Curtiss, 1996).

Research indicates that abusive parents can be distinguished from nonabusive parents by their beliefs and attitudes about childrearing and about their own children (Milner, 2000). Specifically, many abusive parents have limited knowledge of typical child development, and their expectations for their children's developmental abilities are unrealistically high (Azar, Robinson, Hekimian, & Twentyman, 1984). For example, an abusive parent might believe that her 2-year-old child should never have toileting accidents. When the child behaves in a developmentally typical manner and wets her pants, the mother assumes that the child has misbehaved purposefully to annoy the parent. Such attributions of hostile intent are associated with frustration and stress, which, in turn, increase the likelihood that the parent will strike out at the child in anger. In addition, abusive parents tend to view their children in a more negative light than do nonabusive parents, even when observers do not report differences between abused and nonabused children; such findings have been interpreted as abusive parents' negative bias regarding their children's behavior (e.g., Mash & Johnston, 1990).

Family Factors

There are a number of stressful family situations that increase children's vulnerability to physical child abuse. Two of the most notable are intimate partner violence and single parenthood. In published studies, the co-occurrence of intimate partner violence and physical child abuse ranges widely, from 18% to 97%, depending on the definitions of violence and abuse, the populations sampled, and reference periods of assessment. The most often-cited studies indicate that co-occurrence is likely between 30% and 60% in the U.S. and other countries (Knickerbocker, Heyman, Smith Slep, Jouriles, & McDonald, 2007). This co-occurrence could be explained by the presence of common risk factors (i.e., the *common cause hypothesis*), including substance abuse, parental depression, and financial stress. An alternative explanation is that one type of violence contributes to the other (i.e., the *spillover hypothesis*); for example, violence against the mother might interfere with her parenting and increase her likelihood of abusing her child. A third explanation for the co-occurrence of forms of family violence is that children are inadvertently harmed during partner conflicts. Regardless of which explanation is most accurate, partner violence is clearly a significant risk factor for physical abuse (Black et al., 2001).

As noted, some studies (e.g., Sedlak & Broadhurst, 1996) indicate that children of single parents are at higher risk of abuse than are children who live with two biological parents. The rate of child abuse in single-parent households is 27.3 children per 1,000, which is nearly twice the rate for two-parent households (15.5 children per 1,000). An analysis of child abuse cases in a nationally representative sample of 42 counties found that, compared to their peers living with both parents, children in single-parent homes had a 77% greater risk of being physically abused (Goldman, Salus, Wolcott, & Kennedy, 2003). This heightened level of risk may be tied to the higher levels of stress experienced by single parents, who are likely to experience financial constraints and social isolation.

Environmental Factors

Beyond risk factors at the individual child and parent levels, environmental factors, including poverty and unemployment, social isolation, and community characteristics that support violence and fail to encourage nurturing parenting practices, may increase risk for abuse. Most parents or caregivers who live in these types of environments are not abusive. Nonetheless, poverty and unemployment show strong associations with child abuse. Children from families with annual incomes below $15,000 (in 1993) were more than 22 times more likely to be harmed through maltreatment than were children from families with annual incomes above $30,000 (Sedlak & Broadhurst, 1996). In 2000, 85% of states identified poverty and substance abuse as the top two challenges reported by families to child protective service agencies (Child Welfare Information Gateway, 2002).

Several community socioeconomic characteristics are associated with increased levels of child maltreatment (Garbarino, Kostelny, & Grady, 1993), but slightly different sets of neighborhood features predict rates of child abuse for African American, Hispanic, and Caucasian children. To illustrate, high rates of poverty and high density of alcohol outlets predict abuse for African American children, but poverty, unemployment, and single-parent households predict abuse for Hispanic children (Freisthler, Bruce, & Needell, 2007). For all racial and ethnic groups, communities with a larger proportion of residents living in poverty experience higher rates of abuse. The reasons for this association are unclear, but parents in poverty are more likely to live in communities with high levels of violence, and rates of physical abuse are significantly higher among children who live in neighborhoods with violence (Lynch & Cicchetti, 1998). Perhaps poverty creates greater family stress, which, in turn, leads to increased risk of maltreatment. Alternatively, it may be that poor families experience maltreatment at rates similar to other families, but that maltreatment in poor families is reported more frequently, in part because they have more contact with individuals who are legally mandated to report suspected child maltreatment.

Many studies indicate that parents who abuse their children experience isolation and lack of support from others, and this finding is consistent across cultures (Gracia & Gonzalo, 2003). Compared to nonabusive parents, abusive parents show lower levels of community integration, less frequent participation in community social activities, and lower use of formal and informal organizations. Social isolation may contribute to maltreatment because isolated parents tend to have limited financial, material, and emotional support; to lack positive parenting role models; and to feel less pressure to conform to conventional standards of parenting behaviors. Conversely, a high level of social bonding may be protective for families at risk for abuse. For example, rates of child maltreatment tend to be low even in high-poverty neighborhoods when residents know one another, there is a sense of community pride, residents are involved in community organizations, and they feel that they can ask their neighbors for help (Emery & Laumann-Billings, 1998).

Physical Abuse Prevention Approaches

Given the potentially negative impact of physical abuse, effective prevention strategies are crucial. Because abuse is multiply determined, the success of these strategies relies not only on the concerted effort of professionals who work with children and families, but also on the commitment of wider communities and our society at large. Prevention activities vary widely and may be universal, selective, or indicated (see Table 10.1). Increasingly, practitioners are encouraged to use prevention strategies that are evidence based, meaning that the approach has been shown to be successful in a series of well-designed studies. Although research on child abuse prevention strategies is in its relative infancy, there is a considerable body of data (Bethea, 1999; Daro, 1996; MacLeod & Nelson, 2000) to support best practices in prevention (see Table 10.2).

Table 10.1   Description and Illustration of Types of Prevention Strategies

Prevention Level	Target Population	Example
Universal prevention	The entire population, with the aim of preventing child abuse. All individuals, regardless of risk status, are provided with education and/or skills related to positive parenting and awareness of physical abuse. Historically, these strategies have been referred to as "primary" prevention.	Media campaigns to educate the public about the risks associated with shaking babies
Selective prevention	Individuals whose risk for physical abuse is above average due to the presence of risk factors such as teenage pregnancy, long-term poverty, or substance abuse. These strategies are also labeled "secondary" prevention.	Home visiting programs for first-time mothers and fathers (e.g., Nurse-Family Partnership)
Indicated prevention	Parents or other caregivers who have a documented history of physical abuse of their children. These strategies are also referred to as "tertiary" prevention.	Child management skills training for physically abusive parents (e.g., Parent-Child Interaction Therapy)

Table 10.2 Best Practices for Prevention of Physical Child Abuse

- Programs should emphasize and seek to expand on family strengths.
- Parenting instruction and family services should focus on the child's particular developmental level.
- Services should be interactive, providing opportunities for parents to model the behaviors being promoted.
- Programs should place an emphasis on social supports and developing the skills required to access these supports.
- Parent education and support programs should provide in-home services as well as case management.
- Home visitation components must be more than six months in duration.
- Service providers should recognize cultural differences in family functioning and the nature of parent-child interaction and be responsive to this diversity.
- There must be careful attention to fidelity of program implementation.
- Programs should include an evaluation component to inform program processes and outcomes, specifically including measures related to child abuse.

SOURCE: Daro (1996), Guterman (1997), Levental (2005), MacLeod and Nelson (2000).

Public Education and Awareness

Less is known about the impact of public education campaigns than about other child abuse prevention initiatives; however, anecdotal evidence suggests that such programs are promising. For example, as evidenced by the success of mass education efforts on the dangers of shaking a baby (Showers, 1992), the media may be effectively utilized as an outlet for promoting positive parenting and reducing physical child abuse. Similarly, after implementing a school-related child abuse prevention initiative prior to and during the week of report card distribution, including televised public service announcements and informational inserts in report cards, Baltimore experienced a reduction in observed incidents of child maltreatment associated with receiving a bad report card (Mandell, 2000).

Parenting Education and Support

Home Visitation Programs. Home visitation models represent a significantly more intensive prevention strategy than public education approaches. These programs are directed to new parents at risk for abuse and target lack of knowledge about child development. Many parent education and support programs have been developed; the Nurse-Family Partnership (Olds, Henderson, & Kitzman, 1998) and Healthy Families (Duggan et al., 2004) are widely recognized as the most prominent. Both programs include early and frequent home visits, the provision of care within the context of a therapeutic and supportive relationship, an established curriculum, modeling effective parenting, and connecting families to appropriate community services. The Nurse-Family Partnership employs nurses to deliver the intervention, based on the rationale that their professional training and experience have prepared them to make clinical assessments and to offer appropriate guidance to clients. In contrast, Healthy Families utilizes paraprofessionals as the primary service providers, based on the assumption that, as community members, they are best able to establish strong personal connections with families. Data demonstrate that the Nurse-Family Partnership positively impacts parenting attitudes and behavior and reduces reports of child maltreatment. (e.g., Eckenrode et al., 2000). Early evaluations of Healthy Families programs were promising, but recently conducted well-designed studies have produced somewhat disappointing results in terms of prevention of abuse and neglect (see Chaffin, 2004). For example, in an experimental evaluation of the program including approximately 700 participants, families receiving the Healthy Families programming did not significantly differ from control groups in self-reports of physically abusive behaviors (AOR = 1.30) or use of time out as a nonviolent discipline strategy (AOR = 1.01; Duggan et al., 2004).

Another home visitation program that has amassed scientific support is Project 12-Ways/Project SafeCare (Gershater-Molko, Lutzker, & Wesch, 2002). Project 12-Ways was developed as a selective or indicated prevention program, while Project SafeCare was designed for urban families involved in the child welfare system and is offered to families with parenting risk factors and at least one comorbid problem (e.g., parental substance abuse). Both programs involve the use of highly structured training in parenting, assertiveness, self-control, employment, money management, health and nutrition, home safety, and stress reduction. An overview of the program outcomes indicates that participation leads to skill improvements as well as reductions in repeat reports of child abuse (Lutzker, Bigelow, Doctor, Gershater, & Greene, 1998). Although the program is appropriate for families with older children and adolescents, most studies of program effectiveness have focused on families with young children.

Behavioral Parent Training. There is a large body of literature to support the effectiveness of parent training programs, which were originally developed in the 1960s as an intervention for parents of children with oppositional and conduct problems. Because abused children tend to show conduct problems and their parents need assistance in responding appropriately to difficult child behavior, these parent training programs have recently been modified for use with abusive parents and their children. Common goals of these programs are to improve the quality of the parent-child relationship and to increase parents' child management skills. Of note is Parent Child Interaction Therapy (PCIT; Hembree-Kigin & McNeil, 1995), which is provided to parents of young children, typically in a clinical setting. The program relies on a therapist "coach" to train parents in positive parenting skills, delivery of clear age-appropriate instructions, ignoring inappropriate child behavior, and effective use of time out. Initial studies have produced promising results with abusive parents and their young children in terms of improvements in child internalizing problems (e.g., depression and anxiety) and externalizing problems (e.g., conduct and attentional problems; medium effect $\eta^2 = .10$) and reductions in parent stress (medium effect $\eta^2 = .10$; Chaffin et al., 2004; Timmer, Urquiza, Zebell, & McGrath, 2005).

Other Parent Education Programs. In addition to parent training programs that target individual or small groups of parents, other parent education programs adopt a universal approach and strive to educate all parents on strategies such as stress management, coping and parenting skills, appropriate discipline, child development, and safety issues. One such program is the American Psychological Association's Adults and Children Together Against Violence (ACT) Parents Raising Safe Kids program, which emphasizes the importance of parents and other caregivers providing a learning environment that helps to protect young children from violence and injury. The program is designed to be implemented in diverse settings, including schools and community service settings, and to be part of a community's broader framework of parent services (e.g., day care, Head Start, Healthy Families, GED courses). While it is believed that the general parenting education provided by ACT can be beneficial to all parents, regardless of their risk level for abuse, outcome evaluation efforts are in the early phases.

Parent Support Groups. As a result of findings indicating that abusive parents experience social isolation and loneliness, support groups have been developed to offer parents an opportunity to exchange ideas, support, and resources with other parents. Typically, these groups are co-led by parents and a trained facilitator, are open to parents of all ages, and are free. Two of the best-known parent support group programs are Parents Anonymous (Leiber & Baker, 1977), begun in 1969, and Circle of Parents (http://www.circleofparents.org/). Evaluation of these programs has been minimal; however, these programs do show promise in reducing social isolation and improving parenting practices, based on self-reports of parents who participate in the program (Falconer, Haskett, McDaniels, Dirkes, & Siegel, in press).

Early Childhood and Primary Health Care Initiatives

Many programs designed to improve children's school readiness or to improve children's health status have been shown to result in lowered rates of child maltreatment. The best-known early childhood initiative is the Chicago Parent-Child Center model, begun in 1986. Parent education and support are provided through parent resource rooms and home visits designed to increase parents' involvement in their children's education. Other features include comprehensive health and nutrition services, highly skilled teaching staff, and classrooms with low teacher/student ratios. Extensive evaluations of the Centers indicate that children participating in the program for six years show higher academic achievement (medium effects reading $r = .43$; math $r = .45$), better social and emotional adjustment (small effect $r = .23$), and lower rates of child abuse (no effect size reported) than comparison children (Reynolds, 2000). At a 15-year follow-up, youth who had participated in the Centers were 52% less likely to be victims of maltreatment (Reynolds & Robertson, 2003).

Healthy Steps for Children is a universal program of services to improve developmental and behavioral outcomes for young children though pediatric practices. Services are delivered in pediatric offices by nurses, early childhood educators, or social workers. These specialists consult with parents during pediatric care visits, home visits, or phone contacts to provide support and education about parenting and to make referrals to community agencies for needed family services. Parent support groups and call-in child development phone lines also are offered. A trial of several thousand families indicated that parents who participated reduced their likelihood of using spanking (OR = .76) and increased their use of negotiation and other child-centered discipline tactics (OR = 1.16; Minkovitz et al., 2003).

Multi-Component and Comprehensive Programs

There is increasing acknowledgment that community-based models with multiple intervention components are the most promising means of preventing physical child abuse; however, few such programs have been implemented or evaluated. One multicomponent program is the Triple P-Positive Parenting Program, developed by Matthew Sanders and colleagues in Australia and used throughout the world (Sanders, Cann, & Markie-Dadds, 2003). Triple P utilizes a multilevel intervention approach aimed at preventing child behavioral, emotional, and developmental problems as well as child abuse by reducing risk factors and increasing protective factors. The specific interventions range from mass media campaigns to encourage support for new parents (Level 1), to the provision of brief information resources (e.g., tip sheets, videos) and brief targeted intervention by primary care practitioners such as nurses and pediatricians (Levels 2 and 3), to more intensive parenting training programs directed to parents of children with behavioral or developmental challenges (Levels 4 and 5). Parenting skills addressed in the intervention are centered on five core principles: ensuring a safe and engaging environment for the child, creating a positive learning environment, using assertive discipline, formulating realistic expectations of children, and caring for oneself as a parent. Triple P targets five developmental periods, from infancy through adolescence. There is a substantial body of support for this approach, and preliminary results of the first large-scale application of Triple P in the United States are quite promising (Prinz, 2007).

A second approach currently under study is Strong Communities (http://www.clemson.edu/strongcommunities). Gary B. Melton, director of the Institute on Family and Neighborhood Life, and colleagues are examining the impact of this community-based preventive approach in South Carolina. Strong Communities aims to engage neighborhoods, parents, outreach workers, volunteers, and community organizations in a partnership to make child protection an integral part of daily life and to facilitate informal and reciprocal social support within the community. Home visiting and other supports are also further integrated into pediatric well-child visits, community policing, and school-based early childhood programs.

As reflected by these developing approaches, there is increasing acknowledgment that prevention efforts must extend beyond attempts to enhance parenting capacity. Among the range of initiatives that have yet to be fully evaluated are increasing the economic self-sufficiency of families, enhancing communities and their resources, discouraging excessive use of corporal punishment, making health care more accessible and affordable, expanding and improving coordination of social services, improving treatment for alcohol and drug abuse, improving the identification and treatment of mental health problems, increasing the availability of affordable child care, and increasing the value that society places on children (Bethea, 1999).

Treatment of Victims of Physical Child Abuse

Treatment for victims of physical abuse typically involves intensive case management. A human services professional, usually a social worker, coordinates service provision to the family. Typically, the initial step is to secure the physical safety of the child, followed by the provision of other services necessary to secure a safe and nurturing environment for the child. There is wide variation in both the specific services provided as well as the family's response. Although child protective services assume primary responsibility for case management, services for the parent and child are typically provided through outside contractor agencies. Unfortunately, very few approaches to therapy for physically abused children have been examined empirically, so knowledge of effective practices is extremely limited.

One promising approach to intervention for young physically abused children who show evidence of social withdrawal is Resilient Peer Treatment (RPT). This treatment, which takes place in a child care setting, aims to improve social competence by creating positive play experiences with socially skilled peers. In RPT, abused children have the opportunity to learn social skills from a "buddy" and to experience the pleasure of interacting with a friendly peer. Results of a series of studies indicate that RPT leads to increased collaborative play (large effect $\eta^2 = .19$) and reduced solitary play (medium effect $\eta^2 = .14$; e.g., Fantuzzo, Manz, Atkins, & Meyers, 2005). This intervention is relatively low cost, does not stigmatize children, and can be conducted in children's typical day-to-day environment.

Play therapy approaches are used widely; however, their effectiveness has not been well supported empirically (Kaplan, Pelcovitz, & Labruna, 1999). A growing body of clinical research instead supports the use of interventions that focus on the child's specific symptoms. To illustrate, some physically abused children experience symptoms of anxiety. Cognitive behavioral therapies are known to be effective for anxious children (Kendall, Aschenbrand, & Hudson, 2003), and those interventions should be useful for physically abused children as well. It is important to note, however, that many well-supported treatments for childhood disorders include parent involvement; such involvement might be difficult in families characterized by physical abuse. Clearly, involving abusive parents in their children's treatment can present some therapeutic challenges, but there is emerging evidence that several approaches may be effective in responding to physical child abuse.

Foremost among these interventions is Abuse-Focused Cognitive Behavioral Therapy (AF-CBT), an evidence-based practice shown to be effective in assisting school-aged children and their parents to overcome the impact of physical child abuse (Kolko, 2002). AF-CBT integrates cognitive and learning/behavioral interventions with traditional child abuse and family systems therapies, emphasizing education in specific intrapersonal and interpersonal skills to encourage prosocial behavior and discourage coercive or aggressive behavior in individuals and families (Kolko & Swenson, 2002). An increasing number of studies support the effectiveness of AF-CBT for treatment of physical child abuse victims (Cohen, Berliner, & Mannarino, 2003; Kolko, 1996), and AF-CBT is identified as a "best practice" for physically abused children and their families (see Chadwick Center for Children and Families, 2004). For example, Kolko (1996) found significant reductions in child internalizing (small effect $r = .11$) and externalizing (small effect $r = .02$) problems and increases in family cohesion (small effect $r = .16$) and improvements in parent mental health (medium effect $r = .41$) for clients receiving AF-CBT versus routine community services.

Conclusion

As reported in the opening paragraph of this chapter, rates of physical child abuse have dropped steadily over the past decade. In spite of this positive news, many children continue to experience harsh corporal punishment and physical abuse. In the past few decades, advances in research have provided a broader understanding of the etiology of physical abuse, making it clear that abuse results from a highly complex interplay of individual, family, community, and societal factors. Therefore, in order to accelerate the decline in incidents of physical abuse, comprehensive, divergent, multilevel strategies that are congruent with the complexity of the social problem of child abuse must be instituted through community-based programming (Fantuzzo, Weiss, & Coolahan, 1998).

Discussion Questions

1. What is the prevalence of physical child abuse? Are rates of physical abuse rising or falling?

2. Describe three risk factors for physical abuse, and discuss the ways in which these factors interact to increase the likelihood that abuse will occur.

3. If a parent abuses drugs or alcohol, what additional risk factors are likely to occur in the family?

4. Discuss the difference between universal, selective, and targeted prevention programs for child abuse.

5. What are three types of programs shown to have positive effects in prevention of physical abuse?

6. What are the goals of behavioral parent training programs?

7. Define "evidence-based" practices for prevention of abuse and intervention for child victims of abuse.

8. Describe one evidence-based intervention for children who have experienced physical abuse.

9. Describe an *ideal* abuse prevention program for your community, including components to address risk factors for the individual child, the parent, and the community.

Internet Resources

ABA Center on Children and the Law: http://www.abanet.org/child/

Adults and Children Together Against Violence: http://actagainstviolence.apa.org/about/

American Professional Society on the Abuse of Children: http://apsac.org/

Child Welfare League of America (CWLA): http://www.cwla.org/

Children's Safety Network (CSN): http://www.childrenssafetynetwork.org/

Circle of Parents: http://www.circleofparents.org/

Family Violence Prevention Fund (FVPF): http://www.endabuse.org/

International Society for Prevention of Child Abuse and Neglect: http://www.ispcan.org/

National District Attorneys Association: http://www.ndaa.org/

Parent-Child Interaction Therapy: http://pcit.phhp.ufl.edu/

Parents Anonymous: http://www.parentsanonymous.org/

Prevent Child Abuse America: http://www.preventchildabuse.org/

Society for the Advancement of Violence and Injury Research: http://www.savirweb.org/

Triple P-Positive Parenting Program: http://www1.triplep.net/

References

Alizadeh, H., Applequist, K. F., & Coolidge, F. L. (2007). Parental self-confidence, parenting styles, and corporal punishment in families of ADHD children in Iran. *Child Abuse & Neglect, 31,* 567–572.

Azar, S. T., Robinson, D. R., Hekimian, E., & Twentyman, C. T. (1984). Unrealistic expectations and problem-solving ability in maltreating and comparison mothers. *Journal of Consulting and Clinical Psychology, 52,* 687–691.

Belsky, J. (1993). Etiology of child maltreatment: A developmental-ecological analysis. *Psychological Bulletin, 114,* 413–434.

Berger, L., & Brooks-Gunn, J. (2005). Socioeconomic status, parenting knowledge and behaviors, and perceived maltreatment of young low-birth-weight children. *The Social Service Review, 79,* 237–268.

Bethea, L. (1999). Primary prevention of child abuse. *American Family Physician, 59,* 1577–1585.

Black, D. A., Heyman, R. E., & Slep, A. M. (2001). Risk factors for child physical abuse. *Aggression and Violent Behavior, 6,* 121–188.

Briscoe-Smith, A. M., & Hinshaw, S. P. (2006). Linkages between child abuse and attention-deficit/hyperactivity disorder in girls: Behavioral and social correlates. *Child Abuse & Neglect, 30,* 1239–1255.

Bronfenbrenner, U. (1986). Ecology of the family as a context for human development: Research perspectives. *Developmental Psychology, 22,* 723–742.

Brown, J., Cohen, P., Johnson, J., & Salzinger, S. (1998). A longitudinal analysis of risk factors for child maltreatment. *Child Abuse & Neglect, 22,* 1065–1078.

Capalleri, J., Eckenrode, J., & Powers, J. (1993). The epidemiology of child abuse: Findings from the Second National Incidence and Prevalence Study of Child Abuse and Neglect. *American Journal of Public Health, 83,* 1622–1624.

Chadwick Center for Children and Families. (2004). *Closing the quality chasm in child abuse treatment: Identifying and disseminating best practices.* San Diego, CA: Author. Retrieved from http://www.chadwickcenter.org/kauffman.htm

Chaffin, M. (2004). Is it time to rethink Healthy Start/Healthy Families? *Child Abuse & Neglect, 28,* 589–595.

Chaffin, M., Silovsky, J., Funderburk, B., Valle, L. A., Brestan, E. V., Balachova, T., et al. (2004). Parent-child interaction therapy with physically abusive parents: Efficacy for reducing future abuse reports. *Journal of Consulting and Clinical Psychology, 72,* 491–499.

Child Welfare Information Gateway. (2002). *National child abuse and neglect data system (NCANDS) summary of key findings for calendar year 2000.* Washington, DC: Author.

Children's Bureau. (2005). *Child maltreatment.* Washington, DC: U.S. Department of Health and Human Services.

Cohen, J. A., Berliner, L., & Mannarino, A. P. (2003). Psychosocial and pharmacological interventions for child crime victims. *Journal of Traumatic Stress, 16,* 175–186.

Connelly, D. C., & Straus, M. A. (1992). Mother's age and risk for physical abuse. *Child Abuse & Neglect, 16,* 709–718.

Daro, D. (1996). Preventing child abuse and neglect. In J. Briere, L. Berliner, J. A. Bulkley, C. Jenny, & T. Reid (Eds.), *The APSAC handbook on child maltreatment* (pp. 343–358). Thousand Oaks, CA: Sage.

deGruyter, A., Zuravin, S. J., McMillen, C., DePanfilis, D., & Risley-Curtiss, C. (1996). The intergenerational cycle of maltreatment: Continuity versus discontinuity. *Journal of Interpersonal Violence, 11,* 315–334.

Duggan, A., McFarlane, E., Fuddy, L., Burrell, L, Higman, S. M., Windham, A., et al. (2004). Randomized trial of a statewide home visiting program to prevent child abuse: Impact in preventing child abuse and neglect. *Child Abuse & Neglect, 28,* 597–622.

Eckenrode, J., Ganzel, B., Henderson, C. R., Smith, E., Olds, D. L., Powers, J., et al. (2000). Preventing child abuse and neglect with a program of nurse home visitation: The limiting effects of domestic violence. *Journal of American Medical Association, 284,* 1385–1391.

Emery, R. E., & Laumann-Billings, L. (1998). An overview of the nature, causes, and consequences of abusive family relationships: Toward differentiating maltreatment and violence. *American Psychologist, 44,* 121–135.

Endo, T., Sugiyama, T., & Someya, T. (2006). Attention-deficit/hyperactivity disorder and dissociative disorder among abused children. *Psychiatry and Clinical Neurosciences, 60,* 434–438.

Falconer, M. K., Haskett, M. E., McDaniels, L., Dirkes, T., & Siegel, E. C. (in press). Evaluation of support groups for child abuse prevention: Outcomes of four state evaluations. *Social Work with Groups.*

Fantuzzo, J., Manz, P. Atkins, M., & Meyers, R. (2005). Peer-mediated treatment of socially withdrawn maltreated preschool children: Cultivating natural community resources. *Journal of Clinical Child and Adolescent Psychology, 34,* 320–325.

Fantuzzo, J., Weiss, A. D., & Coolahan, K. C. (1998). Community-based partnership-directed research: Actualizing community strengths to treatment child victims of physical abuse and neglect. In J. R. Lutzker (Ed.), *Handbook of child abuse research and treatment* (pp. 213–237). New York: Plenum Press.

Feerick, M. M, Knutson, J. F., Trickett, P. K., & Flanzer, S. M. (Eds.) (2006). *Child abuse and neglect: Definitions, classifications, and a framework for research.* Baltimore: Brookes.

Finkelhor, D., & Jones, L. (2006). Why have child maltreatment and child victimization declined? *Journal of Social Issues, 62,* 685–716.

Finkelhor, D., Ormrod, R., Turner, H., & Hamby, S. L. (2005). The victimization of children and youth: A comprehensive national survey. *Child Maltreatment, 10,* 5–25.

Freisthler, B., Bruce, E., & Needell, B. (2007). Understanding the geospatial relationship of neighborhood characteristics and rates of maltreatment for black, Hispanic, and white children. *Social Work, 52,* 7–16.

Garbarino, J., Kostelny, K., & Grady, J. (1993). Children in dangerous environments: Child maltreatment in the context of community violence. In D. Cicchetti & S. Toth (Eds.), *Child abuse, child development, and social policy* (pp. 167–189). Norwood, NJ: Ablex.

Gershater-Molko, R. M., Lutzker, J. R., & Wesch, D. (2002). Using recidivisim data to evaluate Project Safe Care: Teaching bonding, safety, and health care skills to parents. *Child Maltreatment, 7,* 227–285.

Goldman, J., Salus, M. K., Wolcott, D., & Kennedy, K. Y. (2003). *A coordinated response to child abuse and neglect: The foundation for practice.* Washington, DC: U.S. Department of Health and Human Services, Office on Child Abuse and Neglect, Children's Bureau.

Gracia, E., & Gonzalo, M. (2003). Social isolation from communities and child maltreatment: A cross-cultural comparison. *Child Abuse & Neglect, 27,* 153–168.

Guterman, N. (1997). Early prevention of child physical abuse and neglect: Existing evidence and future directions. *Child Maltreatment, 2,* 12–34.

Haskett, M. E., Ahern, L. S., Ward, C. S., & Allaire, J. (2006). Factor structure and validity of the Parenting Stress Index /Short Form. *Journal of Clinical Child and Adolescent Psychology, 35,* 302–312.

Haskett, M. E., Nears, K., Ward, C. S., & McPherson, A. V. (2006). Diversity in adjustment of maltreated children: Factors associated with resilient functioning. *Clinical Psychology Review, 26,* 796–812.

Haugaard, J. (2006). Characteristics of child maltreatment definitions: The influence of professional and social values. In M. M. Feerick, J. F. Knutson, P. K. Trickett, & S. M. Flanzer (Eds.), *Child abuse and neglect: Definitions, classifications, and a framework for research* (pp. 49–65). Baltimore, MD: Brookes.

Hembree-Kigin, T. L., & McNeil, C. B. (1995). *Parent-child interaction therapy.* New York: Plenum Press.

Kaplan, S. J., Pelcovitz, D., & Labruna, V. (1999). Child and adolescent abuse and neglect research: A review of the past 10 years. Part I: Physical and emotional abuse and neglect. *Journal of the American Academy of Child & Adolescent Psychiatry, 38,* 1214–1222.

Kaufman, J., & Zigler, E. (1987). Do abused children become abusive parents? *American Journal of Orthopsychiatry, 57,* 186–192.

Kendall, P. C., Aschenbrand, S. G., & Hudson, J. L. (2003). Child-focused treatment of anxiety. In A. E. Kazdin & J. R. Weisz (Eds.), *Evidence-based psychotherapies for children and adolescents* (pp 81–100). New York: Guilford Press.

Knickerbocker, L., Heyman, R. E., Smith Slep, A M., Jouriles, E. N., & McDonald, R. (2007). Co-occurrence of child and partner maltreatment. *European Psychologist, 12,* 36–44.

Kolko, D. J. (1996). Individual cognitive behavioral therapy and family therapy for physically abused children and their offending parents: A comparison of clinical outcomes. *Child Maltreatment, 1,* 322–342.

Kolko, D. J. (2002). Child physical abuse. In J. E. B. Meyers, L. Berliner, J. Briere, C. T. Hendrix, C. Jenny, & T. A. Reid (Eds.), *The APSAC handbook on child maltreatment* (2nd ed., pp. 21–54). Thousand Oaks, CA: Sage.

Kolko, D. J., & Swenson, C. C. (2002). *Assessing and treating physically abused children and their families: A cognitive behavioral approach.* Thousand Oaks, CA: Sage.

Lansford, J. E., Dodge, K. A., Pettit, G. S., Bates, J. E., Crozier, J., & Kaplow, J. (2002). A 12-year prospective study of the long-term effects of early child physical maltreatment on psychological, behavioral, and academic problems in adolescence. *Archives of Pediatric Adolescent Medicine, 156,* 824–830.

Leeb, R. T., Paulozzi, L., Melanson, C., Simon, T. R., & Arias, I. (2008). *Child maltreatment surveillance: Uniform definitions for public health and recommended data elements.* Atlanta, GA: National Center for Injury Prevention and Control, Centers for Disease Control and Prevention.

Leventhal, J. D. (2005). Getting prevention right: Maintaining the status quo is not an option. *Child Abuse & Neglect, 29,* 209–213.

Lieber, L. L., & Baker, J. M. (1977). Parents anonymous—Self-help treatment for child-abusing parents: A review and an evaluation. *Child Abuse & Neglect, 1,* 133–148.

Lutzker, J. R., Bigelow, K. M., Doctor, R. M., Gershater, R. M., & Greene, B. G. (1998). An ecobehavioral model for the prevention and treatment of child abuse and neglect: History and applications. In J. R. Lutzker (Ed.), *Handbook of child abuse research and treatment* (pp. 239–266). New York: Plenum Press.

Lynch, M., & Cicchetti, D. (1998). An ecological-transactional analysis of children and contexts: The longitudinal interplay among child maltreatment, community violence, and children's symptomatology. *Development and Psychopathology, 10,* 235–257.

MacLeod, J., & Nelson, G. (2000). Programs for the promotion of family wellness and the prevention of child maltreatment: A meta-analytic review. *Child Abuse & Neglect, 24,* 1127–1149.

Mandell, S. (2000). Child abuse prevention at report card time. *Journal of Community Psychology, 28,* 687–690.

Mash, E., & Johnston, C. (1990). Determinants of parenting stress: Illustrations from families of hyperactive children and families of physically abused children. *Journal of Clinical Child Psychology, 19,* 313–328.

Miller-Perrin, C., & Perrin, R.(1999). *Child maltreatment: An introduction.* Thousand Oaks, CA: Sage.

Milner, J. S. (2000). Social information processing and physical child abuse: Theory and research. In D. J. Hansen (Ed.), *Nebraska symposium on motivation: Motivation and child maltreatment* (Vol. 45, pp. 39–84). Lincoln: University of Nebraska Press.

Minkovitz, C. S., Hughart, N., Strobino, D., Scharfstein, D., Frason, H., Hou, W., et al. (2003). A practice-based intervention to enhance quality of care in the first three years of life: The Healthy Steps for Young Children program. *Journal of the American Medical Association, 290,* 3081–3091.

Myers, J. E. B. (1992). *Legal issues in child abuse and neglect.* Thousand Oaks, CA: Sage.

Olds, D., Henderson, C., & Kitzman, H. (1998). Home visitation II. *Journal of Community Psychology, 26,* 5–21.

Pelham, W. E., & Lang, A. R. (1993). Parental alcohol consumption and deviant child behavior: Laboratory studies of reciprocal effects. *Clinical Psychology Review, 13,* 763–784.

Portwood, S. G. (1998). Factors influencing individuals' definitions of child maltreatment. *Child Abuse & Neglect, 22,* 437–452.

Portwood, S. G. (1999). The impact of individuals' characteristics and experiences on their definitions of child maltreatment. *Child Maltreatment, 4,* 56–68.

Prinz, R. (2007). *Strategies and challenges in population level dissemination.* Paper presented at the annual Helping Families Change Conference, Charleston, SC.

Reynolds, A. J. (2000). *Success in early intervention: The Chicago Child-Parent Centers.* Lincoln: University of Nebraska Press.

Reynolds, A. J., & Robertson, D. L. (2003). School-based early intervention and later child maltreatment in the Chicago Longitudinal Study. *Child Development, 74,* 3–26.

Sanders, M. R., Cann, W., & Markie-Dadds, C. (2003). The Triple-P Positive Parenting Programme: A universal population-level approach to the prevention of child abuse. *Child Abuse Review, 12,* 155–171.

Sedlak, A., & Broadhurst, D. (1996). *Third national incidence study of child abuse and neglect.* Washington, DC: U.S. Government Printing Office.

Showers, J. (1992). "Don't shake the baby": The effectiveness of a prevention program. *Child Abuse & Neglect, 16,* 11–18.

Straus, M. A., Hamby, S. L., Finkelhor, D., Moore, D. W., & Runyan, D. (1998). Identification of child maltreatment with the parent-child conflict tactics scales: Development and psychometric data for a national sample of American parents. *Child Abuse & Neglect, 22,* 249–270.

Straus, M. A., & Stewart, J. H. (1999). Corporal punishment by American parents: National data on prevalence, chronicity, severity, and duration in relation to child and family characteristics. *Clinical Child and Family Psychology Review, 2,* 55–70.

Timmer, S. G., Urquiza, A. J., Zebell, N. M., & McGrath, J. M. (2005). Parent-Child Interaction Therapy: Application to maltreating parent-child dyads. *Child Abuse & Neglect, 29,* 825–842.

Wolfe, D. A. (1999). *Child abuse: Implications for child development and psychopathology* (2nd ed.). Newbury Park, CA: Sage.

Young, N. K., Gardner, S. L., & Dennis, K. (1998). Facing the problem. In *Responding to alcohol and other drug problems in child welfare: Weaving together practice and policy* (pp. 1–26). Washington, DC: Child Welfare League of America Press.

Recommended Reading

Children's Bureau. (2005). *Child maltreatment.* Washington, DC: U.S. Department of Health and Human Services.

Feerick, M. M., Knutson, J. F., Trickett, P. K., & Flanzer, S. M. (Eds.). *Child abuse and neglect: Definitions, classifications, and a framework for research.* Baltimore, MD: Brookes.

Kolko, D. J., & Swenson, C. C. (2002). *Assessing and treating physically abused children and their families: A cognitive behavioral approach.* Thousand Oaks, CA: Sage.

Myers, J. E. B., Berliner, L., Briere, J., Hendrix, T., Jenny, C., & Reid, T. A. (Eds.). *The APSAC handbook on child maltreatment* (2nd ed., pp. 21–54). Thousand Oaks, CA: Sage.

Tricket, P. K., & Schellenbach, C. J. (Eds.). (1998). *Violence against children in the family and the community.* Washington, DC: American Psychological Association.

CHAPTER 11

Sex Offenders

Rape and Child Sexual Abuse

Karen J. Terry, Orestis Giotakos,
Maria Tsiliakou, and Alissa R. Ackerman

Introduction

Sex offenders are a heterogeneous group of individuals. The term *sex offender* describes those who have committed offenses as diverse as child sexual abuse, rape of an adult, transmission of child pornography, exhibitionism, and even consensual sex between teenagers who are far apart in age. These offenders have different motivations for committing their offenses, and, as such, differing responses are appropriate in order to accurately treat, manage, and supervise them. Despite this need, legislation affects them as a single group, and the past two decades have seen a significant increase in laws governing their behavior. The increased penalties against them are based upon two key notions: that sex offenders recidivate at high levels, and that they specialize in sexual offending.

Many studies have shown that these assumptions are inaccurate, however. A meta-analysis by Hanson and Morton-Bourgon (2004) showed

---

EDITOR'S NOTE: Two groups of authors contributed equally to this chapter: Karen J. Terry and Alissa R. Ackerman to the section on child sexual abuse, Orestis Giotakos and Maria Tsiliakou to the section on rape.

low levels of recidivism among sex offenders, with 14% of sex offenders convicted of a new sexual offense within five years and 36% convicted of any new offense during that timeframe. Several researchers have also shown that sex offenders who do recidivate are more likely to commit nonsexual offenses than sexual offenses (Lussier, LeBlanc, & Proulx, 2005; Miethe, Olson, & Mitchell, 2006; Soothill, Francis, Sanderson, & Ackerley, 2000).

Despite the low levels of recidivism based upon conviction rates, it is clear that sexual victimization is a widespread problem, and it is important to understand why people commit sexual offenses and how they can be prevented from doing so. The aim of this chapter is to explore two groups of sexual offenders: child sexual abusers and rapists. Each section provides an overview of the motivations for offending; characteristics of offenders; and various types of treatment, supervision, and management. The chapter concludes with discussion questions about sex offenders and some Internet resources for further research.

Child Sexual Abuse

Despite the declining rates of child sexual abuse in the past few decades (Jones & Finkelhor, 2004), several highly publicized cases of sexual abuse and murder have led to an intense public, political, and academic interest in sex offenders. These emotionally charged cases led to a moral panic (Jenkins, 1998) fueled by media coverage of the "fiends, monsters, and predators" who recidivate at high levels (Douard, 2007; Jenkins, 1998). Child sexual abusers are now subject to incarceration and community supervision at higher rates than ever before (Finkelhor & Ormrod, 2001; Simon & Zgoba, 2006). Many sex offender policies, such as registration and community notification, residency restrictions, sexually violent predator legislation, and mandatory chemical castration for paroled sex offenders, have become popular solutions to the sex offender "problem."

Reactive policies, however, are not necessarily the best way to reduce levels of sexual abuse. It is important to understand the characteristics of abusers and their motivations for offending, which can lead to more effective treatment and management policies for individual offenders. The aim of this section is to provide an overview of child sexual abusers, including the prevalence of child sexual abuse, cycle of offending, typologies of offenders, and treatment and other prevention methods that are currently applied to this population.

CASE STUDY: PANACEA OR PANDORA'S BOX? THE CASE OF JOHN COUEY

Nearly everyone in the U.S. has heard of Jessica Lunsford, the 9-year-old Florida girl who went missing February 23, 2005 and was found dead three weeks later. Jessica was taken from her home, sexually assaulted and buried alive, and died from asphyxiation. Her killer, John Couey, was a registered sex offender who was living across the street from her. High on drugs, he walked into her unlocked house at night and went into her room, told her not to scream, and kidnapped her. He has since been found guilty and sentenced to death. Jessica's father, Mark Lunsford, called for tougher legislation for sex offenders, including 25-year mandatory minimum sentences and lifetime monitoring. Florida passed "Jessica's Law" in 2005; more than 30 states have so far followed suit, and federal legislation is pending.

This scenario should sound familiar. In particular, it sounds very much like the case of Megan Kanka, the 7-year-old New Jersey girl who was sexually assaulted and killed by a recidivist sex offender living across the street from her. When her parents learned that her killer, Jesse Timmendequas, had been convicted of two previous sexual offenses against children, they stated that the community should be notified of serious sexual offenders who are living in the neighborhood. Only then, they claimed, can parents protect their children from dangerous predators. It was their actions, based upon the tragic death of their daughter, that prompted the implementation of "Megan's Law." When one looks at the facts, it seems the Kankas may have been correct; had they known of Timmendequas' whereabouts, they might have warned Megan and she might not have followed him into the house to play with his puppy. But the case of Jessica Lunsford shows the many flaws in this law, and it illustrates why government must be cautious in enacting new legislation.

John Evander Couey had an extensive criminal record. The majority of his crimes were property offenses, including carrying a concealed weapon, disorderly intoxication, driving under the influence, disorderly conduct, fraud, insufficient funds, larceny, and 24 counts of burglary. He did have one conviction for indecent exposure, which made him a registered sex offender, but another arrest for fondling a child under 16 did not lead to a conviction. Despite his being a registered sex offender, his neighbors did not know who he was or anything about his background. How could this happen?

First, the address he registered with the police was not the address where he was living. Though he was registered with an address in Citrus County, he was actually living just 150 yards from Jessica's house. It is difficult to monitor all registered sex offenders and their whereabouts at all times, and the authorities and neighbors were not aware of the danger he posed. Second, even if he had registered the correct address with authorities, he was not considered a "high risk" sex offender. This means that he would be registered, but the community would not be notified of his whereabouts.

This case shows the problems with laws such as Registration and Community Notification Laws (RCNL)—they are viewed as a panacea for monitoring the most dangerous offenders, yet they are not able to protect children from some of the most dangerous predators. Plus, as recent research shows, the most dangerous sex offenders are those who have a large number of prior offenses, both sexual and nonsexual. RCNL simply will not capture those individuals.

Estimates of Child Sexual Abuse

For many reasons, it is difficult to estimate the true prevalence of child sexual abuse; there is a high level of underreporting of offenses, and there is often a long delay before victims disclose the abuse. There are three primary sources of prevalence data: official statistics, victimization surveys, and academic studies. Official statistics are based upon reported cases of abuse. In addition to arrest and conviction data, data on child sexual abuse is also collected by social services and child protection agencies. In 1992, the National Child Abuse and Neglect Data System (NCANDS) of the U.S. Department of Health and Human Services began collecting child sexual abuse data from state child protective services and social services agencies and publishing the annual report *Child Maltreatment*. Child maltreatment reports show a decline in reported incidents from 1992 to 2001 for all reporting states. It is not clear why there was a reduction in reported cases of child sexual abuse; the drop may reflect an actual decrease in the number of cases, or it may be the result of changes in definitions, reporting, and investigation (Jones & Finkelhor, 2004).

Social services agencies and criminal justice institutions each only capture part of the picture, however, because they rely on reported offenses. Victimization surveys and academic studies can help to identify the prevalence of child sexual abuse, even if it is not reported to the police. In one study, for instance, researchers found that only 5.7% of the individuals in their sample who had been sexually abused as children reported their abuse to the police (Boney-McCoy & Finkelhor, 1995). Statistics on prevalence vary, but all show high rates of child sexual abuse. They also generally find that females are sexually abused at a higher rate than males during childhood. A meta-analysis by Bolen and Scannapieco (1999), which summarized many prevalence studies, found that overall rates of sexual victimization were approximately 30% to 40% for girls and 13% for boys in their lifetime.

Victimization studies also show a delay in disclosure of abuse. Lamb and Edgar-Smith (1994) found that although the adults in their study had experienced child sexual abuse before age 10, on average, 64% of the victims only reported this abuse in adulthood. Smith, Letourneau, and Saunders (2000) found that approximately half of the women in their sample who had been raped as children waited more than eight years to disclose the abuse. Arata (1998) found that only 41% of the women in her study, whose average age at the time of victimization was 8.5, reported the abuse at the time it occurred.

There are many factors associated with a delay in disclosure, including the following (Terry & Tallon, 2004):

- The victim's age at the time of abuse. Some studies show that older children are less likely to report the abuse, for fear of social consequences (White et al., 1986, as cited in Campis, Hebden-Curtis, & DeMaso, 1993), while other studies show that developmental maturation facilitates disclosure (DiPietro, Runyan, & Fredrickson, 1997).
- The relationship between the victim and the perpetrator. Victims are less likely to report sexual abuse if they are related to or otherwise close to the abuser (Arata, 1998; Hanson, Saunders, Saunders, Kilpatrick, & Best, 1999; Smith, Letourneau, & Saunders, 2000; Wyatt & Newcomb, 1990).
- The gender of the abuser and the victim. Boys are less likely to report abuse than are girls (Finkelhor, Hotaling, Lewis, & Smith, 1990).
- The severity of abuse. Victims are less likely to report the abuse if it is severe (e.g., involves penetration; Arata, 1998; Gries, Goh, & Cavanaugh, 1996).
- The likely consequences of the disclosure. Those who anticipate negative consequences are less likely to report the abuse (Lamb & Edgar-Smith, 1994; Sorenson & Snow, 1991).

Child Sexual Abusers: Characteristics and Typologies

There are various explanations of the etiology, or causes, of sexual offending. Researchers have attempted to explain this behavior from many theoretical perspectives. Table 11.1 shows a summary of the leading theories of child sexual abuse. However, sex offenders, even child sexual abusers, constitute a heterogeneous population. Because of the complex nature of this behavior, no single theory adequately explains the motivating factors that lead adults to sexually abuse children or the sustaining factors that contribute to the continuation of such abuse (Bickley & Beech, 2001). Nonetheless, understanding the etiology and maintenance of sexual offending is important, in order to implement policies that are appropriate for all types of sexual offenders.

Child sexual abusers may commit offenses for a variety of reasons, but many have common characteristics that include poor social skills; low self-esteem; feelings of inadequacy, humiliation, and loneliness; a sense of worthlessness and vulnerability; an inability to form normal adult relationships or previously frustrating experiences with adult relationships; and problems with potency (Robertiello & Terry, 2007; Terry, 2006b). Some child sexual abusers tend to seek out mutually comforting relationships with children and want the child to accept and enjoy the relationship. Most child sexual abusers also tend to "groom" their victims or manipulate them into complying with the sexual abuse (Terry & Tallon, 2004). Pryor (1996) explains that

Table 11.1 Summary of Theories Explaining Child Sexual Abuse

Theory	Description of Theory
Biological Theory	Concerned with organic explanations of human behavior. Physiological factors (e.g., hormone levels, chromosomal makeup) have an effect of sexual behavior; androgens promote sexual arousal, orgasm, and ejaculation, as well as regulate sexuality, aggression, cognition, emotion and personality; abnormal levels of androgens lead to aggressive sexual behavior.
Psychodynamic Theory	Sexual deviance is an expression of the unresolved problems experienced during the stages of development. The human psyche is composed of three primary elements: the id, the ego, and the superego; sexual deviancy occurs when the id (pleasure principle) is overactive.
Behavioral Theory	Deviant sexual behavior is a learned condition acquired through the same mechanisms by which conventional sexuality is learned; it is acquired and maintained through basic conditioning principles.
Attachment Theory	Humans have a propensity to establish strong emotional bonds with others, and when individuals have some loss or emotional distress, they act out as a result of their loneliness and isolation.
Cognitive-Behavioral Theory	Addresses the way in which offenders' thoughts affect their behavior; focuses on the way in which sex offenders diminish their feelings of guilt and shame by rationalizing it through excuses and justifications.
Integrated Theory	There are preconditions to child sexual abuse, which integrate the various theories about why individuals begin to participate in sexually deviant behavior. Integrated theory addresses the motivation to offend and the rationalization of the behavior; its focus is on the inhibitions of the offenders (internal barriers) and how when these barriers are diminished, distorted thoughts can lead to deviant actions.

SOURCE: Adapted from Terry and Tallon (2004, p. 170).

the main types of grooming behavior are verbal and/or physical coercion, emotional manipulation, seduction, games, and enticements. Because of their poor psychosexual development, child sexual abusers often find comfort in relationships with children who are passive, dependent, nonthreatening, vulnerable, and easy to manipulate (Groth, 1983; West, 1987).

To better understand distinctions between types of child sexual abusers, researchers have created typologies, or classification schemes, based upon offender characteristics and/or victim choice. The reason for creating these typologies is that a greater understanding of the interpersonal and situational characteristics of child abusers will lead to a greater likelihood of controlling such behavior in the future. Groth, Hobson, and Gary (1982) proposed one of the earliest fundamental classification schemes based primarily upon the level of attraction the abuser has to children. They created the *fixated-regressed dichotomy of sexual offending*, in which the *fixated offender* has a persistent, continual, and compulsive attraction to children and the *regressed offender* tends to prefer adult sexual relationships, except when under stress (Groth et al., cited in Terry & Tallon, 2004).

Fixated offenders tend to be exclusively involved with children, have few (if any) age-appropriate sexual relationships, and are often attracted to children from adolescence (Finkelhor, 1984; Groth et al., 1982). It is common for fixated offenders to be diagnosed with pedophilia, which is characterized by recurrent, intense, sexually arousing fantasies of at least six months in duration involving prepubescent children (American Psychiatric Association, 2000). On the other hand, regressed offenders are primarily attracted to agemates and regress to abusing children because of external stressors. These stressors may be situational (e.g., unemployment, marital problems, financial difficulties) or they may result from negative affective states (e.g., loneliness, stress, isolation). Regressed offenders' sexual involvement with children is usually a temporary departure from their primary attraction to adults (Simon, Sales, Kaskniak, & Kahn, 1992). Though fixated offenders are more dangerous because of their exclusive sexual interest in children, most child sexual abusers have more characteristics of regressed offenders than of fixated offenders (Terry, 2006b).

While the fixated-regressed typology has been useful in helping to understand the child sexual abuser's motivation to commit offenses, it is not free from criticism. Some researchers have found that the fixated-regressed distinction is not a dichotomy but rather a continuum because child sexual abusers may have characteristics consistent with both fixated and regressed offenders (Bickley & Beech, 2001). As Robertiello and Terry (2007) note, several researchers have expanded upon the fixated-regressed typology, including Baxter, Marshall, Barbaree, Davidson, and Malcolm (1984), Knight and Prentky (1990), Simkins (1993), and Danni and Hampe (2002) and the FBI (Terry & Tallon, 2004). Some of these more sophisticated typologies further differentiate fixated and regressed offenders by subgroups, while others (e.g., Knight & Prentky, 1990) are multidimensional typologies of child molesters that take into consideration levels of social competence and the meaning of the contact with the child.

Not all research on child sexual abuse focuses on the offenders and victims. Some researchers have recently begun to study the situations in which abuse takes place (Marshall, Serran, & Marshall, 2006; Terry & Ackerman, 2008; Wortley & Smallbone, 2006a). These studies draw upon the literature on situational crime prevention (SCP), which is based on the idea that offenders are rational and will weigh the costs and benefits of the crime (Cornish & Clarke, 1986). The unique environment of the situation will help the potential offender to decide whether or not to commit a particular act (Cornish & Clarke, 1986). In this sense, crime is based upon opportunity, and the crime will not occur if the opportunity is blocked (Felson & Clarke, 1998), such as when the situation presents too much risk, offers too little reward, or requires too much effort.

Wortley and Smallbone (2006a) noted several characteristics of child sexual abuse that can be explained through situational theories. The seven factors they identified are a late onset of deviant behavior, a low incidence of chronic sexual offending, a high incidence of previous nonsexual offenses, a low incidence of stranger abuse, a low incidence of networking among offenders, a low incidence of child pornography use, and a low incidence of paraphilic behavior. They also note that location is an important factor in the commission of sexual offenses, considering that sexual abuse almost always occurs in private and often in the home of the offender. The findings from their study were supported by Terry and Ackerman (2008) when applied to Catholic priests who sexually abused children.

Child Pornography

Most of the literature that focuses on child sexual abuse focuses on child sexual abusers who have physically touched the victims. However, there is also an emerging literature on the characteristics of those who collect and distribute child pornography and seek relationships with children on the Internet. The definition of child pornography varies by country, but in the U.S. it is any visual depiction of actual or simulated vaginal intercourse, oral or anal intercourse, bestiality, masturbation, sexually sadistic or masochistic behavior, or lascivious exhibition of the genitals (U.S. Title 18, Part I, Chapter 110, § 2256). Images are also considered pornographic if the child is the focal point of a sexually suggestive setting, is in an unnatural pose or inappropriate attire, is depicted to suggest coyness or willingness to engage in sexual activity, or is depicted in a way intended to elicit a sexual response in the viewer. Internet sites featuring child pornography are fairly numerous. Japan is a primary location for the production of pornographic material involving children, although other Asian as well as Eastern European countries are common sources of child pornography. The majority of child pornographic films on the Internet depict children from Asia, Africa, and

Latin American countries, whereas the adult men molesting them typically appear to be Europeans and Americans.

There are many methods of distributing child pornography in the Internet. Wortley and Smallbone (2006b, pp. 10–11) summarize the key methods as follows:

- Web pages and Web sites—specific Web sites containing images of child pornography
- Webcams—images of abuse broadcast in real time
- E-mail—distributors may e-mail attachments of child pornography images
- E-groups—members can share and exchange information about new Web sites
- Newsgroups—forums to discuss sexual interest in children with others who have the same interests
- Bulletin Board Systems (BBS)—can host discussions about child pornography, Web sites, advice, etc.
- Chat rooms—may be used to exchange pornography and locate potential victims
- Peer-to-peer (P2P)—permits closed groups to trade images

There are differing levels of severity in child pornographers, as well as different motivations for collecting and/or distributing the materials. Wortley and Smallbone (2006b, pp. 15–17) note the following nine typologies of abusers:

- Browsers—may accidentally see images of abuse but knowingly save the images; no networking, no use of security strategies to avoid detection
- Private fantasizers—create digital images for private use; no networking, no use of secure strategies to avoid detection
- Trawlers—seek images on the Web through open browsers; may network, but employ few strategies to maintain security
- Nonsecure collectors—seek images in nonsecure Web sites or chatrooms; high level of networking, few security strategies
- Secure collectors—members of closed groups who engage in high levels of networking and employ sophisticated security strategies to avoid detection
- Groomers—develop online relationships with children, may send them pornographic images as part of the grooming process
- Physical abusers—sexually abuse children; pornographic images are a part of the abuse process but not the primary focus
- Producers—record abuse images in order to disseminate to networks
- Distributors—disseminate images of abuse; often a financial rather than sexual interest in pornography

As technology has developed and the collectors, producers, and distributors of child pornography have become more sophisticated, the laws have constantly had to adapt. The first federal law to address child pornography specifically was the Sexual Exploitation of Children Act of 1978, which prohibited the distribution of obscene material of minors. Current debates center on the use of "virtual" images (ruled in *Ashcroft v. Free Speech Coalition*, 2002 not to be protected), the monitoring of known sex offenders on social network sites (e.g., MySpace, Facebook), and how to best monitor and control child pornography on the Internet when it is a global, not local, problem.

Sexual harassment of children on the Internet is also a problem that is receiving increased attention. Mitchell, Finkelhor, and Wolak (2001) found that about 20% of child and teenage Internet users had been sexually harassed while using the Internet during the past year, and only 10% of those cases had been reported to police or any other responsible authority. They found also that 70% of parents and 75% of victims didn't know where or how to report those incidents.

Treatment, Management, and Supervision of Child Sexual Abusers

When offenders are convicted of acts of sexual abuse against children, they are punished and mandated to treatment and/or supervision. Treatment is often required for offenders serving some or all of their sentences in the community (e.g., on probation or parole), and today the most common type of treatment for sex offenders is cognitive-behavioral therapy (CBT). CBT developed from an earlier behavioral model of treatment, and it targets the following issues: (1) deviant sexual behavior and interests; (2) a wide range of social skills/relational deficits; and (3) cognitive distortions, which permit the offender to justify, rationalize, and/or minimize the offending behavior (Marshall & Barbaree, 1990b; McGrath, Hoke, & Vojtisek, 1998). It also includes a component of *relapse prevention*, which is a technique used by offenders to help them understand and manage high-risk situations.

Deviant Sexual Behavior and Interests. Combinations of behavioral approaches are frequently used to reduce deviant sexual behavior or fantasies while maintaining and/or increasing sexual arousal to appropriate stimuli. These approaches may include covert sensitization (the pairing of a negative consequence with the sexual arousal stimulus), aversion therapy (the pairing of a sexual arousal stimulus with an aversive event), and masturbatory satiation (masturbating to ejaculation while verbalizing an appropriate sexual fantasy).

Social Skills/Relational Deficits. A key aim of CBT is to enhance offenders' social and relationship skills and help them to understand appropriate social interaction and empathy (Marshall, 1989; Marshall, Anderson, &

Fernandez, 1999; McFall, 1990; Seidman, Marshall, Hudson, & Robertson, 1994). CBT targets issues such as social problem solving, conversational skills, social anxiety, assertiveness, conflict resolution, intimacy, anger management, and self-confidence (Laws & Marshall, 2003).

Cognitive Distortions. An integral part of CBT is cognitive restructuring, which aims to reduce the internal rationalizations, excuses, and justifications that sex offenders make for their behavior (Marshall & Barbaree, 1990b).

Relapse Prevention. Initially developed to treat addictive behaviors such as alcoholism, this approach was subsequently altered for use in the treatment of sex offenders (Eccles & Marshall, 1999; Laws, 1999; Laws, Hanson, Osborn, & Greenbaum, 2000). It proposes that offenders should understand their high-risk situations and be able to manage those situations by making appropriate decisions.

Some treatment plans for sex offenders include multiple treatment approaches, such as combining CBT with pharmacological treatment. Some states, such as California and Florida, even mandate that repeat sex offenders be chemically castrated if they want to be released on parole. Pharmacological treatments usually consist of regular doses of anti-androgens such as Cyproterone Acetate (CPA), Medroxyprogesterone Acetate (MPA), and long-acting analogues of Gonadotropin-Releasing Hormone (GnRH; Berlin, 1983; Bradford, 1990; Grubin, 2000; Rösler & Witztum, 2000). These work by reducing the level of serum testosterone in the male. Other pharmacological treatments are selective serotonin reuptake inhibitors (SSRIs) such as Sertraline, Fluoxetine, Fluvoxamine, Desipramine, and Clomipramine.

Studies have varied in their assessment of treatment efficacy. Overall, it seems that sex offenders who participate in CBT do have lower levels of recidivism, though this is difficult to measure through methodologically sound studies. Looman, Abracen, and Nicholaichuk (2000) found that sex offenders who participated in treatment had a recidivism rate of 23.6%, compared to 51.7% for offenders who did not participate. Nicholaichuk, Gordon, Gu, and Wong (2002) followed a sample of offenders for six years, and those who were treated had a recidivism rate of 14.5%, compared to 33.2% for nontreated offenders. McGrath, Cumming, Livingston, and Hoke (2003) found that sex offenders who participated in treatment were almost six times less likely to be charged with a new sexual offense than were offenders who refused, dropped out, or were terminated from treatment.

Though it is difficult to accurately measure recidivism, most studies show that convicted sex offenders have low recidivism rates whether they participate in treatment or not. The Bureau of Justice Statistics released a report in 2003 that found 5.3% of sex offenders committed another sexual offense within three years. In a meta-analysis of 95 studies assessing recidivism of sex offenders, Hanson and Morton-Bourgon (2004, 2005) found that 13.7% committed another sexual offense within five to six years. Sex offenders who do recidivate are significantly more likely to commit a nonsexual crime than a sexual crime. Hanson and Morton-Bourgon (2004, 2005) found that recidivism rates increase to 36.2% when sexual and nonsexual crimes were taken into consideration. Several recent studies provide support for the finding that sex offenders are more likely to be generalists (those who commit both sexual and nonsexual crimes) than specialists (those who commit only sexual crimes; Lussier et al., 2005; Miethe et al., 2006; Simon, 2000; Smallbone & Wortley, 2004; Soothill et al., 2000; Zimring, Piquero, & Jennings, 2007).

Despite the low rates of recidivism for known sex offenders and the declining number of cases of child sexual abuse since the early 1990s, several high-profile cases of child sexual abuse have led to the implementation of a series of sex offender policies. Registration and community notification laws (RCNL) were first passed in 1996, after Jesse Timmendequas, a repeat sex offender, raped and murdered 7-year-old Megan Kanka, who lived across the street from him (see Case Study: Panacea or Pandora's Box?). New Jersey was the first to pass "Megan's Law," but all 50 states and the federal government followed suit shortly thereafter.

RCNL varies state by state, but generally it mandates that offenders register their home addresses with the police and supply police with basic demographic information. Offenders are assessed at a designated risk level, and the community is notified about high-risk and often moderate-risk offenders. All states now have an Internet registry, with information accessible to anyone who can navigate the Web site (though convicted sex offenders are not supposed to use the registry).

RCNL has evolved quite significantly over the past decade (Terry, 2006a). The most significant requirements include application of RCNL to juveniles in most states, criminal sanctions for offenders who do not comply with RCNL, and the imposition of residency requirements. In many jurisdictions, both local and state, offenders are not allowed to live within a specified distance of schools, playgrounds, or any other place where children congregate. This has created a considerable burden on sex offenders, including forcing them to move from established residences, become homeless, or be driven away from entire towns. Studies are just now beginning to examine the consequences of such restrictions on sex offenders. There is also now a national database, the National Sex Offender Registry (NSOR), with more than 400,000 sex offenders currently listed. The maintenance of NSOR, however, is difficult because it relies on information from state-level data. If state registries do not have accurate, updated information, NSOR will be affected.

Though regulatory in nature, these policies are often punitive or ineffective at reducing criminal behavior because they are applied to a single group of offenders as a one size fits all policy. The effectiveness of these policies, or whether they are based on valid assumptions, is rarely considered (Lotke, 1997). Very few empirical studies have been conducted regarding the effectiveness of legislation that has been passed in the last decade, and studies that have been conducted do not provide support for their effectiveness in preventing future sex crimes.

Rape

The word *rape* originates from the Latin verb *rapere*, which means to seize or take by force, while the Latin term for the act of rape itself is *raptus*. The word originally had no sexual connotation and is still used generically in English. Formerly, rape was legally defined as violent sexual intercourse against a woman's will, specifically involving the penetration of the vagina by the penis. More recent definitions describe rape as coerced sexual intercourse or attempted coerced sex (Koss, 1992), which includes a broader range of behaviors. Morse (1995) suggested that this redefinition of rape occurred because both men and women may be either victims or perpetrators of rape.

Case Study: Helen, Age 18

Helen was 18 years old and a student when she, together with her roommates from campus, decided to attend a party thrown by some fellow students. In the house where the party was held were many people who danced, drank a lot, and used illegal drugs. Helen preferred not to participate in any of these activities and became disenchanted with what was happening at the party. Despite this, she had to stay because the campus was far away, she did not drive, and her friends were somewhere lost in the crowd and seemed to be enjoying themselves. She sat on a couch in the quietest part of the house and waited for the time to pass until she could leave.

Soon enough, a young man of about her age, who didn't seem intoxicated, approached her. He sat next to her, introduced himself as Rodger, and they begun to talk. He observed the cross Helen was wearing on her neck and suggested that sometime they should attend Mass together. Gradually, Helen began to feel comfortable with him; he seemed a very decent boy and a good Christian. After a while, he asked her whether she wanted a drink. She told him that she didn't like alcohol and would prefer a Coca-Cola instead. He returned with the refreshment and suggested they go upstairs where it was quieter and they could talk.

Helen was not concerned by his proposal; she thought she had nothing to be afraid of with so many people around her. They went up to one of the bedrooms of the house, and Rodger left the door slightly open so that Helen would not feel uncomfortable. Soon, Helen began to feel sleepy and felt her strength fade away. She asked Rodger to call her friends so she could leave because she was not feeling very well. Rodger agreed and left the room, closing the door behind him. He returned suddenly and locked the door behind him. Helen tried to stand up and shout but found that she did not have the energy to move. Rodger then raped her without any of the other partygoers being aware of what was happening. Helen reported later that this was the worst night of her life. Her friends found her sometime later and brought her to the hospital. At the hospital, she was told she had been given a "date rape drug," which was mixed in the Coca-Cola she had drunk.

It is estimated that at least 10% to 20% of adult women become victims of sexual assault, with similar estimates for sexual assault against females during childhood (Koss, 1992). Some have estimated that sexual abuse also occurs in a large proportion of physical abuse incidents against children, and it is estimated that only 1 in 10 victims of rape reports the incident (Finkelhor, 1994). Sexually abused persons manifest several acute or lifelong psychosomatic symptoms, including depression, anxiety, sleep problems, social withdrawal, and suicidal behavior. Many experience Post-Traumatic Stress Disorder (PTSD), which is characterized by specific anxiety symptoms, including flashbacks, nightmares, drug abuse, and hypervigilance (Shaw, 1999).

Several studies have shown that rape offenders share some common characteristics, including impulsivity, high general criminal activity, and difficulty in understanding the emotions of others. In addition, the presence of antisocial/psychopathic personality features seems to be a prognostic factor for recidivism of general crimes as well as violent sexual crimes (Hanson & Morton-Bourgon, 2005).

Epidemiology

Russell's (1984) research with random samples of San Francisco women is regarded as among the most thorough measurements of undesired sexual experiences. The prevalence rate of 24%, which was found by Russell, is comparable to the 27.5% prevalence rate found by Koss, Gidycs, and Wisniewski (1987) in a sample survey of American female university students who reported rape or attempted rape victimization from the age of 14. Gavey's (1991) research in New Zealand found a similar percentage (25.3%) of women who reported rape or attempted rape. As Koss (1992) notes, women are four times more likely to be raped by a familiar person than by a stranger. This is consistent with Gavey's (1991) results, which indicate that two-thirds of reported sexual assaults were committed within an ongoing heterosexual relationship, while the percentage rises to 80% if familiar persons, ex-husbands, ex-friends, and ex-lovers are included. According to the international statistics on rape from the UN (Snyder, 2000), one in six women has been raped. Similarly, nearly one in eight African women has suffered sexual assault motivated, in part, by racism.

Male and Female Offenders

Male Offenders

Male against female rape or sexual assault is the most common type of sexual assault. Historically, violence has been attributed to specific characteristics regarding the psychological profiles of the offender and the victim. These have been preserved by a series of myths, which have been characterized as creations of patriarchal societies (Brownmiller, 1975). In such myths, females are presented as vulnerable, sexually provocative, sexually available, and obedient to male desire.

As noted above, rape by familiar persons may be more common than rape by strangers. The term *date rape* refers to rape or nonconsensual sexual activity between people who are acquainted, either platonically or sexually. These cases of sexual assault take place during a social interaction between rapist and victim. Date rapes may be either planned or spontaneous and may involve physical force, the threat of physical force, or the use of intoxicants to subdue the victim. Substances that are used by perpetrators of rape against victims are internationally known as *date rape drugs* or *club drugs,* such as rohypnol and ketamine, and they may be used to neutralize resistance or render the victim unconscious. These drugs are colorless and tasteless substances and often affect memory regarding the event. However, alcohol remains the intoxicant most frequently implicated in substance-assisted sexual assault, as about 80% of date rapes included the use of alcohol by at least one partner and over 50% included the use of alcohol by both partners (Gavey, 1991).

Spousal or *marital rape* is nonconsensual sexual intercourse that is performed by force or by threat of violence or when one partner is unable to give consent. It can occur in any marital arrangement, regardless of age, social status, race, or nationality. No sufficient data exist about the prevalence of rape by husbands, given that it is unlikely that these events are commonly reported (Grandin & Lupri, 1997).

Female Offenders

Female rape offenders are far fewer than males. According to Rowan, Rowan, and Langelier (1990), only 1.5 % from a sample of 600 rapists were women, with most of these offenders involved in the rape of children. Male victims of rape, by either male or female perpetrators, are comparatively rare: It is estimated that 1 in 33 men in the United States has experienced rape or attempted rape (Tjaden & Thoennes, 2000). According to survey research, 1 in 4 homosexual men has been raped or sexually abused by a current or former partner (Cruz, 2003). Also, 1 in 5 male prisoners has experienced rape during his imprisonment (Struckman-Johnson & Struckman-Johnson, 2000).

Male victims of women rapists are comparatively rare, and victims express great difficulty in reporting such incidents (Grandin & Lupri, 1997). Men who have been sexually assaulted by women report experiencing emotions of shame and lowered self-esteem, tend to question their masculinity, and therefore remain silent. The general social perception is that they have not been assaulted but that they acquired pleasure from the sexual interaction, even if they did not consent, and such crimes are not taken seriously (Grandin & Lupri, 1997).

Sexual crimes committed by women are difficult to detect, particularly when they involve incest, because children are usually afraid to speak out against their mother, upon whom they are dependent (Groth, 1979). Finkelhor et al. (1990) suggest that female-perpetrated sexual crimes are difficult to record, more so even than male-perpetrated crimes. They found also that 25% of men who committed sexual crimes reported having been sexually assaulted by a woman. Although arrests of adult women who have committed sexual crimes have declined, the number of adolescent girls who are brought to juvenile courts for sexual crimes has risen. Studies also suggest that an association between psychosis and female sexual crimes exists. Most female offenders are relatively young, ranging between 17 and 24 years old, and come from low economic and educational backgrounds (O'Connor, 1987). Table 11.2 details multiple theories of the etiology of rape behavior.

Psychosocial Features of Sexual Offenders

Family History. A number of family factors have been identified that increase the risk of developing rape behaviors. Interrelated factors, such as bad and distant relationships with parents, unstable or neglectful care, loss of a parent due to death, separation or divorce, and high frequency of physical and sexual abuse, characterize the early childhood experiences of many sexual offenders (Prentky, Knight, Sims-Knight, Straus, Rokous, & Cerce, 1989; Ryan & Lane, 1991; Seghorn, Prentky, & Boucher, 1987).

Education Record. Although their educational achievement varies, rapists most often tend to leave high school prior to graduation. As cognitive abilities may affect the course of sex offender treatment, evaluations should include educational record, general cognitive level, and the existence of learning difficulties. Educational achievement and school behavior can give useful information concerning the cognitive and psychological abilities of an offender in treatment. For example, difficulties in attending to lessons, impulsiveness, lack of goals, low self-esteem, and low persistence can often be detected from academic records. These factors potentially affect the success of treatment for the offender's sexual behavior and can suggest the need for additional educational intervention (Bard, Carter, Cerce, Knight, Rosenberg, & Schneider, 1987).

Table 11.2 Theories of Rape

Theory	Description of Theory
Psychodynamic Theory	Various emotions of fear and sexual or personal inadequacy, and possibly unrecognized homosexual tendencies, interact with aggressiveness and are directed toward the victim, as a substitute for mother, resulting in sexual abuse.
Behavioral Theory	Deviant as well aggressive sexual behavior is a learned condition; sexual stimulation becomes associated with the aggressive response.
Socio-Cognitive Theory	Cognitive errors create thoughts and perceptions characterized by distrust and animosity toward women and eventually result in sexual violence; sexual offenders manifest a difficulty in discriminating between friendliness and sexual provocation and misread female (or male) cues.
Feminist Theory	Rape is a pseudosexual act induced by the sociopolitical domination of men. This form of violence is due to the change of roles that women gradually experience. Social beliefs reinforce sexual aggressiveness; not only rape but also the fear of a potential rape serves as a mechanism of social control.
Socio-Biological Theory	Rape is one strategy for sexual reproduction. Men, in contrast to women, tend to maximize their capacity to reproduce by having sexual intercourse with many different partners. Rape behavior may be influenced by testosterone levels and frustrated sexual drives.
Evolutionary Theory	A large "sexual asymmetry" exists in humans, which means that reproductively, males benefit from sexual intercourse with multiple partners, while females benefit from finding a long-term sexual partner with whom they can raise their children. Males who lack the social capacity to secure consenting relationships will rape; thus, rape is a "last-ditch" effort to reproduce.
The Narcissistic Personality Theory	Individuals with narcissistic personality disorder put their own gratification above the needs of others. Lack of empathy helps narcissists to overcome any compunction that the pain of the victim normally causes. In addition, the narcissistic rapist persuades himself that his victim was satisfied by the sexual intercourse with him.
Biological Theory	Sexual, as well aggressive, behavior seems to be related to circulated androgens. Suppression of the hypothalamic-pituitary-gonadal axis may reduce both testosterone levels and sexually aggressive behaviors. Effective treatment of sexual aggressiveness may involve anti-androgens.

Work Record. A stable work record tends to be a protective element regarding the development of criminal behavior. Most rapists tend to have unstable work records in unskilled professions. Evaluations should thus include work record, focusing on stability, type of work, level of capacity and responsibility, and the overall attitude toward work. These factors might relate to psychological characteristics such as persistence, capacity to tolerate defeat, and the ability to plan and achieve goals. The information provided by the work record could also indicate the need for special interventions aimed at increasing the ability to work (Bard et al., 1987; Bartol, 1991).

Social Record. Many individuals who have a history of dysfunctional attachment to those who have raised them are more likely to present dysfunctional relationships in other areas of life, as well (Hazan & Shaver, 1994). Given that, as noted above, dysfunctional family backgrounds are common among rapists, it is not surprising that rapists have generally problematic social records. For example, low levels of emotional attachment to their colleagues have been reported (Blaske, Borduin, Henggcler, & Mann, 1989), while in one study, 85% had few or no friends at all during adolescence (Tingle, Barnard, Robbin, Newman, & Hutchinson, 1986). Because early childhood experiences have an impact on the development of social stress, evaluation should include the quality, stability, and duration of social relationships; the nature and extent of social isolation; the form of interpersonal relationships; the difficulties that existed during early relationships; and the way the person deals with sexual relationships. The detection of potential deficiencies in a rapist's social life is crucial for planning treatment. For example, Knight and Prentky (1987) found that rapists who present sadistic behaviors, compared with other types of rapists, have more often reported having been assaulted themselves and had poorer social skills, poor ability to find consenting sexual partners, and more unstable interpersonal relationships.

Sexual Record. Men who present high levels of sexual aggressiveness often have had early and more frequent sexual experiences (Koss, 1989) and fewer moralistic beliefs regarding sexuality in general (Marshall, 1989), and also presented greater incidence of paraphilia (Freund, 1990; Marshall, Barbaree, & Eccles, 1991) as well as increased preoccupation with pornography (Carter, Prentky, Knight, Vanderveer, & Bouxher, 1987). A significant number of rapists report having been sexually assaulted during their childhood or having witnessed sexual activity between others, such as caregivers (Dhawan & Marshall, 1996). As noted above, early sexual experience does not imply competence at securing consenting partners. It is important to note, however, that not all individuals who are assaulted during childhood develop sexual aggressiveness (Finkelhor, 1984).

Several researchers observed that rapists tend to be socially isolated and have only a few intimate sexual relationships (Fagan & Wexler, 1988; Marshall, 1989; Tingle et al., 1986). In addition, rapists who reported having higher numbers of sexual relationships describe them as superficial (Marshall, 1989). One common element among rapists is a failure to develop intimate sexual relationships, which leads them to isolation (Tingle et al., 1986). Similarly, rapists, compared with child molesters, present low desire for an intimate relationship with other men and members of their own family (Bumby & Marshall, 1994).

Psychiatric Record. Mental disorders are common among rapists. According to one report, one-third of rapists were diagnosed with depression, while two-thirds were diagnosed with alcoholism (Hillbrand, Foster, & Hirt, 1990). Another study found a high frequency of stress disorders (Dewhurst, Moore, & Alfano, 1992), while Seghorn et al. (1987) found prevalence rates of 7% for schizophrenia, 2% for schizo-affective disorder, 3% for major depression, and 6% for organic impairments, generally documenting higher levels of dysfunction than in the general population. Drug and alcohol abuse is common among rapists. According to one study, 50% of individuals incarcerated for rape were found to have consumed an excessive quantity of alcohol just before the rape (Seto & Barbaree, 1995). Regarding Axis II (Personality Disorders), Seghorn et al. (1987) observed that almost one-third of the sample presented with personality disorders, while other researchers found higher levels, up to 90% (Berner, Berger, Gutierez, Jordan, & Berger, 1992; Giotakos, Markianos, Vaidakis, & Christodoulou, 2003, 2004; Serin, Malcolm, Khanna, & Barbaree, 1994; Stermac & Quinsey, 1986). Models of sexual aggressiveness focus mostly on the antisocial personality characteristics and less on other features (Marshall & Barbaree, 1990a).

Treatment for Rapists

Treatment Programs

Integrated programs for sexual offenders have been developed in the United States, Canada, Australia, and England (Marshall, Fernandez, Hudson, & Ward, 1998). In general, treatment interventions for sexual offenders (commonly organized as group therapy) are divided between those offered in prisons and those performed in the community (including for persons who are on probation or parole). The primary goals include (1) acknowledgment of responsibility, (2) identification of triggers for offending, (3) definition and supervision of individual therapeutic goals, (4) learning prevention methods, and (5) learning techniques from other groups of offenders that reduce rape motivation. The inmate/client also works to acquire training in basic social skills, including communication skills, empathy toward others, anger management, stress management, sexual hygiene, and so on. Each individual in group therapy also attends individual counseling, mainly focused on behavioral plans for controlling aggressive sexual urges. By the end of the intervention, it is expected that the individual will have acknowledged the factors that contribute to the precipitation of the rape behavior, will be capable of detecting situations that might increase the danger of relapse, and will have acquired skills to avoid high-risk situations. It is recommended that therapeutic intervention be continued even after release from prison or probation. It is believed that in order to achieve satisfactory results, the programs should last at least two years.

Outcome studies suggest that almost half the participants receiving at least 54 hours of therapy showed a decrease in paraphilic preoccupation and sexual compulsive behavior and increased empathy toward victims of rape (Marshall, 1989). Alongside psychotherapeutic approaches, several medical interventions have been examined for potential reduction of sexual aggressiveness. Surgical castration, neuroleptics, and estrogen-based medications have been largely dispensed with, due to considerable side effects. The anti-depressants, especially the specific serotonin reuptake inhibitors (SSRIs), demonstrate satisfactory effects. Hormone therapies with anti-androgens and Gonadotropine Releasing Hormone (GnRH) agonists also had a satisfactory outcome in the reduction of sexual aggressiveness (Kafka, 1997; Rösler & Witztum, 1998).

Sex Offenders' Response to Treatment

Evaluation instruments, such as the Sex Offenders Risk Appraisal Guide (SORAG) and Static-99, demonstrate strong ability to predict the relapse of sexual crimes. A recent study from Belgium demonstrated the ability of these instruments to predict future sexual aggression (Ducro & Pham, 2006). However, in a recent five-year follow-up study, Langstrom, Sjostedt, and Grann (2004) found that while these predictive instruments worked well among Europeans, they performed poorly with Africans and Asians. It is possible that different prognostic factors contribute to the relapse of sexual aggression in minorities and emigrants as compared to European Caucasians. A recent study in England with 418 sexual offenders who attended a cognitive-behavioral therapeutic program found that after a surveillance period of five years, antisocial personality was the most significant factor in predicting relapse (Langton, Barbaree, Harkins, & Peacock, 2006). Furthermore, this study showed an association between high levels of antisociality/psychopathy and shorter duration until relapse.

Finally, a recent meta-analysis of 82 studies that examined the relapse in sexual offences in 29,450 people (Hanson & Morton-Bourgon, 2005) showed that generally, deviant sexual behavior and antisocial personality structure are the two major predictors of relapse. This was true not only for violent sexual crimes but also for general criminal activity. Older offenders were less likely to relapse than were younger offenders. In contrast, factors such as psychological distress, failure to take responsibility for criminal activities, empathy toward the victim, and reported motive for therapy had almost no predictive relationship with the relapse in sexual crimes.

Discussion Questions

1. How do we measure the prevalence of sexual victimization? Are prevalence statistics accurate? Why or why not?

2. Many researchers have created typologies of sex offenders. Why is it important to do this? What are some common characteristics of child sexual abusers? What are some common characteristics of rapists?

3. What are the steps that generally occur before a person sexually abuses a child?

4. What are the most effective strategies for preventing sexual abuse? Why?

5. Is it possible that treatment could serve as an alternative to long-term incarceration for rapists? How would this approach impact victims? Is treatment or victim satisfaction a more important issue in regard to consequences of rape behavior?

6. What biological and social forces may contribute to rape?

7. Despite the fact that rape rates have gone down while pornography has become more prevalent, some people argue that pornography, in one form or another, may contribute to sex offenses. What are your thoughts on this?

Internet Resources

Association for the Treatment of Sexual Abusers: http://www.atsa.com

British Association for Sexual and Relationship Therapy: http://www.basrt.org.uk

Bureau of Justice Statistics, Sexual Crimes Data: http://www.ojp.usdoj.gov/bjs/crimoff.htm#sex

Center for Sex Offender Management, U.S. Department of Justice: http://www.csom.org/

Family Research Laboratory: http://www.unh.edu/frl/

International Academy of Sex Research: http://www.iasr.org/index.html

The Kinsey Institute: http://www.indiana.edu/~kinsey/

Klaaskids Foundation: http://www.klaaskids.org/

National Society for the Prevention of Cruelty to Children: http://www.nspcc.org.uk

Parents for Megan's Law (advocacy group): http://www.parentsformeganslaw.com/

Sexual Recovery Institute: http://www.sexualrecovery.com

Stop It Now (Child sexual abuse prevention advocacy group): http://www.stopitnow.com/

Stop Prisoner Rape: http://www.spr.org/

U.S. Department of Justice Sex Offender Database: http://www.nsopr.gov/

Women's Health: http://www.4woman.gov

References

American Psychiatric Association. (2000). *Diagnostic and statistical manual of mental disorders* (Text rev.). Washington, DC: Author.

Arata, C. M. (1998). To tell or not to tell: Current functioning of child sexual abuse survivors who disclosed their victimization. *Child Maltreatment: Journal of the American Professional Society on the Abuse of Children, 3,* 63–71.

Ashcroft v. Free Speech Coalition, 535 U.S. 234 (2002).

Bard, L. A., Carter, D. L., Cerce, D. D., Knight, R. A., Rosenberg, R., & Schneider, B. (1987). A descriptive study of rapists and child molesters: Developmental, clinical, and criminal characteristics. *Behavioral Sciences and the Law, 5,* 203–220.

Bartol, C. (1991). *Criminal behavior: A psychosocial approach.* Englewood Cliffs, NJ: Prentice Hall.

Baxter, D. J., Marshall, W. L., Barbaree, H. E., Davidson, P. R., & Malcolm, P. B. (1984). Deviant sexual behavior: Differentiating sex offenders by criminal and personal history, psychometric measures, and sexual response. *Criminal Justice and Behavior, 11,* 477–501.

Berlin, F. S. (1983). Sex offenders: A biomedical perspective and a status report on biomedical treatment. In J. G. Greer (Ed.). *The sexual aggressor: Current perspectives on treatment* (pp. 83–123). New York: Van Nostrand Reinhold.

Berner, W., Berger, P., Gutierez, K., Jordan, B., & Berger, J. (1992). The role of personality disorder in the treatment of sexual offenders. *Journal of Offender Rehabilitation, 18,* 25–37.

Bickley, J., & Beech, A. R. (2001). Classifying child abusers: Its relevance to theory and clinical practice. *Journal of Offender Therapy and Comparative Criminology, 45,* 51–69.

Blaske, D. M., Borduin, C. M., Henggcler, S. W., & Mann, J. (1989). Individual, family and peer characteristics of adolescent sex offenders and assaultive offenders. *Developmental Psychology, 25,* 846–855.

Bolen, R., & Scannapieco, M. (1999). Prevalence of child sexual abuse: A corrective meta-analysis. *Social Service Review, 73,* 281–313.

Boney-McCoy, S., & Finkelhor, D. (1995). Psychosocial sequelae of violent victimization in a national youth sample. *Journal of Consulting and Clinical Psychology, 63,* 726–736.

Bradford, J. M. W. (1990). The antiandrogen and hormonal treatment of sex offenders. In W. L. Marshall (Ed.), *Handbook of sexual assault: Issues, theories, and treatment of the offender* (pp. 297–310). New York: Plenum Press.

Brownmiller, S. (1975). *Against our will.* New York: Simon & Schuster.

Bumby, K. M., & Marshall, W. L. (1994). *Loneliness and intimacy deficits among incarcerated rapists and child molesters.* Paper presented and the 13th annual research and treatment conference of the Association for the Treatment of Sexual Abusers, San Francisco.

Bureau of Justice Statistics. (2003). *Recidivism of sex offenders released from prison in 1994.* Washington, DC: U.S. Department of Justice.

Campis, L. B., Hebden-Curtis, J., & DeMaso, D. R. (1993). Developmental differences in detection and disclosure of sexual abuse. *Journal of the American Academy of Child & Adolescent Psychiatry, 32,* 920–924.

Carter, D. L., Prentky, R. A., Knight, R. A., Vanderveer, P. L., & Bouxher, R. J. (1987). Use of pornography in the criminal and developmental histories of sexual offenders. *Journal of Interpersonal Violence, 2,* 196–211.

Cornish, D. B., & Clarke, R. V. (1986). *The reasoning criminal.* New York: Springer-Verlag.

Cruz, J. M. (2003). Gay male domestic violence and reasons victims stay. *Journal of Men's Studies, 11,* 309.

Danni, K. A., & Hampe, G. D. (2002). An analysis of predictors of child sex offender types using pre-sentence investigation reports. *International Journal of Offender Therapy and Comparative Criminology, 44,* 490–504.

Dewhurst, A. M., Moore, R. J., & Alfano, D. P. (1992). Aggression against women by men: Sexual and spousal assault. *Journal of Offender Rehabilitation, 18*(3/4), 39–47.

Dhawan, S., & Marshall, W. L. (1996). Sexual abuse histories of sexual offenders. *Sexual Abuse: A Journal of Research and Treatment, 8,* 7–15.

DiPietro, E. K., Runyan, D. K., & Fredrickson, D. D. (1997). Predictors of disclosure during medical evaluation for suspected sexual abuse. *Journal of Child Sexual Abuse, 6,* 133–142.

Douard, J. (2007). Loathing the sinner, medicalizing the sin: Why sexually violent predator statutes are unjust. *International Journal of Law and Psychiatry, 30,* 36–48.

Ducro, C., & Pham, T. (2006). Evaluation of the SORAG and the Static-99 on Belgian sex offenders committed to a forensic facility. *Sex Abuse, 18*(1), 15–26.

Eccles, A., & Marshall, W. L. (1999). Relapse prevention. In W. L. Marshall (Ed.), *The development of cognitive behavioral treatment of sex offenders* (pp. 127–146). London: John Wiley & Sons.

Fagan, J., & Wexler, S. (1988). Explanations of sexual assault among violent delinquents. *Journal of Adolescent Research, 3,* 363–385.

Felson, M., & Clarke, R. V. (1998). *Opportunity makes the thief: Practical theory for crime prevention. Police research series, paper 98.* London: Policing and Reducing Crime Unit, Research, Development and Statistics Directorate.

Finkelhor, D. (1984). *Child sexual abuse: New theory and research.* New York: Free Press.

Finkelhor, D. (1994). The international epidemiology of child sexual abuse. *Child Abuse and Neglect, 18,* 409–417.

Finkelhor, D., Hotaling, G., Lewis, I. A., & Smith, C. (1990). Sexual abuse in a national survey of adult men and women: Prevalence, characteristics, and risk factors. *Child Abuse & Neglect, 14,* 19–28.

Finkelhor, D., & Ormrod, R. (2001, September). Crimes against children by babysitters. *Juvenile Justice Bulletin.* Washington, DC: U.S. Department of Justice.

Freund, K. (1990). Courtship disorder. In W. L. Marshall, D. R. Laws, & H. E. Barbaree (Eds.), *Handbook of sexual assaults: Issues, theories, and treatment of the offender* (pp. 195–207). New York: Plenum Press.

Gavey, N. (1991). Sexual victimization prevalence among New Zealand university students. *Journal of Consulting and Clinical Psychology, 59,* 464–466.

Giotakos, O., Markianos, M., Vaidakis, N., & Christodoulou, G. (2003). Aggression, impulsivity, plasma sex hormones, and biogenic amine turnover in a forensic population of rapists. *Journal of Sex & Marital Therapy, 29*(3), 215–225.

Giotakos, O., Markianos, M., Vaidakis, N., & Christodoulou, G. (2004). Sex hormones and amine turnover of sex offenders, in relation to their temperament and character dimensions. *Psychiatry Research, 127*(3), 185–193.

Grandin, E., & Lupri, E. (1997). Intimate violence in Canada and the United States. *Journal of Family Violence, 12*(4), 417–443.

Gries, L. T., Goh, D. S., & Cavanaugh, J. (1996). Factors associated with disclosure during child sexual abuse assessment. *Journal of Child Sexual Abuse, 5,* 1–20.

Groth, A. N. (1979). *Men who rape: The psychology of the offender.* New York: Plenum Press.

Groth, A. N. (1983). Treatment of the sexual offender in a correctional institution. In J. G. Greer & I. R. Stuart (Eds.), *The sexual aggressor: Current perspectives on treatment* (pp. 160–176). New York: Van Nostrand Reinhold.

Groth, A. N., Hobson, W. F., & Gary, T. S. (1982). The child molester: Clinical observations. In J. Conte & D. A. Shore (Eds.), *Social work and child sexual abuse* (pp. 129–144). New York: Haworth Press.

Grubin, D. (2000). Complementing relapse prevention with medical intervention. In D. R. Laws (Ed.), *Remaking relapse prevention with sex offenders* (pp. 201–212). Thousand Oaks, CA: Sage.

Hanson, R. K, & Morton-Bourgon, K. (2004). *Predictors of sexual recidivism: An updated meta-analysis* (Research Rep. No 2004-02). Ottawa: Public Safety and Emergency Preparedness Canada.

Hanson, R., & Morton-Bourgon, K. (2005). The characteristics of persistent sexual offenders: A meta-analysis of recidivism studies. *Journal of Consulting and Clinical Psychology, 73*(6), 1154–1163.

Hanson, R. F., Saunders, H. S., Saunders, B. E., Kilpatrick, D. G., & Best, C. (1999). Factors related to the reporting of childhood rape. *Child Abuse & Neglect, 23,* 559–569.

Hazan, C., & Shaver, P. (1994). Attachment as an organizational framework for research on close relationships. *Psychological Inquiry, 5,* 1–22.

Hillbrand, M., Foster, H., & Hirt, M. (1990). Rapists and child molesters: Psychometric comparisons. *Archives of Sexual Behavior, 19,* 65–71.

Jenkins, P. (1998). *Moral panic: Changing concepts of the child molester in modern America.* New Haven, CT: Yale University Press.

Jones, L. M., & Finkelhor, D. (2004). *Explanations for the decline in sexual abuse cases. OJJDP Bulletin.* Washington, DC: U.S. Department of Justice.

Kafka, M. P. (1997). A monoamine hypothesis for the pathophysiology of paraphilic disorders. *Archives of Sexual Behavior, 26,* 343–358.

Knight, R. A., & Prentky, R. A. (1987). The developmental antecedents and adult adaptations of rapist subtypes. *Criminal Justice and Behavior, 14,* 403–426.

Knight, R. A., & Prentky, R. A. (1990). Classifying sexual offenders: The development and corroboration of taxonomic models. In W. L. Marshall (Ed.), *Handbook of sexual assault: Issues, theories, and treatment of the offender* (pp. 23–52). New York: Plenum Press.

Koss, M. (1989). Hidden rape: Sexual aggression and victimization in a national sample of students in higher education. In M. A. Pirog-Good & J. Stets (Eds.), *Violence in dating relationships* (pp. 145–168). New York: Praeger.

Koss, M. (1992). The underdetection of rape: Methodological choices influence incidence estimates. *Journal of Social Issues, 48,* 61–75.

Koss, M., Gidycs, C., & Wisniewski, N. (1987). The scope of rape: Incidence and prevalence of sexual aggression and victimization in national sample of higher education students. *Journal Consulting and Clinical Psychology, 55,* 162–170.

Lamb, S., & Edgar-Smith, S. (1994). Aspects of disclosure: Mediators of outcome of childhood sexual abuse. *Journal of Interpersonal Violence, 9,* 307–326.

Langstrom, N., Sjostedt, G., & Grann, M. (2004). Psychiatric disorders and recidivism in sexual offenders. *Sex Abuse, 16*(2), 139–150.

Langton, C., Barbaree, H., Harkins, L., & Peacock, E. (2006). Sex offenders' response to treatment and its association with recidivism as a function of psychopathy. *Sex Abuse, 18*(1), 99–120.

Laws, D. R. (1999). Relapse prevention: The state of the art. *Journal of Interpersonal Violence, 14,* 285–302.

Laws, D. R., Hanson, R. K., Osborn, C. A., & Greenbaum, P. E. (2000). Classification of child molesters by plethysmographic assessment of sexual arousal and a self-report measure of sexual preference. *Journal of Interpersonal Violence, 15,* 1297–1312.

Laws, D. R., & Marshall, W. L. (2003). A brief history of behavioral and cognitive behavioral approaches to sex offenders: Part 1. Early developments. *Sexual Abuse: A Journal of Research and Treatment, 15,* 75–92.

Looman, J., Abracen, J., & Nicholaichuk, T. P. (2000). Recidivism among treated sexual offenders and matched controls: data from the Regional Treatment Centre (Ontario). *Journal of Interpersonal Violence, 15,* 279–290.

Lotke, E. (1997). Politics and irrelevance: Community notification statutes. *Federal Sentencing Reporter, 10,* 64–68.

Lussier, P., LeBlanc, M., & Proulx, J. (2005). The generality of criminal behavior: A confirmatory factor analysis of the criminal activity of sex offenders in adulthood. *Journal of Criminal Justice, 33,* 177–189.

Marshall, W. L. (1989). Intimacy, loneliness, and sexual offenders. *Behavior Therapy and Research, 27,* 491–503.

Marshall, W. L., Anderson, D., & Fernandez, Y. (1999). *Cognitive behavioral treatment of sexual offenders.* London: John Wiley & Sons.

Marshall, W. L., & Barbaree, H. E. (1990a). An integrated theory of the etiology of sexual offending. In W. L. Marshall, D. R. Laws, & H. E. Barbaree (Eds.), *Handbook of sexual assault: Issues, theories, and treatment of the offender* (pp. 257–275). New York: Plenum Press.

Marshall, W. L., & Barbaree, H. E. (1990b). Outcome of comprehensive cognitive-behavioral treatment programs. In W. L. Marshall (Eds.), *Handbook of sexual assault: Issues, theories, and treatment of the offender* (pp. 363–385). New York: Plenum Press.

Marshall, W. L., Barbaree, H. E., & Eccles, A. (1991). Early onset and deviant sexuality in child molesters. *Journal of Interpersonal Violence, 6,* 323–336.

Marshall, W., Fernandez, Y., Hudson, S., & Ward, T. (1998). *Sourcebook of treatment programs for sexual offenders.* New York and London: Plenum Press.

Marshall, W. L., Serran, G. A., & Marshall, L. E. (2006). Situational and dispositional factors in child sexual molestation: A clinical perspective. In R. Wortley & S. Smallbone (Eds.), *Situational prevention of child sexual abuse. Crime prevention studies* (Vol. 19, pp. 37–64). Monsey, NY: Criminal Justice Press.

McFall, R. (1990). The enhancement of social skills. In W. L. Marshall (Ed.), *Handbook of sexual assault: Issues, theories, and treatment of the offender* (pp. 311–327). New York: Plenum Press.

McGrath, R. J., Cumming, G., Livingston, J. A., & Hoke, S. E. (2003). Outcome of a treatment program for adult sex offenders: From prison to community. *Journal of Interpersonal Violence, 18,* 3–17.

McGrath, R. J., Hoke, S. E., & Vojtisek, J. E. (1998). Cognitive-behavioral treatment of sex offenders: A treatment comparison and long-term follow-up study. *Criminal Justice and Behavior, 25,* 203–225.

Miethe, T. D., Olson, J., & Mitchell, O. (2006). Specialization and persistence in the arrest histories of sex offenders: A comparative analysis of alternative measures and offense types. *Journal of Research in Crime and Delinquency, 43,* 204–229.

Mitchell, K., Finkelhor, D., & Wolak J. (2001). Risk factors and impact of online sexual solicitation of youth. *Journal of the American Medical Association, 285,* 3011–3014.

Morse, B. (1995). Beyond the conflict tactics scale: Assessing gender differences in partner violence. *Violence and Victims, 10*(4), 251–272.

Nicholaichuk, T., Gordon, A., Gu, D., & Wong, S. (2002). Outcome of an institutional sexual offender treatment program: A comparison between treated and matched untreated offenders. *Sexual Abuse: A Journal of Research and Treatment, 12,* 139–153.

O'Connor, A. A. (1987). Female sex offenders. *British Journal of Psychiatry, 150,* 615–620.

Prentky, R. A., Knight, R. A., Sims-Knight, J. E., Straus, H., Rokous, F., & Cerce, D. (1989). Developmental antecedents of sexual aggression. *Development and Psychopathology, 1,* 153–169.

Pryor, D. W. (1996). *Unspeakable acts: Why men sexually abuse children.* New York: New York University Press.

Robertiello, G., & Terry, K. J. (2007). Can we profile sex offenders? A review of sex offender typologies. *Aggression and Violent Behavior, 12,* 508–518.

Rösler, A., & Witztum, E. (1998). Treatment of men with paraphilia with a long acting analogue of gonadotropin-releasing hormone. *New England Journal of Medicine, 338,* 416–422.

Rösler, A., & Witztum, E. (2000). Pharmacotherapy of paraphilias in the next millennium. *Behavioral Sciences and the Law, 18,* 43–56.

Rowan, E. L., Rowan, J. B., & Langelier, P. (1990). Women who molest children. *The Bulletin of the American Academy of Psychiatry and the Law, 18*(1), 79–83.

Russell, D. E. H. (1984). *Sexual exploitation: Rape, child sexual abuse, and workplace harassment.* Thousand Oaks, CA: Sage.

Ryan, G., & Lane, S. (1991). *Juvenile sexual offending: Causes, consequences and correction.* Lexington, MA: Lexington Books.

Seghorn, T. K., Prentky, R. A., & Boucher, R. J. (1987). Childhood sexual abuse in the lives of sexually aggressive offenders. *Journal of the American Academy of Child and Adolescent psychiatry, 26*, 262–267.

Seidman, B. T., Marshall, W. L., Hudson, S. M., & Robertson, P. J. (1994). An examination of intimacy and loneliness in sex offenders. *Journal of Interpersonal Violence, 9*, 518–534.

Serin, R. C., Malcolm, P. B., Khanna, A., & Barbaree, H. E. (1994). Psychopathy and deviant sexual arousal in incarcerated sexual offenders. *Journal of Interpersonal Violence, 9*, 3–11.

Seto, M. C., & Barbaree, H. E. (1995). The role of alcohol in sexual aggression. *Clinical Psychology Review, 15*(6), 545–566.

Shaw, J. A. (1999). *Sexual aggression.* Washington, DC: American Psychiatric Press.

Simkins, L. (1993). Characteristics of sexually repressed child molesters. *Journal of Interpersonal Violence, 8*, 3–17.

Simon, L. M. J. (2000). An examination of the assumptions of specialization, mental disorder, and dangerousness in sex offenders. *Behavioral Sciences and the Law, 18*, 175–308.

Simon, L. M. J., Sales, B., Kaskniak, A., & Kahn, M. (1992). Characteristics of child molesters: Implications for the fixated-regressed dichotomy. *Journal of Interpersonal Violence, 7*, 211–225.

Simon, L. M., & Zgoba, K. (2006). Sex crimes against children: Legislation, prevention and investigation. In R. Wortley & S. Smallbone (Eds.), *Situational prevention of child sexual abuse. Crime prevention studies* (Vol. 19, pp. 65–100). Monsey, NY: Criminal Justice Press.

Smallbone, S. W., & Wortley, R. K. (2004). Criminal diversity and paraphilic interests among adult males convicted of sexual offenses against children. *International Journal of Offender Therapy and Comparative Criminology, 48*, 175–188.

Smith, D. W., Letourneau, E. J., & Saunders, B. E. (2000). Delay in disclosure of childhood rape: Results from a national survey. *Child Abuse & Neglect, 24*, 273–287.

Snyder, H. N. (2000). *Sexual assault of young children as reported to law enforcement: Victim, incident, and offender characteristics.* Washington, DC: US Department of Justice, Bureau of Justice Statistics, National Center for Juvenile Justice.

Soothill, K., Francis, B., Sanderson, B., & Ackerley, E. (2000). Sex offenders: Specialists, generalists—or both? *British Journal of Criminology, 40*, 56–67.

Sorenson, T., & Snow, B. (1991). How children tell: The process of disclosure in child sexual abuse. *Child Welfare, 70*, 3–15.

Stermac, L. E., & Quinsey, V. L. (1986). Social competence among rapists. *Behavioral Assessments, 8*, 171–185.

Struckman-Johnson, C., & Struckman-Johnson, D. (2000). Sexual coercion rates in seven midwestern prison facilities for men. *The Prison Journal, 80*(4), 379–390.

Terry, K. J. (2006a). Megan's law: A decade of developments. *Sex Offender Law Report, 7*(5), 67–69.

Terry, K. J. (2006b). *Sexual offenses and offenders: Theory, practice, and policy.* Belmont, CA: Wadsworth.

Terry, K. J., & Ackerman, A. (2008). Child sexual abuse in the Catholic church: Applying situational crime prevention strategies for safe environments. *Criminal Justice & Behavior, 35*(5), 643–657.

Terry, K. J., & Tallon, J. (2004). Child sexual abuse: A review of the literature. In John Jay College Research Team (Eds.), *The nature and scope of sexual abuse of minors by Catholic priests and deacons in the United States, 1950–2002.* Washington, DC: United States Conference of Catholic Bishops.

Tingle, D., Barnard, G. W., Robbin, I., Newman, G., & Hutchinson, D. (1986). Childhood and adolescent characteristics of pedophiles and rapists. *International Journal of Law and Psychiatry, 9,* 103–116.

Tjaden, P., & Thoennes, N. (2000). *Full report of the prevalence, incidence, and consequences of violence against women: Findings from the national violence against women survey.* (Report NCJ 183781) Washington, DC: National Institute of Justice.

West, D. J. (1987). *Sexual crimes and confrontations: A study of victims and offenders.* Aldershot: Gower.

Wortley, R., & Smallbone, S. (2006a). Applying situational principles to sexual offenses against children. In R. Wortley & S. Smallbone (Eds.), *Situational prevention of child sexual abuse. Crime prevention studies* (Vol. 19, pp. 7–36). Monsey, NY: Criminal Justice Press.

Wortley, R., & Smallbone, S. (2006b). *Child pornography on the internet. Problem oriented guides for police, problem-specific guide series number 41.* Washington, DC: U.S. Department of Justice, Community Oriented Policing Services.

Wyatt, G. E., & Newcomb, M. D. (1990). Internal and external mediators of women's sexual abuse in childhood. *Journal of Consulting & Clinical Psychology, 58,* 758–767.

Zimring, F. E., Piquero, A. R., & Jennings, W. G. (2007). Sexual delinquency in Racine: Does early sex offending predict later sex offending in youth and young adulthood? *Criminology & Public Policy, 6,* 507–534.

CHAPTER 12

Hate Crimes

Phyllis B. Gerstenfeld

Weeks later I recall waking up in the hospital with a myriad of emotions, including fear and uncertainty. Most of all, I felt inexplicable humiliation. Not only did I have to face my peers and my family, I had to face the fact that I had been targeted for violence in a brutal crime because of my ethnicity. This crime took place in middle-class America in the year 2006. The reality that hate is alive, strong, and thriving in the cities, towns, and cul-de-sacs of Suburbia, America was a surprise to me.

—David Ritcheson, hate crime victim
(Anti-Defamation League, 2007c)

CASE STUDY: DAVID RITCHESON

David Ritcheson was a 17-year-old Mexican American and had played on his high school football team in a Texas suburb. One evening in April, 2006, he and some acquaintances got together to party. Also present at the party was 18-year-old David Henry Tuck. Tuck had a reputation for violence as well as a long juvenile record. He was rumored to be a racist skinhead, and he had previously been convicted for burning a cross, as well as attacking a Hispanic man at a convenience store. Also present at the party was Keith Robert Turner, a 17-year-old friend of Tuck's with a juvenile record of his own.

At some point during the evening, Tuck punched Ritcheson hard enough to break his jaw. Tuck and Turner then dragged the unconscious Ritcheson outside, stripped him naked, and proceeded to spend several hours beating and torturing him. They kicked him with steel-toed boots, burned

(Continued)

257

(Continued)

him with cigarettes, sodomized him with a patio umbrella pole, poured bleach on him, and started to carve a swastika into his flesh. During the attack, Tuck and Turner shouted out "White power!" and ethnic slurs against Ritcheson ("Prosecutor: Teen attack no hate crime," 2006).

Ritcheson was discovered the next morning by the mother of one of the boys. He was still alive but so badly injured that it was unclear whether he would survive. He spent more than three months in the hospital and required more than 30 surgeries. Both Turner and Tuck were convicted of the attacks; Tuck received a life sentence, while Turner received a sentence of 90 years ("Jury Sentences Texas Teen," 2006).

Ritcheson returned to school and attempted to make up his missing credits so he could graduate. In April, 2007, he testified before Congress in support of a federal hate crime bill. However, he refused counseling to deal with his psychological and emotional pain. On July 1, 2007, David Ritcheson leapt to his death off the tower of a cruise ship in the Gulf of Mexico (Lozano, 2007).

David Ritcheson's case demonstrates many of the difficult issues pertaining to hate crimes. Ritcheson was attacked, it appears, at least in part because of his ethnicity. His attackers were young men acting in a small group. As frequently happens in these cases, prosecutors chose not to bring hate crime charges against the attackers. The federal law that Ritcheson testified in support of—the Local Law Enforcement Hate Crimes Prevention Act of 2007—had been proposed in Congress in various forms for a decade but had never been signed into law. The House of Representatives approved the law in May, 2007, and the Senate was likely to do so as well, but President Bush said he would veto the bill because there was no need for expanded federal hate crime protection (Stout, 2007). And, like other hate crime victims, Ritcheson had to face the trauma of being assaulted because of bias against his ethnicity.

Hate Crime Legislation

Although most people are familiar with the term *hate crime,* a large proportion of the public is unaware of what, exactly, this offense is. One common misconception is that a hate crime is a crime in which the offender hates the victim. Simply put, a hate crime is a criminal act motivated by the victim's personal characteristics, such as race, national origin, or religion (Gerstenfeld, 2004). Hate crime is distinct from *hate speech* in that hate speech involves no underlying criminal act, but rather the utterance, publication, or display of offensive words or symbols directed toward a particular group of people.

Bias is clearly not a recent phenomenon in the United States, and incidents of intimidation, harassment, and violence inspired by bias play a prominent role throughout American history (Petrosino, 1999). In the years following the Civil War, during a surge in xenophobia in the mid-1920s, and again during the Civil Rights era, states and the federal government enacted laws that prohibited some of these incidents. For example, a Georgia law criminalizes wearing masks or hoods in public, and a federal law bars people from interfering with certain activities of other people (such as attending school or being employed) on the basis of race, religion, or national origin (Gerstenfeld, 2004). Not only were prosecutions under these laws rare, but some advocates argued that the laws' limited scopes were insufficient to address the majority of bias-motivated crimes (Jenness & Grattet, 1996).

In 1977, a neo-Nazi group attempted to conduct a march in Skokie, Illinois, a suburb of Chicago with a large Jewish population. The controversy surrounding this proposed event engendered much attention by the media and public and drew attention to the continuing vitality of hatred in the United States. The Anti-Defamation League (ADL), a Jewish organization, began documenting anti-Semitic incidents and drafted a comprehensive model hate crime statute (Greenberg, 1993). The ADL and other anti-bigotry groups lobbied states to enact the law. Their efforts met with success: Oregon and Washington passed hate crime laws in 1981, and most other states soon followed suit. By 2005, all but one state—Wyoming—had at least some form of hate crime legislation (Shively, 2005).

Hate crime laws come in a variety of forms. One of the most common types is the *penalty enhancer*, a law that increases the penalties for criminal acts if those acts are motivated (at least in part) by the victim's group membership (e.g., race, ethnicity, gender, religion). In addition, states may have laws that permit victims of hate crimes to sue offenders and often to receive increased damages if they win, laws that establish training requirements for police officers regarding hate crimes, and laws that require collection of hate crime data.

Although many hate crime statutes were inspired by or modeled on the ADL's proposal, the specifics of those statutes vary considerably from state to state. One of the most significant differences between states is which groups are protected by the laws. Virtually all hate crime laws encompass acts committed because of a victim's race, ethnicity or national origin, or religion. However, only 32 states classify crimes committed because of the victim's sexual orientation as hate crimes, 32 states include disability, and 28 states include gender. Smaller numbers of states include categories such as age, gender identity, and political affiliation (ADL, 2006). The issue of which groups to protect has often been contentious. For example, while an estimated one in five gay and lesbian adults has been victimized based on his or her sexual orientation (Herek, in press), and while there is some evidence that sexual orientation-based crimes tend to be more violent than other hate crimes (Dunbar, 2006), many people strongly oppose including sexual orientation in hate crime laws (Jacobs & Potter, 1998; Johnson & Byers, 2003).

There currently exists no comprehensive federal hate crime statute; although such a law has been repeatedly proposed, it has yet to be passed by

Congress. In fact, the question of whether to include sexual orientation has been one of the major impediments to the enactment of a federal hate crime law (Peek, 2001). There are federal civil rights statutes—some dating to the Reconstruction period—that prohibit specific types of activities, such as interfering with people's housing or employment rights, but these laws are quite limited in scope. The Hate Crimes Sentencing Enhancement Act, enacted in 1994, increases the penalties for federal crimes committed because of the victim's group affiliation, but it is rarely used. In 1999, for example, only 58 cases were prosecuted under this law (Chorba, 2001). The only current federal hate crime law of real significance is the Hate Crime Statistics Act. Enacted in 1990, this law requires the U.S. Department of Justice to collect hate crime data from local law enforcement agencies. The Federal Bureau of Investigation (FBI) has published a report on these data each year since 1992.

Hate crime laws present a number of troubling legal and policy problems. Soon after they were enacted, hate crime penalty enhancers were attacked on constitutional grounds. Perhaps the strongest of the arguments was that because penalty enhancers proscribe only acts based on a particular motive—the motive of bias—these laws violate the First Amendment in that they punish people's thoughts. According to this argument, the only distinction between an offender who vandalizes a home because of the victim's race and another offender who vandalizes a home as a prank is the thoughts going through each offender's head. Yet the first offender may receive more severe punishments under hate crime laws. The United States Supreme Court addressed this argument in 1993 in *Wisconsin v. Mitchell*. In a unanimous decision, the Court found that hate crime laws punish not biased thoughts, but rather the conduct or behavior inspired by those thoughts. While the Constitution prohibits punishment of thoughts, it certainly permits punishment of conduct. The Court also found that hate crimes are qualitatively different—and worse—than other crimes, in that they have a greater impact on victims and communities.

In an earlier case, *R.A.V. v. St. Paul* (1992), the Court held that hate *speech* laws—those that prohibit certain offensive expression, without requiring an underlying criminal act—are unconstitutional in that they violate the First Amendment's free expression protections. Sometimes, the line between hate crime and hate speech is quite indistinct. For example, while burning a cross on one's own property might sometimes be considered a form of protected symbolic speech, it might sometimes constitute intimidation or harassment and thus be subject to prosecution. It depends on the circumstances, such as when and where the cross is burned (*Virginia v. Black*, 2003).

Aside from First Amendment claims, the other major constitutional challenge to hate crime laws is that they may sometimes violate the Fourteenth

Amendment's due process clause. The Supreme Court held in *Apprendi v. New Jersey* (2000) that due process requires any factor that might increase a defendant's sentence to be determined by a jury, and beyond a reasonable doubt, rather than by a judge. This includes hate crime penalty enhancers.

Although the constitutional challenges to hate crime laws have largely been settled by now in the courts, other dilemmas remain. It may be permissible to punish specific motives, but that does not mean doing so is easy, nor wise. In fact, hate crimes are the only crimes that require that the offender's motive be proven as one of the essential elements of the offense. Given the complexity and ambiguity of human motivation, it is often difficult, if not impossible, for victims, police, prosecutors, and juries to accurately determine why people have committed criminal acts. Even when circumstantial evidence suggests that a hate crime has occurred—perhaps the offender uttered racial slurs or belonged to an extremist group—such evidence is not definite proof of bias motivation. In the heat of anger, for instance, people call each other all sorts of names without intending these terms to reflect a systematic bias.

The difficulties in determining an offender's motive cause two significant problems. First, prosecutors may be hesitant to bring hate crime charges unless they are sure they can convince a jury of the defendant's motive. In fact, the statistics bear this out: Hate crime prosecutions are rare, and actual convictions even more so. For example, over 1,300 hate crimes were reported to the police in California in 2006, but hate crime charges were actually filed in only 272 cases, and hate crime convictions were obtained in 140 cases (California Department of Justice, 2007). Because of the relative rarity of these cases, most prosecutors likely have little or no experience prosecuting them, and, to date, no research has been published on successful prosecution strategies for hate crimes.

The second problem is that, faced with an ambiguous situation, people may rely on impermissible extralegal factors when determining a suspect's guilt. Although research specific to decision making in hate crime cases is sparse, a few studies have suggested that the race of the offender and of the victim may affect jurors' decisions in hate crime cases (Craig & Waldo, 1996; Gerstenfeld, 2003; Marcus-Newhall, Blake, & Baumann, 2002; Saucier, Brown, & Mitchell, 2006).

Some commentators have expressed the concern that hate crime legislation might actually harm members of minority communities. It is possible that the laws might inspire complacency in policymakers, discouraging them from taking more meaningful or effective steps to reduce bigotry (Gellman, 1991). Because some members of the public view hate crime laws as some sort of "special protection" for certain minorities—a view encouraged by white supremacist literature and Web sites—the laws might inspire increased resentment of particular groups.

In fact, through the operation of several psychological processes, hate crime laws might even increase prejudice (Gerstenfeld, 2004). In addition, Maroney (1998) argues that the laws could also be used as a tool by the established majority group to disempower minorities. Although all these criticisms appear reasonable, thus far there has been little research either to support or contradict them.

Hate Crime Patterns

One of the recurring problems associated with hate crimes is obtaining an accurate measure of their frequency, trends, and nature. The FBI has issued an annual report on hate crimes for 15 years, and some states, such as California, issue their own reports as well. In 2005, law enforcement agencies reported 7,163 hate crime incidents to the FBI (2006b). As Figure 12.1 illustrates, there have been no dramatic increases or decreases in the number of reported hate crimes since 1995. The exception to this is 2001, which showed a sharp upward spike. This was likely due to a large number of assaults on Muslims, Arabs, and people of Middle Eastern ancestry, which immediately followed the September 11 attacks (Gerstenfeld, 2002; Kaplan, 2006).

On the face of it, hate crime does not appear to be a very common offense. In 2005, there were nearly 17,000 reported murders in the United States, 94,000 reported forcible rapes, and over 862,000 reported aggravated assaults (FBI, 2006a). The small number of hate crimes pales in comparison to these totals. However, the reported numbers underestimate the potential

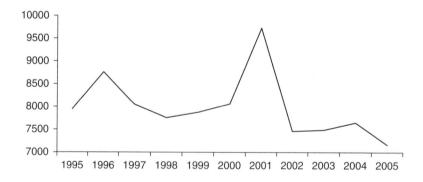

Figure 12.1   Annual Reported Hate Crime Incidents

SOURCE: FBI, 2006b.

impact of hate crimes. As the Supreme Court found in *Wisconsin v. Mitchell* (1993), it is possible that hate crimes have an especially wide and powerful effect on victims and communities.

Moreover, the FBI data show only those offenses that were actually reported to police, and there is good reason to believe hate crimes are severely underreported. Researchers have estimated that only about 20% to 30% of hate crimes are reported to the police (Herek, Gillis, & Cogan, 1999; Levin, 1999; Perry, 2001). Hate crimes are probably less likely than other crimes to be reported (Herek et al., 1999). Reporting rates for hate crimes may be particularly low among some victims. Gays and lesbians may fear having their sexual orientations exposed; undocumented immigrants may fear deportation or lack the English skills to communicate with police. Many victims of hate crimes are members of groups that traditionally have poor relationships with law enforcement, so there may by high levels of distrust or even fear of being revictimized by police. Hate crime victims might not know what hate crimes are, might fear retaliation for reporting, or might be ashamed (Gerstenfeld, 2004; Rayburn, Earleywine, & Davison, 2003).

Even when victims do report an offense to police, that offense will not necessarily be accurately categorized by the officers or by their agency as a hate crime. Police officers may have little training on hate crimes, may have their own biases that affect reporting, may wish to avoid doing extra paperwork, or may be subject to department pressures or policies to either downplay or emphasize hate crimes. Several studies have demonstrated that recording of hate crimes greatly differs from officer to officer and from department to department (Bell, 2002; Boyd, Berk, & Hamner, 1996; Martin, 1995; Nolan and Akiyama, 1999).

Some of the inaccuracies in official hate crime data may be corrected by examining crime victimization surveys rather than police data. However, Rayburn et al. (2003) found that even self-report victimization surveys may severely underestimate true victimization rates. In fact, their study revealed that "certain types of hate crimes may be close to seven times more common than conventional self-report surveys suggest" (p. 1217).

Although hate crime data undoubtedly include only a relatively small proportion of the hate crimes that occur, and although the data must, in general, be interpreted with caution, the data do permit some conclusions to be drawn. As stated above, there is no indication that the rate of hate crimes is increasing at the national level, nor is there real reason to conclude that hate crime legislation has reduced offense rates. There does appear to be a slight downward trend, but this likely reflects the simultaneous downward trend in crime in general, rather than a specific reduction in bias. The data also demonstrate that occasionally there are temporary spikes in hate crime activity, often inspired by events that have transpired in a community or in the nation. Around 1996, for example, there was a surge in the number of church arsons in the United States, and a large proportion of these cases involved black churches burned by white offenders (Soule & Van Dyke, 1999). This surge ebbed away within a few years. As previously mentioned, attacks against certain groups soared in the weeks following September 11, 2001. Kaplan (2006) reported that these attacks greatly reduced in number within about nine weeks. Other triggering factors might be economic troubles, police actions (as in the riots that occurred in Los Angeles in 1992 following the acquittal of police officers for beating motorist Rodney King), or conflicts between ethnic groups in a local community.

Other patterns also are evident in hate crime data. Roughly one-third of reported hate crimes consist of intimidation, and roughly another third involve property damage. About half the offenses target individuals, while the other half target places such as businesses, places of worship, and community organizations. Generally, a small majority of hate crimes are committed out of racial bias, with the remainder spread fairly equally between religious bias, sexual orientation bias, and ethnic bias (e.g., crimes against Latinos or Arabs; FBI, 2006b). These patterns remain quite consistent across time and location, although there is some occasional variation.

Hate Crime Victims

The problems associated with hate crime data, as well as limited amounts of empirical research, make it difficult to draw many strong conclusions about the victims of hate crimes. However, some aspects of hate crime victimization are apparent. It is clear, for example, that members of certain groups are especially likely to become hate crime victims.

In 2005, over 37% of the victims in hate crime cases reported to the FBI were targeted because they were African American (FBI, 2006b). Only about 12.5% of Americans are black, which indicates that blacks are significantly overrepresented among victims (U.S. Census, 2006). This overrepresentation is present in hate crime data in every year and in virtually every jurisdiction in the United States (Gerstenfeld, 1998, 2004). Given the long history of (often institutionalized) bias against African Americans in the United States, these statistics are not unexpected. Indeed, anti-black violence is the archetype of hate crimes in most Americans' minds. What is surprising, however, is that there has been little empirical research focusing specifically on hate crimes against African Americans.

A second group that is especially likely to be targeted for hate crimes is Jews. According to the FBI data, 11% of hate crime victims in 2005 were Jewish. Nearly 70% of religion-based hate crimes were anti-Jewish (FBI, 2006b). As with African Americans, this pattern is consistent over time and jurisdiction, and this group has experienced a very long history of prejudice. According to recent polls by the ADL (2007a, 2007b), 14% of Americans and 35% of Europeans currently hold strong anti-Semitic views. Anti-Semitism also constitutes the basis of much extremist literature and rhetoric, and anti-Semitism is a common theme about which disparate extremist groups have been able to unite (Gerstenfeld, 2004).

Gay, lesbian, bisexual, and transgendered (GLBT) people are also especially likely to experience hate crimes. In 2005, about 14% of hate crimes reported to the FBI were based on the victims' sexual orientation (FBI, 2006b). Because GLBT people may be especially unlikely to report being victimized, it is probable that the true victimization rates are much higher. According to a series of victimization studies, somewhere between 20% and 57% of GLBT people have been threatened or attacked because of their sexual orientation (see, e.g., Berrill, 1992; Herek et al., 1999; von Schulthess, 1992). Some of these crimes, such as the murders of gay college student Matthew Shepard and transgendered teenager Gwen Aurajo, have received extensive media attention.

Among GLBT individuals, hate crimes occur most often against gay men. In 2005, 61% of the GLBT victims of hate crimes were male (FBI, 2006b). The self-report victimization surveys also have demonstrated higher levels of victimization among men than among women (Berrill, 1992; Herek et al., 1999). While the frequency of antigay hate crimes in general is likely partially attributable to cultural, religious, and legal norms that continue to reject homosexuality, scholars have also proposed a variety of explanations for the high rates of violence specifically against gay men. Among these explanations are young men's need to demonstrate their masculinity (Perry, 2001), young men's struggles with their identity and self-attitudes (Herek, 2000), the perceived need to police and maintain traditional gender roles (Perry, 2001), and traditional stereotypes of gay men as weak and vulnerable.

Other groups are also victimized by hate crimes at disproportionately high rates. Among these are Latinos, Asian Americans, Muslims, and immigrants. However, these people do not appear to be targeted as frequently as blacks, Jews, and GLBT people. Moreover, very little empirical research has focused on these groups, so little is known about their victimization patterns and experiences. In the past few years, some advocacy groups have also asserted that there has been an increase in crimes against homeless people (National Coalition for the Homeless, 2007). However, while crimes against the homeless appear to share many characteristics with hate crimes, they do not fall under the legal definition of hate crimes in most states, nor do law enforcement agencies collect data on them.

A persistent issue concerning hate crimes has been their long-term effects upon victims. Certainly, those who suffer any kind of crime may experience physical and emotional harm, but the question is whether hate crimes are *more* harmful. A great many advocates and scholars have asserted that hate crimes are particularly injurious (see, e.g., Lawrence, 1999; Levin & McDevitt, 1993; Weisburd & Levin, 1994). In fact, this was one of the primary arguments given by the Supreme Court in *Wisconsin v. Mitchell* (1993) as to why hate crimes are qualitatively different from ordinary crimes. In reality, however, there is little empirical evidence to support these claims (Gerstenfeld, 2004). It is also plausible that minor crimes, such as vandalism, are more hurtful when they are bias-motivated, but that violent crimes are equally traumatic, regardless of the motive (Jacobs & Potter, 1998). In any case, it is undeniable that victims of hate crime do suffer.

Hate Crime Offenders

Most people assume hate crimes are committed by members of extremist groups—Klan members, skinheads, neo-Nazis, and the like. There are a bewildering variety of hate groups in the United States—the Southern Poverty Law Center (2007a) estimates that 844 hate groups were active in the U.S. in 2006—and many of these groups have a long and notorious history of violence. However, the vast majority of hate crimes—an estimated 84% to 95%—are committed by people who do not belong to organized hate groups (Dunbar, 2003; Dunbar, Quinones, & Crevecoeur, 2005; Levin, 1993).

In general, research indicates that most hate crime offenders are young and male. Although offenders come from many racial and ethnic groups, a majority of them are white (FBI, 2006b). It is unclear whether they tend to have previous criminal histories. Some research suggests hate crime offenders are less likely than other offenders to have previous arrests (Craig, 2002; Franklin, 2000), but in a sample of 204 hate crime offenders studied by Dunbar et al. (2005), 56% had previous convictions. It is possible that Dunbar and colleagues' sample was not representative of hate crime offenders in general; the mean age of the offenders, for example, was 32.7, which is considerably older than other studies have suggested is representative. Because the sample consisted only of offenders who had been identified and arrested for their crimes, it is likely that the offenders in the sample were primarily those whose offenses were more serious and violent.

Although the stereotype of hate crime offenders is that they are uneducated, some studies have found that offending is quite common among college students. In a survey of 489 community college students, Franklin (2000) found that 10% admitted to having attacked or threatened people they thought were gay or lesbian, and nearly one-quarter had verbally harassed them.

A variety of factors contribute to hate crime offending. One of the primary motivations appears to be "thrill-seeking" (McDevitt, Levin, & Bennett,

2002). That is, offenders wish to generate excitement, alleviate boredom, and fit in with and impress their friends (Byers & Crider, 2002; Franklin, 2000). Actual prejudice, while certainly a contributing factor, does not appear to be the main impetus behind many of these crimes. Research indicates that thrill-seeking hate crimes are by far the most common type. In a study by McDevitt et al. (2002), for example, they constituted two-thirds of the total. As a result, hate crimes are more likely than other crimes to involve multiple offenders acting together (Craig, 2002; Dunbar, 2003; Levin, 1993).

Another possible motivation for hate crimes is difficult financial situations. Economic hard times, either for an individual or for a community, may produce strain and encourage scapegoating. Some studies have found a connection between hate crimes and hard times (Gale, Heath, & Ressler, 1999; Hovland & Sears, 1940; Medoff, 1999). Other studies have found that people who commit hate crimes, or who join extremist groups, tend to come from working class or poor backgrounds and tend to be suffering from feelings of isolation and helplessness (Blazak, 2001; Dunbar, 2003; Ezekiel, 1995, 2002). Furthermore, much of the rhetoric of extremist groups centers on economic themes (Gerstenfeld, 2004). Not all scholars are convinced that economics plays a major role in inspiring hate crimes (see, e.g., Perry, 2001). Green and colleagues (Green, Abelson, & Garnett, 1999; Green, Glaser, & Rich, 1998; Green, Strolovitch, & Wong, 1998) have not found a connection between hate crimes and economic deprivation.

Cultural influences also affect hate crime offending. People are constantly exposed to messages that confirm stereotypes and support biases. These messages come from the media, from religion, from politicians and the government, and from social norms. Many of those who repeatedly hear these messages—immigrants are taking our jobs, blacks are violent, homosexuals are immoral, women are sex objects or domestic drones, Muslims are terrorists—are bound to believe them and, in some cases, act on them. What is unclear is why most Americans are exposed to much the same cultural biases, yet only a small number translate those biases into criminal acts.

Situational factors also help to inspire some hate crimes. An example of this is the September 11, 2001 attacks, which triggered a rash of violence against Muslims, Americans of Middle Eastern descent, and even those who were confused with members of these groups, such as Sikhs and South Asians (Christie, 2006). But the situational factors may be local as well. McDevitt et al. (2002) discuss "retaliatory" hate crimes, in which offenders seek vengeance for an actual or rumored attack upon their own group. In Brooklyn's Crown Heights, for instance, confrontations erupted between blacks and Jews in 1991 after a car containing Jews struck and killed an African American child. These confrontations culminated in the stabbing death of a rabbinical student by a black teenager. Several race riots over the last few decades might also fall into this category, including the Los Angeles riots of 1992 as well as riots in Miami in 1980 and Cincinnati in 2001. Each of these cases of civil unrest was triggered by police officers' actions against people of a different race.

Finally, while relatively few hate crimes are committed by members of organized hate groups, the groups' ideologies and activities might inspire nonmembers to commit hate crimes. As mentioned above, there are hundreds of hate groups active in the United States and probably hundreds more abroad. Beginning in 1915, when one of the first—and certainly the most influential in its time—feature-length films, *Birth of a Nation,* had a plotline that glorified and made heroic the Ku Klux Klan, extremist groups have received ample attention from the media. Hate groups have also made heavy use of the Internet as a communication tool. The precise number of hate-based Web sites is impossible to determine, but the Simon Wiesenthal Center (2007) documented nearly 7,000 of them in 2007. Extremist Internet sites are especially problematic in that many of them have content especially meant to appeal to young people and also in that they have enabled disparate and geographically distant groups to connect with one another. Moreover, many of the Web sites take some pains to appear mainstream or objective; unwary Internet surfers might, therefore, become influenced by their messages without realizing the sources (Gerstenfeld, Grant, & Chiang, 2003).

Reducing Hate Crime

Perhaps the most important question regarding hate crimes is how they can be prevented. Merely passing laws against them is likely to have little deterrent effect, especially when the laws are poorly understood by the public and rarely enforced. Moreover, given the rampant racism that pervades inmates in correctional institutions, as well as the ubiquity of racist prison gangs, it is extremely unlikely that those who are incarcerated for hate crimes will be reformed by their prison experiences.

One common approach to dealing with hate crimes has been to focus on law enforcement responses. In addition to legislation requiring law enforcement agencies to collect hate crime data, some jurisdictions provide or require special training for police officers, some departments have special hate crime policies and procedures, and many departments—perhaps several hundred—have special hate crime units. The actual effectiveness of these approaches is unclear. Reporting behaviors by police vary a great deal from place to place, influenced by factors such as presence of advocacy groups, engagement in community policing, geographical region, and police department organizational characteristics (Heider-Markel, 2004;

Jenness & Grattet, 2005; King, 2007; McVeigh, 2003). Giving police more training does not necessarily improve their responses (Sloane, King, & Sheppard, 1998), and many bias crime units exist more in name than in reality (Walker & Katz, 1995).

Another common approach is to provide education and activities designed to reduce prejudice, especially among young people. For example, the Southern Poverty Law Center operates a Teaching Tolerance program, which provides extensive materials and resources for K–12 teachers (http://www.tol erance.org), and the federal Office of Juvenile Justice and Delinquency Prevention has published a middle school curriculum titled "Healing the Hate" (http://www.ncjrs.gov/pdffiles1/165479.pdf). In addition, sometimes media campaigns such as NBC's "The More You Know" have aired on television or appeared in print.

Antiprejudice and diversity education are appealing to many people and might logically be expected to prevent hate crime offending. However, no outcome studies have been performed to assess the true impact of these programs. Furthermore, because the research suggests that bias is not actually the primary motivating factor behind most hate crimes, it is unclear whether simply trying to reduce bias will also reduce hate crimes. In fact, it might make more sense to train young people in methods for resisting peer pressure or to provide youths with better opportunities to avoid boredom and be more comfortable with their own identities.

There have also been community-based, grassroots efforts to fight hate, often initiated in direct response to a particular incident. In several cases, individuals or groups have encouraged members of a community to pledge money to anti-hate causes for every minute that a KKK rally lasted or for every minute that a bigoted speaker spoke. What could have been a very negative situation may, thereby, be subverted for good (Gerstenfeld, 2004). Another example of a grassroots response to hate violence is "Not in Our Town," a movement begun by the people of Billings, Montana after several local hate incidents (O'Neill & Miller, 1995). While grassroots efforts such as these likely have little effect on individual would-be offenders, they may improve community cohesion and heal some of the harms that hate crimes produce.

The civil justice system has been used in some cases as a response to hate crimes as well. Several states explicitly permit victims of hate crimes to sue their attackers. In some cases, victims and their families have been able to obtain multimillion dollar judgments against Klan groups and other organizations or people responsible for engaging in or promoting hate crimes (Dees & Fiffer, 1993; Leavitt, 2001; Stanton, 1992). In July, 2007, for instance, a lawsuit was filed against the Imperial Klans of America after members of that Klan group, who were engaged in recruitment attempts at a county fair in Kentucky, severely beat a Panamanian American teenager (Southern Poverty Law Center, 2007b). In addition to compensating victims for some of their damages, lawsuits such as these might cripple hate groups and curtail their activities. Or they might not—Tom Metzger, against whom a jury handed a $12.5 million judgment in 1990, continues his rather high-profile racist activism and has had several subsequent run-ins with the law.

Perhaps the most promising methods of dealing with hate crimes are those that center on changing the offenders. Massachusetts requires that convicted hate crime offenders participate in a diversity awareness program, and various agencies across the country run diversion and intervention programs (Gerstenfeld, 2004). Recently, some places have used restorative justice approaches, especially victim-offender mediation, in hate crime cases. Among other goals, victim offender mediation seeks to give victims a voice and help offenders understand the harms their actions cause. While there has been no formal assessment of these programs, they do have the potential to make meaningful reductions in hate violence (Coates, Umbreit, & Vos, 2006; Shenk, 2001).

Conclusion

It is impossible to assess the true number of hate crime victims and the full extent of the damage that has been done to them and their communities. By even the most conservative estimates, however, tens of thousands of Americans have, like David Ritcheson, been harassed, threatened, or attacked because of what they look like, how they worship, or whom they love. These crimes have certainly not gone unnoticed: A LexisNexis news search for the term *hate crime* results in 2,798 hits for just the months of June through August, 2007.

Despite media attention to hate crimes, and despite a quarter century of hate crime legislation, there is little indication that the problem has significantly diminished. And although the issue of hate crime has sparked interest in scholars from a wide variety of disciplines, research has addressed most of the questions concerning this issue only superficially, if at all. It is to be hoped that soon, research will help us better understand the implications of hate violence for individuals and communities, as well as assist in the creation of more effective prevention and intervention strategies.

Discussion Questions

1. What are some of the problems that arise when the law attempts to punish specific motives? Given these problems, would you support hate crime legislation? Why or why not?

2. If you were drafting a hate crime law, which groups would you protect? Why? What are the potential problems associated with including or excluding particular groups?

3. Why do many hate crime victims choose not to report the crimes to the police? What are some methods that could be used to improve reporting rates?

4. How would you design a study to evaluate the effects of hate crimes on victims?

5. What do you think would be the characteristics of a successful hate crime prevention program?

6. How would you design a study to evaluate the effectiveness of a hate crime prevention program?

7. Why do people commit hate crimes?

Internet Resources

Anti-Defamation League: http://www.adl.org

FBI Hate Crime Statistics: http://www.fbi.gov/ucr/ucr.htm#hate

Hate Crimes Research Network: http://www.hatecrimes.net

National Gay & Lesbian Task Force: http://thetaskforce.org/issues/hate_crimes_main_page

Southern Poverty Law Center: http://www.splcenter.org

References

Anti-Defamation League. (2006). Anti-Defamation League state hate crime statutory provisions. Retrieved July 25, 2007, from http://www.adl.org/99hatecrime/state_hate_crime_laws.pdf.

Anti-Defamation League. (2007a). *ADL survey: Anti-semitism declines slightly in America; 14 percent of Americans hold "strong" anti-semitic beliefs.* Retrieved August 23, 2008, from http://www.adl.org/PresRele/ASUS_12/4680_12.htm.

Anti-Defamation League (2007b). *ADL survey in six European countries finds anti-semitic attitudes up: Most believe Jews more loyal to Israel than home country.* Retrieved August 23, 2008, from http://www.adl.org/PresRele/ASInt_13/ 5099_13.htm.

Anti-Defamation League. (2007c). *Statement of Mr. David Ritcheson hearing on H.R. 1592, the Local Law Enforcement Hate Crimes Prevention Act of 2007.* Retrieved August 23, 2008, from http://southwest.adl.org/site/PageServer?pagename=swest_david_ritcheson

Apprendi v. New Jersey, 530 U.S. 466 (2000).

Bell, J. (2002). Deciding when hate is a crime: The first amendment, police detectives, and the identification of hate crime. *Rutgers Race & Law Review, 4,* 33–76.

Berrill, K. T. (1992). Anti-gay violence and victimization in the United States: An overview. In G. M. Herek & K. T. Berrill (Eds.), *Hate crimes: Confronting violence against lesbians and gay men* (pp. 19–45). Newbury Park, CA: Sage.

Blazak, R. (2001). White boys to terrorist men: Target recruitment of Nazi skinheads. *American Behavioral Scientist, 44,* 982–1000.

Boyd, E. A., Berk, R. A., & Hamner, K. M. (1996). "Motivated by hatred or prejudice": Categorization of hate-motivated crimes in two police division. *Law & Society Review, 30,* 819–850.

Byers, B. D., & Crider, B. W. (2002). Hate crimes against the Amish: A qualitative analysis of bias motivation using routine activities theory. *Deviant Behavior, 23,* 115–148.

California Department of Justice. (2007). *Hate crime in California, 2006.* Sacramento, CA: Author.

Chorba, C. (2001). The danger of federalizing hate crimes: Congressional misconceptions and the unintended consequences of the Hate Crimes Prevention Act. *Virginia Law Review, 87,* 319–379.

Christie, D. J. (2006). 9/11 aftershocks: An analysis of conditions ripe for hate crimes. In P. R. Kimmel & C. E. Stout (Eds.), *Collateral damage: The psychological consequences of America's war on terrorism* (pp. 19–44). Westport, CT: Praeger.

Coates, R. B., Umbreit, M. S., & Vos, B. (2006). Responding to hate crime through restorative justice dialogue. *Contemporary Justice Review, 9*(1), 7–21.

Craig, K. M. (2002). Examining hate-motivated aggression: A review of the social psychological literature on hate crimes as a distinct for of aggression. *Aggression and Violent Behavior, 7,* 85–101.

Craig, K. M., & Waldo, C. R. (1996). "So what's a hate crime anyway?" Young adults' perceptions of hate crimes, victims and perpetrators. *Law & Human Behavior, 20,* 113–129.

Dees, M., & Fiffer, S. (1993). *Hate on trial: The case against America's most dangerous neo-Nazi.* New York: Villard Books.

Dunbar, E. (2003). Symbolic, relational, and ideological signifiers of bias-motivated offenders: Toward a strategy of assessment. *American Journal of Orthopsychiatry, 73*(2), 203–211.

Dunbar, E. (2006). Race, gender, and sexual orientation in hate crime victimization: Identity politics or identity risk? *Violence & Victims, 21*(3), 323–337.

Dunbar, E., Quinones, J., & Crevecoeur, D. A. (2005). Assessment of hate crime offenders: The role of bias intent in examining violence risk. *Journal of Forensic Psychiatry Practice, 5*(1), 1–19.

Ezekiel, R. S. (1995). *The racist mind: Portraits of American neo-Nazis and Klansmen.* New York: Viking.

Ezekiel, R. S. (2002). An ethnographer looks at neo-Nazi and Klan groups: The racist mind revisited. *American Behavioral Scientist, 46,* 51–71.

Federal Bureau of Investigation. (2006a). *Crime in the United States 2005.* Retrieved August 23, 2008, from http://www.fbi.gov/ucr/05cius/data/table_01.html.

Federal Bureau of Investigation. (2006b). *Hate crime statistics 2005.* Retrieved August 23, 2008, from http://www.fbi.gov/ucr/hc2005/index.html

Franklin, K. (2000). Antigay behaviors among young adults: Prevalence, patterns, and motivators in a noncriminal population. *Journal of Interpersonal Violence, 15,* 339–362.

Gale, L. R., Heath, W. C., & Ressler, R. W. (1999). *An economic interpretation of hate crime.* Unpublished manuscript, University of Southern Louisiana, Lafayette.

Gellman, S. (1991). Sticks and stones can put you in jail, but can words increase your sentence? Constitutional and policy dilemmas of ethnic intimidation laws. *UCLA Law Review, 39,* 333–396.

Gerstenfeld, P. B. (1998). Reported hate crimes in America. *CSU, Stanislaus Journal of Research, 2*(1), 35–43.

Gerstenfeld, P. B. (2002). A time to hate: Situational antecedents of intergroup bias. *Analyses of Social Issues and Public Policy, 2,* 61–67.

Gerstenfeld, P. B. (2003). Juror decision making in hate crime cases. *Criminal Justice Policy Review, 14*(2), 193–213.

Gerstenfeld, P. B. (2004). *Hate crimes: Causes, controls, and controversies.* Thousand Oaks, CA: Sage.

Gerstenfeld, P. B., Grant, D. R., & Chiang, C. (2003). Hate online: A content analysis of extremist internet sites. *Analyses of Social Issues and Public Policy, 3*(1), 29–44.

Green, D. P., Abelson, R. P., & Garnett, M. (1999). The distinctive political views of hate-crime perpetrators and white supremacists. In D. A. Prentice & D. Miller (Eds.), *Cultural divides: Understanding and overcoming group conflict* (pp. 429–464). New York: Russell Sage Foundation.

Green, D. P., Glaser, J., & Rich, A. (1998). From lynching to gay bashing: The elusive connections between economic conditions and hate crime. *Journal of Personality & Social Psychology, 75*, 82–92.

Green, D. P., Strolovitch, D. Z., & Wong, J. (1998). Defended neighborhoods, integration, and racially motivated crime. *American Journal of Sociology, 104*, 372–403.

Greenberg, S. J. (1993). *The evolution of hate crime statutes: Social change through criminal law.* Unpublished manuscript.

Heider-Markel, D. P. (2004). Perception and misperception in urban criminal justice policy: The case of hate crime. *Urban Affairs Review, 39*(4), 491–512.

Herek, G. M. (2000). Sexual prejudice and gender: Do heterosexuals' attitudes towards gay men and lesbians differ? *Journal of Social Issues, 56*(2), 252–266.

Herek, G. M. (in press). Hate crimes and stigma-related experiences among sexual minority adults in the United States: Prevalence estimates from a national probability sample. *Journal of Interpersonal Violence.*

Herek, G. M., Gillis, J. R., & Cogan, J. C. (1999). Psychological sequelae of hate-crime victimization among lesbian, gay, and bisexual adults. *Journal of Consulting and Clinical Psychology, 67*, 945–951.

Hovland, C. I., & Sears, R. (1940). Minor studies in aggression: VI. Correlations of lynchings with economic indices. *Journal of Psychology, 9*, 301–310.

Jacobs, J., & Potter, K. (1998). *Hate crimes: Criminal law and identity politics.* New York: Oxford University Press.

Jenness, V., & Grattet, R. (1996). The criminalization of hate: Comparison of structural and polity influences on the passage of "bias-crime" legislation in the United States. *Sociological Perspectives, 39*, 129–154.

Jenness, V., & Grattet, R. (2005). The law-in-between: The effects of organizational perviousness on the policing of hate crime. *Social Problems, 52*(3), 337–359.

Johnson, S. D., & Byers, B. D. (2003). Attitudes toward hate crime laws. *Journal of Criminal Justice, 31*(3), 227–235.

Jury sentences Texas teen to life for brutal attack on Hispanic youth. (2006, November 18). *USA Today.* http://www.usatoday.com/news/nation/2006-11-18-party-attack_x.htm.

Kaplan, J. (2006). Islamophobia in America? September 11 and Islamophobic hate crime. *Terrorism and Political Violence, 18*, 1–33.

King, R. D. (2007). The context of minority group threat: Race, institutions, and complying with hate crime law. *Law & Society Review, 41*, 189–224.

Lawrence, F. M. (1999). *Punishing hate: Bias crimes under American law.* Cambridge, MA: Harvard University Press.

Leavitt, M. F. (2001). Keenan v. Aryan Nations: Making hate groups liable for the torts of their members. *Idaho Law Review, 37*, 603–639.

Levin, B. (1993). A dream deferred: The social and legal implications of hate crimes in the 1990s. *The Journal of Intergroup Relations, 20*(3), 3–27.

Levin, B. (1999). Hate crimes: Worse by definition. *Journal of Contemporary Criminal Justice, 15*, 1–21.

Levin, J., & McDevitt, J. (1993). *Hate crimes: The rising tide of bigotry and bloodshed.* New York: Plenum Press.

Lozano, J. A. (2007, July 10). Family, friends, remember brutalized teen. *WIBC.com*. http://www.wibc.com/news/article.aspx?id =1175487

Marcus-Newhall, A., Blake, L. P., & Baumann, J. (2002). Perceptions of hate crime perpetrators and victims as influenced by race, political orientation, and peer group. *American Behavioral Scientist, 46*, 108–135.

Maroney, T. A. (1998). The struggle against hate crime: Movement at a crossroads. *New York University Law Review, 73*, 564–620.

Martin, S. E. (1995). "A cross-burning is not just an arson:" Police social construction of hate crimes in Baltimore County. *Criminology, 33*(3), 303–326.

McDevitt, J., Levin, J., & Bennett, S. (2002). Hate crime offenders: An expanded typology. *Journal of Social Issues, 58*, 303–317.

McVeigh, R. (2003). Hate crime reporting as a successful social movement. *American Sociological Review, 68*, 843–867.

Medoff, M. H. (1999). Allocation of time and behavior: A theoretical and positive analysis of hate and hate crimes. *American Journal of Economics and Sociology, 58*, 959–973.

National Coalition for the Homeless. (2007). *Hate, violence, and death on Main Street USA*. Retrieved August 23, 2008, from http://www.nationalhomeless.org/getinvolved/projects/hatecrimes/2006report_2.pdf.

Nolan, J. J., & Akiyama, Y. (1999). An analysis of factors that affect law enforcement participation in hate crime reporting. *Journal of Contemporary Criminal Justice, 15*, 111–127.

O'Neill, P., & Miller, R. (Producers). (1995). *Not in our town* [Motion picture broadcast on PBS]. United States: The Working Group.

Peek, G. S. (2001). Where are we going with federal hate crimes legislation? Congress and the politics of sexual orientation. *Marquette Law Review, 85*, 537–577.

Perry, B. (2001). *In the name of hate: Understanding hate crimes*. New York: Routledge.

Petrosino, C. (1999). Connecting the past to the future: Hate crime in America. *Journal of Contemporary Criminal Justice, 15*, 22–47.

Prosecutor: Teen attack no hate crime. (2006, April 28). *KUTV.com*. http://kutv.com/top stories/topstories_story_118101507.html

R.A.V. v. St. Paul, 505 U.S. 377 (1992).

Rayburn, N. R., Earleywine, M., & Davison, G. C. (2003). Base rates of hate crime victimization among college students. *Journal of Interpersonal Violence, 18*, 1209–1221.

Saucier, D. A., Brown, T. L., & Mitchell, R. C. (2006). Effects of victims' characteristics on attitudes toward hate crimes. *Journal of Interpersonal Violence, 21*, 890–909.

Shenk, A. H. (2001). Victim-offender mediation: The road to repairing hate crime injustice. *Ohio State Journal on Dispute Resolution, 17*, 185–217.

Shively, M. (2005). *Study of literature and legislation on hate crime in America*. Washington, DC: National Institute of Justice.

Simon Wiesenthal Center. (2007). *Digital terrorism and hate 2007* [CD-ROM]. Los Angeles: Author.

Sloane, R. L., King, L., & Sheppard, S. (1998). Hate crimes motivated by sexual orientation: Police reporting and training. *Journal of Gay & Lesbian Social Services, 8*(3), 25–39.

Soule, S. A., & Van Dyke, N. (1999). Black church arson in the United States, 1989–1996. *Ethnic & Racial Studies, 22*, 724–742.

Southern Poverty Law Center. (2007a). *Active U.S. hate groups in 2006*. Retrieved February 5, 2008, from http://www.splcenter.org/intel/map/hate.jsp.

Southern Poverty Law Center. (2007b). *SPLC sues leading Klan group over beating*. Retrieved August 23, 2008, from http://www.splcenter.org/legal/news/article.jsp?site_area=2&aid=277.

Stanton, B. (1992). *Klanwatch: Bringing the Ku Klux Klan to justice*. New York: Mentor Books.

Stout, D. (2007, May 3). House votes to expand hate-crimes protection. *New York Times*.

http://www.nytimes.com/2007/05/04/washington/04hate.html?ex=1184904000&en=caa9df6939ab1d19&ei= 5070

U.S. Census. (2006). *The black population in the United States, 2004.* Retrieved August 23, 2008, from http://www.census.gov/population/socdemo/race/black/ppl-186/tab1.pdf.

Virginia v. Black, 538 U.S. 343 (2003).

Von Schulthess, B. (1992). Violence in the streets: Anti-lesbian assault and harassment in San Francisco. In G. M. Herek & K. T. Berrill (Eds.), *Hate crimes: Confronting violence against lesbians and gay men* (pp. 65–75). Newbury Park, CA: Sage.

Walker, S., & Katz, C. M. (1995). Less than meets the eye: Police department bias-crime units. *American Journal of Police, 14,* 29–48.

Weisburd, S. B., & Levin, B. (1994). "On the basis of sex": Recognizing gender-based bias crimes. *Stanford Law and Policy Review, 5,* 21–43.

Wisconsin v. Mitchell, 508 U.S. 476 (1993).

CHAPTER 13

Murder in a Comparative Context

Jennifer Schwartz

Murder is often perceived as a random occurrence that could happen to anyone at any time, anywhere. This perception might seem validated by the FBI Crime Clock reporting a murder every 31.5 minutes (Federal Bureau of Investigation, 2006) and by news stories detailing random killings, such as the execution-style killing of four college kids in Newark, NJ by robbers and the murderous gun rampage of a Virginia Tech student, both of which occurred in 2007. Despite these images of murder, the reality is that murder most often is not *random* violence. That is, there are statistically identifiable, predictable patterns to murder offending. This chapter explores these statistical patterns of criminal homicide, primarily in the United States, and offers qualitative accounts of various types of murder. This chapter aims to answer the following questions: How common is murder? When and where has murder been most frequent? Who is most likely to commit murder? And, most important, Why would someone take the life of another?

The legal definition of *homicide* is the killing of one person by another, whether intentionally or unintentionally. Homicide includes murder, manslaughter, justifiable homicide, and the accidental killing of one person by another (e.g., hunting accidents). Police use the term *homicide investigation* because whether the killing was a murder or not is undetermined at the time of the body's discovery. Homicides in which the killer could not anticipate or prevent the death are not considered criminal homicide. Examples of noncriminal homicide include a police officer justifiably killing a felon or a citizen killing another in self-defense. In this chapter, the primary focus is murder and nonnegligent manslaughter—intentional, unlawful homicides. *Murder* and *nonnegligent manslaughter* involve willful actions that a reasonable person should realize will likely lead to a fatal outcome (Black, 1990). First- and second-degree murder are distinguished from manslaughter by premeditation, or planning the crime in advance. A murder conviction requires proof of intent to cause great bodily harm or death (i.e., malice aforethought), while a manslaughter conviction is the likely result when there was no prior intent to cause death. For example, a person who planned to beat his victim to death would be charged with murder, whereas a person who lethally assaulted his victim during a passionate argument would probably be charged with manslaughter. Also, a person may be charged with manslaughter if he or she were provoked in a way that would cause a "reasonable person" to lose control. *Negligent manslaughter* (also known as involuntary manslaughter) is defined as recklessness or careless disregard for others without a specific intent to kill, such as driving drunk or severely neglecting a child. State laws defining the specific parameters of murder and voluntary and involuntary manslaughter vary somewhat. Throughout this chapter, I use the terms *murder* and *criminal homicide* to refer to both murder and voluntary (nonnegligent) manslaughter.

Criminologists and sociologists who study crime typically are interested in identifying common, systematic patterns of murder rather than detailing the specifics of unusual or atypical murder cases, such as the Virginia Tech shooting mentioned above. Criminologists use a variety of methods to get a complete and representative picture of homicide offending, ranging from qualitative interviews with a sample of convicted offenders to in-depth analyses of legal documents generated in the criminal justice system to quantitative secondary data analyses of police records. Each methodology elucidates slightly different aspects of homicide offending, making it important to look at multiple sources of evidence.

Regardless of methodology, findings must be interpreted and understood, and this is more easily done with a comparative perspective. A *comparative perspective* simply means examining social phenomena to assess similarities and differences across social groupings, such as nations, time periods, or demographic groups like men and women. Throughout this chapter, gender comparisons are emphasized because this example demonstrates especially well the need to explore both similarities and differences between groups to better understand homicide offending. The general causes and motivations for murder are similar across gender, but there also are important differences in the context and modes of women's and men's criminal homicide offending (Schwartz, 2006b).

The Extent of Homicide Offending

Homicide is a relatively rare phenomenon. In comparison, deaths resulting from heart disease, accidents, and pneumonia are all far more common than deaths resulting from homicide, which is the 10th most common cause of death among men in the U.S. In 2004, police in the U.S. identified 15,935 homicide offenders and 16,137 homicide victims out of a population of about 294 million. The homicide offending rate for 2004 was 5.4 per 100,000 inhabitants (15,935 ÷ 294 million × 100,000 inhabitants). In comparison to other criminal offenses, murder is among the rarest crimes. Only about one-tenth of 1% of all offenses known to the police are murders. In comparison to the approximately 16,000 murders that occurred in 2005, there were over 1 million drunk driving arrests, 850,000 aggravated assault cases known to the police, and 400,000 robberies reported (Federal Bureau of Investigation, 2006).

Given its statistical rarity, and aside from the intrigue surrounding the offense, why do criminologists study homicide offending? This crime is the focus of much research by criminologists, in part because of the severity of the offense. It is significant that the characteristics of homicide events are very similar to those of other forms of violence. In fact, the similarities between murder and aggravated assault in circumstances, victim-offender relationship, and other characteristics have caused some criminologists to deem murder an "overly successful" assault. Therefore, in studying homicide offending, we also learn about the causes and contexts of violence more generally. Criminologists also study homicide because it is the most accurately measured offense (Gove, Hughes, & Geerken, 1985). Bodies rarely go undetected and, despite popular notions, most homicides cases are solved. Historically, more than 90% of U.S. homicide cases were cleared by an arrest, though this percentage has declined in recent years to just under 70% (Federal Bureau of Investigation, 2006). Even so, the clearance rate for murder is higher than for other offenses. For example, burglary and theft cases are rarely solved—an arrest is made in 13% of burglaries reported to the police, 13% of auto thefts, and 18% of larceny-thefts. The clearance rate for aggravated assault, 55%, is somewhat less than the clearance rate for homicide. Consequently, homicide is the offense for which we have the most statistical information on offenders and offenses at the national level. In a practical sense, detailed homicide data are simply more available than data on other crimes, owing to the FBI'S *Supplementary Homicide Reports* (SHR).

Information on homicide in the United States is recorded in the SHR, which contains official, police-recorded statistics on almost all murders and nonnegligent manslaughter incidents in the country (Fox, 2007).

Police voluntarily record information on over 90% of the homicides of which they are aware. The FBI has accurately and consistently compiled these reports since the late 1970s; they include information on victim and offender demographics, their relationship to one another, and situational features of the homicide incident, such as weapon use and motives. Because the SHR includes information on homicides still under investigation, information is incomplete for about 25% of the cases, but by using advanced statistical procedures to gain precision, we can "guess" the characteristics of offenders based on similar solved homicide cases. This procedure infers unknown offender characteristics from recent events with similar victim profiles, situational characteristics, and locale (for more detail, see Fox, 2004). Therefore, the SHR data present a fairly detailed nationwide portrait of homicide incidents, offenders, and victims and how these characteristics have changed over time. These data also allow criminologists, law enforcement, and others to track geographic patterns of homicide. To do so, they often use offender or victimization murder rates that take into account differences across places, time periods, or subgroups in the number of people at risk of offending (or becoming victims). *Murder rates* are a standardized measure of how many murders there are per 100,000 people. International data sources on homicide are more sporadically available than the SHR. INTERPOL, the international police organization, suddenly ceased releasing cross-national offending statistics, for reasons that are not entirely clear. The World Health Organization (WHO) publishes mortality statistics that include figures for criminal homicide victimization. Though countries differ slightly in definitions of homicide and in the quality of data, definitions are far more consistent and data collection efforts more sophisticated for homicide compared to other offenses.

Geographic Comparisons: International and United States Homicide Rates

In comparison to other industrialized nations, the United States has a fairly high murder rate. The U.S. murder rate is about three times higher than that of Canada, the United Kingdom, France, and Australia. The U.S. murder rate is more than three times higher than those of Japan, Germany, Spain, Italy, and the Scandinavian countries, which all have among the lowest homicide rates in the world. In fact, there were fewer than 50 murders last year in Norway (~1 per 100,000 residents) compared to more than 16,000 in the United States (~5.5 per 100,000 residents). Colombia and South Africa, however, have far higher murder rates than the U.S.—10 to 15 times higher. Other countries with high per capita murder rates include

Jamaica, Venezuela, Mexico, and several countries in the former Soviet Republic, such as Russia, Latvia, and Ukraine. Regionally, Africa and the Americas have higher rates of homicide than Asia, Europe, or other regions. That the United States has comparatively high murder rates is puzzling to many, given our high level of wealth, industrialization, and incarceration. There are a variety of explanations, including better record keeping in the U.S., the high level of inequality within a competitive culture, widespread gun ownership, and lack of extensive social welfare.

Within the United States, however, there is much variation in the prevalence of homicide. States in the South and West, for example, tend to have higher rates of homicide offending than other areas of the country, according to FBI data (Federal Bureau of Investigation, 2006). Regardless of region, though, urban areas have higher per capita murder rates than suburban and rural areas. For example, cities have an average homicide rate of 6.9 per 100,000, whereas suburban and rural areas have average homicide rates of around 3 to 4 per 100,000. Recall that rates are standardized measures that take into account population size differences across places. Even among large cities, though, some cities, like Baltimore and Detroit, have very high homicide rates (~40 per 100,000 residents), whereas other cities, such as Seattle, Honolulu, and El Paso, have comparatively low homicide rates (~2–4 per 100,000). Because homicide has predictable geographic patterns, many criminologists focus on types of places rather than types of people in trying to understand homicide offending.

Demographic Comparisons: Gender, Race, and Age

The large majority of perpetrators and victims of homicide are men. According to FBI statistics, homicide offending rates for 2004 were 11.5 per 100,000 men and 1.2 per 100,000 women. Females make up only 10% of homicide offenders and 22% of homicide victims. Among both female and male homicide offenders, young adults (aged 18–24) have the highest rates of offending (and victimization). About 40% of those arrested for murder are between the ages of 18 and 24, though they compose less than 10% of the population. About 8% of murderers are juveniles (under age 18); juveniles are 12% of the population.

Black males have higher homicide rates than white males, and black females have higher homicide rates than white females. The offending rates of white adolescent girls (aged 14–17) are exceptionally low—fewer than 1 in 100,000 girls is arrested for homicide yearly. Black males aged 18–24 have the highest homicide offending rates (203 per 100,000). White males have higher arrest rates than comparably aged women of either race.

Within race groups, black women and white women make up a similar proportion of all homicide offenders—11% of white and 8% of black homicide offenders are women.

Taken together, the most typical criminal homicide offender is a young black male living in an urban environment. Victim characteristics often match closely the offender's demographic characteristics; homicide tends to be intraracial and the victim and offender are usually close in age. Males most often murder other males, though women are also more likely to kill a man. Therefore, men are the large majority of homicide victims (78%), and young adults have the highest risk of victimization, especially young black men. The victimization rate of young adults (aged 18–24) is at least two times greater than the victimization rate of juveniles under 18 or those over 35. These demographic patterns in murder offending and victimization have not changed all that much over time, despite the fact that, overall, the number of homicides has decreased in recent years.

Temporal Comparisons: Changes in Homicide Over Time

Between the mid-1960s and the early 1970s, the homicide rate nearly doubled, from 4 or 5 per 100,000 to 8 or 9 per 100,000 (Fox & Zawitz, 2003). It remained high during the 1970s, peaking in 1980 at more than 10 per 100,000. Though the murder rate declined somewhat after that, it rose again; in 1991, it reached nearly the same level as in 1980. The murder rate then declined, and rates now are lower than in the late 1960s (Fox & Zawitz, 2003). In fact, the current murder rate is almost half what it was at its peak in 1980. Since 2000, there have been no further declines; the national murder rate has been stable for the past five years. (To place current murder trends in a historical perspective, see the Bureau of Justice Statistics' murder trends since the 1900s at http://www.ojp.usdoj.gov/bjs/glance/tables/hmrttab.htm.)

The notable declines in murder took place across all gender, race, and age groups, albeit to somewhat varying degrees. For example, black male offending rates dropped sharply in the mid-1990s and continued to decline into the 2000s. The trends of white males mirrored those of black males, but the decline was not as steep and leveled off by the early 2000s. The changes in homicide rates for black and white females match one another and are characterized by steady declines since the 1980s. Thus, the homicide spike in the early 1990s and the decline thereafter was primarily driven by men's offending patterns (see Blumstein & Wallman, 2005).

Women's rates have declined primarily because of the precipitous drop in women's rates of intimate partner homicide. Interestingly, men's rates of partner homicide did not decline as sharply. Experts attribute the drop in lethal partner violence by women to the increasing availability of non-violent alternatives, such as domestic violence shelters (Browne, 1987). Shifting family formation patterns, such as divorce and delayed marriage, also have placed fewer women at risk of offending against a partner (Dugan, Nagin, & Rosenfeld, 1999). I discuss in more detail below the importance of understanding intimate partner homicide in order to understand female homicide.

The Nature of Murder

Who Are the Killers and How Do They Do It? Offender and Offense Characteristics

Like many offenders, female and male homicide offenders tend to come from economically and educationally disadvantaged backgrounds and communities. Educational attainment is usually low; the average offender does not have a high school diploma (Mann, 1996). Homicide offenders, if employed, tend to be working class; women usually work in the service sector and men will likely have a blue collar occupation (Jurik & Winn, 1990; Scott & Davies, 2002).

Male homicide offenders are likely to have a prior arrest history; in the U.S., more than 75% of men convicted of homicide have previously been arrested, many repeatedly and for felony offenses (Jurik & Winn, 1990). About one-fifth of male homicide offenders have been previously incarcerated (Jurik & Winn, 1990). In contrast, most (70%) female homicide offenders do not have a prior felony record, though many (about 60%) have prior arrests for misdemeanors (Jurik & Winn, 1990; Mann, 1993). These arrests are most often for assault, possibly related to domestic abuse; status violations as a juvenile, such as running away from abuse in the home; or minor property crimes, such as shoplifting, credit card fraud, or check forgery. Very few women in Jurik and Winn's study had ever been previously incarcerated. Female homicide offenders are not immersed in criminal subcultures to the same extent as male homicide offenders (Suval & Brisson, 1974). As further evidence, Figueira-McDonough (1981) found that female homicide offenders were likely to be from a "solid" family background, to have children, and to have a stable living arrangement prior to the offense.

Alcohol is a factor in many, but not most, male decisions to kill. Estimates vary widely, but the best guess is that about 40% of male offenders were drinking alcohol at the time of their offense. This percentage is comparable to that for other violent crimes, such as assault and robbery. About 20% of male offenders were using drugs of some sort at the time of their offense

(Karberg & James, 2005). Female murderers, compared to other female offenders, appear to have somewhat higher levels of problem drinking but lower levels of drug use (Suval & Brisson, 1974). However, women were not necessarily drinking at the time of their offense. Fewer female than male offenders were drinking at the time they committed homicide—perhaps 30% of women compared to 40% of men (Mann, 1993).

For females and males, homicides usually occur on weekends and late at night (Mann, 1996). Female homicide offending usually takes place in her and/or the victim's home; male homicides are more likely to occur in public places, such as in bars or on the street (Jurik & Winn, 1990). This gender difference occurs primarily because women tend to kill intimate partners and children, whereas men tend to kill acquaintances and strangers.

Men are far more likely than women to use guns. In fact, a woman is as likely to use a knife to commit her homicide, a change from 20 years ago when guns were more frequently used by female murderers. Roughly 70% of men's homicides are committed with guns (Fox, 2007). Men's second most common weapon is a knife or other sharp weapon (22%); only about 7% of male murderers used brute force (e.g., strangulation, beating).

Why Do People Kill Each Other? Offender Motivation

The immediate motivation for the majority of both women's and men's homicides is fights and arguments (see Figure 13.1).[1] Nearly half of all homicides committed by men or women were preceded by some sort of argument or fight, such as a conflict over money or property, anger over one partner cheating on another, severe punishment of a child or abuse of a partner, retaliation for an earlier dispute, or a drunken fight over an insult or other affront. As discussed below, though, qualitatively the fights and arguments of women and men differ markedly.

The second most common male homicide circumstance is felony related (see Wilbanks, 1983). About 25% of men's homicides, compared to about 15% of women's homicides, occur while the offender is committing another felony. Almost half the time, the felony-related homicide occurs in the course of a robbery attempt. Note, however, that most robberies do not lead to murder or even to injury. A fraction of 1% of robberies, including attempted robbery, end in homicide; victims are injured in about one-third of robberies, according to the *National Crime Victimization Survey, 2004* (Bureau of Justice Statistics, 2006). Other felony-related homicides occur in the course of drug activity (1 in 5 felony-related homicides for men; 1 in 8 for women) or, less commonly, burglary, arson, sex offenses, or theft (Fox, 2007). Female felony-related homicides are often perpetrated in the context

Panel A: Males

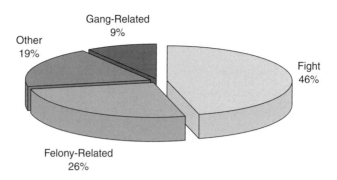

Panel B: Females

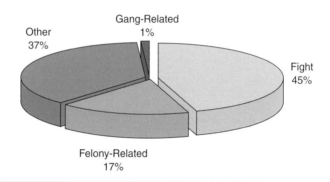

Figure 13.1 Motives for Murder by Sex

SOURCE: Fox (2007).

of prostitution; to some extent, these homicides may be self-defensive because prostitutes may be severely victimized by their clients (e.g., beaten, robbed, raped). Prostitutes also sometimes rob their clients, perhaps with the help of "their man," so prostitution-related homicides may also reflect robberies gone bad.

Female felony-related homicide offenders often co-offend with male partners (Schwartz & Steffensmeier, 2007), though females typically play an assisting role (Jurik & Winn, 1990; Miller, 1998). Many of the women charged with a robbery-related homicide are ultimately considered accessories rather than major actors, and the men usually have brought the weapon (80% of the time) and initiated the violence (Jurik & Winn, 1990). Women who co-offend are often romantically involved with their crime partners (~75%); men, by comparison, mainly co-offend with other men and, therefore, are far less likely to be romantically involved with their crime partner (14%). As we will see again below, women's violence is intimately tied with men's violence because women often offend *with* or *against* their intimates.

The smallest proportion of homicides, for both men and women, are gang related. Only about 1% to 2% of women's homicides are gang related. Less than 50 women in the entire United States were identified as being a participant in a gang-related homicide between 2001 and 2003. For men, the percentage of gang-related homicides is also low, about 9% of the total.

Who Kills Whom? Victim-Offender Relationships

Gender differences in victim-offender relationships are greater than gender differences in motives. Overwhelmingly, females kill family members (see Figure 13.2). In fact, almost 60% of female homicide offenders kill an intimate partner, child, or other family member, such as a (step)parent, (step)sibling, or extended relative. Men, in comparison, kill a family member about 20% of the time. In almost one-third of female homicides, the victim is a boyfriend, husband, or former partner. Children are the next most common targets of women's homicide (19%). In comparison, about 13% of men's homicides are against intimates and 3% are against children.

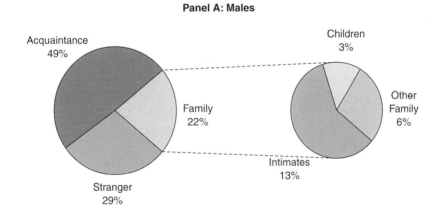

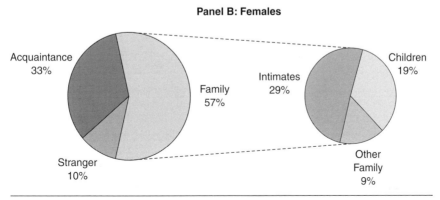

Figure 13.2   Victim-Offender Relationship by Sex

SOURCE: Fox (2007).

Consequently, the large majority of women's victims are men (~75%). Likewise, 75% of males' victims are men, but about half the time, male offenders' targets are acquaintances. Men kill strangers more often (29%) than they kill family members (22%).[2] In contrast, women rarely kill strangers (10%) and only sometimes kill acquaintances (33%; Fox, 2007).

To more directly compare men's and women's homicide offending, I use a measure called the *gender gap*, that is, the female share of homicide offending, relative to the male share.[3] Women's relative involvement in homicide is lowest for stranger homicides; only about 5% to 7% of identified perpetrators of stranger homicide are women. In other words, about 95% of those who kill a stranger are men. This gender gap in homicide is also large for homicide against acquaintances. Less than 10% of homicides against acquaintances were perpetrated by a woman. The gender gap is narrowest for homicides against family members. Over 25% of homicides against family are committed by female offenders; this represents a drop from the 1980s, when 40% were women (Fox, 2007).

CASE STUDY 1: WIFE KILLS HUSBAND

When Teressa was 12, her father beat her until her back was purple because she balked at washing the dishes, covered with maggots, in the sink. At 13, she was raped by a neighbor. She drifted into alcohol and drugs, slept with older men, and stayed out all night, drifting from house to house or living on the streets. Then, at 14, she met Erin through a mutual friend. He, too, was involved with drugs and petty crime. They quickly moved in together—with Erin's mom and six siblings—then were thrown out because Teressa fought with Erin's sister. Teressa was 15 when Erin first behaved violently toward her. In response to her threat to break up with him for flirting with another girl, Erin grabbed Teressa by the hair, dragged her to a bedroom, and held a gun to her. He then put it in his own mouth and put her finger on the trigger. He later apologized profusely, as he often did after a violent fight.

Over the next seven years, Teressa and Erin Turner-Schaefer married and had three children together. He joined and was medically discharged from the Army. Then he worked at Lowe's. During this time, Erin's father, David Schaefer, heard rumors that his son abused Teressa, but he was reassured that everything was fine after talking to his son. "If [Erin] had been hitting her, I would have known it," he said. The police never received reports of abuse, but Teressa's family members and friends said they knew Erin had a history of beating Teressa.

On Sunday, December 11, 2005, the Turner-Schaefers threw a party. Around 11 p.m., everyone had left and the kids, aged 3, 5, and 7 and Erin's brother, 15, were asleep. Teressa was on the phone making sure one of their guests had gotten home safely. Erin overheard part of the conversation and was suspicious that Teressa was having an affair with one of his friends. An argument began.

As Teressa described it, "He pushed my head against the wall and I pushed him away and went to the kitchen to get a bottle of medicine [for my headache]. I was putting water in the glass when I heard him yell 'I'm going to kill you, you [expletive.]' It just scared me. He'd choked me before until I blacked out. It was just a spontaneous act. I grabbed a knife that was drying on a towel on the counter. I turned around just as he lunged."

The six-inch blade sliced through Erin's chest and lung. A family member called the police. When questioned by Prince William Detective Paul Materson, Teressa at first said she didn't know what happened, then that Erin must have been so drunk he stabbed himself, but then she quickly confessed, saying it was an accident. When Detective Materson told Teressa Erin died in the hospital, "She asked me to shoot her."

She pleaded guilty to involuntary manslaughter and served 11 months in county jail with 5 years probation. Circuit Court Judge Rossie Alston said Teressa was "a very decent person" who was amenable to reform, as evidenced by her successful completion of GED and life skills courses while in jail, cooperation with counselors, and attendance at Bible study.

To her victim's family, she said, "I apologize, and despite the problems, Erin and I love each other. . . . I loved him before I knew him; I will continue to love him all my days. . . . The words 'I'm sorry,' I know are little and petty, but if you knew the pain, sorrow, and regret I feel each day, maybe you would know how I feel."

Teressa then returned to her home in Dale City where she had killed Erin a year earlier. Her thoughts were of Erin, but also of how she was going to regain custody of her kids from Erin's mother, find a job even though she had no work experience and a criminal record, learn how to drive, and fill out confusing life insurance claims forms.

Women are more heavily represented as homicide offenders when we examine child victims (aged 0–12).[4] Almost half the offenders arrested for child homicide are women. Female involvement in child homicide declines with victim age: Women commit 50% of infanticides, 33% of murders of toddlers (aged 1–5), and 21% of murders of older kids (aged 6–12). Women more often offend against infants; men more often offend against older children. Overall, toddlers are most vulnerable, making up about half of both women's and men's victims. Toddlers spend much time with mothers and/or caregivers, a riskier situation than school (Mann, 1993); behavioral developments and basic language skills also make this age challenging.

Male-on-Male Violence: Honor Contests and Street Violence

By far the most common homicide situation is male-on-male violence, usually resulting from an argument. The nature of male disputes with other males, however, differs markedly from the types of domestic arguments that spur women to violence. Male-male homicide events often result from what appears to be a minor or trivial provocation, such as a shove, an insult, or the "wrong look," among friends and acquaintances, or, less often, strangers. These events typically occur in a place of leisure, such as a bar, party, barbecue, or park, or on the street, where groups of young men congregate. Insults or threats appear to escalate and develop "spontaneously" into violence, though amplification is often facilitated by the use of alcohol and the presence of an "audience" of young male peers. At some point, both parties come to interpret the exchange as requiring retaliation and mutually agree to aggression (Polk, 1998).

Why would such seemingly trivial slights with so little consequence cause a person to risk death? What seems absurdly trivial to some provides males with the opportunity to demonstrate masculinity through honor contests. Lower-income men may develop a stronger allegiance to street norms and aggressive means of demonstrating masculinity than do middle- and upper-income men, who more strongly subscribe to mainstream norms relating to problem solving. Whereas middle- and upper-income males may have myriad opportunities to "do masculinity," lower-income males living in concentrated urban poverty may, over time and as an adaptation to persistent economic strain, place stronger collective emphasis on more achievable goals than financial success, such as respect and prestige conferred on those with a street reputation (Anderson, 1999; Messerschmidt, 2004). Violations of the "code of the street"—sustained eye contact or a disrespectful demeanor, for example—occasionally can be lethal.

Male homicide offenders are more likely to be immersed in street culture, as evidenced by their tendency to have lengthy arrest and imprisonment histories and long bouts of unemployment. Though male-male status contests are the predominant form of male homicide, two other distinctly male patterns are felony-related homicide and gang-related killings. These types of homicide also stem from male involvement in criminal subcultures. More than 95% of gang homicides are perpetrated by males against males, both of whom are likely to be in (rival) gangs. Motives for gang homicide often are similar to those for non-gang homicide—retaliation in order to save face and to establish social position (Papachristos & Kirk, 2006)—though gang interactions tend to be more conflict oriented than interactions of other groups of youth (Short & Strodtbeck, 1965). Felony-related homicide is also viewed by some as a means of displaying masculinity via demonstrating willingness to engage in risky behavior with the potential for violence (e.g., robbery; Miller, 1998; Polk, 1998). In sum, much of men's violence results from attempts to demonstrate masculinity.

Female-on-Female Violence: Preserving Reputation and Relationships

Roughly 25% of women's homicide victims are other women. Female-on-female violence is often directed against neighbors, their intimates' other sex partner, or friends and acquaintances (Scott & Davies, 2002); however, as many as one-third of female-on-female homicide victims are daughters of the offender. Offenders who kill another woman who is not a relative tend to be younger than the average female offender. Females kill other females in fights over men, to prevent a romance, to preserve their sexual or social reputation, or as a result of an ongoing feud. For example, two neighbors had an ongoing feud over neighborhood matters. On this occasion, the two women were struggling in the kitchen and, as a result, the offender's 3-year-old child was inadvertently injured, though not seriously. The offender responded by stabbing the other woman in the chest once, killing her (Scott & Davies, 2002). Though extreme, this incident also reflects female offenders' greater willingness to aggress to protect a loved one. Other female-female violence may result from fights related to gossip or jealousy, disrespect (e.g., negatively evaluating another girl's appearance), and interactions with another woman's boyfriend—all of which may be regarded generally as reputational challenges, or female honor contests (Miller & Mullins, 2006). Female-on-female homicide is rare, though—these homicides make up less than 2% of total homicides.

Partner Homicide: Women's Self-Help and Men's Attempts to Control

Exploring homicide directed against intimate partners paints a very different portrait of female and male homicide offenders. A woman's decision to kill her partner may be motivated by a desire to protect her children (or herself). Angela Browne's (1987) landmark study of in-depth interviews with women who killed their abusive husbands and women who escaped abuse showed few differences between the two groups of women. Their victims, however, differed: Men who more frequently and severely assaulted or raped their partners, made more death threats, frequently used alcohol or drugs, and abused the children were more likely to be killed. Patterns of violence had escalated more among the women who killed their husbands, prompting Browne to conclude "women's behavior seemed to be primarily in reaction to the level of threat and violence coming in" (p. 127). What appears to trigger the homicide, despite the long history of abuse, is the woman's feeling that her life, or, more important, the safety of her children, is at stake because of an event out of proportion with past "normal" violent events (e.g., physical abuse of a child or discovery of sexual abuse). Indeed, one study reports that as many as 60% of women were being abused at the time they killed their partner (Canestrini, 1987). Another study based on police data and self-reports indicates that women who kill their partners are unlikely to be the first to use force in the event precipitating the homicide (Johnson & Hotton, 2003).

CASE STUDY 2: HUSBAND KILLS WIFE, THEN SELF

Cheryl, a 35-year-old divorced mother of two, met Billy, 45, in 2002, when they both worked as substance abuse counselors. Billy was a fun, athletic man who enjoyed working with children. They fell in love and were married in 2003. "Every time we saw them, they were lovey-dovey" said their boss, Ernest Cantley. Cheryl's family, too, thought the couple was happy. Neighbors, however, knew otherwise. "Billy and Cheryl were lovey-dovey, but behind closed doors it was a mess," said neighbor and friend Mishall Miller. Few knew of Billy's prior arrests for DUI and assault, though Billy's ex-wife, Mildred, became well aware of his volatile, violent side during their two-year marriage. Mildred finally sought a protection from abuse order and divorce when Billy hit her, dragged her out of the bar they were in, slammed her face against the car, and held her hostage in their apartment, threatening to kill her. She escaped while he was in the bathroom.

After their marriage, friends saw a change in Cheryl—she dyed her hair blonde, began dieting, had plastic surgery, and, in 2004, filed for bankruptcy. She also began to complain that her husband tried to control what and when she ate and how she dressed. Even before Billy and Cheryl were married, there were heated arguments. Cheryl's ex-husband called the police in December, 2002 because he was concerned about a verbal argument between the couple he overheard during a phone call, but Cheryl refused to tell her ex-husband where she and Billy were.

Then things started to spin out of control. Police records show that officers responded to at least one domestic disturbance call on March 31, 2005, though neighbors said the police had come to the house at least six times over the past several months. A neighbor said, "Everybody heard them [fighting] . . . [Cheryl] was the kind of person who threw things. She broke a few pictures along the way." Port Orange Commander William Schultz said during the March incident there were signs of an argument but not physical contact, and no arrests were made.

For several months in early 2005, Cheryl tried to get Billy out of the house and, finally, on Tuesday, May 10, she confided to friends that she was going to divorce him. Friend Lavon Berry said Cheryl called her panicked and crying several times that day, saying she had a bad feeling that something was really wrong. Lavon went to the couple's house to watch the kids—and watch Billy get drunk—until Cheryl got home. Billy was totally out of it; when he tried to speak, all he could do was drop his head into his hands and cry.

No one knows what happened over the next 24 hours. On Wednesday evening, Rebecca, Cheryl's daughter, returned home to get permission to play across the street. Sometime between 4:30 and 7:30 p.m., Billy had fired one bullet into Cheryl's head and then one into his own with a .40-caliber gun. Rebecca found them in their bed, facing each other, dead; Billy had the gun still in his hand.

Qualitative analyses suggest that women's homicide and violence is often associated with relational concerns (Steffensmeier & Allan, 1996). Female motives for violence often involve responses to abuse occurring in domestic relationships, risk taking to protect emotional commitments and valued relationships (such as hurting a female rival, as described above), or co-offending with male partners. Moreover, myriad studies show that female violence occurs mainly under extreme stress, such as in the case of aggression against small children, or repeated provocation, such as in response to ongoing domestic abuse and assault (Bailey & Peterson, 1995; Browne, 1987; Dobash, Dobash, Wilson, & Daly, 1992; Schwartz & Steffensmeier, 2007). Men, on the other hand, are more likely than women to kill as a result of jealousy, trivial arguments, or in the course of committing another felony.

Male homicide offenses against partners are dominated by motives of possessiveness, jealousy, and abuse and control. For example, in a study of 155 partner homicides, including both marital and dating relationships, Rasche (1993) found that the offender's inability to accept termination of the relationship was one of the greatest factors in men killing their partners. Men's violence, in these cases, is intended to prevent the woman from leaving, retaliate for her departure, or force her to return. Some studies indicate that women who are separated from their partners are at an elevated risk of violent victimization, including homicide (Johnson & Hotton, 2003).[5] When men kill partners, this often represents the culmination of a prolonged history of abuse. Another motive related to possessiveness is sexual jealousy, such as over a suspected or known infidelity (e.g., love triangles). Motives related to perceived infidelity or termination of the relationship center on themes of male domination and control, whereas the motive of self-defense is more prevalent among female offenders.

A portrait of female homicide offenders as women acting in self-defense and only out of desperation would be one-dimensional, though. For example, some researchers claim that women are as likely as men to engage in violence against their partner (Straus & Gelles, 1990), though the nature and severity of those acts tend to differ by gender (Schwartz & Steffensmeier, 2007). Of the women who killed their partner, 30% were unsuccessful in their claims of self-defense, and some women did have prior criminal records (Mann, 1993). Moreover, some female offenders kill not a partner but another female or even a stranger. And some women are motivated by material wealth and financial gain, revenge, involvement in a criminal subculture or gang, or desire to continue an illicit affair (Weisheit, 1993).

Child Homicide

A predominantly female form of homicide is neonaticide, the killing of a newborn child. These offenders are often young, unmarried women who may conceal pregnancy, give birth alone, and commit homicide using more "delicate" methods such as exposure, suffocation, or strangulation. These women may kill their newborn out of fear of stigmatization should their pregnancy be detected, due to feeling unable to care for the child, or because of extreme stress or mental illness (Gartner & McCarthy, 2006).

Almost uniquely male are murder-suicides and family massacres (familicides), in which a man kills his children, his partner, and possibly himself for reasons such as jealousy, anger, or vindictiveness toward a partner; loss of children through separation; or the inability to financially support his family (Alder & Polk, 1996). The victims are usually biological children who are killed with a gun (Daly & Wilson, 1988). Like the women who commit neonaticide, these men may express feelings of anger, pain, powerlessness, and that matters have gone beyond their control.

Both types of homicide often indicate planning, such as the infanticide of a child found "dressed in an infant suit, wrapped in a blanket, and placed inside a gunnysack . . . in a garbage dump. Death was caused by asphyxia and exposure" (Gartner & McCarthy, 2006, p. 101). Yet, other homicides seem to occur with little forethought, and the offender shows signs of irrationality or mental illness.

The more common scenario for child homicide, for both women and men, is not a premeditated killing; rather, it is the end result of harsh punishment. Consider the following two examples, the first a female description, the second a male description.

> I was packing up my stuff [to move] and my son was acting up and I didn't know what to do 'cause I don't understand nothing about disciplining a child 'cause how I was raised by my own family, how they abused me and I didn't know what to do, so I took it out on my son and sent him to his room and I made him go to bed and he went to bed. I went near and he wasn't breathing, he stopped breathing, wouldn't breathe. I know he was sleeping and he didn't wake up. I hit him, I only hit him twice in the head with my hand. I don't know, with my shoe, my flat shoe in the head twice and that was it, and I sent him to his room 'cause I didn't want to hit him no more. . . . It was very hard for me 'cause I didn't know what to do. The only thing I knew was to take him to the doctor when he needed to go to the doctor and feed him and keep him clean, that was it. I didn't know how to love him, 'cause I didn't have, didn't love myself, I didn't know how to love him. (Crimmins, Langley, Brownstein, & Spunt, 1997, p. 58)

> Austin was sitting on the floor eating a packet of chips and he started crying. I picked him up and whacked him on the bum three or four times with an open hand. I put him down and he was still crying. I picked him up and shook him (to) shut him up. . . . I didn't lose my cool, I was just annoyed. . . . I was just annoyed because I couldn't hear the video. He was getting on my nerves. (Alder & Polk, 1996, pp. 404–405)

Though these statements do not reflect it, the homicides of these and other preschool children tend to be more brutal than those of infants killed by their mothers, as evidenced by multiple wounds, more severe injury, and prolonged histories of abuse (Mann, 1993). Many of the women, usually those who are primary caregivers, report having felt socially isolated, trapped by their responsibilities at a young age. The male child homicide offenders shared more in caregiving responsibilities than most men (Alder & Polk, 1996). The males were often stepfathers or other men living with the mother and children.

Female child homicide offenders, often married or partnered, tend to commit the crime alone, in the bathroom or bedroom, using manual force (hitting, kicking, choking, drowning; Mann, 1993). Female offenders are seldom under the influence of drugs or alcohol at the time. Women filicide offenders often claim innocence or that it was an accident, although many victims have multiple wounds. Half the women arrested for child homicide, particularly those who killed a toddler (aged 2–5), had recorded child abuse histories. A large minority of the women reported having been abused themselves as children. In 80% of cases, offenders are convicted of a lesser charge than murder, suggesting less culpability or some mitigating circumstances.

Men initially attempt to deny or cover up their role in child homicide, sometimes persuading their partners to support their story. Case files (Alder & Pollok, 1996) include male offenders saying "I was just playing," that the child was "accident-prone," or that "the child fell downstairs." The child's death was seldom premeditated, but the physical evidence often showed signs of prior abuse and that extreme aggressive acts precipitated the child's death.

Often, these families are enmeshed in stressful circumstances: money troubles and unemployment, frequent fights between partners, or residence in a high-poverty community. As many as 70% of murdered children resided in severe urban poverty. This suggests that child homicide is, in part, rooted in social organization—or disorganization.

Understanding Homicide Offending Patterns

When trying to understand how one person can kill another, many people probably look for something inside the individual: mental illness or insanity, profound rage or inability to control one's emotions, or some other individual "deficiency." Individual risk factors are important, but individual factors alone cannot explain geographic, temporal, or demographic homicide patterns (see Nash, 1995). Because murder is not an idiosyncratic event but is distributed in a patterned way, macro-level sociologists focus on social forces *outside* the individual that influence his or her evaluations of homicide (violence) as a viable solution to a problem or situation. Researchers look for *contextual effects,* patterns of social organization and social arrangements that promote or discourage homicide.

Accumulated research has identified a set of contextual features associated with homicide, including family structure, concentrated poverty and inequality, and racial heterogeneity (see reviews in Parker, McCall, & Land, 1999; Pratt & Cullen, 2005). These social-structural sources of homicide are similarly related to women's and men's lethal violence (Schwartz 2006a, 2006b, 2008; Steffensmeier & Haynie, 2000a, 2000b). These factors also are related to all sorts of homicide offending, including partner homicide, child homicide, and gang killings (Gauthier, Chaudoir, & Forsyth, 2003; Kubrin, 2003; Papachristos & Kirk, 2006).

The detrimental effects of these structural conditions may result from *social disorganization,* which occurs when residents lack the informal social control capabilities to prevent violence. For example, communities with many single-parent families likely have fewer public guardians and weaker parental control networks. Contextual effects are also interpreted from a *strain/relative deprivation* perspective that highlights the stress-producing aspects of poor social and economic conditions. For example, communities with many single-parent families are likely to be economically disadvantaged because single-parent households are usually less well off than dual-parent families. Living in concentrated poverty might, over time, lead to altered success goals that are more achievable than occupational status, such as reputational status conferred by demonstrating violence and street smarts (Anderson, 1999). Inequality and perceptions of an unjust distribution of wealth can lead to hostility and weakened support for mainstream norms such as the restrained use of violence (Blau & Blau, 1982).

Conclusion

Homicide is rare, but it is more common in some groups, places, or time periods than in others. Homicide offending (and victimization) is more common among young, African American males living in urban settings and those living in the South and West. Homicide is least common among women, the young and old, and those living in rural areas. The motives of homicide offenders tend to be similar: People are most often killed by someone they know in the course of an argument or fight occurring late at night on a weekend. Homicide offenders and victims tend to be concentrated more heavily in communities characterized by economic and social disadvantages.

Homicide patterns, including victims, motivation, and commission, differ across groups in some important ways. For example, men and women kill in ways that uniquely reflect their gender roles and opportunities. Thus, women's aggression tends to be directed at those who are closest to them: intimate partners and children with whom these women spend much of their time. Only rarely do women kill strangers. When a woman kills, it is likely she is under extreme pressure and/or provoked by fear for her life or for the sake of someone close to her (e.g., children), though sometimes her motives are less altruistic. Men's homicide occurs more often in the context of the criminal underworld. Men's relational patterns of homicide are more heavily weighted by friends and acquaintances or strangers, and the event typically takes place in public, perhaps where alcohol and an audience are present. Men often kill over matters that appear to be trivial—minor insults or minimal physical contact—yet these challenges are viewed by participants as requiring a response in order to defend one's masculinity. When a man kills his partner, it is rarely out of mortal fear but usually in response to jealousy or other control motive.

The occurrence of criminal homicide, of all sorts and for all groups, is higher in places with entrenched, concentrated poverty, inequalities, and more vulnerable family structures. Solutions often do not address the difficult-to-observe social forces that influence individual decision making and situational characteristics regarding the use of violence in various circumstances. Perhaps the failure to address social-structural sources of homicide offending is, in part, attributable to the popular misperception that homicide is a random occurrence among strangers when, in fact, most real-world murder mysteries have a fairly predictable ending.

Notes

1. Increasingly, the circumstances surrounding homicides are unknown or unrecorded (16% were unknown or unrecorded in 1980, compared to 30% in 2004), often because the homicide is unsolved. In unsolved cases, the victim and offender are usually strangers; most stranger homicides are perpetrated by men. Sometimes, however, the offender is known even though the circumstances are not. In 90% of these cases, the offender is male. Given these patterns, the inability to assign a motive to the homicide likely has a larger effect on what we know about men's homicide than women's homicide.

2. This likely underestimates the percentage of male homicides committed against strangers because this type of case is least likely to be solved or have offender characteristics recorded. The percent of stranger homicides committed by women is probably somewhat underestimated as well, but given the comparatively small numbers of women who offend against strangers ($N = 321$), the effects are more apparent in men's statistics.

3. We calculate the gender gap as female rate ÷ (male rate + female rate) × 100. The resulting percentage is interpreted as the percentage of homicide offenders who are women. This percentage subtracted from 100 yields the percentage of offenders who are men.

4. The majority of child victims were killed by a family member; the few who were killed by a stranger were highly likely to have been killed by a male (Alder & Polk, 1996).

5. It is important to note that some scholars attribute female declines in partner violence to declining rates of marriage and increased rates of divorce (i.e., decreased exposure to risk), though the increased presence of resources for domestic violence victims has helped as well (Browne, 1987; Dugan et al., 1999; Rosenfeld, 1997). However, it is equally important to note that changing marital and family structures do not appear to have decreased women's risk of partner victimization.

Discussion Questions

1. How "random" is murder? Is fear of this crime justified? For whom?

2. Statistically, what are the most common forms of murder? Is this what you expected before you read this chapter? Why or why not?

3. In what ways are men's and women's homicide offending similar? Different? What are the sources of these differences?

4. Do you think gun control laws would help reduce the number of murders? What other social policies could decrease the number of murders? Would gun control (or other policies) be effective for all sorts of homicide? Explain.

Internet Resources

Bureau of Justice Statistics, Homicide Rate Trends: http://www.ojp.usdoj.gov/bjs/glance/tables/hmrttab.htm

Bureau of Justice Statistics, Sourcebook of Criminal Justice Statistics:
http://www.albany.edu/sourcebook/index.html

Easy Access to the FBI's Supplementary Homicide Reports 1980–2005:
http://www.ojjdp.ncjrs.gov/ojstatbb/ezashr/

FBI, Crime in the United States 2004, Murder: http://www.fbi.gov/ucr/
cius_04/offenses_reported/violent_crime/murder.html

References

Alder, C., & Polk, K. (1996). Masculinity and child homicide. *The British Journal of Criminology, 36,* 396–411.

Anderson, E. (1999). *Code of the street.* New York: Norton.

Bailey, W., & Peterson, R. D. (1995). Gender inequality and violence against women: The case of murder. In J. Hagan & R. D. Peterson (Eds.), *Crime and inequality* (pp. 174–205). Palo Alto, CA: Stanford University Press.

Black, H. C. (1990). *Black's law dictionary* (6th ed.). St. Paul, MN: West.

Blau, J. R., & Blau, P. M. (1982). The cost of inequality: Metropolitan structure and violent crime. *American Sociological Review, 47,* 114–129.

Blumstein, A., & Wallman, J. (2005). *The crime drop in America.* New York: Cambridge University Press.

Browne, A. (1987). *When battered women kill.* New York: Free Press.

Bureau of Justice Statistics. (2006). *Criminal victimization in the United States–Statistical tables.* Retrieved from http://www.ojp.usdoj.gov/bjs/abstract/cvusst.htm.

Canestrini, K. (1987). *1986 female homicide commitments.* Albany: New York State Department of Correctional Services.

Crimmins, S., Langley, S., Brownstein, H. H., & Spunt, B. J. (1997). Convicted women who have killed children. *Journal of Interpersonal Violence, 12,* 49–69.

Daly, M., & Wilson, M. (1988). *Homicide.* Hawthorne, NY: Aldine de Gruyter.

Dobash, R., Dobash, R. E., Wilson, M., & Daly, M. (1992). The myth of sexual symmetry in marital violence. *Social Problems, 39,* 71–91.

Dugan, L., Nagin, D., & Rosenfeld, R. (1999). Explaining the decline in intimate partner homicide: The effects of changing domesticity, women's status, and domestic violence resources. *Homicide Studies, 3,* 187–214.

Federal Bureau of Investigation. (2006). *Crime in the United States, 2005.* Washington, DC: U.S. Department of Justice.

Figueira-McDonough, J. (1981). Community structure and female delinquency rates: A heuristic discussion. *Youth and Society, 24,* 3–30.

Fox, J. A. (2004). Missing data problems in the SHR: Imputing offender and relationship characteristics. *Homicide Studies, 8,* 214–254.

Fox, J. A. (2007). *Uniform crime reports United States: Supplementary homicide reports, 1976–2004* [Computer file].Compiled by Northeastern University, College of Criminal Justice. ICPSR20100-v1. Ann Arbor, MI: Inter-university Consortium for Political and Social Research.

Fox, J. A., & Zawitz, M. W. (2003). Homicide trends in the United States. *Bureau of Justice Statistics.* Retrieved July 31, 2006, from http://www.ojp.usdoj.gov/bjs/homicide/homtrnd.htm

Gartner, R., & McCarthy, B. (2006). Killing one's children: Maternal infanticide and the dark figure of homicide. In K. Heimer & C. Kruttschnitt (Eds.), *Gender and crime: Patterns in victimization and offending* (pp. 91–114). New York: New York University Press.

Gauthier, D., Chaudoir, N., & Forsyth, C. (2003). A sociological analysis of maternal infanticide in the United States, 1984–1996. *Deviant Behavior, 24,* 393–404.

Gove, W. R., Hughes, M., & Geerken, M. (1985). Are uniform crime reports a valid indicator of index crimes? An affirmative answer with minor qualifications. *Criminology, 24,* 451–501.

Johnson, H., & Hotton, T. (2003). Losing control: Homicide risk in estranged and intact intimate relationships. *Homicide Studies, 7,* 58–84.

Jurik, N., & Winn, R. (1990). Gender and homicide: A comparison of men and women who kill. *Violence and Victims, 5,* 227–242.

Karberg, J., & James, D. J. (2005). Substance dependence, abuse, and treatment of jail inmates, 2002. *Bureau of Justice Statistics.* Retrieved September 26, 2006, from http://www.ojp.usdoj.gov/bjs/pub/pdf/sdatji02.pdf

Kubrin, C. (2003). Structural covariates of homicide rates: Does type of homicide matter? *Journal of Research in Crime and Delinquency, 40,* 139–170.

Mann, C. R. (1993). Maternal filicide of preschoolers. In A. V. Wilson (Ed.), *Homicide: The victim-offender connection* (pp. 227–246). Cincinnati, OH: Anderson.

Mann, C. R. (1996). *When women kill.* Albany: State University of New York Press.

Messerschmidt, J. (2004). *Flesh and blood: Adolescent gender diversity and violence.* Totowa, NJ: Rowman & Littlefield.

Miller, J. (1998). Up it up: Gender and the accomplishment of street robbery. *Criminology, 36,* 37–66.

Miller, J., & Mullins, C. W. (2006). Stuck up, telling lies, and talking too much: The gendered context of young women's violence. In K. Heimer & C. Kruttschnitt (Eds.), *Gender and crime: Patterns of victimization and offending* (pp. 41–66), New York: New York University Press.

Nash, R. P. (1995). *Alcohol and homicide: A deadly combination of two American traditions.* New York: State University of New York Press.

Papachristos, A. V., & Kirk, D. S. (2006). Neighborhood effects on street gang behavior. In J. F. Short & L. A. Hughes (Eds.), *Studying youth gangs* (pp. 63–84). New York: AltaMira Press.

Parker, K. F., McCall, P. L., & Land, K. C. (1999). Determining social-structural predictors of homicide: Units of analysis and related methodological concerns. In M. D. Smith & M. A. Zahn (Eds.), *Homicide: A sourcebook of social research* (pp. 107–124). Thousand Oaks, CA: Sage.

Polk, K. (1998). Males and honour contest violence. *Journal of Homicide Studies, 3,* 6–29.

Pratt, T. C., & Cullen, F. T. (2005). Assessing macro-level predictors and theories of crime: A meta-analysis. *Crime and Justice, 32,* 373–450.

Rasche, C. E. (1993). "Given" reasons for violence in intimate relationships. In A. V. Wilson (Ed.), *Homicide: The victim-offender connection* (pp. 75–100). Cincinnati, OH: Anderson.

Rosenfeld, R. (1997). Changing relationships between men and women: A note on the decline in intimate partner homicide. *Homicide Studies, 1,* 72–83.

Schwartz, J. (2006a). Effects of diverse forms of family structure on women's and men's homicide. *Journal of Marriage and Family, 68,* 1292–1303.

Schwartz, J. (2006b). Family structure as a source of female and male homicide in the United States. *Homicide Studies, 10,* 253–278.

Schwartz, J. (2008). Effects of two sources of male capital on female and male rates of violence: The institutions of family men and old heads. *Sociological Perspectives, 51,* 91–117.

Schwartz, J., & Steffensmeier, D. (2007). The nature of female offending: Patterns and explanations. In R. Zaplin (Ed.), *Female offenders: Critical perspective and effective interventions (pp. 43–75).* Boston: Jones & Bartlett.

Scott, L., & Davies, K. (2002). Beyond the statistics: An examination of killing by women in three Georgia counties. *Homicide Studies, 6,* 297–324.

Short, J. F., & Strodtbeck, F. L. (1965). *Group process and gang delinquency.* Chicago: University of Chicago Press.

Steffensmeier, D. J., & Allan, E. (1996). Gender and crime: Toward a gendered theory of female offending. *American Review of Sociology, 22,* 459–487.

Steffensmeier, D. J., & Haynie, D. (2000a). Gender, structural disadvantage, and urban crime: Do macrosocial variables also explain female offending rates? *Criminology, 38,* 403–438.

Steffensmeier, D. J., & Haynie, D. (2000b). The structural sources of urban female violence in the United States. *Homicide Studies, 4,* 107–134.

Straus, M. A., & Gelles, R. J. (1990). *Physical violence in American families: Risk factors and adaptations to violence in 8,145 families.* New Brunswick, NJ: Transaction.

Suval, E. M., & Brisson, R. C. (1974). Neither beauty nor beast: Female criminal homicide offenders. *International Journal of Criminology & Penology, 2,* 23–34.

Weisheit, R. (1993). Structural correlates of female homicide patterns. In A. V. Wilson (Ed.), *Homicide: The victim-offender connection* (pp. 191–206). Cincinnati: Anderson.

Wilbanks, W. (1983). The female homicide offenders in the U.S. *International Journal of Women's Studies, 6,* 302–210.

CHAPTER 14

Serial Murder

Maria Ioannou

The phenomenon of serial murder, although a rare form of homicide, has attracted an increased degree of interest in the last decades. Theodore Bundy, John Wayne Gacy, Henry Lee Lucas, Kenneth Bianchi and Angelo Buono (the "Hillside Stranglers"), David Berkowitz (the "Son of Sam"), Jeffrey Dahmer, Richard Ramirez (the "Night Stalker"), and Albert DeSalvo (the "Boston Strangler") are a few of the serial killers that have both terrorized and fascinated the public.

CASE STUDY: DR. HAROLD SHIPMAN

Harold Frederick Shipman (1946–2004) does not fit the stereotype of the serial killer. He was a British general practitioner who was the most prolific serial killer in the United Kingdom. His victims were most often elderly women (about 80% of his victims were female). His youngest victim was Peter Lewis, a 41-year-old man. Shipman came to the attention of the police when, in 1998, a colleague reported the high death rate of his patients. In particular, she was concerned about the large number of cremation forms for elderly women that he had needed countersigned. She said he was "killing" his patients, although she was not sure whether it was negligent or intentional. An investigation was launched but was soon dropped due to lack of evidence. However, the daughter of one of his victims suspected that something was wrong when she discovered that the will that her mother made excluded her totally and left a large sum of money to Shipman. The victim's body was exhumed and examined and was found to contain traces of diamorphine (a pain medication). In addition, Shipman's typewriter was identified as the one that was used to create the will. As a result, there was an investigation of the other deaths Shipman had certified. A pattern emerged of his administering lethal overdoses of diamorphine, signing patients' death certificates, and then forging medical records to indicate they had been in poor health. He was convicted in January 2000 of murdering 15 people

---

by lethal injections of diamorphine and sentenced to 15 concurrent life sentences. The official inquiry into his career concluded that between 1971 and 1998, he had probably killed 250 people, 218 of whom were positively identified. In total, 459 people died while under his care. It is uncertain how many of these were Shipman's victims, as he was often the only person to certify a death. Much of Britain's legislation concerning health care and medicine was reviewed and heavily modified as a direct and indirect result of Shipman's crimes, especially after the findings of the Shipman Inquiry. In 2004, Shipman was found hanged in his cell at Wakefield Prison. The cause of death was suicide.

Shipman consistently denied his guilt, disputing the scientific evidence against him. He never commented on why he committed these murders and never made any statements about his actions. No obvious motive was apparent, so a discussion about motive can only be speculative.

Serial murder may appear to be a new phenomenon, but we have a few examples from past centuries: Gilles de Rais, a Frenchman who lived during the 15th century, killed several hundred young children, drank their blood, and engaged in necrophilia. At the time, it was believed he had made a pact with the devil. Peter Stubb, who lived in 16th-century Germany, ate his own son, murdered 13 young children, and engaged in cannibalism and sexual torture. Jack the Ripper, in 19th-century London, killed five prostitutes and was never caught.

Serial killers are individuals who can be responsible for horrific crimes while at the same time leading quite normal lives, a fact that produces discomfort, fear, and awe in most people. Most were shocked when it was revealed that the person executed in 1989 for the murder of at least 30 young women was Theodore Bundy, a charming and intelligent young man; similarly, John Wayne Gacy, esteemed in his community for his charity work, was discovered to have tortured and killed 33 young men and buried them under his home.

The media, the film industry (e.g., *Silence of the Lambs*), and many researchers are mainly responsible for the mythology and fiction blurred with fact that surrounds serial murder. "Along with manipulation, domination and control, a significant motivator for almost all serial killing is sexual, even if, as with Son of Sam David Berkowitz, the crimes themselves are not overtly so" (Douglas & Olshaker, 1999, p. 238). Statements like this surely don't help in dispelling the serial murder myths, as serial murders that do not fit this stereotype are discounted. Serial killers who rape, torture, sodomize, and mutilate their victims attract an inordinate amount of attention from the press, the public, and professionals. Although they may be the most fascinating type of serial killer, they are hardly the only ones. Serial killing occurs all over the world in many different forms, committed by many different sorts of people. For example, according to this stereotype, Dr. Harold Shipman (see Case Study: Dr. Harold Shipman) wouldn't be labeled a serial killer even though he was one of the most prolific murderers in the history of the UK—and probably the world (Esmail, 2005, p. 1843).

Definition of Serial Murder

The term *serial murder* was first coined in the early 1980s by FBI profilers. There is no universally accepted definition of serial murder because there has always been much confusion as to what serial murder is. Researchers have debated the number of victims needed to constitute serial murder. Some authors now suggest that a minimum of two victims is serial murder. Egger (1984) stated that serial murder occurs when one or more individuals commits a second murder. However, other authors believe the minimum number of victims should be set at three (Hickey, 1997), four (Fox & Levin, 1998), or even five (Dietz, 1986), though three victims is commonly considered sufficient (Douglas, Burgess, Burgess, & Ressler, 1992; Ferguson, White, Cherry, Lorenz, & Bhimani, 2003; Hickey, 2002; Keeney & Heide, 1994).

Holmes and Holmes (1998) state that serial murder may be defined as the unlawful killing of three or more human beings over a period of time. For the offence to be considered serial murder, a cooling-off period, during which the offender does not kill, must occur between each offence. The cooling-off period is a distinguishable time interval between each murder, which can be days, weeks, months, or even years (Bartol, 1995) and is the key feature that distinguishes the serial killer from other multiple killers (Ressler, Burgess, & Douglas, 1988). When the time is right for him and he has cooled off from his last homicide, the serial killer selects his next victim and proceeds with his crime. Theodore Bundy is an example of a serial killer who killed 30 or more times over a period of many years in at least five different states. Serial sexual murder involves evidence of sexual activity before, during, and/or after death (Meloy, 2000). Not all serial murderers are sexual murderers.

Serial murder is a type of multiple murder and mustn't be confused with the other two types, mass murder and spree murder. All of these terms are used interchangeably, but there are fundamental differences between these three forms of multicide. *Mass murder* is an offence in which at least four victims are killed in the same general location at one time (Delisi & Sherer, 2006; Fox & Levin, 2003). *Spree murder* is a single event with multiple victims in two or more locations and no emotional cooling-off period between murders; it often occurs in conjunction with other criminal behavior (Delisi & Sherer, 2006; Fox & Levin, 2003; Holmes & Holmes, 1998; Rush, 2003). A spree murder can be of short or long duration.

The differences between these categories are the time between killings and the geographic area in which the murders occur (Delisi & Sherer, 2006; Douglas et al., 1992; Hickey, 2002). Serial homicide offenders kill their victims over an extended period of time, spanning years or even decades, and take, at times, significant breaks between killings. Spree killers murder their victims during a truncated period of time—hours or days—often in conjunction with other criminal activity. Mass killers murder victims at a discrete time and place. Mass killing occurs quickly and often yields the most victims; it happens without warning and usually ends with the offender killing himself or herself.

Prevalence Rates of Serial Murder

There are varying estimates of the incidence of serial murder. Holmes and DeBurger (1988) claimed that as many as 3,500 to 5,000 people are victims of serial murder each year in the U.S. and that serial killers are responsible for up to two-thirds of unsolved homicides as well as a portion of missing persons cases. This estimate is much too high, and it has been criticized (Egger, 1998; Gresswell & Hollin, 1994) for its attribution of unsolved murders to serial killers (Fox & Levin, 1998); roughly 14% to 20% of all criminal homicides committed each year across the entire country are unsolved (Bartol, 1995), while serial killers are estimated to commit only 1% to 2% of all homicides in the United States. In a more conservative estimate, Hickey (1991) places the risk at 0.2 per 100,000 population, and general estimates show that the number of multiple murderers (serial, mass, and spree) active in the United States is from 30 to more than 100 at any given time. During the 1970s and early 1980s, there were about 35 serial killers active in the U.S. (U.S. Department of Justice, 1983, cited in Harrower, 1998).

Hickey (1997) conducted one of the most exhaustive measurements of the prevalence and trends in serial murder. He assembled a historical database going back to 1800 and showed a slowly rising trend from 1800 through the 1960s; he found that since 1970, the number of cases has increased dramatically. In contrast to the Justice Department's estimate of thousands of victims annually, Hickey enumerated only 2,526 to 3,860 victims slain by 399 serial killers between 1800 and 1995 and 974 to 1,398 victims from 1975 to 1995, which is 49 to 70 per year, although his data collection didn't involve undetected cases (Fox & Levin, 1999). In the UK, Gresswell and Hollin (1994) estimate that there are up to four serial killers active at any one time and that between 1982 and 1991 there were 196 victims of multicide in England and Wales. Jenkins (1988) estimates that in England, serial murder accounted for 1.7% of murders between 1940 and 1985, increasing to a rate of 3.2% between 1970 and 1993.

In general, there is an indication that since the 1970s there has been an increase in serial killing (Canter, Missen, & Hodge, 1996), and this may be attributed to the improvement in communication and computer networks in law enforcement agencies and the fact that they have become better equipped to identify links between victims killed by the same murderer. Nevertheless, there is agreement among experts in law enforcement and academia that serial murder has increased; at least, there has been an increase in homicides committed by strangers and for unknown motive.

The truth is that it is almost impossible to measure the precise prevalence of serial murder today for many reasons: serial murderers usually target strangers; they take great care to cover up their crimes by disposing of their victims' bodies; many of the homicides may remain open missing persons reports; in many cases, the victims come from marginal groups, such as homeless people and prostitutes, and their disappearances may never be reported; in many cases, homicide cases are not linked by law enforcement authorities (Egger, 1998) because they are not recognized as the work of the same offender. Murders committed by a serial killer are difficult to solve because they typically lack either motive or evidence. The Unabomber, Theodore Kaczynski, was careful to cover his tracks for nearly two decades, despite a massive task force investigating his bombings.

Offender Characteristics

Virtually every book examining and reviewing the topic of serial murder devotes considerable attention to Theodore Bundy, the charming, attractive, intelligent, and well-spoken law student who brutally killed dozens of women from Washington to Florida in the mid-1970s and was able to lure victims and elude the police for years. But Bundy is more the exception than the rule. Serial killers span a broad range of human qualities including appearance, social class, and intelligence. But most of them are fairly average; contrary to the popular stereotype, serial killers tend, in many respects, to be "extraordinarily ordinary" (Levin & Fox, 1985).

Hickey (2002), in a review of basic demographics of serial homicide cases from 1800 to 1995 that included 337 males and 62 females, dispelled the myths that all serial homicide offenders are white, male, insane, very intelligent, or travel great distances to commit their crimes (Salfati & Bateman, 2005). Despite the fact that serial killers come from a variety of different ethnic backgrounds (Egger, 2002; Hickey, 2002), they tend to share some traits in common. Hickey (2002) found most to be about 30 years old, Caucasian, and male. Offenders are more likely to be Caucasian than African American, in numbers consistent with the relative proportion of Caucasians and

African Americans in the U.S. population (Godwin, 2000; Keeney & Heide, 1994; Ressler, Burgess, Douglas, Hartman, & D'Agostino, 1986).

In another study, Hickey (1991) conducted a meta-analysis of studies concerning 169 American offenders and found that the average age was 28.5 and 85% were white. Half the offenders were categorized as local, and they were found to come from a wide variety of educational and occupational backgrounds, but the majority were not highly educated, tended to be in unskilled jobs, and almost 60% had a history of prior criminal activity. Unlike the typical violent individual who demonstrates a propensity for violence at an early age, serial murderers generally begin their careers of repetitive homicide at a relatively late age. Jenkins (1988) concludes that most start their careers between the ages of 24 and 40. The median age of arrested serial murderers is 36 (Bartol, 1995). Arrests typically occur about four years after they begin killing. This, of course, does not mean that their first contacts with the criminal justice system occurred at so late an age. While serial murderers often have extensive police records, the records reflect petty theft, embezzlement, and forgery, rather than a history of violence (Jenkins, 1988). In a study of 217 American serial murderers, Canter et al. (1996) found that 75% had previous convictions and nearly half had been arrested as juveniles.

Method of killing is one area that has drawn much attention. Hickey (1991) found that 61% of offenders used a combination of methods, as these murders are often a process rather than a simple act. The methods used by the killers to perpetrate their murders were varied and included shooting, stabbing, strangulation, and blunt force with instruments and/or hands. Likewise, several healthcare providers used more than one method to kill patients. For example, Beverly Allitt injected insulin, potassium chloride, and air, and used suffocation. In most of the cases, healthcare providers used injection (insulin, potassium chloride, morphine, neuro-muscular paralyzing agents, etc.), suffocation, drowning, air embolus (injecting air into a vein), oral medications, tampering with equipment, and poisoning. Kraemer, Lord, and Heilbrun (2004) found in their comparative analysis of single and serial homicide that gunshot wounds followed by stab wounds were the most frequently occurring causes of death in single homicides (56% cumulatively). In serial homicides, however, strangulation was the most frequent cause of death (47%), while stab wounds and gunshot wounds each accounted for 15% of the deaths.

Some research has looked at the periodicity in an offender's urge or wish to commit murder. In the great majority of cases, intervals between murders in a series range from a few days to a year or even longer. A common pattern has been for a year or more to elapse after the first killing, which is followed by three or four further murders in a year. The only rule of periodicity that does appear to have some validity is that in the career of each murderer, the rate of killing has accelerated over time. John Christie, for example, committed his first known murder in 1943. The second was over a year later. Five years elapsed before the third and fourth murders, in 1949. The chief variable in his decision to kill appears to have been the presence of his wife. When she left to visit a relative, he would kill. In 1952, he killed his wife and then killed three more women in a two-month period.

Victim Characteristics

According to research, most victims of serial homicide are young, vulnerable, Caucasian women (Egger, 1998; Godwin, 2000; Hickey, 1997). Kraemer et al. (2004) found that serial homicide victims were most likely female (67%) and Caucasian (71%) and were an average of 33 years old. Hickey (1991) reported that the majority of the victims are adult strangers, with young women ranking the highest in preference. Prime targets are hitchhikers, women living alone, prostitutes, young children, and the elderly (Levin & Fox, 1985). Children (under 18 years old) form another victim category. In Hickey's study, 24% of serial offenders killed at least one child, and Godwin reported that 27% of victims were under the age of 17.

Serial homicide is usually intraracial, with offenders killing victims of their own race (Godwin, 2000; Hazelwood & Douglas, 1980; Hickey, 1997). The racial proportions of serial homicide victims are roughly equivalent to the proportion of different races in the U.S. population. "For example, in Godwin's study, 80% of the victims were Caucasian, 16% were African American, and 4% were members of other racial groups" (Kraemer et al., 2004, p. 327). Holmes and DeBurger (1988) also note that serial murder predominantly involves white males killing white females. There are exceptions, of course. Jeffrey Dahmer, a white male, killed at least nine African American males. While most homicide cases involve people who know each other, serial homicide is typically a stranger-to-stranger crime (Egger, 1998; Fox & Levin, 1999; Godwin, 2000). Godwin found that 90% of the victims in his study were strangers to their assailants and Hickey (1997) reports 62% were strangers. Of course, there are many exceptions. Gary Evans was an intelligent white male who killed his friends and business partners.

Choice of victim seems to be determined by victim vulnerability and offender opportunity. Killers prefer potential victims who offer easy access, are transient, and can disappear without causing much alarm or concern (Bartol, 1995). Prostitutes are the most vulnerable, which explains their extremely high rate of victimization by serial killers. In many cases, when a prostitute disappears the search for her can be delayed weeks or months, either because her disappearance never results in an official report or because the case is treated as a missing person case rather than a homicide, leaving the police with a corpse difficult to identify. The Green River killer murdered about 50 prostitutes between 1982 and 1984, leaving the police with little more than the skeletal remains of his victims. Another group, known as "angels of death," are caretakers, nurses, and doctors who take advantage of the frailty and dependence of their elderly victims by suffocating or poisoning them. In 1987, Donald Harvey confessed to poisoning to death 60 patients, most of them elderly, over a period of years in a number of Cincinnati-area institutions. Hospital homicides like these are particularly difficult to detect and solve because deaths of patients, especially the elderly, are not uncommon and suspicions are rarely aroused.

Serial Murder Typologies

There have been a handful of attempts to classify serial murder. These typologies classify offenders on the basis of a mixture of features including inferred motives, crime scene evidence, and offender background characteristics.

The Federal Bureau of Investigation (FBI; Ressler et al., 1986) conducted one of the most widely cited classification studies and, based on interviews with 36 offenders, identified two types of serial killer: organized and disorganized. An *organized offender* possesses good intelligence and social and sexual competence, lives with a partner, is likely to be employed, uses a vehicle, and follows his crime in the media. He leads a planned and orderly life, and this is reflected in the way he commits his crimes. The organized crime scene reveals evidence of a carefully planned crime, control, use of restraints, and use of a weapon he has brought with him and subsequently removed from the crime scene. A *disorganized offender* is characterized by average intelligence, sexual incompetence, and social immaturity; is less likely to be employed; lives alone; drives an old car or has no car; has minimal interest in the news reports of his crimes; kills spontaneously; and leaves a haphazard crime scene. The disorganized crime scene shows evidence of an impulsive and unplanned attack; use of minimal restraint; and no attempt to conceal the body, which is left at the crime scene with forensic evidence (Ressler et al., 1988; see Tables 14.1 and 14.2). The FBI initially divided their sample into 24 organized and 12 disorganized offenders.

The model had many critics because many methodological flaws were identified in relation to the reliability and validity of the interviews and the ways in which conclusions were drawn from them. The widespread citation of this typology is based on an informal, exploratory study of 36 offenders put forward as exemplars, rather than a specific test of a representative

Table 14.1 Profile Characteristics of Organized and Disorganized Murderers

Organized	Disorganized
Good intelligence	Average intelligence
Socially competent	Socially immature
Skilled work preferred	Poor work history
Sexually competent	Sexually incompetent
High birth order	Low birth order
Father's work stable	Father's work unstable
Inconsistent childhood discipline	Harsh discipline in childhood
Controlled mood during crime	Anxious mood during crime
Use of alcohol with crime	Minimal use of alcohol
Precipitating situational stress	Minimal situational stress
Living with partner	Living alone
Mobility, with car in good condition	Lives/works near crime scene
Follows crime in news media	Minimal interest in news media
May change jobs or leave town	Minimal change in lifestyle

SOURCE: Ressler et al. (1988).

Table 14.2 Crime Scene Differences Between Organized and Disorganized Murderers

Organized	Disorganized
Offense planned	Spontaneous offense
Victim a targeted stranger	Victim or location known
Personalizes victim	Depersonalizes victim
Controlled conversation	Minimal conversation
Crime scene reflects overall control	Crime scene random and sloppy
Demands submissive victim	Sudden violence to victim
Restraints used	Minimal use of restraints
Aggressive acts prior to death	Sexual acts after death
Body hidden	Body left in view
Weapon/evidence absent	Evidence/weapon often present
Transports victim or body	Body left at death scene

SOURCE: Ressler et al. (1988).

sample of a general population of serial murderers (Canter, Alison, Alison, & Wentink, 2004). Canter et al., using a multidimensional scaling procedure, examined the FBI's model and found that *organized* and *disorganized* are not opposing dichotomous categories. A subset of organized features was found in most serial murders, with disorganized features being much rarer and not forming a distinct type. They employed four descriptor terms that consider whether the victim has suffered mutilation, execution, sexual control, or plunder (see Figure 14.1).

Holmes and Holmes's (1998) model was the result of further work carried out on the original model proposed by Holmes and DeBurger (1988). They identified four types of serial killers, based on motives: the visionary, the mission-oriented, the hedonistic, and the power/control killer. The *visionary serial killer* kills in response to the commands of voices or visions from demons, angels, the devil, or God telling him to kill a particular individual or particular types of people. This killer is often considered to be suffering from psychosis. The *mission-oriented serial killer* believes that it is his mission to rid the world of a group or groups of people who must be destroyed or eliminated because they are judged to be unworthy or undesirable, for example, prostitutes, children, the elderly, or a specific ethnic group. He sees no visions, hears no voices, and functions on a day-to-day

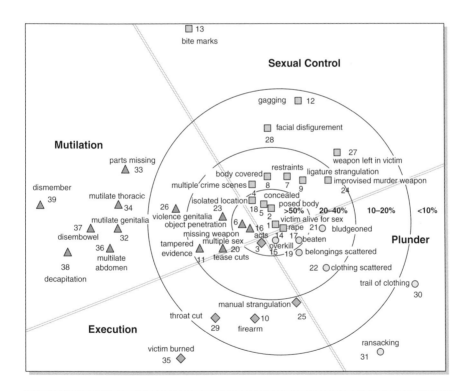

Figure 14.1   SSA of 39 Organized/Disorganized Criteria Interpreted to Show Four Styles of Interaction With Victim

SOURCE: Canter et al. (2004).

NOTE: Contours indicate overall frequencies.

basis without demonstrating psychopathology. The *hedonistic serial killer* seeks pleasure and benefits from killing and derives satisfaction from the murder event. This type is divided into three subtypes: the lust killer, the thrill killer, and the comfort killer. The *lust killer* kills for sexual gratification; sex is the focal point of the murder, even after he has killed the victim. This type of murderer derives pleasure from the process of the murderous event. Various acts, such as cannibalism, necrophilia, and dismemberment, are prevalent in this type of murder. His motives are sexual and sadism is an integral part of his behavior. The *thrill killer* murders for the pleasure and excitement of killing. Once a victim is dead, this murderer loses interest. This type of killing often involves a long process of extended acts of torture. The *comfort killer* murders for profit and material gain. Last, the *power/control serial killer* derives satisfaction from having complete control over the victim. His motives are driven by the need for power and dominance over another human being. Control and domination are the primary motives, even if his behavior has a sexual component.

Canter and Wentink's (2004) content analysis of crime scene evidence from 100 U.S. serial murders raised several concerns about the reliability and validity of the data collection, the lack of direct empirical testing, the lack of definition of behaviors, and overlap of criteria between types. They subjected the content categories to Smallest Space Analysis (SSA) in order to empirically evaluate the model and found only limited support for it. They found that the power or control killings were typical of the sample as a whole and occurred in more than 50% of the cases; thus, power or control killings did not form a distinct type. Limited support was found for the aspects of lust, thrill, and mission styles of killing. However, a model of serial killing emerges that places much more emphasis on how the offender interacts with the victim than on inferences about the motivations of the offender. One interpretation is that the offender's interactions with the victim reflect the role that the offender assigns to the victim (Canter, 1994). Mutilation is typical of the *victim as object* (the offender has no consideration for the victim; the offender merely treats him or her as an object with which to play, e.g., Fred West), ransacking is typical of the *victim as vehicle* (the offender has more awareness of the victims, who often share symbolic importance and similar characteristics, but frenzied violence may be evident, e.g., Jack the Ripper), and restraints are typical of the *victim as person* (the offender may believe he can have an intimate relationship with the victim and that he is taking on the role of a hero).

Other models of serial homicide include those of Keppel and Walter (1999; Power-Assertive Rape-Murder, Power-Reassurance Rape-Murder, Anger-Retaliatory Rape-Murder, and Anger-Excitation Rape-Murder);

Jenkins (1988), who noted two types of serial murderers, the *predictable type* and the *respectable type*, largely determined by the presence or absence of a violent criminal history and whether or not alcohol abuse featured in their day-to-day life; Dietz (1986), who offered a more detailed set of discriminations based largely on the presumed psychopathology that was the basis of the killings, distinguishing between serial murderers who were psychopathic sexual sadists, crime spree killers, organized crime killers, psychotics, and custodial poisoners; and Fox and Levin's (1998) motivational typology, which identified five motives: power, revenge, loyalty, profit, and terror (see Table 14.3).

It should be noted that typologies, in general, should be approached with extreme caution. Researchers develop a number of different typologies in an attempt to systematically examine how and why different individuals become serial killers and how they differ from each other. But the typology approach to classification, which seeks to identify strict categories, has been criticized because few individuals are found who conform to these rigid classifications (Gibbons, 1988). A requirement of typological systems is that each offender belong to only one type or category. Such rigidity denies the possibility of variation in an offender's behavior and ignores the potential for development or change in an offender's behavior or actions. The schemes that include less strict categories have generally being found to be more successful (Canter, 1994). The studies of Canter et al. (2004) and Canter and Wentink (2004) reveal the value and importance of developing reliable and valid classification systems for considering serial homicide.

Table 14.3   Examples of Motivations for Serial Murder

Motivations	Example
Power	Inspired by sadistic fantasies, a man tortures and kills a series of strangers to satisfy his need for control and dominance.
Revenge	Grossly mistreated as a child, a man avenges his past by slaying women who remind him of his mother.
Loyalty	A team of killers turn murder into a ritual to prove their dedication and commitment to one another.
Profit	A woman poisons to death a series of husbands in order to collect their life insurance.
Terror	A profoundly paranoid man commits a series of bombings to warn the world of impending doom.

SOURCE: Fox and Levin (1998).

Theories of Serial Murder

A number of theorists and researchers have examined serial murder and tried to explain this phenomenon using concepts from several scientific disciplines; the major contributions have come from psychology, psychiatry, sociology, criminology, anthropology, and biology. To review accurately and adequately all the studies and theories on serial murder from each relevant discipline, or to discuss every single variable associated with serial murder, is beyond the scope of this chapter. However, the roles of sex, childhood abuse, relationship with parents, and mental disorder appear in several theories that attempt to explain serial murder and will be discussed below.

Sexual Motive

A number of investigators and researchers feel that the sexual component is of great importance to understanding serial murder. It has been suggested that in order to achieve sexual gratification, the sexual sadist will torture, kill, and mutilate. He uses multiple means of torture, psychological and physical, to heighten his sexual arousal. The sight of suffering and the helplessness of the victims increasingly excite him. Some offenders even construct soundproof torture chambers equipped with video equipment and other paraphernalia such as restraints, torture racks, whips, blindfolds, weapons, and gags. Many sexual sadists keep records of their crimes in the form of writings, drawings, or photographs. Paraphilias, such as sexual sadism, cannibalism, exhibitionism, fetishism, and necrophilia, are most frequently associated with the serial sexual murderer. For instance, in a sample of 25 serial murderers, Prentky et al. (1989) found that voyeurism was present in 75%, fetishism in 71%, cross-dressing in 25%, and indecent exposure in 25%. Many sexual serial killers collect memorabilia, souvenirs, or trophies (e.g., diaries, clothing, photos, jewelry, even body parts belonging to their victims) that hold special meaning for them. Danny Rolling, who in 1991 butchered five young college students in Florida, removed and kept the nipples of some of his female victims (Fox & Levin, 1994, 1996).

Pornography and fantasy have also been associated with serial murder, in a few theories. According to FBI researchers, for example, 81% of the 31 sexual predators they interviewed reported an active interest in violent pornography (Ressler et al., 1988). Prentky et al. (1989) compared 25 serial sexual murderers with 17 single sexual murderers and found that for 86% of the serial killers and 23% of the single murderers, fantasy preceded their offences. John Wayne Gacy, who killed and buried 33 young men and boys, owned a large collection of pornographic videotapes. Theodore Bundy claimed on Death Row that pornography turned him into a vicious killer.

But support is not strong for this theory. While some serial murders are sexual murderers, most are not.

Childhood Abuse

Many scientists and journalists tend to search for clues in the killer's childhood that might explain the brutal murders. Psychological, physical, and/or sexual abuse has often been linked with violent criminals. Ressler et al. (1988), in their interviews with 36 murderers, found evidence of psychological abuse in 23 cases and physical trauma in 13 cases. Hickey (1997) reported that among a group of 62 male serial killers, 48% had been rejected as children by a parent or some other important person in their lives. Hazelwood and Warren (1995) report that in their study of 41 serial rapists, 76% said they had been sexually abused as children. Fred West and his wife Rosemary killed and tortured at least 12 young women, including his first wife and two of his daughters, over 20 years. Both he and his wife are said to have suffered serious sexual and emotional abuse as children.

Relationship With Parents

Some explanations focus on dysfunctional parent-child relationships. One feature that emerges in the study of serial killers is a pathological relationship with their parents, especially the mother, who is viewed as dominating, controlling, and, on occasion, incestuous. The father, on the other hand, is viewed as absent or violent. MacDonald (1963) hypothesized a triad of symptoms—enuresis, fire setting, and cruelty to animals—that were seen as reactions to parental rejection, neglect, or brutality. Shortly after the capture of Hillside Strangler Kenneth Bianchi, psychiatrists speculated that he tortured and murdered young women as an expression of hatred of his mother, who had allegedly brutalized him as a youngster (Fox & Levin, 1994). Theodore Bundy was raised by his grandparents because his mother gave birth to him while she was still young, and for many years she pretended to be his sister. He was 23 years old when he discovered the truth. Psychiatrists, after his execution, suggested that his victims served as surrogates for the real target he sought, his mother. Edmund Kemper came from an abusive home and was belittled by a domineering mother who occasionally locked him in the basement when he failed to meet her standards. At the age of 15, he killed both his grandparents, but after a few years of treatment he was released into his mother's care. While he was attending sessions with his parole officer and psychiatrist and it looked like he was making progress, he was murdering female hitchhikers, dismembering them, and saving various body parts, some of which he cooked. He eventually killed and decapitated his mother and had sex with the corpse. He claimed that after this act he was "liberated" and didn't feel the need to kill any longer.

Mental Disorder

There is a perception by the public that serial murderers are mad or psychotic. Very few serial killers have been driven by psychosis (e.g., Herbert Mullen killed at least 10 people in 1972, obeying voices that ordered him to make human sacrifices to avert an earthquake). With a few notable exceptions, most serial killers do not suffer from a profound mental disorder, such as schizophrenia. Most serial killers are not insane or psychotic in either a legal or medical sense. Most understand the difference between right and wrong and know the nature and quality of their criminal acts.

One mental disorder that has been associated or used in the defense of a few serial killers is Dissociative Identity Disorder (formerly known as multiple personality disorder), which is the existence within the person of two or more distinct personalities or personality states that recurrently take control of behavior. Kenneth Bianchi (one of the Hillside Stranglers) claimed to be suffering from Dissociative Identity Disorder and used this as his defense. Under hypnosis, he purported to reveal the personality "Steve Walker," a vicious individual who killed 12 women. In the end, it was revealed that Steve Walker was, in fact, a student from whom Bianchi had stolen personal documents, so he dropped his insanity defense and pleaded guilty.

Of mental disorders, the one associated most with serial murder and violent crime in general is psychopathy, which reflects a disorder of personality rather than of the mind. Serial murderers are often labeled psychopaths or sociopaths without a proper clinical diagnosis. Psychopathy comprises a collection of interpersonal, affective, and behavioral features pertaining to the selfish, callous, and remorseless use of others and an impulsive, chronically unstable, and antisocial lifestyle (see Table 14.4 for a full list of the criteria). These traits and behavioral criteria are measured by the Psychopathy Checklists (Hare, 1991). It was claimed that Henry Lee Lucas was devoid of any feelings or concern for his victims; "Killing someone is just like walking outdoors," he said (Jeffers, 1992, p. 45).

Describing the etiology of crime is a difficult task, and some serious research in the area acknowledges that the creation of a serial murderer is a *process* (Canter, 1994; Hickey, 2001). While it was found that some of the above variables correlate with serial murder, correlation does not imply causation. Furthermore, most of the research lacks a comparison group of nonoffenders. For example, it is impossible to conclude that serial killers

Table 14.4   The Revised Psychopathy Checklist (PCL-R)

1. Glibness/superficial charm	11. Promiscuous sexual behavior
2. Grandiose sense of self-worth	12. Early behavior problems
3. Need for stimulation/proneness to boredom	13. Lack of realistic, long-term goals
	14. Impulsivity
4. Pathological lying	15. Irresponsibility
5. Conning/manipulative	16. Failure to accept responsibility for own actions
6. Lack of remorse or guilt	
7. Shallow affect	17. Many short-term marital relationships
8. Callous/lack of empathy	18. Juvenile delinquency
9. Parasitic lifestyle	19. Revocation of conditional release
10. Poor behavioral controls	20. Criminal versatility

SOURCE: Hare (1991, 2003).

have suffered as children to any greater extent than others. While some of the offenders seem to have suffered child abuse, only a small proportion of abused children go on to become violent offenders. And there are many individuals who weren't abused as children who become serial killers.

Female Serial Murderers

Women are rarely viewed by the public as killers; however, although it is relatively rare, there have been a considerable number of female serial murderers throughout history. Much of what we know about why women kill emphasizes the victimization they confront at the hands of a spouse or partner (Egger, 2002; Hickey, 1997; Kelleher & Kelleher, 1998). People often assume that a female could not have wanted to deliberately cause harm. Predatory homicide perpetrated by women (i.e., homicide motivated by reasons other than self-defense or repeated victimization) has not received extensive attention in the relevant literature. Unless the female serial killer fits the profile of a typical male serial killer, it is most likely that she will not be labeled a serial killer. This may be why Aileen Wuornos was labeled by the FBI "America's first female serial killer" (Hickey, 2002), which is not true.

Hickey (1991) identified 34 documented female serial murderers active between 1795 and 1988, and 82% of them had acted after 1900. He found that their average age was 32, the number of victims ranged from 8 to 14, 97% were white, and 18% were nurses. Holmes and Holmes (1998) found that female serial killers were "geographically stable" and lived in the same area where they committed their offences. Even their motivation differs: Hickey (1991) reported that 50% killed for money and 47% mentioned motives of enjoyment and revenge. Insurance benefits, inheritances, and trusts are often the motives for their crimes.

Most women kill people they know. Only about one-third of female serial murderers kill strangers, in contrast to males, who almost exclusively prefer strangers (Holmes, Hickey, & Holmes, 1991). Most victims of female serial murderers are husbands, former husbands, or suitors (the female killers are known as "black widows"). Belle Gunness murdered an estimated 14 to 49 husbands or suitors (Holmes et al., 1991) and Nannie Doss killed 11 husbands and family members (Bartol, 1995). Many female serial murderers are "quiet" killers working in a caring capacity in which the victim is dependent on them (the female killers are known as "angels of death"). Gwendolyn Graham and Catherine Wood suffocated to death at least six nursing home patients under their care. Marybeth Tinning killed nine of her own children one at a time, in order to draw attention. One of the very few female serial killers to target strangers was Aileen Wuornos, a Florida prostitute who shot to death seven men between 1989 and 1990 and was executed for her crimes in 2002. Aileen Wuornos had been severely neglected as a child and had been repeatedly raped (Hickey, 1997). Both her selection of the victims and her style of killing resembled that of a predatory male serial killer.

Research has shown that female serial murderers use less violent methods to kill their victims, and the preferred methods are poisoning (Hickey, 1991; Wilson & Hilton, 1998), lethal injection, and suffocation. Many of them kill with an accomplice, usually a male; for example, Charlene Gallego, the wife of serial killer Gerald Gallego, who helped Gerald select, abduct, and murder at least 10 individuals (Holmes et al., 1991). Rosemary West, wife of Fred West, and Myra Hindley, partner of Ian Brady, are two more examples.

There have been very few attempts to classify female serial murderers, because the majority of available typologies were developed for male serial murderers. Holmes and Holmes (1998) described five types of female serial murderers according to motives and pattern of offences: visionary, comfort, hedonistic, power seeker, and disciple. The *comfort killer* tends to be the most prevalent and includes offenders who kill acquaintances. The *hedonistic killer* is rare. Kelleher and Kelleher (1998) proposed another classification system: black widow, angel of death, revenge killer, profit or crime killer, sexual predator, team killer, question of sanity, unexplained, and unsolved. But as with the male typologies, one should be cautious when using such labels.

Geographical Offender Profiling

Geographical offender profiling involves predicting the home location of an offender based on information about where that offender has committed his or her crimes (Canter & Larkin, 1993; Snook, Canter, & Bennell, 2002). Although the actions of serial killers are difficult to explain, they may have quite direct and everyday reasons for their choice of victim, the murder site, and the body recovery site. While their actions are, in many cases, extreme, that doesn't mean their spatial behaviors will be extreme as well; these will result from their daily activities because criminals behave like any other individual, operating where they know the area and feel safe. The psychological importance of the home (Canter & Larkin, 1993) and familiarity with their surroundings (Brantingham & Brantingham, 1981) influence the spatial decision making of serial murderers.

Based on interviews and analysis of over 400 cases of serial murder, Holmes and DeBurger (1988) proposed a distinction between geographically stable and geographically transient serial killers. *Geographically stable killers* live in the same area for some time and kill and dispose of bodies in the same or a nearby area. *Geographically transient killers* travel continuously from one area to the next and dispose of bodies in far-flung places. Canter and Larkin (1993) have drawn a fundamental distinction between two types of serial criminal offender in terms of the offender's spatial behavior during the execution of his or her series of crimes. *Marauders* operate in an area that is proximate to the home base; *commuters* commit crimes in locations perceived to be distant from the offender's place of residence. In short, while marauders commit their offences in their own neighborhood, commuters go beyond this habitual zone and commit their offences in more remote residential areas.

In the modern mythology of serial murder, the killer is characterized as a nomad whose killing spree takes him hundreds of thousands of miles a year as he drifts from state to state and region to region, leaving scores of victims in his wake. This may be true of some well-known and well-traveled killers like Theodore Bundy, but it is not true of the majority (Levin & Fox, 1985). Hickey (1991) identified three types of serial killers, based on mobility: traveling serial killers who cross states to murder their victims, local serial killers who kill in their home states, and serial killers who kill in their homes or places of work. He found that most of the male offenders were categorized as local killers.

While researchers (Canter, 2003, 2004; Rossmo, 1995, 1997) have stressed the importance of the geographical behavior of serial criminals, empirical research is limited (Labuschagne, 2006). Results from studies on different types of crimes have shown that offenders generally select targets not very far from their homes. Indeed, most offenders, including burglars, rapists, thieves, and robbers, select targets within 5 km of their home (Snook, Cullen, Mokros, & Harbort, 2005). A study of serial rapists shows that the home can be used to define the area in which crimes were committed; Canter and Gregory (1994) showed that very few offenders commuted to other areas to commit their crimes and that in 86% of the cases, the home was within a circle defined by the two crimes furthest from each other.

For serial murderers specifically, research shows that they usually select victims much closer to their homes than the drifter image implies. A limited amount of information is available regarding serial murderers' spatial decisions, and a few studies have quantified the distance between where serial murderers live and where they offend (Canter, Missen, & Hodge, 1996; Godwin & Canter, 1997; Hickey, 1991; Lundrigan & Canter, 2001). Godwin and Canter (1997), studying U.S. serial killers, showed that victim encounter locations were, on average, 2 km from the offender's home, and body recovery locations were 23 km from the offender's home. Lundrigan and Canter (2001) reported that the median and average home-to-crime distances for American serial murderers were 15 km and 40 km, respectively, whereas the median and average home-to-crime distances for UK serial murderers were 9 km and 18 km, respectively. Based on these findings, it appears that serial murderers indeed offend farther from their homes than do other types of criminals, but they still offend relatively close to home. There are also suggestions that "serial offenders commit crimes farther from their home as series lengthen" (Snook et al., 2005, p. 150). For example, John Duffy initially targeted victims from his neighborhood but selected victims farther from his home as he killed more people (Canter, 1994). "Closely associated with series chronology is the belief that serial offenders live in closer proximity to their first crime location than their subsequent crime locations" (Snook et al., 2005, p. 150). Where the victim has last been seen is very important; research shows that the location of initial contact with the victim may be of more direct assistance in helping to delimit the area in which the offender resides than the sites at which victims' bodies are discovered.

More research is needed in this area because an understanding of the processes that shape serial killers' journeys to crime could be a very important investigative tool.

Offender Profiling

Offender profiling is the process of linking offence behaviors to characteristics of the offender (Canter, 1994). In order to establish that a single offender has committed more than one homicide, the homicides must be linked together. While forensic evidence, such as DNA or fingerprints, is the preferred means for linking offences, it is often unavailable to the investigation team (Canter, 1994). During the early 1970s, Special Agents of the FBI's Behavioral Science Unit (BSU) began profiling criminals by using crime scene information to deduce certain offender characteristics. But, even if the term was new, offender profiling wasn't. In 1888, Thomas Bond, a surgeon, compiled a detailed description of Jack the Ripper, and during the Second World War, William Langer, a psychiatrist, compiled a profile of Adolf Hitler.

But does offender profiling work? Whether it is effective or not is a key question, and historically, there are famous successes and failures. One of the best-known failures in the U.S. was the case of Albert DeSalvo (known as the Boston Strangler). A profile suggested the offender was a male homosexual school teacher living alone. As it turned out, Albert DeSalvo was a heterosexual construction worker living with his family. In the UK, the Rachel Nickell case is seen as a failure of offender profiling (see Case Study: Rachel Nickell).

CASE STUDY: RACHEL NICKELL

On July 15, 1992, Rachel Nickell was walking on Wimbledon Common, South London when she was attacked. Her attacker cut her throat, stabbed her 49 times, and sexually assaulted her while her young son was present. The investigation quickly targeted Colin Stagg, an unemployed man from Roehampton who was known to walk his dog in the area. Because the police didn't have any scientific evidence to link Mr. Stagg to the scene, they asked criminal psychologist Paul Britton to create an offender profile of the killer. They decided that Stagg fit the profile and asked Britton to assist in designing a covert operation. An operation was put together in which a female police officer befriended the suspect, promising him an intimate relationship in exchange for a description of his sexual fantasies and a confession that he murdered Rachel. The confession was not forthcoming, but Stagg was still arrested and charged. When the case reached the court, the judge said that the police had tried to incriminate a suspect by deceptive conduct of the grossest kind. The entrapment evidence was excluded, the case fell apart, Stagg was acquitted, and in 2008 he was awarded £706,000 (approximately $1,300,000) for damages. On November 28, 2007, a 41-year-old man, Robert Napper, was charged with Nickell's murder.

Holmes (1989) cites FBI data that reveal that in 1981, arrests were made in 88 of 192 cases in which profiles were generated, but the profile contributed to the arrest in only 17% of the 88 cases.

One of the major criticisms of profiling is its current lack of scientific foundation, its vagueness, and its lack of usefulness to investigators (Egger, 1998; Levin & Fox, 1985). In the UK, offender profiling has been dominated by the work of David Canter, who was approached by the police in 1985 to assist them in a notorious serial murder case, the "Railway Rapist." During

1982 and 1986, a man raped and murdered women in the south of England. Canter's profile described the offender and where he lived so accurately that the police were able to arrest John Duffy, who was subsequently convicted in 1988 of three murders and seven rapes (see Table 14.5). He was sentenced to 30 years in prison, and since then, a further 12 years have been added to his sentence for a further 17 convictions for rape. This was the first case that David Canter was asked to help with and the first application of investigative psychology, which is concerned with psychological input to the full range of issues that relate to the management, investigation, and prosecution of crime (Canter, 2004). Canter's approach to profiling is much more rooted in psychological principles than is the approach of the FBI, and he emphasizes the need for a systematic research approach to the relationship between offender crime actions and offender characteristics, describing profiling based on crime scene analysis as "more of an art than a science" (Canter, 1989, p. 12). He uses psychological principles and empirical approaches to draw thematic models of crime actions and link them to the offender's characteristics and has applied the thematic models to different types of crimes (Canter & Fritzon, 1998; Canter & Heritage, 1990; Salfati & Canter, 1999). This is done by using "pools" of behaviors that all have the same underlying psychological meaning, as first outlined by Canter (2000). For example, an offender is gagging his victim in one crime and binding her in another. The offender is using different individual behaviors, but both behaviors have the same underlying psychological meaning: control (see Canter & Heritage, 1990). Following the work of Canter (2000), Hodgskiss (2003) found that serial murderers' offence behaviors could be divided into thematic models.

Table 14.5   Profile Drawn by David Canter

Main Points of Canter's Profile	Characteristics of John Duffy
Lived in area circumscribed by the first three cases since 1983	Lived in the area suggested (Kilburn)
Probably lives with wife/girlfriend, possibly without children	Was recently separated from his wife
Aged mid to late 20s	Aged late 20s
Semi-skilled or skilled job involving weekend work	He was a traveling carpenter
Has knowledge of the railway system	He worked for British Rail
Previous criminal record for violence (maybe arrested between October, 1982 and January, 1984)	Arrested for raping his wife at knife point

Except for a few attempts, there hasn't been much research on linking serial homicides. Bateman and Salfati (2007) examined 35 serial homicide behaviors utilized by 90 offenders in 450 serial homicide cases, to examine whether these offenders consistently performed the same behaviors across their series of homicides, which is essential when linking homicides together and to a common offender. The study showed the difficulty in doing this, questioning current theories that suggest that signatures or specific key behaviors are important to understand the consistency in an offender's behavior across crimes.

But one has to be cautious when it comes to offender profiling. A profile cannot identify a suspect for investigation, nor can it eliminate a suspect who does not fit the profile. Human behavior in general, and criminal behavior specifically, is extremely variable, making precise predictions problematic. If an offender profile can be drawn based on systematic, scientific research, it will allow the investigator to identify and prioritize suspects, but an overreliance on the contents of a profile can misdirect a serial murder investigation, sometimes quite seriously.

Conclusion

A considerable number of theorists and researchers looked into serial murder, and a plethora of theories, typologies, and risk factors have been reported; abuse, adoption, abandonment, learning and physical disabilities, academic failure, pornography, and rejection may be important factors, but they are neither necessary nor sufficient to make someone a serial murderer. Biological, psychological, and sociological theories have tried to explain the phenomenon, but no single explanation is adequate to account for all serial murderers, especially as there are many different types of offenders with different motives. Human behavior in general, and criminal behavior in particular, are so varied that determining a single motive is problematic.

Despite the many theories, books, and media coverage, there have been very few well-designed, empirically based studies on serial murder. Most of the knowledge we have is based on clinical observations, investigative reports, interviews with very small samples, and anecdotal data (Bartol, 1995). There have been very few studies attempting to link offence characteristics to offender characteristics, which is crucial if we want offender profiling to become something more than an art and intuition. There is a need for systematic research in order to understand serial murder. There is a need to shift away from traditional misconceptions of the mad, sexually sadistic individual and look in the direction of the ordinary person and his individual, unique story. As Theodore Bundy once said, "We are your sons, and we are your husbands, and we grew up in normal families" (Lamar, 1984).

Discussion Questions

1. Discuss different serial murder typologies and how and whether they can be utilized for investigative purposes.

2. Is it possible to identify the characteristics of an offender from the crime scene?

3. Describe the main differences between male and female serial murderers.

4. Do you think that offender profiling is an effective investigative tool? Discuss the advantages and disadvantages of the different approaches that are currently used in drawing an offender's profile.

5. How can geographical profiling assist police during serial murder investigations?

Internet Resources

CrimeLibrary.com: http://www.crimelibrary.com/

Elizabeth Bathory: http://www.crimelibrary.com/serial_killers/predators/bathory/countess_1.html

Federal Resources on Missing and Exploited Children: http://www.ncjrs.gov/pdffiles1/ojjdp/206555.pdf

Serial Killers and Mass Murderers: http://crime.about.com/od/serial/Serial_Killers_and_Mass_Murderers.htm

Ted Bundy: http://www.crimelibrary.com/serial_killers/notorious/bundy/index_1.html

References

Bartol, C. R. (1995). *Criminal behavior: A psychosocial approach.* Upper Saddle River, NJ: Prentice Hall.

Bateman, A., & Salfati, G. (2007). An examination of behavioral consistency using individual behaviors or groups of behaviors in serial homicide. *Behavioral Sciences and the Law, 25,* 527–544.

Brantingham, P. L., & Brantingham, P. J. (1981). *Environmental criminology.* Beverley Hills, CA: Sage.

Canter, D. (1989). Offender profiles. *Psychologist, 2*(1), 12–16.

Canter, D. (1994). *Criminal shadows.* London: HarperCollins.

Canter, D. (2000). Offender profiling and criminal differentiation. *Legal and Criminological Psychology, 5,* 23–46.

Canter, D. (2003). *Mapping murder: The secrets of geographical profiling.* London: Virgin Books.

Canter, D. (2004). Geographic profiling of criminals. *Medico-legal Journal, 72,* 53–66.

Canter, D. V., Alison, L. J., Alison, E., & Wentink, N. (2004). The organized/disorganized typology of serial murder: Myth or model? *Psychology, Public Policy, and Law, 10*(3), 293–320.

Canter, D., & Fritzon, K. (1998). Differentiating arsonists: A model of firesetting actions and characteristics. *Legal and Criminal Psychology, 3,* 73–79.

Canter, D. V., & Gregory, A. (1994). Identifying the residential location of rapists. *Journal of the Forensic Science Society, 34,* 169–175.

Canter, D., & Heritage, R. (1990). A multivariate model of sexual offence behaviour: Developments in "offender profiling." *The Journal of Forensic Psychiatry, 1*(2), 185–212.

Canter, D., & Larkin, P. (1993). The environmental range of serial rapists. *Journal of Environmental Psychology, 13,* 63–69.

Canter, D., Missen, C., & Hodge, S. (1996). Are serial killers special? A case for special agents. *Policing Today, 2*(1), 22–28.

Canter, D. V., & Wentink, N. (2004). An empirical test of the Holmes and Holmes serial murder typology. *Criminal Justice and Behavior, 31*(4), 489–515.

Delisi, M., & Sherer, A. M. (2006). Multiple homicide offenders: Offence characteristics, social correlates, and criminal careers. *Criminal Justice and Behaviour, 33*(3), 367–391.

Dietz, P. E. (1986). Mass, serial and sensational homicide. *Bulletin of the New York Academy of Science, 62,* 477–491.

Douglas, J., Burgess, A., Burgess, A., & Ressler, R. (1992). *Crime classification manual.* Lexington, MA: Lexington Books.

Douglas, J., & Olshaker, M. (1999). *Anatomy of motive.* New York: Pocket Books.

Egger, S. A. (1984). A working definition of serial murder and the reduction of linkage blindness. *Journal of Police Science and Administration, 12,* 348–356.

Egger, S. A. (1998). *The killers among us: An examination of serial murder and its investigation.* Upper Saddle River, NJ: Prentice Hall.

Egger, S. (2002). *The killers among us: An examination of serial murder and its investigation* (2nd ed.). Upper Saddle River, NJ: Prentice Hall.

Esmail, A. (2005). Physician as serial killer—the Shipman case. *New England Journal of Medicine, 352,* 1843–1844.

Federal Bureau of Investigation. (1969). *Crime in the United States: The Uniform Crime Reports.* Washington, DC: U.S. Government Printing Office.

Federal Bureau of Investigation. (1995). *Crime in the United States: The Uniform Crime Reports.* Washington, DC: U.S. Government Printing Office.

Ferguson, C. J., White, D. E., Cherry, S., Lorenz, M., & Bhimani, Z. (2003). Defining and classifying serial murder in the context of perpetrator motivation. *Journal of Criminal Justice, 31,* 287–292.

Fox, J. A., & Levin, J. (1994). *Overkill: Mass murder and serial killing exposed.* New York: Plenum Press.

Fox, J. A., & Levin, J. (1996). *Killer on campus.* New York: Avon.

Fox, J. A., & Levin, J. (1998). Multiple homicide: Patterns of serial and mass murder. *Crime and Justice, 23,* 407–455.

Fox, J. A., & Levin, J. (1999). Popular myths and empirical realities. In D. Smith & M. Zahn (Eds.), *Homicide: A sourcebook of social research* (p. 165). Thousand Oaks, CA: Sage.

Fox, J. A., & Levin, J. (2003). Mass murder: An analysis of extreme violence. *Journal of Applied Psychoanalytic Studies, 5,* 47–64.

Gibbons, D. C. (1988). Some critical observations on critical types and criminal careers. *Criminal Justice and Behaviour, 15,* 8–23.

Godwin, G. M. (2000). *Hunting serial predators: A multivariate classification approach to profiling violent behavior.* Boca Raton, FL: CRC Press.

Godwin, G. M., & Canter, D. (1997). Encounter and death: The spatial behaviour of U.S. serial killers. *Policing: International Journal of Police Strategy and Management, 20,* 24–38.

Gresswell, D. M., & Hollin, C. R. (1994). Multiple murder: A review. *British Journal of Criminology, 34*, 1–14.

Hare, D. (1991). *Hare psychopathy checklist–revised.* New York: Multi-Health Systems.

Hare, R. D. (2003). *Hare psychopathy checklist-revised (PCL-R): Technical manual* (2nd ed.). Toronto: Multi-Health Systems.

Harrower, J. (1998). *Applying psychology to crime.* London: Hodder & Stoughton.

Hazelwood, R. R., & Douglas, J. E. (1980). The lust murderer. *FBI Law Enforcement Bulletin,* 18–22.

Hazelwood, R., & Warren, J. (1995). The serial rapist. In R. Hazelwood & A. W. Burgess (Eds.), *Practical aspects of rape investigation.* Boca Raton, FL: CRC Press.

Hickey, E. W. (1991). *Serial murderers and their victims.* Belmont, CA: Wadsworth.

Hickey, E. W. (1997). *Serial murderers and their victims* (2nd ed.). Belmont, CA: Wadsworth.

Hickey, E. W. (2001). *Serial murderers and their victims.* Belmont, CA: Wadsworth.

Hickey, E. (2002). *Serial murderers and their victims* (3rd ed.). Belmont, CA: Wadsworth.

Hodgskiss, B. (2003). Lessons from serial murder in South Africa. *Journal of Investigative Psychology and Offender Profiling, 1*(1), 67–94.

Holmes, R. (1989). *Profiling violent crimes.* Newbury Park, CA: Sage.

Holmes, R. M., & DeBurger, J. (1988). *Serial murder.* Newbury Park, CA: Sage.

Holmes, S. T., Hickey, E., & Holmes, R. M. (1991). Female serial murderesses: Constructing differentiating typologies. *Journal of Contemporary Criminal Justice, 7,* 245–256.

Holmes, R. M., & Holmes, S. T. (1998). *Serial murder* (2nd ed.). Thousand Oaks, CA: Sage.

Jeffers, P. H. (1992). *Profiles in evil.* London: Warner Books.

Jenkins, P. (1988). Serial murder in England 1940–1985. *Journal of Criminal Justice, 16,* 1–15.

Keeney, B. T., & Heide, K. M. (1994). Gender differences in serial murderers: A preliminary analysis. *Journal of Interpersonal Violence, 9,* 37–56.

Kelleher, M. D., & Kelleher, C. L. (1998). *Murder most rare: The female serial killer.* Westport, CT: Praeger.

Keppel, R. D., & Walter, R. (1999). Profiling killers: A revised classification model for understanding sexual murder. *International Journal of Offender Therapy and Comparative Criminology, 43*(4), 417–437.

Kraemer, G. W., Lord, W. D., Heilbrun, K. (2004). Comparing single and serial homicide offenses. *Behavioural Sciences and the Law, 22,* 325–343.

Labuschagne, G. N. (2006). The use of a linkage analysis as evidence in the conviction of the Newcastle serial murderer, South Africa. *Journal of Investigative Psychology and Offender Profiling, 3*(3), 183–191.

Lamar, J. V. (1984). Trail of death. *Time,* pp. 123–126.

Levin, J., & Fox, J. A. (1985). *Mass murder: America's growing menace.* New York: Plenum Press.

Lundrigan, S., & Canter, D. (2001). A multivariate analysis of serial murderers' disposal site location choice. *Journal of Environmental Psychology, 21,* 423–432.

MacDonald, T. M. (1963). The threat to kill. *American Journal of Psychiatry, 120,* 125–130.

Meloy, J. R. (2000). The nature and dynamics of sexual homicide: An integrative review. *Aggression and Violent Behaviour, 5*(1), 1–22.

Prentky, R. A, Burgess, A. W., Rokous, F., Lee, A., Hartman, C., Ressler, R., et al. (1989). The presumptive role of fantasy in serial sexual homicide. *American Journal of Psychiatry, 147*(7), 887–891.

Ressler, R. K., Burgess, A. W., & Douglas, J. E. (1988). *Sexual homicide.* Lexington, MA: Lexington Books.

Ressler, R. K., Burgess, A. W., Douglas, J. R., Hartman, C. R., & D'Agostino, R. B. (1986).

Sexual killers and their victims: Identifying patterns through crime scene analysis. *Journal of Interpersonal Violence, 1,* 288–308.

Rossmo, D. K. (1995). Place, space, and police investigations: Hunting serial violent criminals. In J. E. Eck & D. L. Weisburd (Eds.), *Crime and place: Crime prevention studies* (Vol. 4, pp. 217–235). Monsey, NY: Criminal Justice Press.

Rossmo, K. (1997). Geographic profiling. In J. L. Jackson & D. A. Bekerian (Eds.), *Offender profiling: Theory, research and practice* (pp. 159–176). New York: John Wiley and Sons.

Rush, G. E. (2003). *The dictionary of criminal justice* (6th ed.). New York: Dushkin/McGraw-Hill.

Salfati, C. G., & Bateman, A. L. (2005). Serial homicide: An investigation of behavioural consistency. *Journal of Investigative Psychology and Offender Profiling, 2*(2), 121–144.

Salfati, G., & Canter, D. (1999). Differentiating stranger murders: Profiling offender characteristics from behavioural styles. *Behavioural Sciences and the Law, 17,* 391–406.

Snook, B., Canter, D., & Bennell, C. (2002). Predicting the home location of serial offenders: A preliminary comparison of the accuracy of human judges with a geographic profiling system. *Behavioral Sciences and the Law, 20,* 109–118.

Snook, B., Cullen, R. M., Mokros, A., & Harbort, S. (2005). Serial murderers' spatial decisions: Factors that influence crime location choice. *Journal of Investigative Psychology and Offender Profiling, 2*(3), 147–164.

Wilson, W., & Hilton, T. (1998). Modus operandi of female serial killers. *Psychological Reports, 82,* 495–498.

Recommended Reading

Books

Canter, D. (1994). *Criminal shadows.* London: HarperCollins.

Canter, D. (2003). *Mapping murder: The secrets of geographical profiling.* London: Virgin Books.

Hickey, E. (2002). *Serial murderers and their victims* (3rd ed.). Belmont, CA: Wadsworth.

Ressler, R. K., Burgess, A. W., & Douglas, J. E. (1988). *Sexual homicide.* Lexington, MA: Lexington Books.

Journals

Bateman, A., & Salfati, G. (2007). An examination of behavioral consistency using individual behaviors or groups of behaviors in serial homicide. *Behavioral Sciences and the Law, 25,* 527–544.

Canter, D. (2000). Offender profiling and criminal differentiation. *Legal and Criminological Psychology, 5,* 23–46.

Canter, D. V., Alison, L. J., Alison, E., & Wentink, N. (2004). The organized/disorganized typology of serial murder: Myth or model? *Psychology, Public Policy, and Law, 10*(3), 293–320.

Delisi, M., & Sherer, A. M. (2006). Multiple homicide offenders: Offence characteristics, social correlates, and criminal careers. *Criminal Justice and Behaviour, 33*(3), 367–391.

Fox, J. A., & Levin, J. (1998). Multiple homicide: Patterns of serial and mass murder. *Crime and Justice, 23,* 407–455.

Gresswell, D. M., & Hollin, C. R. (1994). Multiple murder: A review. *British Journal of Criminology, 34,* 1–14.

Keppel, R. D., & Walter, R. (1999). Profiling killers: A revised classification model for understanding sexual murder. *International Journal of Offender Therapy and Comparative Criminology, 43*(4), 417–437.

Lundrigan, S., & Canter, D. (2001). A multivariate analysis of serial murderers' disposal site location choice. *Journal of Environmental Psychology, 21,* 423–432.

PART III

Victims, Prevention, and Treatment

CHAPTER 15

Victimology

Arthur J. Lurigio

Introduction

Criminal victimization is common in the United States and has been part of the American landscape since colonial times (Friedman, 1993). Millions of Americans have fallen victim to violent, property, or other kinds of crimes each year (Herman & Waul, 2004). The number and type of crimes reported to the police and in victimization surveys wax and wane, for reasons that baffle criminologists and other experts. Changes in crime rates are usually correlated with changes in the economy, illegal drug markets, crime control strategies, and the population's age distribution (Blumstein & Wallman, 2000). Specifically, a high unemployment rate, the introduction of a new illicit drug sold by rival gangs, the adoption of public-order policing tactics, and a large population between the ages of 16 and 25 almost always signal a significant growth in arrests nationwide. However, these changes never fully account for why crimes are committed or who will become a crime victim.

CASE STUDY: SUSAN

On Wednesday, December 12, 2001, at 4:09 p.m., Susan T.'s (age 40) life changed instantaneously and forever. A successful small business owner and divorced mother of an 11-year-old son, Thomas, Susan lived in a beautifully decorated townhouse in a quiet suburb northwest of Chicago. Her one-year relationship with her live-in boyfriend, James F. (age 53), had been volatile. According to Susan's close friends, the relationship had recently become more tense and dissatisfying for them both. They argued incessantly about James's jealousy and Susan's

(Continued)

(Continued)

lack of attention to financial matters, especially those related to the shared costs of their home. During the previous year, the couple had repeatedly broken up and reconciled. Susan told her best friend Carol L. that she was "very unhappy with James" and had decided to "kick him out of the house." At Thanksgiving dinner, Susan's family noticed that she was uncharacteristically quiet and seemed sad, which was in stark contrast to her usual ebullient personality.

On the afternoon of December 12, Susan and James's longstanding argument about money escalated to a high-pitched level. Having come home from school to become an involuntary witness to the argument from another room, Susan's son observed that his mother was sitting on the bottom steps facing the front door and leading to the upstairs of the townhouse. James hovered over her, demanding that she return his investment in the home ($60,000) and pay the credit card debt ($1,500) that she had recently incurred. Although he apparently had never struck Susan, James faced anger management problems (he was arrested twice for domestic battery charges in his previous marriage). At approximately 4:05 p.m., his words and gestures became more menacing, and he threatened Susan with physical violence. Susan warned James that she would ask her ex-husband (Thomas's father) to retaliate if he hurt her. As a result of her counterthreat, James became livid, and Susan yelled for Thomas to call his father. When Thomas was unable to reach him, Susan pleaded with Thomas to call 911, which he did immediately.

Enraged, James stormed out of the house. Within seconds, he returned with a handgun (a 9-mm semi-automatic). Thomas heard him pull back the gun's chamber and saw him point the weapon at his mother's left temple. Thomas reported that the gunfire sounded "like a firecracker." James shot Susan once. He fled the scene, jumped into his jeep, and sped out of the driveway. Susan slid down the stairs on her backside as blood gushed from her head wound. The ambulance and police arrived within five minutes of Thomas's emergency call. Thomas gave the police descriptive information about James's vehicle and license plate number as well as the direction in which he fled. Susan was rushed to the closest local hospital. Recognizing the severity of her wounds, the medical staff stabilized her, and she was transported by special ambulance to a hospital with a major trauma and neurological intensive care unit (ICU).

Soon after James shot Susan, he was cornered in a police road block. He exchanged shots with the police. In a desperate effort to escape, he then turned his vehicle around, aimed it at a police officer, and pressed the accelerator to the floor. By 4:18 p.m., James was dead, shot twice in the head by police officers, leaving behind his elderly mother and two children in their twenties. His car careened into a pond with his body slumped over the steering wheel. The shootings were the lead story on the local 10:00 p.m. evening news. In televised and newspaper interviews, neighbors expressed shock and outrage, characterizing James and Susan as a "friendly, upbeat couple." Susan's distraught parents and siblings and their spouses were dumbfounded; they had no knowledge of Susan and James's heated arguments or impending separation.

The physicians who examined Susan in the second hospital's emergency room noted that she had an entry wound in her left temporal lobe and an exit wound, three inches away, in her left occipital lobe. In the first several hours after the shooting, Susan's condition was extremely critical. She lost a considerable amount of blood and was transfused and intubated; she remained unresponsive, but her vital signs became relatively stable. The neurosurgeons' news was grim.

Susan's prognosis was poor; her odds of living through the night were 50-50. Surgery was scheduled for the next morning. Fortunately, a CAT scan revealed that the bullet had not crossed the brain's left or right hemispheres, which is almost always fatal. Despite two surgeries—the first lessened the pressure in her cranium that was caused by brain swelling and the second removed skull fragments from her brain and repaired the damage from the wounds by grafting bone matter and skin from her hip to her head—the bullet was left in her brain; it could not be removed because of its proximity to a major artery.

Susan was moved to the neurological ICU and placed in a medically induced coma for four days. She subsequently remained in a natural coma for nearly two weeks before slowly regaining consciousness. Susan started by tracking her visitors with her eyes and showed some recognition of her family members and the ICU nurses who had cared for her since her arrival at the hospital. Although she was conscious and breathing on her own, Susan could not speak, sit up, or move her right arm or leg, which were also insensitive to pain and pressure. Susan was hospitalized for six weeks and lost nearly 30 pounds, subsisting on a feeding tube.

She was transferred to an internationally recognized rehabilitation institute. She started forming unintelligible sentences and greeting visitors with a smile. Her hair, which had been shaved off for her surgeries, began to grow back. Her family joked that "with her crew cut, she looked just like her brother Chris." Every day, she engaged in hours of painful rehabilitative exercises and participated in speech therapy.

During this time, Susan's family attempted to sue James's estate, but the case was dismissed. Susan was released from the inpatient care after eight weeks and returned to her parents' house, where she lived under their care for several more months. Her excellent rehabilitation services, which included six additional weeks of outpatient services, made it possible for Susan to regain partial use of her right leg and engage in very simple conversations; however, she had difficulty understanding numbers and could not count or read. Her young nieces spent many hours teaching Susan to read from their children's books, reading her pages and pointing to the names of words and pictures. Throughout her ordeal, Susan remained upbeat and maintained an unstinting sense of humor and optimism.

Today, Susan lives in her own condominium with her son. She made the down payment using the profit from the sale of her previous home—the site of the attempted murder. Her parents pay her monthly mortgage and utility bills. Susan received $24,000 in victim compensation from the Illinois Attorney General's Office's Crime Victim Compensation Program, the maximum settlement allowed by statute. She received an initial payment of $12,000 and 12 monthly installments of $1,000 each, until the maximum benefit was paid. Because of her disability, Susan also receives monthly social security benefits and, for her healthcare costs, she receives Medicaid, Medicare, and Kid's Care—an Illinois benefit program for children under 18 years old. To enable Susan to maintain her independence and obviate the need for nursing home care, the state pays a specially trained home care aide to assist her with shopping, transportation, home maintenance, and other chores.

As of October, 2007, Susan must still use a cane to walk. She tries to get around without the cane as often as she can and practices walking unassisted daily. She has never regained the use of her right hand. However, she cooks for herself and her son, keeps a tidy house, and has a part-time job at Target, where she retrieves misplaced merchandise and returns it to its proper place on the shelves. She takes the bus to work. She thoroughly enjoys her job, which gives her a sense of accomplishment and self-worth. Susan has a boyfriend, Phil, who joins her in the care of the condominium and runs errands for her, as needed. Their favorite activities are visiting friends and going out to dinner. Meanwhile, Thomas is seeing a psychiatrist for chronic depression, insomnia, and anxiety problems stemming from his mother's shooting and its life-altering consequences. He has difficulty with school and experiences frequent nightmares.

In the United States, crime rates steadily declined from the mid-1980s to the mid-1990s, continuing this downward trend into the 21st century. During this period, the national homicide rate—a barometer that public officials and residents use to gauge the overall safety of their communities—dropped to a 30-year low (Blumstein & Wallman, 2000). In addition, between 1993 and 2005, the violent and property crime rates decreased 58% and 52%, respectively (Catalano, 2006). From 1991 to 2004, the violent crime rate fell nearly 40%, from 758 per 100,000 persons to 463 per 100,000 persons (Federal Bureau of Investigation, 2006). Consequently, by 2004, the overall crime rate was roughly the same as it was in 1970, and the murder rate had fallen to its lowest level since 1965 (Bureau of Justice Statistics, 2006a).

Such fairly steady reductions in crime over the past 15 years should be welcome news to Americans. Nevertheless, the volume of violent crimes committed annually in the United States is still at a staggering level, compared to other industrialized nations (Farrington, Langan, & Tonry, 2004), and fear of crime is as rampant as ever in this country (Warr, 2000). Whatever its causes—and despite recent drops in crime—criminal victimization continues to transform people's lives, leaving a host of human misery in its wake that affects not only the victims but also their partners, family members, friends, and neighbors (Herman & Waul, 2004; Skogan, Lurigio, & Davis, 1990).

The current chapter focuses on the nature, extent, and cost of crime in the United States as well as the efforts that have been made to alleviate victim harm and suffering and to promote victims' rights. The chapter is divided into two major sections. The first section discusses how crime data are collected and disseminated; it presents recent statistics on reported crime and victimization rates and on the tangible and intangible costs of criminal victimization. The first section also examines the risk of victimization and the victim's responsibility for the incident. The second section describes the crime victims' movement and the initiation of legal reforms and services on behalf of crime victims and their families; it focuses on the President's Task Force on Victims of Crime, the Victims of Crime Act, victims' rights, and victim compensation and services programs, implemented to help victims recover from trauma and economic burden.

Nature, Extent, and Costs of Crime

Uniform Crime Report

Crime in the United States is primarily measured and reported through two mechanisms: the Uniform Crime Report (UCR) program and the National Crime Victimization Survey (NCVS). The UCR program was created in 1929 by the International Chiefs of Police Association, in order to establish a standard and reliable methodology for collecting and communicating crime data throughout the United States. The Federal Bureau of Investigation (FBI) assumed responsibility for the UCR program in 1930.

The UCR program obtains information on crimes that are reported to or discovered by the police; police department administrators compile these data in monthly reports that are submitted to the FBI for analysis and dissemination. The focus of the UCR program is eight major "street" crimes, known as Part I Index Crimes: homicide, rape, robbery, and aggravated assault, identified as violent crimes; and burglary, theft, motor vehicle theft, and arson, identified as property crimes. A major limitation of the UCR program is that it gathers only "official" crime data, consisting of offenses that come to the attention of police officers and are recorded in police departments' records; unreported crimes are thus not included (Schmalleger, 2007). The UCR program can present crime data for the nation as a whole, or it can disaggregate the information by regions of the country, states, counties, and cities or towns.

Reported Crime

According to the UCR data, in 2006, more than 1.4 million violent crimes were reported in the United States—a rate of 474 violent crimes for every 100,000 persons. The most frequently reported violent crime was aggravated assault (61%), followed by robbery (32%), rape (6%), and murder (1%). Firearms were used in nearly 70% of homicides, 42% of robberies, and 22% of aggravated assaults. In addition, property crimes were much more numerous than violent crimes, totaling more than 9.9 million offenses—a rate of 3,335 property crimes for every 100,000 persons. More than two-thirds of property crimes were thefts (FBI, 2006).

Both property and violent crimes were more likely to occur in major metropolitan areas than in suburban and rural areas. The highest percentages of both property and violent crimes occurred in the South, followed by the Western, Midwestern, and Northeastern regions of the country. The proportion of murders that occurred in the South (43%) was more than three times greater than the proportion that occurred in the Northeast (12%; FBI, 2006). The only exception was motor vehicle theft, which was most prevalent in the Western region of the United States.

The FBI established its Crime Clock to roughly estimate the relative frequency of Part I Index Crimes during fixed time intervals. However, the clock's data do not literally suggest that such crimes occur with any precise temporal regularity (Schmalleger, 2007). In 2005, the Crime Clock indicated that a violent crime was committed every 23 seconds and a property crime every 3 seconds. In other words, someone was killed every 30 minutes, raped every 6 minutes, and robbed every 1 minute. A car was stolen every 25 seconds, a house was burglarized every 15 seconds, and property was stolen every 5 seconds (FBI, 2005).

National Crime Victimization Survey

The NCVS, administered by the Bureau of Justice Statistics and conducted by the Census Bureau, was designed to illuminate the "dark figure" of crime, namely, offenses that never come to the attention of the police. The NCVS asks questions mostly about Part I Index Crimes, except for arson and homicide, but it does not measure crimes against businesses (i.e., commercial crimes). Each year, approximately 150,000 NCVS interviews are conducted with persons aged 12 or older to gather detailed information about both reported and unreported crimes as well as data on victims (such as age, gender, and race), offenders (such as age and the offender's relationship to the victim), and the crime itself (such as any weapons used, the location of the offense, and the economic costs and physical injuries caused by the victimization). With regard to overall trends, the findings of the UCR and NCVS are closely matched; for example, both show that property crimes are much more numerous than violent crimes, crime rates are higher in cities than in suburbs, and young men are the most likely victims and perpetrators of violent offenses. Indeed, when crime goes up in one data set, it goes up in the other, and vice versa.

Victimizations. According to the NCVS, an estimated 23 million individuals were victimized (some multiple times) in 2005, most of whom (18 million, or 78%) were victims of property crimes (burglary, theft, and motor vehicle theft). The remainder (5 million, or 22%) were victims of violent crimes (rape, robbery, and aggravated assault), which are generally more serious with respect to victim and societal harm. In a hierarchical counting scheme, the NCVS records only the most serious crime committed against an individual who suffered repeat victimizations. Many people are indirect or vicarious victims of crime, negatively affected when they know or have heard about someone who has been victimized. Direct and vicarious victimization fuels fear of crime, which keeps residents indoors at night, affecting "commerce (retail business), road use, leisure activities, and social interaction" (Warr, 2000, p. 481). Deserted streets encourage more victimization, creating a vicious cycle of crime, disorder, and neighborhood decline (Skogan, 1990).

Reporting Crime. In 2005, victims reported to the police less than half the violent victimizations and only 40% of the property victimizations experienced that year (Catalano, 2006). A victim's decision to report a crime to the police is essential to solving the crime, for several reasons. Without a victim's report, the police might receive sketchy or no information about an offense or alleged offender; limited information hampers their ability to concentrate resources against certain crimes or suspects or in certain parts of the community (i.e., "bad" neighborhoods). The absence of a report also precludes an arrest, clearing an incident, or removing from the street criminals who could victimize other residents. In addition, most victim service and compensation programs rely on police referrals. Thus, by not reporting a crime, victims are depriving themselves of ameliorative care and private insurance claims, which require a police report (Skogan, 1984).

The decision to report a crime has little to do with victim characteristics (e.g., race, gender, or income) and a lot to do with the crime incident itself (Skogan, 1984). The seriousness of the victimization is an important factor in the decision to report a crime to the police. For example, in the 2005 NCVS, the most common reasons that victims did not report a crime to the police were the offender was unsuccessful (it was an attempted, rather than a completed, crime) or the property was recovered (the incident involved minimal or no financial loss; Bureau of Justice Statistics, 2006c). Further explanations for not reporting a crime included victims' perceptions that the incident was "not important enough" to report or that the incident was "a private or personal matter." Moreover, victims did not call the police if they believed that the "police would not want to be bothered" with the incident or that the police are "ineffective or biased" (Bureau of Justice Statistics, 2006b). Others did not report their victimization because they distrust the police or want to avoid being labeled a "victim" (Bachman & Saltzman, 1995; Feldman-Summers & Ashworth, 1991).

Victim Characteristics. Crime is more likely to strike certain residents than others; the likelihood of victimization is determined by who an individual is, where that individual lives, and how much money that individual earns. For example, the most likely victims of violent crime in 2005 were young men—especially those under the age of 24. Young African American men were particularly vulnerable to homicide, while young African American women were more often victims of rape and sexual assault than were older, non-African American women. In general, men were more likely to be attacked by strangers, whereas women were more likely to be attacked by someone they knew. Interestingly, persons who identified themselves as members of two or more races were significantly more likely to be victims of violent crime, compared to persons who identified themselves as white, African American, or Latino (Catalano, 2006).

In addition, poor people (i.e., those with an annual income of less than $7,500) were more likely to be victims of robbery and assault, compared to people with incomes of $35,000 or more. Never-married persons had higher rates of victimization than those in other marital status categories. City dwellers experienced the highest rates of both property and violent crime, followed by suburbanites and rural dwellers. Finally, homeowners were more immune to every type of property crime than were renters (Catalano, 2006).

NCVS data also suggest a relationship between occupation and victimization risk (Karmen, 2004). For example, the occupations safest from robbery are farmers, engineers, elementary school teachers, psychologists, and college professors (Warchol, 1998); among the most at risk are taxi drivers, amusement park workers, car wash attendants, and musicians (Block, Felson, & Block, 1985). Irrespective of occupation, the risk of being a crime victim accumulates over a lifetime (Koppel, 1987). For example, as Karmen (2004) observed,

> Over a span of about 60 years, nearly everybody will experience at least one theft, and most people may eventually suffer three or more thefts, according to the projections made on the basis of rates that prevailed in the 1970s and 1980s. (p. 81)

Households. The NCVS also reports annual crime by counting the number of households struck by crime, enabling researchers to examine the concentration or distribution of crime around the country. In 2005, 14%—16 million households—had at least one member aged 12 or older who experienced one or more violent or property victimizations. Approximately 12% of the households experienced a property crime, while approximately 2% experienced a violent crime. Where people live and their racial and ethnic origins were found to be related to household victimization; households in the Western United States were more likely than households in other regions of the country to be touched by one or more crimes, while households in urban areas were involved in criminal victimization more often than those in suburban and rural areas. Households with larger numbers of members and those headed by Latinos also experienced greater numbers of victimizations (Klaus, 2007).

Lifestyle, Risk, and Victim Responsibility

Several explanatory models suggest that lifestyle affects the risk of criminal victimization (Hindelang, Gottfredson, & Garofalo, 1978). For example, frequenting bars in high-crime areas and exiting them alone and intoxicated in the middle of the night creates a recipe for becoming a victim of armed robbery or some other type of violent crime. Taxi drivers and musicians often work late hours in or around bars in high-crime areas—lifestyle factors that might explain their high rates of robbery victimization. In contrast, spending quiet evenings in a secure suburban home, reading a book by the fireplace, is likely to keep a person out of harm's way. Elementary school teachers and college professors have an affinity for activities that keep them in safe environments, which might explain their lower likelihood of being victims of robbery. Between these extremes is a continuum of risk that varies with people's characteristics, behaviors, and the settings in which they interact with others.

Routine Activities Theory. Cohen and Felson's (1979) routine activities theory posits that the concurrence of three elements increases the likelihood of criminal victimization: motivated offenders, suitable targets, and the absence of capable guardians. The risk of victimization increases when offenders and targets are in proximity to one another, providing offenders with ready opportunities for offenses. The likelihood of victimization also increases when offenders are undeterred by other persons who might intervene or identify them, as well as when they have easy egress from the scene. Together, these conditions facilitate the commission of a criminal act.

Fattah's Model. Fattah's (1991) model of the risk of criminal victimization, one of the most comprehensive of its kind, consists of 10 basic factors that include the dimensions (and convergences) of person, place, and time. The model also attributes the risk of victimization to behaviors, which can be provocative, thereby increasing the likelihood of violent crime, or negligent, thereby increasing the likelihood of property crime. Scenarios that are more or less conducive to crime are determined by personal characteristics that are correlated with victimization, such as age and gender; the communities in which people live, such as high- or low-crime neighborhoods; the places in which people socialize and the times they are in such places, for example, "places of public entertainment, where the risks of becoming a victim are higher than at work or at home" (p. 19); and the inclination of an individual to engage in high-risk behaviors, such as soliciting a prostitute or purchasing illegal drugs.

Karmen's Typology. Karmen's (2004) typology of victim responsibility consists of six categories of victims that are defined by increasing blameworthiness or shared responsibility, ranging from complete innocence to active participation in the crime. Karmen illustrates how this typology applies to auto theft. The members of the first category, *conscientiously resisting victims,* are totally blameless. These car owners install the latest and most expensive anti-theft devices and avoid parking in unsafe places. Nonetheless, professional car thieves, who have perfected techniques to circumvent such measures, eventually steal the car.

The next two categories of victims are not as wary as the first. The second type of victims, known as *conventionally cautious victims,* lock the doors of their automobiles, remove valuables from plain view, and ensure that the keys have been removed from the ignition. Although their cars are protected, they are not "extra-theft resistant" (Karmen, 2004, p. 108). Experienced thieves have little difficulty breaking into and stealing these vehicles. In contrast, the *carelessly facilitating victims,* the third category, set the stage for theft through gross negligence. These victims leave the doors unlocked and the keys in the ignition—unintentional but costly behaviors. No experience in thievery is necessary to drive off with their vehicles.

The next three types of victims are willing participants in auto theft; as such, the label *victim* seems unbefitting in their cases. *Precipitative initiators* want their vehicles to be stolen. These people have determined that a stolen car is worth more (e.g., in terms of the *Kelley Blue Book* value) than the car remaining in their possession; hence, to encourage thieves to steal the car, precipitative initiators purposely leave the doors unlocked and the keys in the ignition. To further encourage thieves, they park their vehicles in high-crime areas and on dimly lighted streets. *Provocative conspirators* go a step further; they hire offenders to steal, damage, or destroy their cars as willing accomplices in insurance fraud. The final category of "victims" consists of *fabricating stimulators* who insure a nonexistent vehicle and later report it as stolen to their insurance company, thereby committing a flagrant act of fraud.

Costs of Victimization

Monetary Loss. Criminal victimization is costly and can abruptly and irrevocably change people's lives (Shapiro, 1999). Victims of property crime suffer the loss of valuables or must pay for or replace damaged property; meanwhile, victims of violent crime—who are physically or emotionally injured—endure medical expenses or disabilities that can result in missed days of work and lost wages. In 2004, 95% of property crimes resulted in economic losses, totaling nearly $15 billion, while the costs of violent crime exceeded $1 billion (Bureau of Justice Statistics, 2006a). In 2005, more than $360 million worth of property was stolen during robberies, nearly $4 billion during thefts, and nearly $3 billion during burglaries (FBI, 2005).

In the mid-1990s, the National Institute of Justice launched the most comprehensive quantitative analysis of the tangible and intangible costs of crime ever conducted (Miller, Cohen, & Wiersema, 1996). Researchers found that from 1987 to 1990, crime cost $450 billion annually: $18 billion for medical and mental health care costs; $87 billion for other tangible costs, such as lost (or damaged) property, lost income, and lost work productivity; and $345 billion for costs associated with diminished quality of life (e.g., pain, suffering, fear, and avoidance behaviors).

Fear of Crime. The less tangible costs of crime include lasting psychological harm that destroys victims' ability to feel safe in their own homes or neighborhoods. Victimization can produce feelings of vulnerability, dread, chronic anxiety, and depression. Victims often struggle to regain a lost sense of control in their lives that is critical to well-being. As noted earlier, fear of crime can be harmful to entire communities. Forty years ago, the President's Commission on Law Enforcement and the Administration of Justice (1967) asserted, "The most damaging of the effects of violent crime is fear, and that fear must not be belittled" (p. 3). Today, fear of crime remains a ubiquitous and defining element in American culture (Warr, 1994).

Fear of crime is largely an emotional reaction and is rarely based on a rational determination of the odds of being attacked (Warr, 2000). Perceived vulnerability trumps actual risk in terms of people's crime-related feelings and behaviors (Stiles, Halim, & Kaplan, 2003). For example, older white women express considerable fear of violent crime, despite being at low risk for such victimization. In contrast, younger men of color express little fear of violent crime, even though they are at high risk for such victimization (Pastore & Maguire, 2002).

The mass media are greatly responsible for exaggerating the risk of criminal victimization and fueling fear of crime (Graber, 1980; Warr, 2000). Exceptional and sensational crimes, such as multiple or serial homicides, are featured repeatedly on the news (Graber, 1980). Moreover, crimes that appear to be random events or that involve attacks on strangers—which are atypical—are also given an inordinate share of newspaper space and airtime on news and entertainment programs. Repeated exposure to vivid depictions or descriptions of violent or heinous crimes leads to widespread fear and avoidance behaviors (Heath, 1984; Warr, 1994).

In addition to being inundated with fear-inducing news stories about crime, the average American television viewer faces a daily barrage of crime-related programs and dramatic (fear-mongering) advertisements for a variety of security devices or systems designed to keep his or her home safe from would-be intruders (Glassner, 1999). Regular television viewers of reality crime shows, such as *Cops, America's Most Wanted,* and *American Justice,* report being more fearful "about the probability of being sexually assaulted, beaten, knifed, and getting killed" than other television viewers (Haghighi & Sorensen, 1996, p. 29).

Emotional Harm. Many victims of serious crime are diagnosed with Post-Traumatic Stress Disorder (PTSD), a psychiatric problem that affects thoughts, feelings, and behaviors. Victims' "pain and suffering" defy quantification but are among the most deleterious consequences of crime (DiMaggio & Galea, 2007). PTSD symptoms include intense anxiety, depression, recurrent and distressing dreams and recollections of the event, flashbacks of the episode, persistent symptoms of physiological reactivity (e.g., exaggerated startle responses, hypervigilance, and sleep difficulties), impairment in social and occupational functioning, and disrupted interpersonal relationships (American Psychiatric Association, 2004).

Compared to nonvictims, crime victims experience significantly higher rates of current (10% versus 4%) and lifetime (25% versus 9%) PTSD (Kilpatrick & Acierco, 2003). The risk of developing PTSD is highest among victims of the most serious crimes: 49% among rape victims, 24% among other types of sexual assault victims, and 32% among aggravated assault victims (Sidram Foundation, 2004). Furthermore, crime victims have extremely high rates of comorbid psychiatric disorders; for example, in one study, 88% of male crime victims and 79% of female crime victims with symptoms of PTSD also met the diagnostic criteria for depression, substance use disorders, and phobias (Kilpatrick & Acierno, 2003)

The families and friends of homicide victims are another group (secondary victims) who are vulnerable to PTSD. Research has demonstrated that the current and lifetime prevalence rates of PTSD among surviving family members and friends of homicide victims are 10% and 22%, respectively (Thompson, Norris, & Ruback, 1998). As Herman and Waul (2004) observed, "Merely hearing about the victimization of a neighbor, friend, acquaintance, or coworker can also result in secondary victimization effects, such as increased anxiety and fear of crime" (p. 11).

Assistance for Crime Victims

Crime Victims' Movement

Clearly, crime victims experience a variety of adverse consequences; victims can be traumatized and often require ameliorative care. Consequently, the recognition of crime victims as a group with special needs and interests gained widespread notoriety and momentum in the crime victims' movement, which emerged from a confluence of events. Initially, the purpose of the victims' movement was to reintegrate victims into the criminal justice system by inviting them to participate in the prosecution of their cases (Davis, Smith, & Henley, 1990). According to Young and Stein (2004), five major factors—a combination of political, social, research, and legal developments—were responsible for the early growth of the movement.

Victimology. The first factor was the emergence of the field of victimology. Victimology is the scientific study of crime victims, their relationship with offenders, and the situations and behaviors that place them at risk for criminal victimization. Victimologists also study the harmful consequences of crime and the effectiveness of victim service programs (Karmen, 2004). Schafer's (1968) book, *The Victim and His Criminal,* released in the midst of the enormous crime wave of the 1960s, was a seminal publication that spurred interest in victimology as an area worthy of scholarly attention and a source of knowledge that could help better understand and stifle the unexpected and unprecedented explosion in crime sweeping the United States, which continued, mostly unabated, for the next 20 years. However, in the 1990s, critics attacked the field of victimology for becoming more ideological and less scientific and for urging victims to embrace the "victim identity," which critics believed perpetuated victim suffering and interfered with their recovery (Karmen, 2004).

Victim Compensation. The second factor in the early growth of the victims' movement was the development of victim compensation programs, inaugurated in New Zealand and Great Britain. In the United States, the first victim compensation programs appeared in California and New York in the mid-1960s and were predicated on the notion that crime victims are needy citizens who deserve government assistance. Compensation programs were characterized as "welfare programs" for crime victims. In these programs, the state assumed responsibility for victims' care and accepted blame for their plight because of "[its] long inattention to poverty and social injustice," considered to be among the root causes of crime (Goldberg, 1970, p. 176). By the 1970s, the notion of victim compensation as a vehicle for victim healing was replaced by the notion of victim compensation as a vehicle for attaining justice and encouraging victim participation in the criminal justice system; as such, filing a police report and cooperating with the prosecution became prerequisites for receiving state funds to pay medical bills or replace lost wages (Young & Stein, 2004).

Women's Movement. The third factor spurring the victims' movement was the women's movement, which empowered female victims of sexual assault and domestic violence to demand more respectful and humane treatment in the court system. The women's movement also provided victim advocates with examples of effective strategies for bringing public attention to social and political issues; such strategies led to the creation of laws and public policies that benefited female crime victims (Young & Stein, 2004). The early focus on the emotional devastation of sexual assault victims paved the way for research on the emotional suffering of crime victims in general (Lurigio, 1987), "increasing public sensitivity to the psychological effects of crime on victims, particularly feelings of powerlessness, isolation, and guilt" (Friedman, 1985, p. 791).

System Failure. The fourth factor propelling the victims' movement was the criminal justice system's failure to control crime and bring offenders to justice. Confidence in the system began to erode with the rising crime rates of the 1960s and reached a nadir with Martinson's (1974) widely cited and controversial review of the impact of correctional programs, which concluded that "nothing works" with regard to the rehabilitation of criminals; "with few and isolated exceptions, the rehabilitative efforts that have been reported so far [have] had no appreciable effect on recidivism" (p. 25). The court system's effectiveness was also challenged as a greater proportion of cases were lost and an increasing number of crime victims walked away from the legal process disheartened and dissatisfied (Friedman, 1985). Most prosecutorial failures were caused by once-cooperative witnesses who turned their backs on the court system because they received shoddy treatment from police officers, prosecutors, and judges (Cannavale & Falcon, 1976).

In other words, the system that was supposed to assist crime victims and punish offenders instead harmed victims further by neglecting their basic needs and making their cooperation in the court process difficult and emotionally painful (Bard & Sangrey, 1979). As Sales, Rich, and Reich noted (1984), victims were expected to participate in a court system that had "treated them with less respect that it [had] treated the offender" (p. 114). Victims' negative experiences were so common that Symonds (1980) argued that their participation in the criminal justice system resulted in a "second wound," which was also referred as "secondary victimization" (Lurigio, Skogan, & Davis, 1990).

Grassroots Efforts. The final factor affecting the growth of the victims' movement was the proliferation of grassroots organizations and shelters founded mostly by crime victims, for crime victims or their surviving family members. These organizations supported victims in their efforts to recover from the trauma and hardship encountered in the aftermath of crime. In addition, they advocated for changes in laws that led to more government services and victim protection and compensation programs (Young & Stein, 2004). According to Davis and Henley (1990),

> Operating with close ties to the community rather than to the criminal justice system did have some advantages. Grass-roots programs were tied to service networks within the community. Being outside of the criminal justice system, the programs had the credibility to work with victims distrustful of the system, including those who didn't report crimes to authorities. (p. 162)

The victims' movement spawned the implementation of various reforms and interventions to enhance public sensitivity to crime victims as well as improve their treatment—both in and out of the criminal justice system. Numerous victim service programs were established independently or in conjunction with police departments and prosecutors' offices, in order to satisfy victims' needs for compensation, justice, and support (Davis & Henley, 1990). The favorable attention to crime victims that arose during the 1970s occurred at the national, state, and local levels.

President's Task Force on Victims of Crime

President Ronald Reagan took a historic step forward in the federal government's support of crime victims by proclaiming National Victims of Crime Week in 1981. One year later, advocacy for crime victims gained further impetus with the President's Task Force on Victims of Crime (1982), which was formed in response to a presidential executive order that called for a nationwide study of the criminal justice system's treatment of crime victims. Its members argued, "If we take the justice out of the criminal justice system, we leave behind a system that serves the criminal" (p. vi).

The task force members interviewed crime victims and experts in the budding field of victim assistance and ultimately proposed 68 recommendations in five general areas: executive and legislative action at the federal and state levels; federal action; action for criminal justice system professionals (police officers, prosecutors, judges, and parole board members); action for other organizations (hospitals, churches, schools, mental health agencies); and an amendment to the federal constitution, augmenting Sixth Amendment rights for crime victims, such as guaranteeing that "the victims in every criminal prosecution shall have the right to be present and to be heard at all critical stages of judicial proceedings" (Hook & Seymour, 2004, p. 113).

Victims' Rights

In 1982, Congress passed the Omnibus Victim and Witness Protection Act, which mandated consideration of victim impact statements at sentencing in all federal criminal cases. The Act also required protection of victims and witnesses from defendant intimidation and offender restitution for victims. In addition, the act promulgated guidelines for the fair and humane treatment of victims and recommended stricter bail laws (Davis & Henley, 1990).

The Supreme Court first acknowledged the rights of crime victims in *Morris v. Slappy* (1983). In this case, the court held that a victim's rights had been properly affirmed when it reversed a court of appeal's ruling to overturn a verdict against a defendant. The defendant argued that his due process rights were violated when a judge refused to reschedule his case because his original public defender was unavailable on his court date (Viano, 1987). In reversing the lower court's decision, the Supreme Court stated,

[The] court [of appeals] wholly failed to take into account the interest of the victim of these crimes, and . . . in the administration of criminal justice, courts may not ignore the concerns of victims . . . this is especially so when the crime is one calling for public testimony about a humiliating and degrading experience. [103 S. Ct. 1618]

In 1984, Congress passed the Victims of Crime Act (VOCA), "ending nearly 20 years of floor debates, lobbying, political posturing, maneuvering, and last-minute compromises" (Karmen, 2004, p. 318). According to Newmark (2006), "With the passage of VOCA, the federal government reasserted its role in the victim assistance field and provided significant resources for its continued expansion" (p. 6). VOCA established a federal Crime Victims Fund, which consisted exclusively of revenue from the payment of fines, penalties, and bond forfeitures from offenders convicted of federal crimes. Most important, VOCA generates millions of dollars to support state victim compensation and assistance programs (Deem, Nerenberg, & Titus, 2007; Gaboury, 1992). To be eligible for VOCA funding, state programs must, for example, encourage victim cooperation in the prosecution and conviction of defendants; include victims of drunk driving or domestic violence among those eligible for benefits; expand accessibility to services, particularly for victims in underserved populations; and maximize resources in order to reduce the various costs of crime (Gaboury, 1992; Newmark, 2006).

Currently, VOCA allows funds to be used to compensate victims of financial crimes, such as fraud, cybercrimes, identity theft, and the financial abuse of the elderly. As described on the Web site of the Office for Victims of Crimes (2006), victims of financial crimes are an underserved population eligible for direct assistance in several areas, including mental health assistance, respite care, and advocacy services. VOCA funds can also be awarded to states for public education and publications to prevent financial victimization (Deem et al., 2007).

Justice for All Act

In 2004, President George W. Bush signed into law the Justice for All Act (H.R. 5107, Public Law 108-405). The purposes of the Act include the protection of crime victims' rights and the elimination of the backlog of DNA samples gathered from convicted offenders and crime scenes as well as those collected for inclusion in a federal DNA repository. Furthermore, the Act amended the federal Criminal Code to accord crime victims several specific rights, such as the right to be notified of any public court proceeding or parole hearing and the right to receive victim restitution. The Act also allows federal crime victims—under certain circumstances—to petition the court to reconsider plea agreements or sentences (Office for Victims of Crime, 2006).

In the past two decades, all states have passed laws in support of victims' rights as well as a victims' bill of rights (National Center for Victims of Crime, 2007), such as the Illinois Bill of Rights for Victims and Witnesses of Violent Crime (Illinois Criminal Justice Information Authority, 2007). The Illinois Constitution (Article 1, Section 8.1) states that crime victims "have rights to be treated with fairness and respect for their dignity and privacy throughout the criminal justice process and to obtain certain information from the criminal justice system." For purposes of the legislation, the Illinois Rights of Crime Victims and Witnesses Act (725 ILCS 120) defines a crime victim as a person who has been injured or experienced the loss or damage of property as the result of a violent crime. The Act's provisions also apply to immediate family members of homicide or other violent crime victims and the witnesses to violent crime who testify for the prosecution.

Similar to laws passed in other states, the Illinois Act includes the following crime victims' rights: to receive a written explanation of their legal rights at first contact with the criminal justice system; to be notified when the state begins the prosecution process; and to be given information about social services and how to apply for victim compensation to pay for medical expenses and lost or damaged property (Illinois Criminal Justice Information Authority, 2007). Once defendants are convicted, victims have the right to address the court or submit a written statement regarding the crime's impact on their lives, which the judge can take into consideration in rendering a sentencing decision.

Victim Service and Compensation Programs

Service Programs. As noted previously in this chapter, the victims' movement in the United States emerged in the 1970s. A major component of the movement was the creation of victim service and compensation programs. Fueled by grassroots efforts and spurred by Law Enforcement Assistance Administration (LEAA) funding, victim service programs proliferated in the United States and in numerous other countries, especially Great Britain and countries in Europe. Between 1970 and 1975, LEAA spent more than $22 million on such programs, which are typically housed in police departments and prosecutors' agencies in order to facilitate victim cooperation "in the apprehension, prosecution, and conviction of criminals" (Davis, Lurigio, & Skogan, 1999, p. 101). Since the 1970s, victim service programs have received millions of VOCA dollars earmarked for victim assistance and compensation.

Victim service programs offer a variety of services, from crisis intervention for victims who are struggling to adjust to postvictimization trauma, to emergency aid for victims with immediate practical needs (e.g., new locks, shelter, clothing, food, or cash), to court advocacy for victims who are overwhelmed by the complexities of the court and legal system (Skogan, Davis, & Lurigio, 1991). In a study of a small sample of crime victim programs, Davis et al. (1999) analyzed victim interviews to identify four major categories of victim needs: crime prevention (e.g., protection from the offender), household logistical support (e.g., repairs of broken locks or doors), counseling/advice/advocacy (e.g., psychological treatment), and property replacement (e.g., assistance with insurance claims).

Victims reported that the most common source of assistance for meeting such needs was family members or friends. Approximately 4% of victims indicated that they received help from a victim service program to meet their crime prevention, logistical, or property replacement needs. Nearly one-fourth reported that a victim service program helped with their counseling-related needs (Davis et al., 1999). Consistent with the results of Friedman, Bischoff, Davis, and Person (1982), Davis et al. (1999) found that the neediest victims (those with the most problems) were the most likely to receive assistance from a victim service program.

Compensation Programs. All 50 states (as well as the District of Columbia, Guam, Puerto Rico, and the Virgin Islands) currently have victim compensation programs, which receive one-third of their funding from federal VOCA funds; the remainder of the funds is generated from offender fines and fees (National Association of Crime Victim Compensation Boards, 2007; Newmark, 2006). Each year, these programs serve nearly 200,000 victims and family members, spending approximately $450 million to foster victim recovery. Victim compensation programs vary in terms of their rationales and resources (Karmen, 2004); however, most programs have a number of basic requirements and features, and all are intended primarily to alleviate the financial consequences of crime (Parent, Auerbach, & Carlson, 1992). Programs typically award compensation only to "innocent" crime victims; that is, any evidence of victim precipitation or "contributing misconduct" precludes victim compensation. Moreover, to be eligible for compensation, victims are required to report the crime promptly and cooperate with the police.

Programs concentrate their resources on serving victims of the most serious crimes—robbery, rape, and child abuse—and most of their funds pay for these victims' medical bills (Newmark, 2006). Property crime victims are ineligible for compensation. Programs deduct money that victims have received from private insurance companies and government entitlement programs, such as Medicaid, from final compensation awards and usually set the maximum award allotted to crime victims at $25,000 (Karmen, 2004; National Association of Crime Victim Compensation Boards, 2007). Furthermore, state residency is not a requirement for compensation; for example, a resident of Kansas who is victimized in Florida can apply for compensation from Florida's program.

Conclusion

Criminal victimization is common in the United States and affects the lives of millions of Americans and their families each year. Crime is measured and reported by the federal government through the UCR Program, which is administered by the FBI, and the NCVS, which is conducted by the

Census Bureau and measures crime against individuals and households. Although both of these data collection strategies have marked a steady decline in crime rates over the past 25 years, they have also demonstrated that the United States continues to lead the industrialized world in the number of violent crimes committed annually.

Crime is extremely costly; the tangible costs include lost property and wages while the intangible costs include significant psychological distress that can persist for many years after the incident and fear of crime, which restricts individual freedom and diminishes the quality of life in entire communities. The risk of victimization is related to personal characteristics, such as gender, race, and age, as well as place of residence. Young men of color who live in urban environments are at much higher risk of victimization (especially from violent crime) than older white women who live in rural areas. A person's lifestyle can also affect the likelihood of victimization through neglectful or provocative behaviors.

In the 1970s, the crime victims' movement brought attention to victims' suffering and their need for services. Spurred by the women's movement, the field of victimology, and the grassroots efforts of crime victims to empower themselves and other victims, the crime victims' movement helped garner support and resources for crime victims at the local, state, and federal levels. The President's Task Force on Victims of Crime led to legislation, such as the Victims of Crime and Justice for All Acts, that protects victims' rights and funds victim compensation and service programs.

Discussion Questions

1. Which crime reporting program, the UCR or NCVS, provides more useful information for crime-control purposes?

2. What can the media do to lower crime rates and fear of crime in the United States?

3. How did the conservative politics of the Reagan and Bush administrations benefit crime victims and extend their rights?

4. What aspects of criminal victimization are related to the emotional trauma that many crime victims suffer?

5. Can the emphasis on the rights of crime victims go too far and infringe on the constitutional rights of defendants or convicted offenders?

6. Can holding victims responsible for their attacks (victim blaming) be harmful to victims?

7. Discuss how the material in the chapter helped you better understand and contextualize the case study.

Internet Resources

Bureau of Justice Statistics: http://www.ojp.usdoj.gov/bjs/

Federal Bureau of Investigation: http://www.fbi.com

Federal Bureau of Investigation's Office for Victim Assistance: http://www.fbi.gov/hq/cid/victimassist/home.htm

Federal Bureau of Investigation Uniform Crime Reports: http//www.fbi.gov/ucr/ucr.htm

Mothers Against Drunk Driving: http://www.madd.gov

National Center for Victims of Crime: http://www.ncvc.org

National Crime Victimization Survey: http://www.ojp.usdoj.gov/bjs/cvict.htm#ncvs

National Victim Assistance Academy: http://www.nvaa.org

Office for Victims of Crime: http://www.ojp.usdoj.gov/ovc/

References

American Psychiatric Association. (2004). *Diagnostic and statistical manual* (Text rev.). Washington, DC: Author.

Bachman, R., & Saltzman, L. E. (1995). *Violence against women*. Washington, DC: Bureau of Justice Statistics.

Bard, M., & Sangrey, D. (1979). *The crime victims' handbook*. New York: Brunner/Mazel.

Block, R., Felson, M., & Block, C. (1985). Crime victimization rates for incumbents of 246 occupations. *Sociology and Social Research, 69*, 442–449.

Blumstein, A., & Wallman, J. (2000). *The crime drop in America*. New York: Cambridge University Press.

Bureau of Justice Statistics. (2006a). *Crime and justice data on-line: Crime 1974–2004*. Washington, DC: U.S. Department of Justice.

Bureau of Justice Statistics. (2006b). *Criminal victimization in the United States, 2004: Statistical tables* (Table 81). Washington, DC: U.S. Department of Justice.

Bureau of Justice Statistics. (2006c). *Criminal victimization in the United States, 2005: Statistical tables* (Table 105). Washington DC: U.S. Department of Justice.

Cannavale, F. J., & Falcon, W. D. (1976). *Witness cooperation*. Lexington, MA: Lexington Books.

Catalano, S. M. (2006). *Criminal victimization, 2005*. Washington, DC: U.S. Department of Justice, Bureau of Justice Statistics.

Cohen, L. E., & Felson, M. (1979). Social change and crime rate trends: A routine activities approach. *American Sociological Review, 44*, 588–608.

Davis, R. C., & Henley, M. (1990). Victim service programs. In A. J. Lurigio, W. G. Skogan, & R. C. Davis (Eds.), *Victims of crime: Problems, policies, and programs* (pp. 157–171). Newbury Park, CA: Sage.

Davis, R. C., Lurigio, A. J., & Skogan, W. G. (1999). Services for victims: A market research study. *International Review of Victimology, 6*, 101–115.

Davis, R. C., Smith, B. E., & Henley, M. (1990). *Victim impact statements: Their effects on court outcomes and victim satisfaction*. New York: Victim Services Agency.

Deem, D., Nerenberg, L., & Titus, R. (2007). Victims of financial crime. In R. C. Davis, A. J. Lurigio, & S. Herman (Eds.), *Victims of crime* (3rd ed., pp. 125–146). Los Angeles: Sage.

DiMaggio, C., & Galea, S. (2007). The mental health and behavioral consequences of terrorism. In R. C. Davis, A. J. Lurigio, & S. Herman (Eds.), *Victims of crime* (3rd ed., pp. 147–160). Los Angeles: Sage.

Farrington, D. P., Langan, P. A., & Tonry, M. (2004). *Cross-national studies in crime and justice.* Washington, DC: U.S. Department of Justice, Bureau of Justice Statistics.

Fattah, E. A. (1991). Victimology: Past, present, and future. *Criminologie, 33,* 1–33.

Federal Bureau of Investigation. (2005). *Crime in the United States, 2005.* Washington, DC: Author.

Federal Bureau of Investigation. (2006). *Crime in the United States, 2006.* Washington, DC: Author.

Feldman-Summers, S., & Ashworth, C. D. (1991). The victim-offender relationship and calls to the police in assaults. *Criminology, 37,* 931–947.

Friedman, L. M. (1993). *Crime and punishment in American history.* New York: Basic Books.

Friedman, L. N. (1985). The crime victim movement in its first decade. *Public Administration Review, 45,* 790–794.

Friedman, K., Bischoff, H., Davis, R. C., & Person, A. (1982). *Victims and helpers: Reactions to crime.* Washington, DC: U.S. Government Printing Office.

Gaboury, M. T. (1992). Implementation of federal legislation to aid victims of crime in the United States. In E. Viano (Ed.), *Critical issues in victimology: International perspectives* (pp. 224–232). New York: Springer.

Glassner, B. (1999). *Culture of fear: Why Americans are afraid of the wrong things.* New York: Bare Books.

Goldberg, A. J. (1970). Preface: Symposium on governmental compensation for victims of violence. *Southern California Law Review, 43,* 164–182.

Graber, D. A. (1980). *Crime news and the public.* New York: Praeger.

Haghighi, J., & Sorensen, J. (1996). American's fear of crime. In T. Flanagan & D. R. Longmire (Eds.), *Americans view crime and justice* (pp. 16–30). Thousand Oaks, CA: Sage.

Heath, L. (1984). Impact of newspaper crime reports on fear of crime: A multimethodological investigation. *Journal of Personality and Social Psychology, 47,* 263–276.

Herman, S., & Waul, M. (2004). *Repairing the harm.* Washington, DC: National Center for Victims of Crime.

Hindelang, M., Gottfredson, M., & Garofalo, J. (1978). *Victims of personal crime.* Cambridge, MA: Ballinger.

Hook, M., & Seymour, A. (2004). *A retrospective of the 1982 President's Task Force on Victims of Crime.* Washington, DC: Office for Victims of Crime.

Illinois Criminal Justice Information Authority. (2007). *Illinois bill of rights for victims and witnesses of violent crime.* Springfield, IL: Author.

Karmen, A. (2004). *Crime victims: An introduction to victimology* (5th ed.). Belmont, CA: Wadsworth.

Kilpatrick, D. G., & Acierno, R. (2003). Mental health needs of crime victims: Epidemiology and outcomes. *Journal of Traumatic Stress, 16,* 127–141.

Klaus, P. (2007). *Crime and the nation's households, 2005.* Washington, DC: U.S. Department of Justice, Bureau of Justice Statistics.

Koppel, H. (1987). *Lifetime likelihood of victimization: Bureau of Justice Statistics technical report.* Washington, DC: U.S. Department of Justice.

Lurigio, A. J. (1987). Are all victims alike? The adverse, generalized, and differential impact of crime. *Crime and Delinquency, 33,* 454–467.

Lurigio, A. J., Skogan, W. G, & Davis, R. C. (Eds.). (1990). *Victims of crime: Problems, policies, and programs.* Newbury Park, CA: Sage.

Martinson, R. (1974). What works: Questions and answers about prison reform. *Public Interest, 35,* 22–54.

Miller, T. R., Cohen, M. A., & Wiersema, B. (1996). *Victims lost and consequences: A new look.* Washington, DC: U.S. Department of Justice, National Institute of Justice.

Morris v. Slappy, 103 S. Ct. 1610 (1983).

National Association of Crime Victim Compensation Boards. (2007). *Crime victim compensation: Resources for recovery.* Alexandria, VA: Author.

National Center for Victims of Crime. (2007). *Rights of crime victims.* Retrieved from http://www.ncvc.org/ncvv/main.

Newmark, L. C. (2006). *Crime victims' needs and VOCA-funded services: Findings and recommendations from two national studies.* Washington, DC: U.S. Department of Justice, Office of Justice Programs.

Office for Victims of Crime. (2006). *OVC fact sheet: The Justice for All Act.* Washington, DC: U.S. Department of Justice, Office of Justice Programs.

Parent, D., Auerbach, B., & Carlson, K. (1992). *Compensating crime victims: A summary of policies and practices.* Washington, DC: U.S. Department of Justice.

Pastore, A. L., & Maguire, K. (Eds.). (2002). *Sourcebook of criminal justice statistics, 2001.* Washington, DC: U.S. Department of Justice, Bureau of Justice Statistics.

President's Commission on Law Enforcement and the Administration of Justice. (1967). *The challenge of crime in a free society.* Washington, DC: U.S. Government Printing Office.

President's Task Force on Victims of Crime. (1982). *Report of the President's Task Force on Victims of Crime.* Washington, DC: U.S. Government Printing Office.

Sales, B., Rich, R. F., & Reich, J. (1984). Victims of crime and violence: Legal and policy issues. In A. S. Kahn (Ed.), *Victims of crime and violence* (pp. 113–154). Washington, DC: American Psychological Association.

Schafer, S. (1968). *The victim and his criminal: A study in functional responsibility.* New York: Random House.

Schmalleger, F. (2007). *Criminal justice today: An introductory text for the 21st century.* Upper Saddle River, NJ: Pearson-Prentice Hall.

Shapiro, E. (1999). *Cost of crime: A review of the research studies.* St. Paul, MN: Minnesota House of Representatives.

Sidram Foundation. (2004). *Post-traumatic stress disorder fact sheet.* Towson, MD: Author.

Skogan, W. G. (1984). Reporting crimes to the police: The status of world research. *Journal of Research in Crime and Delinquency, 21,* 113–137.

Skogan, W. G. (1990). *Disorder and decline: Crime and the spiral of decay in American neighborhoods.* New York: Free Press.

Skogan, W. G., Davis, R. C., & Lurigio, A. J. (1991). The impact of victim service programs. In G. Kaiser, H. Kury, & H. J. Albrecht (Eds.), *Victims and criminal justice, 3,* 97–114.

Skogan, W. G., Lurigio, A. J., & Davis, R. C. (1990). Criminal victimization. In A. J. Lurigio, W. G. Skogan, & R. C. Davis (Eds.), *Victims of crime: Problems, policies, and programs* (pp. 7–22). Newbury Park, CA: Sage.

Stiles, B. L., Halim, S., & Kaplan, H. B. (2003). Fear of crime among individuals with physical limitations. *Criminal Justice Review, 28,* 233–234.

Symonds, M. (1980). The "second injury" to victims. *Evaluation and Change, 42,* 36–38.

Thompson, M. P., Norris, F. H., & Ruback, R. B. (1998). Comparative distress levels of inner-city family members of homicide victims. *Journal of Traumatic Stress, 11,* 223–242.

Viano, E. (1987). Victim's rights and the constitution: Reflections on a bicentennial. *Crime and Delinquency, 33,* 438–451.

Warchol, G. (1998). *BJS special report: Workplace violence, 1992–1996.* Washington, DC: U.S. Department of Justice.

Warr, M. (1994). Public perceptions and reactions to violent offending and victimization. In A. J. Reiss & J. A. Ruth (Eds.), *Understanding and preventing violence* (Vol. 4, pp. 137–151). Washington, DC: National Academy Press.

Warr, M. (2000). Fear of crime in the United States: Avenues for research and policy. In D. Duffee (Ed.), *Crime and justice 2000* (pp. 451–490). Washington, DC: U.S. Department of Justice, Office of Justice Programs, National Institute of Justice.

Young, M., & Stein, J. (2004). *The history of the crime victims' movement in the United States.* Washington, DC: U.S. Department of Justice, Office of Justice Programs, Office for Victims of Crime.

CHAPTER 16

Prevention and Treatment of Violent Offending/Offenders

Mary Clair, Lisa Faille, and Joseph V. Penn

CASE STUDY: MIKE

Mike is a 15-year-old male who has had multiple school suspensions for fighting with peers and being disrespectful to teachers. He misses school on average two to three days per week and smokes "weed" (marijuana) with his friends. More recently, he has been staying out "later and later" on school nights. Sometimes he doesn't come home on weekends. At age 13, he stole a video game from a store, for which he was arrested but not charged. At age 8, he set a small fire in the closet in his room. He was diagnosed with ADHD at age 7, but he discontinued treatment after a few days because he didn't like the way the medicine made him feel.

Mike's mother was 23 when she had him. He was her third child. Mike's father has a history of significant alcohol and cocaine use. Mike's parents separated when he was 4 years old, after Mike's father severely beat his mother. Mike witnessed the entire assault. His mother required emergency medical treatment and hospitalization. Mike's father was subsequently incarcerated, and Mike has had little contact with him since then. Mike's mother, who continues to struggle as a single parent of three, reports that Mike has a "rebellious streak." School reports identify that as early as the first grade, Mike had numerous incidents of lying, arguing, defiance, and shoving peers. Mike repeated third grade, and despite a special education designation and services, he is currently at risk of repeating the current academic year due to poor attendance and failing grades. Mike's mother made an appointment with a child psychiatrist; however, the doctor had a three-month waiting list. At the time of the appointment, she no longer had a car and did not take Mike to his appointment.

Violence Prevention in Youth

Unfortunately, the scenario described in the Case Study is common among youth who are considered at risk for committing offending behaviors. The remainder of this chapter will describe programs and treatments that are often used with these youth and will identify the most promising and effective treatments for this population.

Identifying and addressing the predictors of youth violence within a biopsychosocial framework and utilizing evidence-based approaches is critical for prevention efforts. Unfortunately, the empirical research in this area is limited. There are few high-quality longitudinal studies of the predictors of youth violence in general. Much of the adult literature is extrapolated to juvenile populations and settings. For example, there is a notable paucity of current research regarding school violence and targeted school violence (Murakami, Rappaport, & Penn, 2006).

Over the past two decades, there has been growing attention paid to youth crime and violence in the United States. Recently, there has been some collaboration among government agencies, educators, court systems, law enforcement, mental health services, academic centers, researchers, concerned citizens, and primary care professionals in this regard. Although existing data suggests an overall decline in rates of youth violent crimes and juvenile homicides since the mid-1990s, youth violence is still a widespread problem. In the aftermath of the Columbine High School multiple victim school shooting in 1999, the Virginia Tech college campus shooting in 2007, and other high-profile violent events, there has been increased attention paid to the need to identify and prevent future violent acts by youth offenders.

Although psychiatrists, psychologists, and other mental health professionals cannot predict long-term dangerousness with definitive accuracy, they can often identify risk factors associated with an increased likelihood of violent behavior and, in particular, they can predict violent behavior in the short term. Exploration of the youth's violence history should include such variables as how chronic or recent the behavior is, as well as the frequency, severity, and context of violent behavior. The clinician should clarify the youth's history of exposure to domestic violence, past physical and sexual abuse and other traumatic events, perpetration of violence against others (e.g., cruelty to animals, bullying, fire setting, sexual assaultive behaviors), substance abuse, and other risk factors for future violence. In addition, a standardized approach should be used to elicit a history of weapon possession, access to and use of weapons preincarceration, and assaultive or threatening behaviors against peers or staff prior to or during incarceration (Penn & Thomas, 2005).

So what are some different protective factors or interventions that can be implemented for "at risk" youths? Which youth are most likely to grow up to become violent perpetrators, and which will be productive members of society? Existing research has yet to fully answer these questions. However, one of the fundamental theoretical premises for violence prevention in juveniles is that violence can be a learned behavior and can, therefore, be unlearned, or better yet, not learned in the first place. For example, thwarting the acquisition of violent behaviors at an early age is crucial because children who are exposed to violence have an increased risk for future violence. Additionally, youth who present with childhood-onset mental illnesses such as Oppositional Defiant Disorder (a pattern of negative, hostile, and defiant behavior) are at risk to develop a more severe disruptive disorder, Conduct Disorder (a repetitive and persistent pattern of behavior in which the basic rights of others or major age-appropriate societal norms or rules are violated); substance abuse; and other psychiatric comorbidity. Similarly, conduct-disordered youth are at an increased risk of becoming adults with Antisocial Personality Disorder (a pervasive pattern of disregard for, and violation of, the rights of others that begins in childhood or early adolescence and continues into adulthood), antisocial traits or behaviors, and violent offending.

At what age should violence prevention initiatives begin, and who should receive such interventions? Some violence prevention programs have been implemented in elementary school-aged children, even as early as kindergarten. Two programs that are aimed at violence prevention are Second Step: A Violence Prevention Curriculum (Beland, 1992; Fitzgerald & Edstrom, 2006) and Promoting Alternative Thinking Strategies (PATHS; Kusche & Greenberg, 1994). These programs are psychoeducational in nature and are taught in the classroom by elementary school teachers as part of the curriculum. The programs are geared toward increasing children's ability to manage difficult feelings and promoting effective thinking and planning skills. Both Second Step (Grossman et al., 1997; McMahon & Washburn, 2003; Taub, 2002) and PATHS (Kam, Greenberg, & Kusché, 2004; Kam, Greenberg, & Walls, 2003; Kelly, Longbottom, Potts, & Williamson, 2004) have been shown to increase prosocial behavior, socio-emotional competence, inhibition, and problem-solving skills in children, which are the very skills that are the antithesis of violence. Moreover, Kam et al. (2004) found a significant decrease in teacher's ratings of internalizing symptoms (Cohen's $d = .22$).

Another type of violence prevention program that is home based rather than school based emphasizes parenting skills. The Triple P–Positive Parenting Program is one such program. It targets parents by training them to respond positively and nonviolently to their children's behavior, and it is specifically intended as an alternative to aggressive parenting. Triple P has been successful at reducing dysfunctional, coercive parenting behavior and the ensuing behavioral problems in the children of these parents (Sanders, 1999; Sanders, Cann, & Markie-Dadds, 2003; Sanders, Markie-Dadds, &

Turner, 2003). Again, the premise for this program is that if violence is not modeled in the home, it will then be less likely that the child will learn violence and grow up to perpetuate violence in society.

Ineffective Treatment for Violence

The discussion of violence treatment initiatives must include the stark realization that incarceration as a sole deterrent may not be effective in preventing violence. This is unfortunate because detention and imprisonment are the crux of our current adult and juvenile penal systems. Many government and policy leaders suggest that incarceration for violence—"if you do the crime, you will do time"—serves as a motivation to not recommit aggressive behaviors, yet this is often not the case. Locking an offender behind bars separates that individual from society for a specified period of time (usually a period of time that is shorter than the imposed sentence). Consequently, other members of society are given a false sense of security. Although studies have not focused exclusively on violent crime, a 10% rise in incarceration rates for a given state in the U.S. results in only a 2% to 4% decrease in crime rates (Levitt, 1996; Spelman, 2000, 2005). In short, incarceration without rehabilitation is generally ineffective at reducing crime.

Interventions other than incarceration have been investigated for at-risk or delinquent youths. However, numerous interventions, even some very well-intended ones, have been empirically shown to be ineffective at reducing youth violence and criminal behavior. One type of school-based intervention that does little to reduce violence is Drug Abuse Resistance Education (DARE), which is a youth drug prevention program that is administered in schools nationwide. Unfortunately, in spite of the significant amount of support it receives from teachers, police, and other civic leaders, it has demonstrated little impact on the prevention of drug use (Lynam, Milich, & Zimmerman, 1999; Rosenbaum, Flewelling, & Bailey, 1994; Thombs, 2000). Additionally, nonpromotion to successive grades has an adverse effect on violence reduction, as an individual's motivation for school achievement can be diminished when a sense of failure in school is fostered, and negative school attitudes can be a risk factor for violence (Brier, 1995; Lipsey & Derzon, 1998; Peacock, McClure, & Agars, 2003). Clearly, there are many difficult issues for educators, administrators, policymakers, parents, and families regarding promotion and nonpromotion of potentially at-risk youth.

Community-based programs have also made efforts at violence reduction. One program, called Scared Straight, is intended to deter future crime by exposing youths to prisons, incarcerated adults, and/or parolees, with the hypothesis that these youth would be shocked and subsequently deterred by the consequences for crime. However, the desired result does not appear to occur on a consistent or sustained basis. Conversely, it has consistently been shown that Scared Straight programs do more harm than good, as participating youths actually had higher rates of recidivism (Farrington & Welsh, 2005; Petrosino, Turpin-Petrosino, & Buehler, 2005; Petrosino, Turpin-Petrosino, & Finckenauer, 2000), which may be due to the unintended "normalizing" of incarceration. Another type of community-based intervention that has been implemented throughout the country is gun buyback programs. They also tend to be very expensive and have resulted in little violence reduction in the communities that participate in these programs (Sherman, Gottfredson, MacKenzie, Eck, Reuler, & Bushay, 1997).

Within the penal system, efforts have also been made to reduce violence among delinquent youths. One such method has been boot camps, which are named after the camps for training military recruits that serve as the inspiration for the design of the program. Boot camps are live-in programs that emphasize structure, intense discipline, and physical labor. The rules are enforced by staff who often incorporate physical exertion, yelling, and other strategies that could be described by some as being verbally and/or physically abusive to youths. Indeed, it has come to light that boot camps are riddled with staff abuses, and two adolescents have died in these camps (Clines, 1999). Thus, it is perhaps not surprising that boot camps have not been shown to be an effective violence intervention technique (Benda, 2005; Cullen, Blevins, & Trager, 2005; Mackenzie, Brame, McDowall, & Souryal, 1995). In some cases, participation in boot camps has been correlated with increased recidivism (Jones, 1997; Peters, Thomas, & Zamberlan, 1997). Lastly, boot camps are often much more costly to run and operate than detention facilities. Thus, they are not cost effective, particularly when they are used as an alternative to probation (Peters et al., 1997).

Also, within the penal system, a response to violence that has been shown to be particularly harmful to youth is the process of being waived (transferred) to adult court. Juveniles whose crimes are deemed to be particularly deplorable or who have lengthy criminal records are tried and convicted in an adult court, and those juveniles serve their sentence in an adult correctional institution. Adult penal institutions are rarely geared toward the needs of teenage youth. Accordingly, juveniles in adult facilities often do not receive the educational, psychological, or even medical services that their same-age peers in juvenile facilities receive. Moreover, youths who are waived to adult court tend to have higher rates of recidivism than their counterparts who remain in the juvenile system (Bishop, Frazier, & Lanza-Kaduce, 1996; Myers, 2003; Winner, Lanza-Kaduce, & Bishop, 1997).

Furthermore, juveniles tend to be very vulnerable in adult facilities. Youths in adult correctional facilities are at increased risk of being sexually victimized by adult inmates, physically assaulted by corrections officers, and assaulted by someone using a weapon (Forst, Fagan, & Scott, 1989; Mathis, 2007). Even more disturbing is that among youths in the adult corrections system, suicide rates are five times the national average and eight times higher than rates for juveniles who are not in the adult system (Austin, Johnson, & Gregoriou, 2000). One study, using data from 1978, estimated rates of suicide for juveniles in adult correctional facilities to have been as high as 2,041 per 100,000, in contrast with estimated suicide rates for juveniles in youth correctional facilities at 57 per 100,000 (Memory, 1989). One reason for such differences in suicide rates is that juveniles may feel much more hopeless regarding their legal situations and future in general when they are locked up with adults.

Finally, these adult institutions are geared for adult criminals, with typically inadequate funding for services and programs for youths and inadequately trained custodial and mental health staff (who are not specifically trained for or do not have experience in working with adolescents or do not have an appreciation for their unique social, physical activity, educational, and other developmental needs). Aside from the above-cited empirically based increased risk of suicide, there are myriad associated liability and administrative issues, such as physical assaults (with risks of injuries to these youths and also to correctional staff), accidental and nonaccidental injuries, and the risk of resulting costly civil litigation.

Treatment Is Not One Size Fits All

When appropriate individual or group violence reduction programs are offered to the individual, either during or after incarceration, there may be barriers to their successful implementation. These treatments aim to decrease the frequency and intensity of violence, change antisocial beliefs and attitudes that support violence, and increase interpersonal skills that would decrease violent behaviors. Whether they are correctional or community-based programs, treatment programs often do not cater to the mentally ill, and they can be hard to manage for the dually diagnosed individual (e.g., someone with a psychological diagnosis and co-occurring substance abuse problem). Someone who is dually diagnosed may need much greater monitoring in the community to ensure medication compliance and program attendance. Moreover, violence reduction programs are typically geared toward men and often fail to address the treatment needs of the 14% of all 2.1 million violent offenders who are female (U.S. Department of Justice, 1999). For instance, a violence treatment curriculum that does not address issues related to violence and parenting will fall far short of helping the violent female offender, who may also be the primary caregiver of young children. Moreover, violence prevention programs that require a female offender, who may also be a mother, to attend weekly meetings but do not offer day care are likely to be poorly attended. Indeed, treatment for violence is too frequently conceptualized as a one-size-fits-all intervention, which does not take into account the unique barriers to receiving treatment that the mentally ill, persons with co-occurring substance abuse diagnoses, and women face. Undoubtedly, there is a great need for violence intervention programs that are specifically geared to serving these populations.

Effective Treatments for Violence

After reading the previous section, you may be wondering, "What *does* work with individuals who engage in violent behaviors?" Fortunately, the past several decades of evidence-based research have yielded several effective programs and treatments, and the remainder of this chapter will describe them in detail.

Effective Treatments for Youth

Parent Management Training. Youth who engage in violent or aggressive behaviors may be evaluated and diagnosed with Conduct Disorder (CD). This disorder is characterized by aggression to people and animals, destruction of property, deceitfulness or theft, and serious violations of rules (American Psychiatric Association, 2000). One of the preliminary and most evidence-based treatment interventions for youth with CD is Parent Management Training (PMT).

Patterson (1982) is often credited with developing PMT (Welsh & Farrington, 2007), but other researchers (e.g., Eyberg, University of Florida; Forehand, University of Georgia; and Webster-Stratton, University of Washington) have also contributed to its development (Kazdin, 1997). It is often used with preadolescent children aged 3 to 12 who engage in aggressive or oppositional behaviors; however, PMT has been investigated in many randomized clinical trials with youth ranging from 2 to 17 years of age (Kazdin, 1997).

In general, PMT aims to teach parents how to alter their interactions with their children to increase prosocial behavior and decrease deviant behavior (Kazdin, 1997). Components of the treatment include providing parents with an understanding of social learning principles, implementing mild punishment such as time outs, and implementing reinforcement programs for desired or target behaviors in the home. Moreover, combining PMT with problem-solving skills training for the child has been more effective than PMT alone (Kazdin, Siegel, & Bass, 1992). PMT has also been found to produce positive results cross-culturally in a Latino population (Martinez &

Eddy, 2005) and is being implemented nationwide in Norway (Ogden, Forgatch, Askeland, Patterson, & Bullock, 2005).

Overall, results from the many investigations include improvements in child behavior, as noted on parent and teacher reports, in direct observations of behaviors at home and at school, and in institutional records. Conduct behaviors are reduced to nonclinical levels of functioning at home and at school, with treatment gains often being maintained up to three years after treatment. Not only has PMT been shown to decrease the undesired behaviors of the identified youth, it has also been shown to improve the behaviors of siblings as well as improve maternal psychopathology, particularly depression (Kazdin, 1997). In addition to individual studies finding significant results with PMT, a review of 82 controlled research studies of psychosocial treatments for CD youth was conducted to establish evidence-based treatments for CD. Studies were evaluated using the stringent criteria developed by the Division 12 (Clinical Psychology) Task Force on Promotion and Dissemination of Psychological Procedures, and two studies emerged that met the criteria for well-established treatment: parent management training programs based on Patterson and Guillion's (1968) manual *Living With Children* (Alexander & Parsons, 1973; Bernal, Klinnert, & Schultz, 1980; Wiltz & Patterson, 1974) and a videotape modeling parent training program (Brestan & Eyberg, 1998; Spaccarelli, Cotler, & Penman, 1992; Webster-Stratton, 1984, 1994).

Diversionary Programs for Youth

Juvenile Hearing Boards. Often, youth with CD find themselves in trouble with the law; however, instead of incarceration, diversionary programs are often the first line of intervention for youth. Diversionary programs attempt to divert the individual to community interventions rather than incarceration or out-of-home placements. One type of diversionary program that is used in many communities is a Juvenile Hearing Board. These boards are essentially an extension of the Family Court system and allow municipalities to manage minor nonviolent offenses, such as vandalism or truancy, committed by youth 18 years of age and under. The boards comprise community volunteers, and typical sanctions include community service, counseling, and restitution. Two main advantages of these boards are (1) they allow the Family Court to focus on more serious crimes and (2) they divert first-time youthful offenders from involvement in Family Court. Although empirical data is limited regarding the efficacy of these types of programs, one evaluation indicated that only 5% of their youth re-offended after 3 months and 9% re-offended after 6 months (Minugh & Breeden, 2005). Certainly, more research is needed to determine whether these boards are the most efficacious mechanism to reduce recidivism for first-time, nonviolent offenders, but it appears they may be cost effective, beneficial programs for these youth.

Mental Health Courts and Drug Courts for Youth. Once an individual becomes involved in the court system, he or she is often mandated for treatment. This simply means that there may be further legal consequences if he or she refuses to comply with treatment (Dill & Wells-Parker, 2006). Often, mandated treatments are imposed with the goal that these individuals will learn more adaptive coping skills and behaviors, thus reducing their threat to the community. Youth who engage in more serious crimes or who have significant mental health needs may be mandated for treatment in other types of diversionary programs, such as mental health courts and drug courts.

The purpose of mental health and drug courts is to provide supervised mental health or substance abuse treatment to offenders in the community, rather than impose incarceration. These courts employ a multidisciplinary team approach that develops treatment plans, monitors compliance and progress, and makes recommendations to the courts. Most courts accept individuals with charges ranging from misdemeanors to felonies; however, they usually restrict the offenses to nonviolent crimes. Progress is monitored through judicial review hearings, community supervision, home visits, and electronic monitoring. Many courts use incentives and rewards, such as reduced frequency of review hearings and termination of probation, and also impose sanctions for noncompliance, such as temporary placement in detention or electronic monitoring. It should be noted that despite widespread use of mental health courts, no large-scale examination of the success of these courts has been conducted with the juvenile population; however, a few courts are utilizing evidence-based services. Seneca County, OH and King County, WA provide Multisystemic Therapy (MST), which will be described later in this chapter, to youth who participate in their mental health courts (Cocozza & Shufelt, 2006).

There is also a dearth of research on drug courts. However, there is some emerging support for their effectiveness when juvenile drug courts are integrated with evidence-based practices. A randomized clinical trial of 161 youth who met diagnostic criteria for substance abuse or dependence was conducted (Henggeler, Halliday-Boykins, Cunningham, Randall, Shapiro, & Chapman, 2006). The youth were randomly assigned to one of four conditions: family court with standard community service (i.e., group-based substance abuse treatment, FC), drug court with standard community services (DC), drug court with multisystemic therapy (DC/MST), or drug court with MST with contingency management (DC/MST/CM). Regarding substance use, the results indicate that DC was more effective than FC, DC/MST was slightly more effective than DC, and DC/MST/CM was slightly more effective than DC/MST. Biological measures (i.e., urine drug screens) also indicated similar results, with positive drug screens in the first four months at rates of 69%, 28%, and 18% for DC, DC/MST, and DC/MST/CM, respectively. Regarding self-reported criminal behaviors, the youth in the DC conditions engaged in significantly fewer status offenses and crimes against persons as compared to the youth in the FC condition. Interestingly, however, no differences were found between the groups regarding re-arrest rates. The investigators hypothesized that the re-arrest rates for the DC conditions were inflated due to the intense supervision of these youth, whereas the youth in the FC condition experienced less surveillance and accountability for their behaviors.

Multisystemic Interventions for Youth. For youth who have a more extensive history of engaging in delinquent behaviors, more intensive interventions may be necessary. For these youth, the most effective treatments involve the multiple systems in their lives. Four treatments—functional family therapy, multidimensional treatment foster care, multisystemic therapy, and wraparound services—have not only been identified in the empirical literature but have also been identified by the U.S. Surgeon General as promising and effective treatments with juvenile offenders (U.S. Department of Health and Human Services, 2001).

Functional Family Therapy. Functional family therapy (FFT) was developed for youth aged 11 to 18 who are at risk of, or already engaging in, delinquent or disruptive behaviors (Alexander, Jameson, Newell, & Gunderson, 1996; Alexander & Parsons, 1982). FFT is a comprehensive treatment that involves multiple steps and phases and typically involves 8 to 30 hours of direct services to the youth and parent, depending on the needs of the family. There are three phases: engagement/motivation phase, behavior change phase, and generalization phase. The generalization phase is often the most difficult but most important. The therapist becomes more of a facilitator as the family begins to apply the skills consistently and in all areas of life. As a result, the family begins to function more independently, with less reliance on the therapist (McMahon & Kotler, 2006).

Research supporting FFT was begun in the 1970s by Alexander and colleagues (Alexander & Parsons, 1973; Klein, Alexander, & Parsons, 1977; Parsons & Alexander, 1973). These initial studies included primarily status offenses and did not include the cognitive and affective components that are now a hallmark of the therapy. In a sample of 86 youth, the families that received FFT improved their communication skills and had significantly lower recidivism rates (26%) when compared to no-treatment controls (50%), client-centered family groups (47%), and eclectic psychodynamic family therapy (73%).

The current model of FFT has been applied to more challenging youth who have offended multiple times and have been incarcerated. Barton, Alexander, Waldron, Turner, and Warburton (1985) found in their 15-month follow-up that the youth in FFT were less likely to commit another offense, as compared to youth in group homes. When additional offenses were committed, they committed significantly fewer offenses compared to the youth residing in group homes.

FFT has also been used with various populations and measured longitudinally. Gordon, Arbuthnot, Gustafson, and McGreen (1988) modified the current model to their sample of delinquent youths residing in a rural community, with similar results. At the 2 ½-year follow up, the recidivism rate for the FFT group was 11% while the recidivism rate for the probation-only comparison group was 67%. Similar rates were found when the youths were 20 to 22 years old. The youth who received FFT recidivated at a rate of 9%, while the comparison group recidivated at a rate of 41% (Gordon, Graves, & Arbuthnot, 1995). A group of Swedish investigators also found similar results. At the one-year follow up, 33% of the youth in the FFT condition relapsed while 65% of the comparison group that received treatment as usual relapsed (Hansson, Cederblad, & Alexander, 2002).

Multidimensional Treatment Foster Care. While FFT primarily incorporates biological or custodial parents in the treatment process, the Multidimensional Treatment Foster Care (MTFC) model engages the foster family and youth, as well as the biological/adoptive family members. This treatment model provides services to youth who have a long history of offending behaviors, as an alternative to less effective options such as incarceration, group homes, and residential facilities. The overarching goal of MTFC is to decrease offending behaviors while increasing participation in prosocial activities. The objectives for MTFC include setting fair and consistent limits with predictable consequences for infractions while providing a positive relationship with at least one adult and simultaneously decreasing access to delinquent peers. The three mechanisms that MTFC contributes to successful outcomes are a proactive approach to reducing problem behaviors, a consistent and reinforcing environment, and a separation and stratification of staff roles (Fisher & Chamberlain, 2000).

In addition to providing services to the foster families, MTFC also provides services to the biological families of the youths. Parent training and other services are provided to family members, with the goal of improving family relationships in addition to decreasing offending behaviors in preparation for reunification with the family. Additionally, the youth involved in MTFC receive skills-based training in areas such as anger management and problem solving. Relevant adjunctive services are also provided to meet the individual needs of the family and youth (Fisher & Chamberlain, 2000; McMahon & Kotler, 2006).

Chamberlain, Moreland, and Reid (1992) conducted a study that compared foster care families that received an additional stipend as well as MTFC to foster care families that only received a stipend. They found that the MTFC foster families had increased retention rates of foster parents, decreased reports of problem behaviors, increased reports of effectively managing problem behaviors, and decreased number of placements in a two-year period. A more recent study investigated 79 boys who were assigned to either MTFC or group care. At one-year follow-up, significant differences were found in runaway rates, length of time in placement, arrest rates, length of time incarcerated, and self-reported problem behaviors, and at four-year follow-up, the boys in the MTFC group continued to have significantly fewer arrests. Antisocial behavior and delinquency were mediated by family management skills and peer associations, accounting for approximately one-third of the variance in boys' subsequent antisocial behavior (Chamberlain, Fisher, & Moore, 2002).

Many outcome studies on juvenile offenders focus on males; female juvenile offenders often receive little attention in the literature. However, Chamberlain and colleagues (Chamberlain, Leve, & DeGarmo, 2007; Leve & Chamberlain, 2005; Leve, Chamberlain, & Reid, 2005) have focused their investigations on both male and female juvenile offenders. One recent study investigated the treatment effects on delinquent peers because they are a known risk factor for youth misbehavior. The results indicated that both male and female youth who received MTFC had fewer delinquent peers at 12-month follow up than the group care comparison group (Leve & Chamberlain, 2005).

A one-year follow-up investigation of another study yielded results that indicated females in MTFC had significantly greater reduction in days in locked settings and caregiver-reported delinquency than girls in group care (Leve et al., 2005). At the two-year follow-up, maintenance effects continued for the MTFC group, as measured by days in locked settings, number of criminal referrals, and self-reported delinquency (Cohen's $d = .65$). However, for both groups, older females exhibited less delinquency at the two-year follow up (Chamberlain et al., 2007).

Multisystemic Therapy. Another intervention that is used primarily with reoffending youth is Multisystemic Therapy (MST). MST is a multicomponent, family-based intervention that addresses the youth's behavior in multiple settings. Treatment techniques may include family therapy, marital therapy, parent training, school consultation, and cognitive-behavioral therapy (McMahon & Kotler, 2006).

Focusing on changing the social ecology of the youth and family, MST is usually provided in the youth's natural environments, which include the home, school, and community. Because it is such an intense clinical undertaking, caseloads are typically small. Although the therapists function in a team of three to four practitioners, each has his or her own caseload, typically averaging between three and six families. At least one practitioner on the treatment team is available 24 hours a day. Family participation and collaboration are paramount, so appointments are scheduled at the convenience of the family. Daily contact is made with the family, whether by phone or face to face. The treatment is time limited, usually three to five months, depending on the needs of the family (Henggeler, Schoenwald, Borduin, Rowland, & Cunningham, 1998).

MST has nine principles guiding its intense, comprehensive treatment. The first principle is *Finding the Fit*. The therapist utilizes the assessment to understand the relationship between the identified problem behavior and the systems involved. The assessment enables the therapist to understand all the factors and systems that directly or indirectly influence the problem behavior. The second principle, *Positive and Strength Focused*, focuses on a strengths-based approach to facilitate change. This type of approach helps foster cooperation and collaboration, identify protective factors, and increase confidence in family members. The third principle, *Increasing Responsibility*, indicates that interventions are developed to decrease irresponsible behaviors of family members while enhancing responsible behaviors. This includes the parents and the child because increases in parents' responsible behaviors typically increase responsible behavior in the child. The fourth principle, *Present Focused, Action Oriented, and Well-Defined*, suggests that target behaviors must be well-defined and the interventions for the behaviors must be present focused and action oriented. MST focuses on the "here and now" in order to facilitate and maintain change. Furthermore, as the fifth principle, *Targeting Sequences*, suggests, MST interventions identify what maintains and reinforces the behavior. The sixth principle, *Developmentally Appropriate*, reminds therapists that the interventions must be developmentally appropriate and fit the needs of the youth. For example, the developmental needs of a 17-year-old may require a focus on transitioning to adulthood, while the needs of a 14-year-old may be to develop relationships with prosocial peers. The seventh principle, *Continuous Effort*, means the interventions require weekly, if not daily, efforts by all family members. This allows barriers to be identified rapidly, problems to be resolved quickly, and progress to be monitored frequently to provide the opportunity for feedback and positive reinforcement. The eighth principle, *Evaluation and Accountability*, recommends that the effectiveness of the intervention be evaluated by multiple informants, and multiple methods should be used to measure the identified behavior. This approach provides multiple perspectives on the progress of the intervention, and the therapist assumes accountability for any barriers to success. The last principle, *Generalization,* proposes that the generalization and maintenance of therapeutic change are achieved through caregiver empowerment. Empowerment of the family is the cornerstone of MST and is based on the premise that a family that is empowered will have the ability to effectively manage challenges that arise and navigate successfully through the multiple systems involved in their lives (Henggeler et al., 1998).

Of the evidence-based treatments for juvenile offenders, MST is perhaps the most rigorously investigated. Support for MST has been found not only in efficacy studies (which are typically clinical trials performed in university settings) but also in effectiveness studies (studies conducted in "real world" community settings; Timmons-Mitchell, Bender, Kishna, & Mitchell, 2006). MST has been used by a variety of populations, such as abusive/neglectful parents, juvenile sexual offenders, violent and chronic juvenile offenders, substance abusing juvenile offenders, and psychiatrically disturbed adolescents (Curtis, Ronan, & Borduin, 2004). A meta-analysis conducted by Curtis et al. (2004) included studies on the aforementioned populations, and the results indicated that the youths and families that received MST were functioning better than 70% of the youths and families in the control conditions. Interestingly, larger effects were found in studies of graduate student therapists involved in efficacy trials than in studies of therapists in the community. Additionally, most of the studies involved the direct oversight of one of the two principal developers of MST, Dr. Scott Henggeler and Dr. Charles Borduin. To investigate whether similar results could be replicated without the direct oversight of the principal developers, Timmons-Mitchell et al. (2006) conducted a randomized clinical trial of MST with 93 juvenile offenders. The youth were assigned to MST or treatment as usual (TAU), and the youth who received MST had decreased rates of recidivism as well as improved functioning in the home, at school, and in the community. However, effect sizes were similar to those of the effectiveness studies reported in Curtis et al. (2004). As reported previously, MST is also being integrated in drug courts with promising outcomes.

Wraparound Programs. Wraparound programs are another multisystemic service that shows promise in reducing recidivism and arrests in adjudicated juveniles. Wraparound Milwaukee is an example of a premier program that has yielded impressive results. It has five core components: (1) it is a strengths-based approach to children and families, (2) it involves the family in the treatment process, (3) it involves needs-based service planning and delivery, (4) it involves individualized service plans, and (5) it utilizes objective measures to evaluate the program (Kamradt, 2001). The treatment team includes the Care Coordinators, Child and Family Team, Mobile Urgent Treatment Team, and provider network.

Unlike the aforementioned programs, to our knowledge, Wraparound Milwaukee has not been a part of any randomized clinical trials; however, as previously mentioned, it does evaluate the success of its program based on objective clinical measures and objective data. According to Kamradt (2001), the use of residential treatment has decreased 60% since the initiation of Wraparound Milwaukee, and inpatient psychiatric hospitalizations have decreased by 80%. To evaluate clinical progress, the Child and Adolescent Functional Assessment Scale (CAFAS; Hodges, 1994) was used to measure youths' change in functioning at home, at school, and in the community. The youths' average score on the CAFAS at the time of enrollment was in the high range of impairment, and after one year of enrollment, the score decreased to the moderate level of impairment. However, it is unclear whether the change is statistically significant or simply a regression to the mean. There was a reduction in recidivism for the following offenses one year prior to enrollment as compared to one year post-enrollment: sex offenses (12%), assaults (15%), weapons offenses (8%), property offenses (27%), and drug offenses (2%). Additionally, there was a reduction in the percentages of clients who were referred for felonies (23%) and misdemeanors (36%), from a three-year period prior to enrollment to three years following dis-enrollment, indicating that treatment gains were maintained three years post-enrollment.

Diversionary Programs for Adults

Mental Health Courts and Drug Courts for Adults. Like juveniles, adults also have mental health and drug courts that follow similar models. Studies regarding mental health courts for adults have only recently begun to emerge. According to Kaplan (2007), a recent study indicated that mental health courts are successful in increasing mental health services while decreasing jail time and costs to taxpayers. For certain subpopulations, they appear more effective. For example, cost savings were greatest for those with felony charges, those suffering from psychotic disorders, and those functioning poorly due to their mental illness (Ridgely, Engberg, Greenberg, Turner, De Martini, & Dembosky, 2007).

Some preliminary support also exists for adult drug courts. A meta-analysis of 55 investigations tentatively suggests that those who participate in drug court are less likely to recidivate for all types of offenses, as compared to those who receive traditional interventions such as probation, with an odds ratio of 1.66 (an odds ratio greater than 1 suggests that the odds of an offense are lower for the drug court condition as compared to the other conditions, indicating the effectiveness of the drug court). Furthermore, drug courts that use a pre-plea model (diversion; odds ratio = 1.86) or post-plea model (suspended sentence; odds ratio = 1.71) were more effective than courts that used mixed approaches or had no incentive for completion of the requirements. Moreover, courts that used a single substance abuse treatment provider (odds ratio = 1.73) had slightly larger effects than those that used multiple providers. However, all of these results should be interpreted with caution, due to the generally weak methodologies of the majority of the studies (Wilson, Mitchell, & MacKenzie, 2006).

Diversionary Programs for Adults With Severe Mental Illness

Unfortunately, individuals with severe mental illness continue to serve time in correctional facilities rather than receive necessary and appropriate treatment. They are also more likely to be incarcerated for misdemeanors and for longer periods of time, as compared to non-mentally ill individuals. Clinical factors such as comorbid substance abuse, treatment nonadherence, and homelessness, in addition to systemic factors such as deinstitutionalization (i.e., when individuals are removed from a facility, usually a state hospital, and treated in the community) and fragmented services are some of the factors that contribute to the frequent and extended incarceration of those with mental illness (Lamberti, Weisman, Schwarzkopf, Price, Ashton, & Trompeter, 2001). Fortunately, diversionary programs for adults with severe mental illness are becoming the treatment of choice.

At the ground, or entry level, police-based jail diversion programs have been designed to address the disproportionately high numbers of mentally ill individuals being arrested and incarcerated. These programs focus on improving the ability of police departments to respond to calls involving mentally ill individuals. A Crisis Intervention Team (CIT) is a model that involves specialized training for police officers and was started in Memphis, TN in 1998. It was initially adopted by a few large cities, such as Houston, TX; Portland, MA; Seattle, WA; and Albuquerque, NM. There have been recent statewide dissemination efforts in Colorado, Connecticut, Florida, Georgia, Illinois, and Ohio (Munetz, Morrison, Krake, Young, & Woody, 2006). Other models involve partnerships between law enforcement and mental health workers; the Psychiatric Emergency Response Team (PERT) in San Diego, CA and the Police Team with Mental Health Expertise in Birmingham AL are two such examples (Lamberti & Weisman, 2004). While these programs are reporting favorable results, they have yet to undergo rigorous randomized investigations.

One challenge of these programs is the lack of follow-up and maintenance of the community services that are essential for these individuals (Lamberti et al., 2001). In contrast, Assertive Community Treatment programs (ACT) have been found to be effective at engaging individuals with community-based services. Due to their delivery of intensive healthcare and social services, the number of emergency room and hospital visits has decreased; however, there has been little effect on incarceration (Lamberti et al., 2001).

Modified therapeutic communities are another diversionary program for adults with severe mental illness and comorbid substance use disorders. These communities develop independent living skills, foster employment, and promote appropriate utilization of social services while providing mental health and substance abuse treatment (Lamberti et al., 2001).

To address the revolving door phenomenon of these individuals cycling between correctional facilities, hospitals, and homelessness, a hybrid of care that incorporates jail diversion, ACT, and modified therapeutic community was developed at the University of Rochester Department of Psychiatry, in collaboration with local community agencies (Weisman, Lamberti, & Price, 2004). Project Link, a university-led consortium of five community agencies, links healthcare, social services, and criminal justice systems with the goals of decreasing jail and hospital recidivism while promoting community adjustment for adults with severe mental illness who have been involved with the criminal justice system (Lamberti et al., 2001). A mobile treatment team includes a forensic psychiatrist, a dual-diagnosis treatment residence, and a culturally sensitive staff. Results of 41 one-year completers indicated a decrease in the mean number of jail days and hospital stays, with significant results in the average number of arrests per patient and in the average number of incarcerations and hospitalizations per patient. No assaults or suicide attempts were reported for this sample during this study period. Another nationally recognized program that utilizes ACT and has produced similar results is the Thresholds Jail Program in Chicago, IL (Lamberti & Weisman, 2004).

Therapeutic Interventions for Incarcerated Juvenile and Adult Offenders

Thus far, the goal of the treatments discussed is to prevent the incarceration of juvenile and adult offenders. However, this is not always possible, and so the question becomes, "What types of treatments are effective for treating youth and adults who are incarcerated?" The remainder of the chapter is dedicated to discussing effective treatments for incarcerated juvenile and adult offenders, often referred to as correctional treatment.

When mental health treatment is provided in a correctional environment, there are three principles that are addressed: risk, need, and responsivity. In this context, *risk* refers to the level of treatment services an individual receives based on the risk level of the offender; high-risk offenders receive more intensive services while low-risk offenders receive minimal services. *Need* refers to both criminogenic needs, which are risk factors associated with reducing criminal activity, and noncriminogenic needs that are not related to criminal activity, such as self-esteem. *Responsivity* refers to service delivery and indicates that services should be delivered in a mode that matches the learning style of the offender (Dowden & Andrews, 2000). A meta-analysis conducted by Dowden and Andrews found that the effects of the treatment increased with increased adherence to each principle. Interestingly, the two most targeted criminogenic needs, fear of official punishment and vague emotional/personal problems, were negatively associated with the effect size, and programs that targeted these needs had increased, but not statistically significant, levels of recidivism. On the contrary, programs that targeted negative affect/anger and relapse prevention skills were positively and significantly associated with effect size, while programs targeting antisocial attitudes had a trend toward reducing violent reoffending. Another meta-analysis (Andrews & Dowden, 2006) that focused primarily on risk found that the risk principle is much stronger for females and young offenders and that the risk principle only enhanced programs that adhered to the principles of need and responsivity. It was also found that criminal justice interventions that did not include human service elements produced negative results regardless of the level of offender risk. Keeping these principles in mind, the following are evidence-based interventions for incarcerated populations.

Motivational Interviewing. Offenders often do not attend treatment of their own volition, so treatment is often court mandated. Research indicates that confrontational styles and interventions are not effective at eliciting behavior change and actually enhance resistance. One study found that a directive-confrontational approach resulted in twice the resistance and half as many positive behavior changes as a client-centered supportive approach (Miller, Benefield, & Tonigan, 1993). However, as noted in the previous sections of this chapter, this approach has been the style of choice of many working with offenders. An opposing, client-centered approach, Motivational Interviewing (MI), has recently emerged as a promising technique with the criminal justice population.

MI is "a client-centered, directive method for enhancing intrinsic motivation to change by exploring and resolving ambivalence" (Miller & Rollnick, 2002, p. 25). Rather than a set of techniques, MI is a communication style, a style of "being with people," which is often referred to as "the spirit of MI." Collaboration, evocation, and autonomy (rather than confrontation, education, and authority) are at the core of MI and facilitate resolving ambivalence while propelling the person toward change. MI has a longstanding empirical history in the treatment of substance abuse, but over the past several decades it has been used in various other settings, and more recently, it has been used in the treatment of offenders.

One of the first studies, Project Match (Project Match Research Group, 1997), was a multisite study with offenders and nonoffenders that investigated the client characteristics and the "fit" with alcohol treatment. The study compared Twelve-Step Facilitation, CBT, and MET (Motivational Enhancement Therapy, which is MI with feedback), and results indicated that outpatients high on anger ratings who received MET had better post-treatment drinking outcomes. The nonconfrontational nature of MET was indicated as one of the potential sources of success with those high on anger ratings (Mattson, 1998). Adult and juvenile offenders often have difficulty with anger regulation; thus, the efficacy with angry individuals has strong implications for criminal justice populations (Feldstein & Ginsburg, 2006).

There have been several recent investigations of MI used with incarcerated adolescents. A pilot study of the Family Check-Up (FCU; Dishion & Kavanaugh, 2003) was conducted with 10 incarcerated youth (Slavet, Stein, & Klein, 2005). The FCU is an assessment and feedback session based on the principles of MI and designed to enhance parents' recognition of risky behaviors engaged in by their child and to provide support in reducing those behaviors. After the intervention, the youth were more confident in their ability to resist drug use, and the parents were more confident in their ability to impact the risky behaviors of their child. Moreover, both the youth and parents reported being satisfied with the treatment. In another study that investigated whether MI enhanced substance abuse treatment engagement, MI was compared with a relaxation training (RT) control condition in a sample of incarcerated youth (Stein, Colby, Barnett, Monti, et al., 2006). The youth were randomly assigned to either individual condition (MI or RT), which was then followed by the standard of care group-based treatments that targeted criminal and substance-using behaviors. Results indicate that MI significantly mitigated negative substance abuse treatment engagement. The final study found that after release, incarcerated youth who received MI as compared to relaxation training had lower rates of drinking and driving and of being a passenger in a car with someone who had been drinking. Similar but nonsignificant results were found regarding marijuana-related risky driving (Stein, Colby, & Barnett, 2006). Not only is MI being used in efficacy trials, many large-scale MI training initiatives are being delivered to probation and parole personnel in many jurisdictions in Canada, United States, Britain, and Sweden (Feldstein & Ginsburg, 2006).

Cognitive-Behavioral Therapy. One of the most evidence-based psychotherapy treatments provided to incarcerated offenders is Cognitive-Behavioral Therapy (CBT). The basic tenet of CBT is the focus on the interrelationship between thoughts, feelings, and behaviors. Often, CBT is used to address specific deficits, such as problem solving and anger regulation, and behaviors such as substance abuse. Two recent meta-analyses, conducted by Pearson, Lipton, Cleland, and Yee (2002) and Wilson, Bouffard, and MacKenzie (2005), demonstrated that CBT is an effective intervention for reducing recidivism and criminal behavior in offenders. Regarding effects of the treatment, Pearson et al. reported a weighted mean $r = .144$ and the corresponding BESD of 57.2% success in the experimental group and 43.8% in the comparison group (BESD = Binomial Effect Size Display). Wilson et al. found a moderate effect size across a variety of CBT programs whose quality was generally considered low (mean effect = .51); however, when only higher quality studies were investigated, a moderate effect size was also found (mean effect size = .32). A recent meta-analysis further advanced the research by identifying the factors associated with effective treatment (Landenberger & Lipsey, 2005). The meta-analysis included 58 experimental and quasi-experimental studies of CBT with adult and juvenile offenders; however, the majority of the studies were conducted with primarily male, adult samples. Treatment was delivered in a correctional facility in almost half the studies and typically lasted less than 20 weeks. In most cases, treatment providers had little mental health background and minimal CBT training and provided one of the "brand name" manualized CBT programs, such as Moral Reconation Therapy (Armstrong, 2003), with multiple treatment elements, such as cognitive restructuring and behavior modification. The results yielded no differences between adult and juvenile samples, between "brand name" CBT protocols and generic forms of CBT, or between genders. The results further indicate that the treatment group had a 25% decrease in recidivism as compared to the control group. The factors related to recidivism reduction were treatment of high-risk offenders, high-quality treatment, and CBT programs that included anger control and interpersonal problem solving, but not victim impact and behavior modification.

Another recent study in New Zealand (Polaschek, Wilson, Townsend, & Daly, 2005) investigated a CBT program for high-risk violent offenders and found that offenders who completed the program were less likely to violently reoffend. Offenders who received the program and reoffended did so in the first year post-release; however, the length of time before reoffending was twice as long as in the comparison group that did not participate in the program.

Substance Abuse Treatment. Substance abuse treatments at different levels were discussed throughout this chapter, such as preliminary interventions through drug courts and more comprehensive interventions with juveniles through MST and with severely mentally ill adults through modified therapeutic communities. However, the high prevalence of substance abuse with criminal behaviors warrants its own section. The National Institute on Drug Abuse (NIDA, 2006) developed specific guidelines for drug abuse treatment for criminal justice populations. According to NIDA, the guiding principles for effective drug treatment include motivation to change, developing problem-solving skills, skill building for resisting drug use and criminal activity, developing constructive non-drug using activities to replace drug using and criminal activity, and learning and understanding the consequences of one's behavior. Also, targeting "criminal thinking" (attitudes and beliefs that support criminal behavior) using cognitive skills training may result in decreased drug abuse and criminal activity. Monitoring drug use with methods such as urinalysis is also recommended. Moreover, programs that combine cognitive-behavioral interventions with transition to and follow-up with community-based services have also been shown to be effective and are recommended (MacKenzie, 2000).

Conclusion

Despite the ongoing use of programs and interventions that have been shown to be ineffective with juvenile and adult offenders, many evidence-based treatments are emerging and being implemented with these populations. In general, for both adults and juveniles, diversionary programs are the first line of intervention. More intensive programs that employ a multi-systemic approach and utilize a cognitive-behavioral intervention are recommended. However, much work is still needed in evaluating, implementing, and disseminating these treatments.

Discussion Questions

1. What kinds of approaches to treating and preventing violence *don't* work? What are some reasons that these approaches may fail?

2. What are some potential difficulties in assessing treatment outcome for offenders?

3. It is commonly heard within the criminal justice community that treatments for offenders are not very effective. Yet the psychological community often claims that treatments can be effective. What accounts for this discrepancy? How high an effect size should treatments have before they are considered "effective"?

4. What are your thoughts on the use of mental health courts? What types of offenders ought to have the option of diversion into the mental health system rather than the criminal justice system?

Internet Resources

American Medical Association, "Violence Prevention": http://www.ama-assn.org/ama/pub/category/3242.html

National Institutes of Mental Health: http://www.nimh.nih.gov/

Psi Chi, "What is Forensic Psychology?": http://www.psichi.org/pubs/articles/article_58.asp

World Health Organization, Department of Violence and Injury Prevention and Disability: http://www.who.int/violence_injury_prevention/en/

References

Alexander, J. F., Jameson, P. B., Newell, R. M., & Gunderson, D. (1996). Changing cognitive schemas: A necessary antecedent to changing behaviors in dysfunctional families? In K. S. Dobson & K. D. Craig (Eds.), *Advances in cognitive-behavioral therapy* (pp. 174–191). Thousand Oaks, CA: Sage.

Alexander, J. F., & Parsons, B. V. (1973). Short-term behavioral interventions with delinquent families: Impact on family process and recidivism. *Journal of Abnormal Psychology, 81,* 219–225.

Alexander, J. F., & Parsons, B. (1982). *Functional family therapy.* Monterey, CA: Brooks/Cole.

American Psychiatric Association. (2000). *Diagnostic and statistical manual of mental disorders* (Text rev.). Washington, DC: Author.

Andrews, D. A., & Dowden, C. (2006). Risk principles of case classification in correctional treatment: A meta-analytic investigation. *International Journal of Offender Therapy and Comparative Criminology, 50*(1), 88–100.

Armstrong, T. A. (2003). The effect of moral reconation therapy on the recidivism of youthful offenders: A randomized experiment. *Criminal Justice and Behavior, 30*(6), 668–687.

Austin, J., Johnson, K. D., & Gregoriou, M. (2000). *Juveniles in adult prisons and jails: A national assessment.* Washington, DC: Bureau of Justice Assistance.

Barton, C., Alexander, J. F., Waldron, H., Turner, C. W., & Warburton, J. (1985). Generalizing treatment effects of functional family therapy: Three replications. *American Journal of Family Therapy, 13,* 16–26.

Beland, K. (1992). *Second step: A violence prevention curriculum for grades 1–5, revised.* Seattle, WA: Committee for Children.

Benda, B. B. (2005). Introduction: Boot camps revisited: Issues, problems, prospects. *Journal of Offender Rehabilitation, 40*(3–4), 1–25.

Bernal, M. E., Klinnert, M. D., & Schultz, L. A. (1980). Outcome evaluation of behavioral parent training and client-centered parent counseling for children with conduct problems. *Journal of Applied Behavioral Analysis, 13,* 677–691.

Bishop, D. M., Frazier, C. E., & Lanza-Kaduce, L. (1996). The transfer of juveniles to criminal court: Does it make a difference? *Crime & Delinquency, 42*(2), 171–191.

Brestan, E. V., & Eyberg, S. M. (1998). Effective psychosocial treatments of conduct-disordered children and adolescents: 29 years, 82 studies, and 5,272 kids. *Journal of Consulting and Clinical Psychology, 27*(2), 180–189.

Brier, N. (1995). Predicting antisocial behavior in youngsters displaying poor academic achievement: A review of risk factors. *Journal of Developmental & Behavioral Pediatrics, 16*(4), 271–276.

Chamberlain, P., Fisher, P. A., & Moore, K. (2002). *Multidimensional treatment foster care: Application of the OSLC intervention model to high-risk youth and their families.* Washington, DC: American Psychological Association.

Chamberlain, P., Leve, L. D., & DeGarmo, D. S. (2007). Multidimensional treatment foster care for girls in the juvenile justice system: 2-year follow-up of a randomized clinical trial. *Journal of Consulting and Clinical Psychology, 75*(1), 187–193.

Chamberlain, P., Moreland, S., & Reid, K. (1992). Enhanced services and stipends for foster parents: Effects on retention rates and outcomes of children. *Child Welfare, 71,* 387–401.

Clines, F. X. (1999, December 19). Maryland is latest of states to rethink youth "boot camps." *The New York Times.* Retrieved September 10, 2007, from http://www.lexis nexis.com.revproxy.brown.edu/

Cocozza, J. J., & Shufelt, J. L. (2006). *Juvenile mental health courts: An emerging strategy.* Delmar, NY: National Center for Mental Health and Juvenile Justice.

Cullen, F. T., Blevins, K. R., & Trager, J. S. (2005). The rise and fall of boot camps: A case study in common-sense corrections. *Journal of Offender Rehabilitation, 40*(3–4), 53–70.

Curtis, N. M., Ronan, K. R., & Borduin, C. M. (2004). Multisystemic treatment: A meta-analysis of outcome studies. *Journal of Family Psychology, 18*(3), 411–419.

Dill, P. L., & Wells-Parker, E. (2006). Court-mandated treatment for convicted drinking drivers. *Alcohol Research and Health, 29*(1), 41–48.

Dishion, T. J., & Kavanaugh, K. (2003). *Intervening in adolescent problem behavior: A family centered approach.* New York: Guildford Press.

Dowden, C., & Andrews, D. A. (2000). Effective correctional treatment and violent reoffending: A meta-analysis. *Canadian Journal of Criminology, 42*(4), 449–467.

Farrington, D. P., & Welsh, B. C. (2005). Randomized experiments in criminology: What have we learned in the last two decades? *Journal of Experimental Criminology, 1*(1), 9–38.

Feldstein, S. W., & Ginsburg, J. I. D. (2006). Motivational interviewing with dually diagnosed adolescents in juvenile justice settings. *Brief Treatment and Crisis Intervention, 6*(3), 218–233.

Fisher, P. A., & Chamberlain, P. (2000). Multidimensional treatment foster care: A program for intensive parenting, family support, and skill building. *Journal of Emotional and Behavioral Disorders, 8*(3), 155–164.

Fitzgerald, P. D., & Edstrom, L. V. (2006). Second Step: A violence prevention curriculum. In S. Jimerson & M. Furlong (Eds.), *The handbook of school violence and school safety: From research to practice.* Mahwah, NJ: Erlbaum.

Forst, J., Fagan, J., & Scott, B. T. (1989). Youth in prison and training schools: Perceptions and consequences of the treatment-custody dichotomy. *Juvenile and Family Court Journal, 40,* 1–4.

Gordon, D. A., Arbuthnot, J., Gustafson, K. E., & McGreen, P. (1988). Home-based behavioral-systems family therapy with disadvantaged juvenile delinquents. *American Journal of Family Therapy, 16,* 243–255.

Gordon, D. A., Graves, K., & Arbuthnot, J. (1995). The effects of functional family therapy for delinquents on adult criminal behaviors. *Criminal Justice and Behavior, 33,* 60–73.

Grossman, D. C., Neckerman, H. J., Koepsell, T. D., Liu, P. Y., Asher, K. N., Beland, K., et al. (1997). Effectiveness of a violence prevention curriculum among children in elementary school: A randomized controlled trial. *Journal of the American Medical Association, 277*(20), 1605–1611.

Hansson, K., Cederblad, M., & Alexander, J. F. (2002). *A method for treating juvenile delinquents: A cross cultural comparison.* Manuscript submitted for publication.

Henggeler, S. W., Halliday-Boykins, C. A., Cunningham, P. B., Randall, J., Shapiro, S. B., & Chapman, J. E. (2006). Juvenile drug court: Enhancing outcomes by integrating evidence-based treatments. *Journal of Consulting and Clinical Psychology, 74*(1), 42–54.

Henggeler, S. W., Schoenwald, S. K., Borduin, C. M., Rowland, M. D., & Cunningham, P. B. (1998). *Multisystemic treatment of antisocial behavior in children and adolescents: Treatment manuals for practitioners.* New York: Guildford Press.

Hodges, K. (1994). *Child and adolescent functional assessment scale.* Ypsilanti: Eastern Michigan University, Department of Psychology.

Jones, M. (1997). Is less better? Boot camp, regular probation and rearrest in North Carolina.

American Journal of Criminal Justice, 21(2), 147–161.

Kam, C. M., Greenberg, M. T., & Kusché, C. A. (2004). Sustained effects of the PATHS curriculum on the social and psychological adjustment of children in special education. *Journal of Emotional & Behavioral Disorders, 12*(2), 66–79.

Kam, C. M., Greenberg, M. T., & Walls, C. T. (2003). Examining the role of implementation quality in school-based prevention using the PATHS curriculum. Promoting alternative thinking skills curriculum. *Prevention Science, 4*(1), 55–63.

Kamradt, B. (2001). *Wraparound Milwaukee: Aiding youth with mental health needs.* Washington, DC: Office of Juvenile Justice and Delinquency and Prevention.

Kaplan, A. (2007). Mental health courts reduce incarceration, save money. *Psychiatric Times, 24*(8), 1–2. Retrieved August 21, 2008, from http://www.psychiatrictimes.com.

Kazdin, A. E. (1997). Parent management training: Evidence, outcomes, and issues. *Journal of the American Academy of Child and Adolescent Psychiatry, 36*(10), 1349–1356.

Kazdin, A. E., Siegel, T., & Bass, D. (1992). Cognitive problem-solving skills training and parent management training in the treatment of antisocial behavior in children. *Journal of Consulting and Clinical Psychology, 60*, 733–747.

Kelly, B., Longbottom, J., Potts, F., & Williamson, J. (2004). Applying emotional intelligence: Exploring the promoting alternative thinking strategies curriculum. *Educational Psychology in Practice, 20*(3), 221–241.

Klein, N. C., Alexander, J. F., & Parsons, B. V. (1977). Impact of family systems intervention on recidivism and sibling delinquency: A model of primary prevention and program evaluation. *Journal of Consulting and Clinical Psychology, 45*, 469–474.

Kusche, C. A., & Greenberg, M. T. (1994). *The PATHS curriculum.* Seattle, WA: Developmental Research and Programs.

Lamberti, J. S., & Weisman, R. L. (2004). Persons with severe mental disorders in the criminal justice system: Challenges and opportunities. *Psychiatric Quarterly, 75*(2), 151–164.

Lamberti, J. S., Weisman, R. L., Schwarzkopf, S. B., Price, N., Ashton, R. M., & Trompeter, J. (2001). The mentally ill in jails and prisons: Towards an integrated model of prevention. *Psychiatric Quarterly, 72*(1), 63–77.

Landenberger, N. A., & Lipsey, M. W. (2005). The positive effects of cognitive-behavioral programs for offenders: A meta-analysis of factors associated with effective treatment. *Journal of Experimental Criminology, 1*, 451–476.

Leve, L. D., & Chamberlain, P. (2005). Association with delinquent peers: Intervention effects for youth in the juvenile justice system. *Journal of Abnormal Child Psychology, 33*(3), 339–347.

Leve, L. D., Chamberlain, P., & Reid, J. B. (2005). Intervention outcomes for girls referred from juvenile justice: Effects on delinquency. *Journal of Consulting and Clinical Psychology, 73*, 1181–1185.

Levitt, S. D. (1996). The effect of prison population size on crime rates: Evidence from prison overcrowding litigation. *Quarterly Journal of Economics, 111*(2), 319–351.

Lipsey, M. W., & Derzon, J. H. (1998). Predictors of violent and serious delinquency in adolescence and early adulthood: A synthesis of longitudinal research. In R. Loeber & D. P. Farrington (Eds.), *Serious and violent juvenile offenders: Risk factors and successful interventions* (pp. 86–105). Thousand Oaks, CA: Sage.

Lynam, D. R., Milich, R., & Zimmerman, R. (1999). Project DARE: No effects at 10-year follow-up. *Journal of Consulting and Clinical Psychology, 67*(4), 590–593.

MacKenzie, D. L. (2000). Evidence-based corrections: Identifying what works. *Crime and Delinquency, 46*(4), 457–471.

Mackenzie, D. L., Brame, R., McDowall, D., & Souryal, D. (1995). Boot camp prisons and recidivism in eight states. *Criminology, 33*(3), 327–358.

Martinez, C. R., & Eddy, J. M. (2005). Effects of culturally adapted parent management training on Latino youth behavioral outcomes. *Journal of Consulting and Clinical Psychology, 73*(4), 841–851.

Mathis, K. J. (2007). American Bar Association: Adult justice system is the wrong answer for most juveniles. *American Journal of Preventive Medicine, 32*(4, Supp. 1), S1–S2.

Mattson, M. E. (1998). *Finding the right approach.* New York: Plenum Press.

McMahon, R. J., & Kotler, J. S. (2006). Conduct problems. In D. A. Wolfe & E. J. Mash (Eds.), *Behavioral and emotional disorders in adolescents* (pp. 153–225). New York: Guilford Press.

McMahon, S. D., & Washburn, J. J. (2003). Violence prevention: An evaluation of program effects with urban African-American students. *Journal of Primary Prevention, 24,* 43–62.

Memory, J. (1989). Juvenile suicides in secure detention facilities: Correction of published rates. *Death Studies, 13,* 455–463.

Miller, W. R., Benefield, G., & Tonigan, J. S. (1993). Enhancing motivation for change in problem drinking: A controlled comparison of two therapist styles. *Journal of Consulting and Clinical Psychology, 61,* 455–461.

Miller, W. R., & Rollnick, S. (2002). *Motivational interviewing: Preparing people for change* (2nd ed.). New York: Guilford Press.

Minugh, P. A., & Breeden, K. R. (2005). *Juvenile hearing boards evaluation brief.* Retrieved September 16, 2007, from http://www .mjdatacorp.com/presentations_reports/cf_ jhb_brief.pdf.

Munetz, M. R., Morrison, A., Krake, J., Young, B., & Woody, L. M. (2006). State mental health policy: Statewide implementation of the crisis intervention team program: The Ohio model. *Psychiatric Services, 57,* 1569–1571.

Murakami, S., Rappaport, N., & Penn, J. V. (2006). An overview of juveniles and school violence. In C. Scott (Ed.), *Psychiatric clinics of North America* (pp. 725–741). Philadelphia: Elsevier.

Myers, D. L. (2003). The recidivism of violent youths in juvenile and adult court: A consideration of selection bias. *Youth Violence and Juvenile Justice, 1*(1), 79–101.

National Institute on Drug Abuse. (2006). *Principles of drug abuse treatment for criminal justice populations: A research-based guide.* Retrieved September 16, 2007, from http://www.nida.nih.gov/PDF/PODAT_CJ/ PODAT_CJ.pdf.

Ogden, T., Forgatch, M. S., Askeland, E., Patterson, G. R., & Bullock, B. M. (2005). Implementation of parent management training at the national level: The case of Norway. *Journal of Social Work, 19*(3), 317–329.

Parsons, B. V., & Alexander, J. F. (1973). Short-term family intervention: A therapy outcome study. *Journal of Consulting and Clinical Psychology, 41,* 195–201.

Patterson, G. R. (1982). *Coercive family process.* Eugene, OR: Castalia.

Patterson, G. R., & Guillion, M. E. (1968). *Living with children: New methods for parents and teachers.* Champaign, IL: Research Press.

Peacock, M. J., McClure, F., & Agars, M. D. (2003). Predictors of delinquent behaviors among Latino youth. *Urban Review, 35*(1), 59–72.

Pearson, F. S., Lipton, D. S., Cleland, C. M., & Yee, D. S. (2002). The effects of behavioral/cognitive-behavioral programs on recidivism. *Crime and Delinquency, 48*(3), 476–496.

Penn, J. V., & Thomas, C. R. (2005). AACAP Work Group on Quality Issues: Practice parameter for the assessment and treatment of youth in juvenile detention and correctional facilities. *Journal of the American Academy of Child & Adolescent Psychiatry, 10,* 1085–1098.

Peters, M., Thomas, D., & Zamberlan, C. (1997). *Boot camps for juvenile offenders program summary.* Washington, DC: U.S. Department of Justice, Office of Juvenile Justice and Delinquency Prevention.

Petrosino, A., Turpin-Petrosino, C., & Buehler, J. (2005). Scared Straight and other juvenile awareness programs for preventing juvenile delinquency. *The Scientific Review of Mental Health Practice, 4*(1), 48–54.

Petrosino, A., Turpin-Petrosino, C., & Finckenauer, J. O. (2000). Well-meaning programs can have harmful effects! Lessons from experiments of programs such as Scared Straight. *Crime & Delinquency, Special Issue, 46*(3), 354–379.

Polaschek, D. L. L., Wilson, N. J., Townsend, M. R., & Daly, L. R. (2005). Cognitive-behavioral rehabilitation for high-risk violent offenders: An outcome evaluation of the Violence Prevention Unit. *Journal of Interpersonal Violence, 20*(12), 1611–1627.

Project Match Research Group. (1997). Project Match secondary a priori hypotheses. *Addiction, 92,* 1671–1698.

Ridgely, M. S., Engberg, J., Greenberg, M. D., Turner, S., De Martini, C., & Dembosky, J. W. (2007). *Justice, treatment, and cost: An evaluation of the fiscal impact of Allegheny County Mental Health Court.* Santa Monica, CA: RAND. Retrieved August 21, 2008, from http://www.rand.org/pubs/technical_reports/2007/RAND_TR439.pdf.

Rosenbaum, D. P., Flewelling, R. L., & Bailey, S. L. (1994). Cops in the classroom: A longitudinal evaluation of drug abuse resistance education (DARE). *Journal of Research in Crime and Delinquency, 31*(1), 3–31.

Sanders, M. R. (1999). The Triple P-Positive parenting program: Towards an empirically validated multilevel parenting and family support strategy for the prevention of behavior and emotional problems in children. *Clinical Child and Family Psychology Review, 2*(2), 71–90.

Sanders, M. R., Cann, W., & Markie-Dadds, C. (2003). The Triple P-Positive Parenting Program: A universal population-level approach to the prevention of child abuse. *Child Abuse Review, 12*(3), 155–171.

Sanders, M. R., Markie-Dadds, C., & Turner, K. M. T. (2003). Theoretical, scientific and clinical foundations of the Triple P-Positive Parenting Program: A population approach to the promotion of parenting competence. *Parenting Research and Practice Monograph, 1,* 1–21.

Sherman, L. W., Gottfredson, D., MacKenzie, D., Eck, J., Reuler, P., & Bushay, S. (1997). *Preventing crime: What works, what doesn't, what's promising: A report to the United States Congress.* Retrieved from http://www.cjcentral.com/sherman/sherman.htm.

Slavet, J. D., Stein, L. A. R., & Klein, J. (2005). Piloting the family check up with incarcerated adolescents and their parents. *Psychological Services, 2*(2), 123–132.

Spaccarelli, S., Cotler, S., & Penman, D. (1992). Problem-solving skills training as a supplement to behavioral parent training. *Cognitive Therapy and Research, 16,* 1–18.

Spelman, W. (2000). What recent studies do (and don't) tell us about imprisonment and crime. *Crime and Justice, 27,* 419.

Spelman, W. (2005). Jobs or jails? The crime drop in Texas. *Journal of Policy Analysis and Management, 24,* 133–165.

Stein, L. A. R., Colby, S. M., & Barnett, N. P. (2006). Effects of motivational interviewing for incarcerated adolescents on driving under the influence after release. *American Journal on Addictions, 15*(Supp. 1), 50–57.

Stein, L. A. R., Colby, S. M., Barnett, N. P., Monti, P. M., Golembeske, J. C., Lebeau-Craven, R., et al. (2006). Enhancing substance abuse treatment engagement in incarcerated adolescents. *Psychological Services, 3*(1), 25–34.

Taub, J. (2002). Evaluation of the Second Step violence prevention program at a rural elementary school. *School Psychology Review, 31,* 186–200.

Thombs, D. L. (2000). A retrospective study of DARE: Substantive effects not detected in undergraduates. *Journal of Alcohol and Drug Education, 46*(1), 27–40.

Timmons-Mitchell, J., Bender, M. B., Kishna, M. A., & Mitchell, C. C. (2006). An independent effectiveness trial of multisystemic therapy with juvenile justice youth. *Journal of Clinical Child and Adolescent Psychology, 35*(2), 227–236.

U.S. Department of Health and Human Services. (2001). *Youth violence: A report of the Surgeon General.* Rockville, MD: Author.

U.S. Department of Justice. (1999). *Women offenders.* Retrieved from http://www.ojp .usdoj.gov/bjs/pub/ascii/wo.txt

Webster-Stratton, C. (1984). Randomized trial of two parent-training programs for families with conduct-disordered children. *Journal of Consulting and Clinical Psychology, 52,* 666–678.

Webster-Stratton, C. (1994). Advancing video-tape parent training: A comparison study. *Journal of Consulting and Clinical Psychology, 62,* 583–593

Weisman, R. L., Lamberti, J. S., & Price, N. (2004). Integrating criminal justice, community healthcare, and support services for adults with severe mental illness. *Psychiatric Quarterly, 75*(1), 71–85.

Welsh, B. C., & Farrington, D. P. (2007). Scientific support for early prevention of delinquency and later offending. *Victims and Offenders, 2,* 125–140.

Wilson, D. B., Bouffard, L. A., & MacKenzie, D. L. (2005). A quantitative review of structured, group-oriented, cognitive-behavioral programs for offenders. *Journal of Criminal Justice and Behavior, 32*(2), 172–204.

Wilson, D. B., Mitchell, O., & MacKenzie, D. L. (2006). A systematic review of drug court effect on recidivism. *Journal of Experimental Criminology, 2,* 459–487.

Wiltz, N. A., & Patterson, G. R. (1974). An evaluation of parent training procedures designed to alter inappropriate aggressive behavior of boys. *Behavior Therapy, 5,* 215–221.

Winner, L., Lanza-Kaduce, L., & Bishop, D. M. (1997). The transfer of juveniles to criminal court: Reexamining recidivism over the long term. *Crime & Delinquency, 43*(4), 548–563.

Index

About the Editor

Christopher J. Ferguson, PhD, is an assistant professor of clinical and forensic psychology at Texas A&M International University. He earned his PhD in clinical psychology from the University of Central Florida and is licensed as a psychologist in Texas. His research focuses on biological and social causes of violent behavior. Most recently, he has been working on positive and negative effects of video game play. Aside from research on violent crime, he enjoys writing speculative fiction, some published examples of which can be found at http://members.aol.com/dukearagon/fiction.html.

About the Contributors

Alissa R. Ackerman is a criminal justice doctoral student at John Jay College of Criminal Justice/CUNY Graduate Center. Her research interests include the supervision and management of sex offenders.

Kevin M. Beaver, PhD, earned his PhD from the University of Cincinnati in 2006 and was awarded the Graduate Research Fellowship from the National Institute of Justice. He is currently an assistant professor at the College of Criminology and Criminal Justice at Florida State University. His research examines the ways in which the environment intersects with biological and genetic factors to produce delinquent and criminal behaviors. Recent publications have appeared in *American Journal of Public Health, Behavioral and Brain Functions, Criminal Justice and Behavior, Criminology, Journal of Adolescent Research, Journal of Quantitative Criminology, Justice Quarterly,* and *Social Biology,* among others. He is also co-editor (with Anthony Walsh) of *Biosocial Criminology: New Directions in Theory and Research* (Routledge, 2008).

Francisco Javier Chacartegui-Ramos is employed by the Scientific Police Department in the city of Seville, Spain as a CSI Technician Deputy Inspector. He has worked as a crime scene specialist on many violent crimes that were later solved and now specializes in fingerprint identification and latent print identification, lending his expertise to material required by judicial authorities. A recipient of the Police Medal of Merit, he also has received over 20 Public Service Awards in recognition of his assistance in crime resolution.

Mary Clair, PhD, is an assistant research professor at the Cancer Prevention Research Center at the University of Rhode Island. She received her doctoral degree in clinical psychology from Drexel University and completed a two-year adolescent forensic postdoctoral fellowship at the Center for Alcohol and Addiction Studies in the Department of Psychiatry and Human Behavior at Brown University. Her clinical and research interests include adolescents involved with the juvenile justice system.

Jeanette M. Daly, RN, PhD, is an assistant research scientist in the Department of Family Medicine, University of Iowa. She has worked in acute care and also has seven years of work experience in long-term care as Director of Nursing and three years as a National Institute on Aging postdoctoral fellow through the University of Iowa Center on Aging. She has evaluated patients who have been abused and has implemented the investigative process for victims. The focus of her research has been the relationship of the law to elder abuse in domestic and long-term care settings.

Sarah L. Desmarais, PhD, is a postdoctoral research fellow in the Department of Health Care and Epidemiology, University of British Columbia and the Child & Family Research Institute. She obtained a PhD with a specialization in law and forensic psychology from Simon Fraser University in 2008. Funded by the Social Sciences and Humanities Research Council of Canada, the Michael Smith Foundation for Health Research, the Interdisciplinary Women's Reproductive Health Training Program, the Consortium for Applied Research and Evaluation in Mental Health, and the Canadian Institutes for Health Research, her research examines factors affecting intervention in forensic and healthcare settings. Current research projects include an evaluation of the effectiveness of an intimate partner violence intervention, delivered in the context of primary care, in reducing violence against and improving health outcomes of pregnant women, as well as an examination of predictors of successful community reintegration among women released from correctional settings. Since 2005, she has been a researcher with the B.C. Mental Health & Addiction Services. She is also a member of an international research team whose focus is to reduce violence perpetration, victimization, and self-harm among persons with mental disorders.

Lee Ellis, PhD, received his PhD at Florida State University. He has taught criminology and other courses in the sociology department at Minot State University in Minot, North Dakota since 1976. Besides criminology, his research interests include the study of social stratification, sex differences in behavior, and research methods. He is the lead author of *Sex Differences: Summarizing More than a Century of Scientific Research* (Psychology Press, 2008) and *Crime Correlates* (Elsevier, 2009). The latter provides a fully documented summary of what is currently known about variables that are statistically associated with criminal and delinquent behavior.

Lisa Faille, PhD, is a graduate of the postdoctoral fellowship, Rhode Island Training School/RI Department of Children, Youth, and Families and the Department of Psychiatry and Human Behavior, Brown University, Providence. She is a licensed clinical psychologist for the Adult Corrections Institution of the Rhode Island Department of Corrections, Cranston,

Rhode Island and an adjunct psychology professor at Roger Williams University, Newport, Rhode Island.

Phyllis B. Gerstenfeld, PhD, is professor and chair of criminal justice at California State University, Stanislaus, where she has taught since 1993. She earned a JD and a PhD in psychology at the University of Nebraska–Lincoln. She is known internationally for her research and publications on hate crimes, and her other areas of research include juvenile justice and psychology and law. Her books include *Hate Crimes: Causes, Controls, and Controversies* (Sage, 2004) and *Crimes of Hate: Selected Readings* (Sage, 2004).

Andrea Gibas is a clinical psychology graduate student in the law and forensic psychology program at Simon Fraser University, British Columbia, Canada. Funded by the Canadian Institutes for Health Research, Andrea's research and clinical interests primarily focus on intimate partner violence. In particular, she is currently involved in research that examines structured risk assessments for intimate partner violence and stalking, safety planning, and the development of a clinical intervention to assist victims of intimate partner violence. Andrea has worked at Correctional Service of Canada, Youth Forensic Psychiatric Services, and the Forensic Psychiatric Services Commission. She also works closely with local police officers who are conducting intimate partner violence risk assessments.

Orestis Giotakos, PhD, graduated in 1985 from the Military Medical School, University of Thessaloniki, Greece, and he has been working as a military psychiatrist since 1992. In 1998, he obtained a MSc in neuroscience at the Institute of Psychiatry, University of London. In 2003, he received his doctorate in sexual aggression at the Medical School, University of Athens. He has conducted several investigations and has written a number of articles and books on sexual aggression and on psychopathology and prevention strategies. He is president of the Hellenic Society for Research and Prevention of Sexual Abuse (http://www.obrela.gr).

Martin Gottschalk, PhD, is an associate professor in the Department of Criminal Justice at the University of North Dakota. He received his PhD in criminal justice at the University at Albany, State University of New York, in 2002. His research uses evolutionary theory and the many disciplines that inform it to help understand criminal behavior, moral/legal behavior, and the human punitive response.

Mary E. Haskett, PhD, is currently a professor of psychology at North Carolina State University and a faculty member at the Center for Developmental Science at UNC-Chapel Hill. She received her PhD in clinical and school psychology from Florida State University, and she completed a predoctoral internship at the Medical University of South Carolina, where she received a NIH training fellowship from the National Crime Victims Research and Treatment Center. She is interested in the linkages between parenting and young children's social and emotional adjustment; specifically, she investigates the adjustment of children who have experienced harsh, abusive parenting. Her work also focuses on examining factors that contribute to abusive parenting, with the goal of contributing to prevention and intervention efforts. Her research is supported by grants from NIMH and NICHD.

Maria Ioannou, MSc, PhD, CPsychol, is a chartered forensic psychologist and currently works as a research fellow at the International Centre for Investigative Psychology at the University of Liverpool. She is the assistant editor of the *Journal of Investigative Psychology and Offender Profiling* and the chair of the Membership and Fellowship Nominations Committee of the International Academy of Investigative Psychology. She has assessed intervention programs for reducing and preventing crime for a range of different forms of criminality and groups of offenders and has consulted with police forces and other agencies. Her research interests include the emotional experience of offending, criminal narratives, psychological characteristics of offenders, the relationship between personality and crime, mental disorder and crime, stalking behavior, sexual offences, and homicide. Her work has been presented nationally and internationally.

Patricia Kerig, PhD, is a professor of psychology and the Director of Clinical Training at Miami University. She received her degree in clinical psychology from the University of California at Berkeley, with a specialization in children and families. After completing an internship at Stanford Children's Hospital and a postdoctoral fellowship at the University of Colorado Health Sciences Center, she held faculty positions in the departments of psychology at Simon Fraser University and UNC-Chapel Hill. Her research has focused on understanding and ameliorating the effects on youth of exposure to trauma, interparental conflict, family violence, maltreatment, and divorce. She is interested in the ways in which these risks affect relationships among family members and relationships outside the family. She also studies resilience and believes that uncovering the protective factors that enable children to overcome the risks associated with family stress and trauma will help us to design empirically supported interventions.

John C. Kilburn, Jr., PhD, is currently chair of the Department of Behavioral, Applied Sciences and Criminal Justice as well as an associate professor of sociology and criminal justice at Texas A&M International University. He previously served on the faculty at Eastern Connecticut State

University. He earned his MA and PhD degrees in sociology from Louisiana State University. As a graduate student in Baton Rouge, Louisiana, he served as a consultant to the Mayor-President Task Force on Fear and Violence and has continued to study violence in various forms including partner and caregiver violence, handguns, effectiveness of prevention programs, and neighborhood reactions to violence. He is currently working on a manuscript that explores halfway houses as both public goods and neighborhood nuisances. His previous research has appeared in journals such as *Urban Affairs Review, Criminal Justice Review,* and *Social Forces.*

Jenifer Lee, PhD, received her PhD in criminology from Indiana University of Pennsylvania in 2005. Her dissertation focused on law students' perceptions of African American, gay, and lesbian hate crime victims. Currently, she is an assistant professor of criminology at Mount Saint Mary College in Newburgh, New York. She has presented at national conferences in areas including the media and school violence, prosecutorial decision making and hate crimes, and the use of Web-based surveys in social science research. Her research interests include hate crimes and hate crime victims, prostitution, and diversity in higher education. Her work has appeared in the *International Journal of Cultural Studies* and *Deviant Behavior.*

José León-Carrión, PhD, is a professor of neuropsychology and director of the Human Neuropsychology Laboratory at the University of Seville, Spain and is also director of the university's Postgraduate Program in Neuropsychology. He designs rehabilitation programs and coordinates the R+D+I Department at the Center for Brain Injury Rehabilitation in Seville. He served as president of the Academy for the Advancement of Brain Injury Rehabilitation, is vice-chairman of the executive committee of the International Brain Injury Association, and is a member of the World Academy for Multidisciplinary Neurotraumatology and the European Brain Injury Society. He served as president of the Second World Congress on Brain Injury and has participated in conferences worldwide. A member of several journal editorial boards, he is also recognized for international books and articles on assessment and rehabilitation of brain injury and neuropsychology textbooks. He is executive director of the Revista Española de la Neuropsicología and currently serves as a reviewer and consultant for the U.S. Department of Defense Traumatic Brain Injury Grant Program.

Kristen M. Lewis, MA, is enrolled in the doctoral program in school psychology at North Carolina State University. She obtained her MA in psychology from the University of North Carolina at Wilmington. Her research interests include family violence, parenting stress, positive parenting interventions, children's causal attributions, and depression. She supervises undergraduate researchers in data collection for a NICHD-funded study examining pathways from parenting to children's social and academic adjustment. In addition, she has served as the primary instructor for several undergraduate psychology classes. Her dissertation is designed to explore the effects of a parenting intervention (Triple P) for graduate students who are balancing graduate school and parenting young children.

Arthur J. Lurigio, PhD, is a psychologist and Associate Dean for Faculty in the College of Arts and Sciences and a professor of criminal justice and psychology at Loyola University Chicago, where he received tenure in 1993. He is also a member of the Graduate Faculty and Director of the Center for the Advancement of Research, Training, and Education at Loyola University Chicago, and a Senior Research Advisor at Illinois Treatment Alternatives for Safe Communities. In 2003, he was named a faculty scholar, the highest honor bestowed on senior faculty at Loyola University Chicago. His research is primarily in the areas of offender drug abuse and dependence problems, mental disorders and crime, community corrections, police-community relations, criminal victimization, and victim services. In recognition of the overall outstanding contributions of his research to criminology and criminal justice practices, he received the University of Cincinnati Award in 1996 and the Hans W. Mattick Award in 2003.

Cricket Meehan, PhD, is the Coordinator of School Mental Health Projects at Miami University's Center for School-Based Mental Health Programs. She received her PhD in clinical psychology from the University of Central Florida. Her clinical and research interests revolve around working in local communities to conduct needs assessments, develop and identify programs based on recognized needs, conduct program evaluations, secure resources and funding for mental health organizations, train in-the-field mental health practitioners in the latest empirically supported treatment protocols, provide advocacy for mental health interests in the public policy and legislation sectors, and bridge the gap between pragmatic treatment and academic research in psychology. She currently provides technical assistance to local elementary and middle schools to plan, implement, and sustain evidence-based prevention programs. In addition, she leads the Southwest Ohio Regional Action Network affiliate of the Ohio Mental Health Network for School Success.

Tonia L. Nicholls, PhD, obtained a PhD with a specialization in law and forensic psychology from Simon Fraser University in 2002. The Social Sciences and Humanities Research Council of Canada and the Michael Smith Foundation for Health Research funded her three-year postdoctoral fellowship in the Department of Psychiatry, University of British Columbia and the B.C. Institute Against Family Violence. She is an assistant professor in the Department of Psychiatry, University of British Columbia and senior research fellow at the Forensic Psychiatric Services Commission, B.C. Mental Health & Addiction Services. Her scholarly work has earned her Brain Star awards from the Institute of Neurosciences, Mental Health, and Addictions (Canadian Institutes of Health Research); the American Psychological Association Award for Distinguished Professional Contribution by a Graduate Student; and the Canadian Psychological Association President's New Researcher Award. Her research interests include women in conflict with the law, the assessment and management of violence, and intimate partner abuse. In 2007, she received a Michael Smith Foundation for Health Research Career Scholar award.

Joseph V. Penn, MD, CCHP, is Director of Mental Health at the University of Texas Medical Branch Correctional Managed Health Care, Huntsville, Texas. He was previously Director of Child and Adolescent Forensic Psychiatry, Rhode Island Hospital, Providence, Rhode Island; Director of Psychiatric Services, Rhode Island Training School, Cranston, Rhode Island; and Clinical Associate Professor, Department of Psychiatry and Human Behavior, Brown Medical School, Providence, Rhode Island.

Sharon G. Portwood, PhD, currently serves as executive director of the Institute for Social Capital, professor of Public Health Sciences, and adjunct professor of psychology at the University of North Carolina at Charlotte. She received her JD from the University of Texas School of Law in 1985, and after more than 10 years as a practicing trial attorney she received her PhD in psychology from the University of Virginia in 1996. She has authored journal articles, book chapters, and a textbook on topics including the prevention of youth and family violence, child maltreatment, the intersection between child maltreatment and domestic violence, and law and policy responses to crimes committed by and against children. Her work has been presented both nationally and internationally. She has provided consulting and training on program implementation and evaluation to a wide variety of agencies and organizations at the federal, state, and local level. She is a fellow in the American Psychological Association and past president of the American Psychological Association's section on child maltreatment.

Jennifer Schwartz, PhD, is an assistant professor of sociology at Washington State University. Her research focuses on gender and other correlates of crime; stratification, family structure, communities, and crime; and how social change impinges on trends in crime and social control. Her work in these areas has been published in *Criminology, Journal of Marriage and Family, Homicide Studies,* and *Sociological Perspectives.* Currently, she is examining how trends in women's drunk driving have been altered by changes in women's lives and changes in DUI laws and enforcement. She is also studying whether girls and women are becoming more violent or are being arrested more often for low-level violent behaviors in which they have always participated.

Karen J. Terry, PhD, is an associate professor in the Department of Law, Police Science, and Criminal Justice Administration at John Jay College of Criminal Justice and the executive officer of the Doctoral Program in Criminal Justice, CUNY. She holds a doctorate in criminology from Cambridge University. She has authored several publications on sex offender treatment, management, and supervision, including *Sex Offender Registration and Community Notification: A "Megan's Law" Sourcebook* (Civic Research Institute, 2003) and *Sexual Offenses and Offenders: Theory, Practice and Policy* (Wadsworth, 2006). She has been involved with numerous research projects regarding sexual offenses and offenders. She was the principal investigator for a study on the nature and scope of child sexual abuse in the Catholic Church and is currently the principal investigator for a study on the causes and context of the Catholic Church sexual abuse crisis. She is also the editor of the periodical *Sex Offender Law Report*, published bi-monthly by the Civic Research Institute.

Maria Tsiliakou, PhD, graduated in 1998 from the Law School of Democritus, University of Thrace, Greece, and she has been working as a lawyer since 2000. In 2004, she obtained a MA in criminology at Panteion University of Athens, Greece. In 2008, she received her doctorate in alternative justice and sexual offenders from Panteion University of Athens, Greece. She is a professor at the Police Academy and teaches criminology. She is responsible for the public relations of the Hellenic Society for Research and Prevention of Sexual Abuse (http://www.obrela.gr), and she is a member of the European and Greek Criminological Societies. She has worked as a legal advisor for the International Organization for Migration, and she is a legal advisor for NGO Solidarity. She has written a number of articles and books.